Introduction to

COMPETITION LAW

Introduction to

COMPETITION LAW

E. Susan Singleton LLB

Solicitor

Pitman

To my husband, Martin and our children,
Rachel, Rebecca and Benjamin

Pitman Publishing
128 Long Acre, London WC2E 9AN

A Division of Longman Group UK Limited

First published in Great Britain in 1992
© E.S. Singleton 1992

British Library Cataloguing in Publication Data
Singleton, E. Susan
Introduction to Competition Law.
I. Title
341.7

ISBN 0 273 03438 3

Typeset, printed and bound in Great Britain

Contents

Preface

Competition law increasingly impinges on business life. The achievement of a single common market by 1 January 1993 requires strict enforcement of European competition law to ensure a level playing field, with no enterprises enjoying unfair advantages arising from price fixing or market sharing cartels. The removal of barriers to trade and the free movement of goods within the Community are central aims of the European Commission.

EC competition law is enforced vigorously – heavy fines of millions of pounds are levied for infringement of the rules. In July 1991 a record fine of £52m was ordered against Tetra Pak.

EC law is increasing in volume and complexity. There are general exemptions for many categories of agreement. In 1989 the know-how and franchising general exemptions came into force. From 21 September 1990 the Merger Regulation has applied, requiring prior notification of large EC mergers. Case law continues to develop, with the supremacy of EC law over UK law confirmed in the European Court of Justice decision in July 1991 in *Factortame* and the partial reversal by the Court, in the 1990 *Hag (No 2)* decision, of the common origin doctrine.

In the United Kingdom national competition law applies in tandem with that of the EC. The Government has proposed a radical overhaul of UK competition law, replacing it with an EC based model. The existing law continues to be applied, with illegal cartels in many industries being investigated and, where companies are already subject to orders of the Restrictive Practices Court, proceedings being initiated to fine heavily those in contempt of court and even to jail involved individuals.

No lawyer or student of the law can ignore competition law, which will go to the heart of the drafting of many commercial agreements, from joint ventures to disposals of businesses and patent licences to franchising and distribution, specifying in many cases the only permitted restrictive provisions in such agreements.

I would like to thank my family for their forbearance, assistance and encouragement in the writing of this book.

In this book 1 ECU has been taken to be 70p (£1 = ECU1.42). 'He' is used to encompass both male and female.

The law is as stated at 1 August 1991.

E. Susan Singleton, Harrow, August 1991

Table of cases

Table of investigations
Competition Act 1980 and Fair Trading Act 1973

Table of statutes and statutory instruments

Terms and abbreviations used in the text

CFI Court of First Instance (EC)

CMLR Common Market Law Reports, EC law reports

Commission European Commission

DG1V Directorate General 1V, of the European Commission, the department responsible for competition matters

Director or DGFT The Director General of Fair Trading

DTI Department of Trade and Industry

EC European Community

ECLR European Competition Law Review

ECR European Court Reports, EC law reports

EIPR European Intellectual Property Review, journal

FT Financial Times

FTA Fair Trading Act 1973

IBL International Business Lawyer, journa

MMC Monopolies and Mergers Commission

NLJ New Law Journal

OFT Office of Fair Trading

OJ The Official Journal of the European Communities, where decisions, regulations, directives and notices of the Commission are published

R&D Research and development

RPA Resale Prices Act 1976

RPC Restrictive Practices Court

RTPA Restrictive Trade Practices Act 1976

SJ Solicitors Journal

The Treaty The Treaty of Rome, founding the EC

PART 1

UK and EC competition law

1

Introduction

Competition law regulates the market power of companies and individuals. Its practical effects are that it requires that companies refrain from agreements restrictive of competition, such as collusion to agree the level of prices which companies will charge to their customers or who will serve which customers. It determines whether one company will be entitled to merge with another and restricts the freedom of large, dominant companies to charge excessive prices or discriminate against particular customers.

It has a substantial impact upon the drafting of agreements as diverse as patent licences and sale and purchase agreements for the acquisition of companies. It must be borne in mind when meetings with competitors are proposed or joint ventures envisaged. Varying political purposes behind competition law ensure that over time it changes to achieve whatever objectives are important to those with the power to enforce and determine such law.

Ignoring the competition rules can lead to large fines being levied by the European Commission of up to 10 per cent of the turnover of the companies concerned. In July 1991 Tetra Pak was fined a record £52m for competition law infringement.[1] Restrictions in agreements may be void and, under UK law, where a company infringes a Restrictive Practices Court order, individuals are at risk of being jailed by the court for contempt of court. Also in 1990, in *Re Ready Mixed Concrete*,[2] individuals involved in illegal market sharing and price fixing arrangements were brought before the Restrictive Practices Court and personally fined.

THE RATIONALE

The regulation of the agreements and behaviour of companies in an economic context is an interference with the free market. However, such interference is deemed justifiable in the interests of consumers. Efficient companies or organisations producing goods which the public want will necessarily increase their share of the market for those goods. Perfect competition is rarely achieved where many manufacturers of goods compete in supplying the same goods to customers. Often a dominant company will emerge, producing products of such quality and in such demand that goods produced by their competitors cease to be bought at all. All competition is eliminated. The efficient company, in business to make large profits, will therefore be in a position where it can exploit its position, particularly if it is difficult or expensive for other companies to enter the particular product area, i.e. there are high barriers to entry.

A company in such a dominant position could increase prices substantially, knowing that it has eliminated its competitors, who have gone out of business

[1] See FT 25 July 1991

[2] [1991] ICR 52, but see *DGFT v Smiths Concrete Ltd* (CA), judgement July 1991

because of their inferior products. It could impose unfair conditions on customers and supply shoddy goods and the incentive to undertake research and development to produce goods which are better than others in the market would be removed. Clearly if prices became much too high the goods would not be bought at all, unless there were no substitute for them and they were essential goods. The market, in the form of consumers, would still be able to make a choice, but in this case only a choice between buying these goods or none at all.

Restrictive agreements between two competitors could enable them to eliminate competition. Where two or more companies between themselves hold a high percentage of the market and they agree a minimum level of prices for their products, then the normal effects of two keen competitors are removed. They would not be competing on price. Consumers would be required to pay whatever price they determined or accept whatever terms or conditions of sale were presented to them following a restrictive agreement between the competitors. The positive benefits of competition in the market place would be removed.

Mergers are principally regulated in the UK on competition grounds. Why should Government interfere in the choice of two companies that they become one or that one acquire the share capital or assets of the other? Again the reason is on grounds of competition. The two original separate companies may between them supply 50 per cent each of a certain product in the UK. Their concentration would mean that the new entity would control the whole of that product and would no longer be subject to the same market regulation. It would be able to behave unilaterally,[3]

The EC Commission has stated that competition law within the EC:

> provides for the establishment of a system to ensure that competition in the common market is not distorted. The objective of market integration is as important as the traditional role which competition plays in free market economies, ensuring efficient allocation of resources, stimulating enterprises to make the best use of their know-how and skills and encouraging them to develop new research techniques and products.[4]

In connection with EC competition law, social and economic factors are important, but the principal objective is the achievement of the Single European Market, with no national barriers to trade, where goods can move freely between nations.

COMPETITION LAW – THE ECONOMIC ANALYSIS

No analysis of the rationale of competition law would be complete, even within the bounds of this introductory text, without some discussion of the so-called Harvard and Chicago schools.

The Harvard school enjoyed greatest influence and acclaim in the middle of this century, particularly in the 1960s. Where high market shares were enjoyed, it was assumed that restrictive agreements must be in place and it would be difficult to enter the particular market, because of high barriers to entry. The structure of the market was the principal factor in the analysis.

This approach fitted the then political situation, where the prevailing will

3 See Liesner J. & Glynn D. – *Does Anti-trust Make Economic Sense?* [1987] ECLR 344 and Hawk B.E. – *The American (Anti-trust) Revolution: lessons for the EEC?* [1988] ECLR 53

4 *EEC Competition Policy in the Single Market*, 2nd ed., March 1989, Office for Official Publications of the European Communities, p.13

See *Commercial Solvents*
974] 1 CMLR 309

was for a deconcentration of power and protection for individuals trading in particular markets. This approach has been largely followed by the European Commission,[5] with a system of prohibition of anti-competitive agreements and a system for notifying agreements for close examination by competition law authorities, whether agreements were between competitors engaged in the same level of the market, i.e. horizontal arrangements, or between suppliers and distributors or others at different levels of supply, i.e. vertical arrangements.

With the start of the 1970s, the Chicago school gained acceptance in the USA with a very different approach. By this method, barriers to entry and apparent market share were not necessarily relevant. An examination of a company's prices in relation to its costs is undertaken to ascertain its real market power. Companies may have a large market share at one particular moment in time, but this may be illusory or transient.

This policy translates into enforcement which regulates only the large horizontal cartel arrangements and mergers and leaves restrictive vertical agreements unregulated. Efficiency is seen to flow from vertical arrangements and licences of intellectual property rights.

This school does not, however, reflect the current EC policy towards competition law, although some influences of this US Chicago school can be discerned from some Commission decisions. The European Commission, although granting exemptions for some types of vertical arrangements which fall within very limited criteria as to the clauses which may be included in such agreements, closely regulates all vertical and horizontal arrangements and will look not just at market power or the efficiency benefits wrought by a particular arrangement, but also, and particularly, at the effects on consumers.

The Commission may have regard to economic, political and social factors in reaching decisions, such as any impact on levels of unemployment. Although such social factors will not necessarily be decisive, regard will be had to them to a greater extent than would be the case in equivalent circumstances under US competition law, which is more influenced by the Chicago school.

HISTORY

See *Whish* p. 49 and *Dyer's*
ase (1414) YB 11 Hen 5 fo 5
l 26

Competition law has developed principally since the Second World War in the UK, although the courts have considered restrictions as being in restraint of trade at common law since about 1200.[6] The modern cradle of competition law has been the USA, with competition law dating back many decades to the Sherman Act of 1890. Known as 'anti-trust' in the USA it developed from US attempts to demolish 'trusts' or anti-competitive cartels, groups of the main manufacturers in particular industries who banded together to strengthen their hold on such industries and ensure that high prices and amenable terms and conditions were retained. US legislation was aimed at breaking such trusts, hence the term 'anti-trust'.

Turning to the UK, after the Second World War when cartels in most industries were rife and had been regarded benignly for some time, the

Labour Government of Atlee determined to take action to stem such anti-competitive arrangements. The Monopolies and Restrictive Practices (Inquiry and Control) Act 1948 established a Monopolies and Restrictive Practices Commission in the UK. The relevant Minister could refer to this Commission the supply, processing or export of goods of any description. Before a reference of this sort could be made to the Commission, it was necessary that one third of all goods of a particular description were supplied by a person or group of persons who conducted their affairs such as to restrict competition.

The Commission reported as to whether the fulfillment of these statutory conditions operated against the public interest. There was power by statutory instrument to make orders remedying the situation.

The Restrictive Trade Practices Act 1956 was enacted because of the slow operation of the existing legislation and was very much the forerunner of the present Restrictive Trade Practices Act 1976.

The Resale Prices Act 1964 outlawed the imposition of minimum resale price maintenance, except for books and medicines.

Mergers were brought within control for the first time under the Monopolies and Mergers Act 1965, which permitted a reference of mergers to the Monopolies Commission. It also provided that the supply of services, which were not regulated under the original Monopolies and Restrictive Practices (Inquiry and Control) Act 1948, be referable to the Commission in the same way as were monopolies and mergers in relation to the supply of goods.

Finally the last piece of historic, as opposed to current, UK competition legislation was the Restrictive Trade Practices Act 1968, which amended the 1956 Act and ensured that there could be civil liability for breach of statutory duty where the restrictive practices legislation was breached, thereby increasing the sanctions to which parties to such arrangements might be subject. This Act also brought in regulation of 'information agreements', such as those for an exchange of information concerning the prices charged for goods and also gave the Minister powers to exempt from the RTPA certain beneficial agreements.

In the EC the Treaty establishing the European Coal and Steel Community was signed by France, Germany, Italy, Belgium, the Netherlands and Luxembourg at Paris on 18th April 1951. This Treaty of Paris founded the Coal and Steel Community which exists to this day and is considered in Chapter 11. Articles 65 and 66 of the Treaty of Paris proscribe anti-competitive agreements between undertakings and abuses of a dominant position.

The Treaty establishing the European Economic Community (EEC), the Treaty of Rome, signed in Rome on 25th March 1957 by Germany, France, Italy, Luxembourg, Belgium and the Netherlands, founded the EEC. Subsequently Denmark, Ireland, Greece, the UK, Portugal and Spain acceded to the Treaty bringing the total number of Member States to 12.

The EEC itself has, for convenience, become known simply as 'the EC', the expression used throughout the book to denote the European Economic Community.

EC COMPETITION LAW

See Chapters 2 and 3

Articles 85 and 86 of the Treaty of Rome are the principal instruments of EC competition policy.[7]

Article 85(1)

Article 85(1) prohibits as incompatible with the common market agreements which have as their object or effect the prevention, restriction or distortion of competition within the Common Market and which may affect trade between Member States. Specific reference is made to agreements to fix prices, to limit production, markets or technical development, to share markets, to apply dissimilar conditions to equivalent transactions and to make the conclusion of contracts subject to acceptance by other parties of supplementary obligations with no connection with the contract.

Article 85(1) regulates anti-competitive agreements. It is an 'effects based' doctrine, i.e. it looks to the commercial effect of restrictive provisions and not to the form of the agreement and how the restrictions are phrased. It is not possible to draft around the Treaty if the anti-competitive effect is just the same.

Article 85(3)

Article 85(2)

OJ 1962 13/204

Restrictions are void if Article 85(1) is infringed.[8] It is possible under Article 85(3) to justify restrictions to the European Commission, which polices EC competition policy, if an individual notification of the agreement is made to the Commission by the parties to the agreement under Regulation 17.[9] Such a specific exemption may be available where the provisions of the agreement contribute to economic progress, allow consumers to benefit and only contain restrictions which are indispensable and there is no opportunity to eliminate all competition.

Block exemptions

Common restrictive agreements may benefit from a 'block exemption', a general exemption for agreements of a typical type, where the conditions of an exemption Regulation are complied with.

The Commission has issued a number of block exemption Regulations in categories such as exclusive distribution and purchasing, patent and know-how licensing, franchising, research and development agreements and specialisation. These typically set out restrictions which are exempted by the Regulation, those provisions which would not infringe Article 85(1) and those provisions the presence of which in the agreement would render the block exemption inapplicable. The Regulations remove the need to notify these common types of agreement, provided their terms fall within the wording of the exemption.

Where parties to an agreement wish to include a provision not permitted under the relevant regulation, the parties will have to notify the agreement to the Commission for exemption under Article 85(3). If they do not do so then the restrictions will be void and the parties are at risk of Commission fines and the adverse publicity companies suffer when such cases appear in the newspapers.

Where an agreement is notified, the Commission will determine whether it fulfils the conditions necessary for it to be exempted under Article 85(3). If it does, then the restriction will be enforceable. If it does not, then the restrictions will be void, but the parties will be protected from fines, from the date when the notification was made.

Article 86

Article 86 regulates individual behaviour by companies and individuals who have a dominant position in the EC or a substantial part of the EC, where that dominant position is abused, such as by imposing unfair prices, limiting production or technical development, applying dissimilar conditions to equivalent transactions and making the conclusion of contracts subject to the acceptance of supplementary obligations.

Again there must be an effect on trade between Member States. Chapter 3 considers abuses of a dominant position in some detail. Enjoyment of a strong market position is not of itself forbidden, but 'abuse' of that position is outlawed. Companies enjoying a high market share therefore have to be particularly careful to ensure that they act fairly to all their customers and suppliers, do not discriminate against them or force them to buy additional goods which they do not want. They must also ensure that they do not refuse to supply goods where there is no objectively justifiable reason for such a refusal, which could otherwise amount to an abuse of a dominant position.

Free movement of goods rules

The free movement of goods rules (Articles 30 – 36 of the Treaty of Rome)[10] are designed to ensure the free movement of goods in the EC. Article 30 provides:

> Quantitative restrictions on imports and all measures having equivalent effect shall, without prejudice to the following provisions, be prohibited between Member States.

This principle that goods should not be restricted from moving freely round the common market is an important one in the context of the idea of the common market, that it would truly be a 'common market', a market common to all. Article 36 ensures that the free movement of goods provisions in the Treaty do not prevent the protection of industrial and commercial property, although it is important to note that the free movement of goods provisions concern all goods, not just those protected by patents or other forms of intellectual property.

Other provisions

Article 2 of the Treaty of Rome, in part, states:

> The Community shall progressively bring about the conditions which will of themselves ensure the most rational distribution of production at the highest possible level of productivity, while safeguarding continuity of employment and taking care not to provoke fundamental and persistent disturbances in the economies of Member States.

10 See Chapter 10

Article 3(f) provides for the institution of a system ensuring that competition in the common market is not distorted.

These provisions lay the foundations for the competition provisions of the Treaty in Articles 85 and 86.

Mergers

From 21st September 1990, mergers with 'a community dimension' must be notified in advance to the Commission for clearance before they take place. In the UK, the Fair Trading Act 1973 provides for a system of voluntary pre-notification of mergers. Competition law relating to mergers is considered in detail in Chapter 4.

Regulations, Notices and Directives

Competition legislation in the EC comprises Regulations and Notices. The European Commission, described below, also issues Directives.

Regulations have direct effect in the Member States without the need for any national legislation to bring them into force. Directives are directed to the Member States who are required to enact national legislation to achieve the objectives of the Directive, but the exact wording and method of bringing the Directive into force is left to Member States. In some circumstances Directives have been held to be directly effective where a Member State has not enacted the Directive within the time specified in the Directive. In those circumstances, individuals as against the State may claim rights under the unenacted Directive, although not against private enterprises as was the case in *Marshall*.[11] In the competition field there are a number of block exemption Regulations, considered in more detail later, which directly apply in each Member State.

As well as Directives and Regulations, the Commission also issues Notices, which can be useful in the competition field. These set out the Commission's views on areas such as agency, sub-contracting, the exclusive distribution and purchasing block exemptions and other competition related matters. A Notice is not legally binding on the Commission as a Regulation is, but is a good indication of the Commission's likely stance towards a particular form of agreement.

1 *Marshall* v *Southampton Area Health Authority* [1986] CMLR 140, [1986] 2 WLR 80 and see *Foster* v *British Gas* [1991] 2 CMLR 217

Penalties

Infringements can be punished by fines and restrictions in anti-competitive agreements will be void. The European Commission, described below, has powers to demand information and also to search premises, occasionally without notice in so-called 'dawn raids'.

The Commission

The rules of competition of the EC described above are enforced by the European Commission, the executive arm of the Community. The Commission has 17 members. They are nominated by their respective governments. There are a considerable number of additional civil servants working at the Commission to assist the Commissioners.

Different sectors are involved in the work that the Commission does and the Commission is therefore divided into Directorates General. DG1V deals with competition policy.

The Courts of Justice and First Instance

The judicial arm of the EC is the Court of Justice and the Court of First Instance, both operating from Luxembourg. The Court of First Instance (CFI) is the first appellate court for competition cases brought by individuals and the Court of Justice is the final court to which appeal can be made on a point of law concerning a decision of the Commission. There may also be references to the Court of Justice (but not the CFI) from national courts on points of interpretation of the Treaty, known as Article 177 references as Article 177 of the Treaty provides for such references, on:

(a) the interpretation of the Treaty;
(b) the validity and interpretation of acts of the institutions of the Community;
(c) the interpretation of the statutes of bodies established by an act of the Council, where those statutes so provide.

Where such a question is raised before any court or tribunal of a Member State, that court or tribunal may, if it considers that a decision on the question is necessary to enable it to give judgement, request the Court of Justice to give a ruling thereon.

The Court of Justice comprises judges and advocates general. The advocates general, of which there are six, offer advice and opinions to the judges, who themselves reach the decisions of the court. The Court has judges drawn one from each of the twelve member states of the EC and one additional judge, making a total of thirteen.

The CFI was set up under the Single European Act,[12] which came into force on 1 July 1987. The Single European Act enacted institutional reform of the EC. It inserted a new Article 168a into the Treaty of Rome empowering the Council to set up a court of first instance. This provides:

> At the request of the Court of Justice and after consulting the Commission and the European Parliament, the Council may, acting unanimously, attach to the Court of Justice a court with jurisdiction to hear and determine at first instance, subject to a right of appeal on points of law only and in accordance with the conditions laid down by the Statute, certain classes of action or proceedings brought by natural or legal persons. That court shall not be competent to hear and determine actions brought by Member States or by Community institutions or questions referred for a preliminary ruling under Article 177.

Only actions brought by private persons or companies can be entertained and Article 177 references must be brought to the Court of Justice. Appeals from a decision of the CFI are on points of law only. There are 12 members of the CFI, who are chosen from persons whose independence is beyond doubt and (by Article 168(a)(3)) who 'possess the ability required for appointment for high office'. Members are appointed for a term of six years and retiring members may be reappointed. The first members of the CFI were appointed one from each Member State, although there is no obligation for such a spread of nationality.

12 OJ 1987, L169/1, see also the decision of the Council establishing the CFI of 24 October 1988, OJ 1989 C215/1 and [1989] 3 CMLR 458 – corrected version and rules of procedure

The Council of Ministers

As well as the Commission and the Courts, there is the Council of the European Communities. The Council is the legislature of the Community. It formulates policy, which is implemented by Regulations and Directives which are proposed by the Commission. Ministers responsible for competition policy in each of the Member States comprise the Council of Europe which meets three times a year.

European Parliament

The fourth limb is the European Parliament, which has a rather limited role compared to the UK Parliament. Members are elected every five years. The Parliament's role is to give advice and to be consulted, but its political importance is growing.[13]

3 See Articles 2 to 6 of the reaty of Rome for the setting p of such institutions

The Economic and Social Committee

The Economic and Social Committee was established under Articles 193 – 198 of the Treaty of Rome. It prepares opinions on Directives, Regulations and other Community legislation and is made up of about 200 workers, employers, consumers and academics.

UK COMPETITION LAW

UK competition law is embodied in the Restrictive Trade Practices Act 1976 (RTPA), the Competition Act 1980, the Fair Trading Act 1973 and the Resale Prices Act 1976.

The Restrictive Trade Practices Act 1976

The RTPA has most immediate impact on agreements. It applies to agreements between two parties carrying on business in the UK in the supply of goods or two parties carrying on business in the UK in the supply of services. The Act will only apply where there are restrictions on two parties. Restrictions as to goods are listed in section 6 and restrictions as to services are listed in section 11. Typical clauses in agreements caught would include a restriction on competition, agreeing the prices at which two suppliers will supply goods or which customers they will serve.

The RTPA is a 'form based' piece of legislation and will apply wherever there are restrictions on not less than two parties even if there is no adverse impact on competition and the agreement only falls within the Act by virtue of its wording. For this reason it may often be possible to rephrase a clause to avoid the impact of the RTPA. This distinguishes UK competition from that of the EC, which is an effects based doctrine, looking to the commercial effect of restrictions not their form.

The Government has proposed abolishing the RTPA in its White Paper, considered in Chapter 6, and replacing it with legislation similar to the EC model. The advantage of the form based system is that the law sets out exactly the restrictions allowed, although the often obstruse wording of the RTPA can make such advantage illusory. With EC law economic factors are relevant; questions need to be asked of the parties as to their market share and an attempt must be made to determine what is the relevant market for particular products.

The RTPA will apply only where there are restrictions on two parties to the agreement, as will be seen in Chapter 2. It will not apply where there are any number of restrictions on one party and none on the other. It contains a series of exemptions, for very limited categories of agreement, which contain only listed restrictions, such as patent and know-how licences, exclusive supply arrangements and export agreements.

Once an agreement falls within the RTPA, it must be registered at the Office of Fair Trading before the restrictions take effect, otherwise the restrictions will be void and any person damaged by the agreement may bring an action for breach of statutory duty against the parties, although few such actions have been brought. The Government hopes to encourage such private actions as a means of enforcement and envisages such a right being a central part of the new legislation on restrictive trade practices proposed in the Government's White Paper.

Registration of restrictive agreements involves sending them to the OFT. Whereas under EC law it is necessary to make a notification on Form A/B (or Form CO for mergers), supplying the Commission with a considerable amount of commercial information concerning the parties and their market shares, under the RTPA only the agreements must be furnished, although if merger clearance is sought then a similar exercise to that required under EC competition law is necessary.

Once an agreement has been registered, a decision will be taken as to whether it should be referred to the Restrictive Practices Court. In many cases, where restrictions are insignificant, a direction under section 21(2) of the Act will be made. The agreement will be placed upon the Public Register and no further action will be taken. Where the agreement is restrictive then a reference may be made to the Court, which has power to grant orders that the parties must not enter into any registrable agreement again without first registering it or that they must not enter into any agreement to 'like effect' to that which they have entered into. Breach of such an order would be contempt of court for which the companies involved could be fined and individuals with responsibility for subsequent restrictive agreements could be fined or even jailed.[14]

14 See Chapter 2

There are provisions under section 10 of the RTPA for restrictions to be justified under the so-called 'gateways', although cases are rarely fought under the gateways before the court. In practice companies will agree modifications to agreements or accept undertakings rather than proceed with the expense and management time needed to fight a case before the Restrictive Practices Court.

The Competition Act 1980

Under the Competition Act 1980, particular practices by individuals and firms can be investigated to establish whether a course of conduct amounts to an anti-competitive practice under the Act. There are no offences specified in the legislation. There have been investigations into refusals to supply and excessive or discriminatory pricing. For most agreements the Competition Act is not of immmediate relevance. There is no requirement to modify the drafting of an agreement to avoid provisions of the Competition Act. There is a risk of a reference whenever an anti-competitive practice is embarked upon.

There is a two-stage approach to a Competition Act reference. The Director General of Fair Trading carries out a preliminary investigation to establish whether a particular course of conduct amounts to an anti-competitive practice, which can be referred to the Monopolies and Mergers Commission. The Director can accept undertakings from the participating companies not to pursue a course of conduct in the future instead of making a reference to the MMC. If on a reference to the MMC it is found that an anti-competitive practice has been operated which is contrary to the public interest, then the Secretary of State can ask the Director to seek undertakings from the parties or can make an order prohibiting the practice or remedying or preventing its adverse effects.

There are *de minimis* limits such that small companies or those with a small market share are not investigated in this way.

The Fair Trading Act 1973

The Fair Trading Act (FTA) regulates monopolies and mergers in the UK. The MMC can investigate whenever a monopoly situation exists[15] or whenever a qualifying merger takes place.[16] It is possible under the FTA to notify a merger to the MMC in advance of its occurring so as to obtain clearance of it before it goes ahead.

15 See Chapter 3
16 See Chapter 4

The Resale Prices Act 1976

The Resale Prices Act (RPA) prohibits collective resale price maintenance and individual minimum resale price maintenance. Resale price maintenance occurs where a supplier of goods requires that the purchaser resell goods at a fixed price or a minimum resale price. Clearly such a practice restricts competition in that the reseller is not free to determine the prices at which he may sell the goods. Any term of a contract for the sale of goods which purports to establish a minimum price at which the goods can be resold is void under the RPA.

It is also unlawful to withhold supplies from a dealer who has sold the goods at a price below the resale price of the goods sold to him, unless he is loss leading, i.e. he has sold goods within the last twelve months not to make a profit but instead to attract customers to his shop to purchase other goods or otherwise for the purposes of advertising the business of the dealer.

These are the four principal UK statutes which regulate competition in the UK, the equivalents of Articles 85 and 86 of the Treaty of Rome.

The Office of Fair Trading

The OFT is a UK Government body staffed by civil servants. It is responsible for consumer affairs and competition policy enforcement. In the competition field it is the Competition Policy Division of the OFT which administers the Director's responsibilities under the Acts referred to above. In 1990 the OFT received 1,514 complaints and enquiries about anti-competitive practices.

Under the FTA, the OFT examines mergers and monopolies. In 1990 the

OFT examined 369 merger cases, either completed mergers, proposals, requests for 'confidential guidance' or merger notices.

The Director General of Fair Trading

The Director General of Fair Trading is currently Sir Gordon Borrie. His role is to head the OFT. His function under the RTPA is to prepare and maintain the register of restrictive trading agreements to which the RTPA applies and to bring before the Restrictive Practices Court all restrictive agreements, although many agreements are granted a direction under section 21(2), where they are not of such significance as to render a reference to the Court necessary.

The Director also has powers to investigate restrictive practices and bring various proceedings as laid down in the RTPA. He also has functions under the Competition Act and Resale Prices Act and advises the Secretary of State in connection with mergers under the Fair Trading Act.

The Monopolies and Mergers Commission

The Monopolies and Mergers Commission (MMC) was established under section 1 of the Monopolies and Restrictive Practices (Inquiry and Control) Act 1948 as the Monopolies and Restrictive Practices Commission and then became the Monopolies Commission. With the advent of the FTA, it became (by section 4 of the FTA) the Monopolies and Mergers Commission. By section 4(2) of the FTA, the MMC must have not less than 10 and not more them 25 regular members, who are appointed by the Secretary of State. This figure has been increased over the years and in 1989 the maximum number of members of the MMC was increased by order from 32 to 50. Schedule 3 of the FTA sets out the details of the structure of the MMC, its officers – chairman, deputy chairmen – and the terms of appointment of members. It has one chairman and three deputy chairmen. In 1990 35 reports were completed by the MMC into mergers and monopolies.[17]

Whenever an enquiry is launched by the MMC a team of staff under a Team Manager is nominated to assist the group of Commission members undertaking the enquiry. The MMC has legal advisers, industrial advisers, team managers, accountant and economic advisers to assist it in its work.

Finance for the MMC is provided by the Department of Trade and Industry. The MMC's expenditure for its financial year 1988/89 was £4.418m.

Restrictive Practices Court

The Restrictive Practices Court[18] is the court with responsibility for making orders under the Restrictive Trade Practices Act. It was established under section 2 of the 1956 RTPA and is now established under the Restrictive Practices Court Act 1976. The Court consists of judicial and lay members, although on matters of law the views of the judicial members prevail. The Court can make orders under the RTPA and make injunctive orders where there has been a default in the furnishing of particulars of registrable agreements.

A brief outline of the sources of competition law and the bodies and

17 See MMC 1990 Annual Review, available from the MMC, 48 Carey Street, London WC2A 2JT

18 See Stevens and Yamey – *The Restrictive Practices Court: a study of the judicial process and economic policy*, Weidenfeld and Nicholson, 1965 and Cunningham – *The Fair Trading Act 1973*, Sweet & Maxwell, 1974 and Supplement, 1978

institutions concerned with it has been given, with an introduction to the rationale for such regulation.

This book examines the basic competition statutes and regulations referred to above for both the UK and EC in Chapters 2 and 3. Chapter 4 looks at competition law as it specifically applies to mergers and in particular examines the EC Merger Regulation, which came into force on 21st September 1990 and the voluntary system for pre-notification of UK mergers, which has applied since April 1990. Chapter 5 addresses the issues arising from breach of competition law, such as penalties and investigations. In Chapters 6 and 7, the proposed new system for UK competition law is discussed, competition law abroad is examined and compliance procedures considered, whereby infringement of the rules may be avoided by careful prior action.

The second part of the book looks at specific types of agreement such as distribution agreements, licensing of intellectual property, research agreements and others which have been regulated specifically by the competition authorities.

FURTHER READING

History

Brock – *The Control of Restrictive Practices from 1956*, McGraw-Hill, 1966
Stevens and Yamey – *The Restrictive Practices Court: a study of the judicial process and economic policy*, Weidenfeld and Nicholson, 1965
Whish R. – *Competition Law*, Butterworths, 2nd ed., 1989

Economics

Hawk B.E. – *The American (Anti-trust) Revolution: lessons for the EEC?* [1988] ECLR 53
Liesner J. & Glynn D. – *Does Anti-trust make economic sense?* [1987] ECLR 344
Merkin and Williams – *Antitrust Policy in the United Kingdom and the EEC*, Sweet & Maxwell, 1984
Swann – *Competition and Industrial Policy in the European Community*, Methuen, 1983
Whish (*op cit*)

General texts

Chitty on Contracts, Volume II, Sweet & Maxwell, 26th ed., 1990
Cunningham – *The Fair Trading Act 1973*, Sweet & Maxwell, 1974 and Supplement, 1978
Korah V. – *An Introductory Guide to EEC Competition Law and Practice*, ESC Publishing, 4th ed., 1990

Institutions

Millett T. – *The Court of First Instance of the European Communities*, Butterworths, 1990
Neville Brown L. – *The Court of Justice of the European Communities*, Sweet & Maxwell, 3rd ed., 1989

2

Anti-competitive agreements

Competition law regulates both formal, written agreements between companies and individuals and oral agreements, arrangements in the broadest sense and understandings. EC competition law applies automatically in the UK and runs in parallel with UK competition law. Both bodies of law may be applicable to one transaction. National competition authorities may take action against an agreement pending before the European Commission, provided national law does not prejudice the full application of Community law.[1]

Clearly not all agreements are anti-competitive. The EC and UK approaches are quite different. EC competition law is an effects based system. The effect on actual or potential competition is the paramount concern, whatever the form of the agreement. The current UK system looks to the form of the arrangement, as to whether set criteria are met, whether the agreement leads to a decrease in competition or not. This can have the result that innocuous agreements from the competition point of view are caught by the legislation.

As there are such anomalies and because of other problems, such as the difficulties of enforcement of the current UK competition legislation, it is proposed to replace the Restrictive Trade Practices Act with a new UK system based on the EC effects based model.[2]

ARTICLE 85

Under Article 85(1) of the Treaty of Rome it is provided:

1. The following shall be prohibited as incompatible with the common market: all agreements between undertakings, decisions by associations of undertakings and concerted practices which may affect trade between Member States and which have as their object or effect the prevention, restriction or distortion of competition within the common market, and in particular those which:

(a) directly or indirectly fix purchase or selling prices or any other trading conditions;

(b) limit or control production, markets, technical development, or investment;

(c) share markets or sources of supply;

(d) apply dissimilar conditions to equivalent transactions with other trading parties, thereby placing them at a competitive disadvantage;

(e) make the conclusion of contracts subject to acceptance by the other parties of supplementary obligations which, by their nature or according to commercial usage, have no connection with the subject of such contracts.

1 See *Wilhelm* v *Bundeskartellamt* [1969] CMLR 100, [1969] ECR 585 and Van Bael & Bellis *Competition law of the EEC*, CCH Editions, 2nd ed., 1990, p.258

2 See the Government's White Paper, *Opening Markets: New Policy on Restrictive Trade Practices*, Cm 727, July 1989, which summarises the proposals for change

Article 85 will only apply where the object or effect of the agreement is to prevent, restrict or distort competition. Therefore an agreement which seeks to restrict competition, but fails in its objective could theoretically be caught. So could an agreement be caught where its effect is that competition is in practice distorted, notwithstanding that it was not the intention of the parties so to do. A distortion of competition would include not only a reduction in competition, but also an enhancement.

In assessing an agreement in order to discern whether it falls within Article 85 the European Commission[3] will look at the agreement itself and all the facts, including details of the relevant market.

Effect on trade between Member States and *de minimis*

Article 85 will only apply where trade between Member States[4] is affected. This does not mean that agreements between two enterprises situated in the same Member State will not be caught by the legislation. An agreement between two UK companies may affect interstate trade if it results in the home market being even harder to penetrate or has the effect that imports or exports are impeded. An 'effect' may mean an adverse or even beneficial effect and does not have to be a substantial effect. The agreement under consideration must, however, cause the volume of trade between Member States to increase rather than decrease. There must be a significant effect on the market.[5]

Where an agreement, at least potentially, has an effect on trade between Member States and contains restrictions of the sort prohibited by Article 85, the restrictions will be void.[6]

The Commission has issued a Notice,[7] which is not binding as a Regulation would be, but which indicates where Article 85 would apply to agreements which are not of much economic significance.

The Commission, at first through case law,[8] laid down the factors which might determine whether an agreement had the necessary effect on trade between Member States, which is a precondition for the application of both Articles 85 and 86. Whether appreciable effects are apparent by the arrangement under consideration is a question of fact in each case. The Commission will look to whether the parties have a strong market share, if not, then it is unlikely that the agreement would be held to have an effect on trade between Member States. However, it can be difficult to define the market in relation to which the parties have a small or large market share. Case law generally reached the position whereby 5 per cent was regarded as a large enough share of any market above which the parties' behaviour may have the necessary effect on trade between Member States, which must be an appreciable effect.

In 1970 the Commission issued the Notice referred to previously, setting out its views in connection with appreciable effect. The latest version of this Notice is Commission Notice of 3 September 1986 on agreements of minor importance which do not fall under Article 85(1) of the Treaty establishing the European Economic Community.[9]

In the Notice the Commission sets out its opinion that agreements with no appreciable effect on competition would not be caught by Article 85(1) at all.

3 The European Commission consists of independent members nominated by the governments of the Member States. The Commission's work is undertaken by a number of departments known as Directorates General. DG1V deals with competition law matters

4 The Member States are Belgium, Denmark, France, Germany, Greece, Ireland, Italy, Luxembourg, Netherlands, Portugal, Spain and the United Kingdom

5 In *Völk* v *Vervaëke* [1969] CMLR 273, the Court stated that 'an agreement falls outside the prohibition in Article 85(1) when it has only an insignificant effect on the markets, taking into account the weak position which the persons concerned have on the market of the product in question'. See also *Louis Erauw-Jacquery* v *La Hesbignonne* [1988] 4 CMLR 576

6 Article 85(2) provides 'Any agreements or decisions prohibited pursuant to this Article shall automatically be void'

7 Published in the Official Journal at C231/2, 12 September 1986

8 *Consten and Grundig* v *Commission* [1966] CMLR 418, [1966] ECR 299, case law continues – *Re Roofing Felt* [1991] 4 CMLR 96 & 130 (cartel in single Member State does not mean no effect on interstate trade)

9 Published in the Official Journal at C231/2, 12 September 1986

The Commission sets out quantitative criteria to assist those assessing minor agreements in connection with Article 85. The definition is not an 'absolute yardstick; in fact, in individual cases even agreements between undertakings which exceed these limits may still have only a negligible effect on trade between Member States or on competition, and are therefore not caught by Article 85(1)'.[10]

The Commission goes on to state:[11]

> Where, due to exceptional circumstance, an agreement which is covered by the present Notice nevertheless falls under Article 85(1), the Commission will not impose fines.

Fines will not be levied against companies which have failed to notify an agreement because the parties wrongly took the view that it fell within the Notice, unless the failure was due to negligence.

This seems to be a very satisfactory basis on which to proceed. Companies have the certainty of fixed limits in the Notice and, even if the Notice is not applied in a particular case, they will not be fined. Often there are complications. The Notice is not legally binding in any event and it depends in part on a definition of the market concerned. Often the Commission has defined the relevant market very narrowly, as will be seen in Chapter 3. What market the Commission will pick is often unclear. The market for the supply of wine glasses may be the glassware market generally, the drinking glass market or even the specialised cut-glass market, perhaps only relating to wine glasses. The Commission will look at what products are substitutes for each other in the eyes of customers, but the test is by no means clear.

In many cases, in practice, the best advice must be that it is dangerous to rely on the Notice at all, and much safer to notify the agreement or modify its terms so that it does not fall within Article 85(1) at all. The Notice does have some utility however, particularly when the markets are clearly discernible and the agreement is of little economic or commercial significance. Consideration is therefore given below to the terms of the Notice.

Agreements will not, by Article 7 of the Notice, fall within Article 85(1) where:

> – the goods or services which are the subject of the agreements (hereinafter referred to as 'the contract products'), together with the participating undertakings' other goods or services which are considered by users to be equivalent in view of their characteristics, price and intended use, do not represent more than 5% of the total market for such goods or services (hereinafter referred to as 'products') in the area of the common market affected by the agreement and
> – the aggregate annual turnover of the participating undertakings does not exceed 200 million ECU (£140m).

It is important to note that the two tests of market share and turnover are not alternatives. Companies will only be able to benefit from the Notice and find their agreements do not fall within Article 85 where there is a market share under 5 per cent and the turnover of all the companies is low. Where one party to an agreement is a large multi-national corporation it will never be able to benefit from the Notice, although as the Notice states, there may be circumstances where agreements which fall outside the Notice limits are also of such insignificant effect as not to fall within Article 85(1).

10 Notice, para. I.3

11 Notice, para. I.5

If the turnover figure is exceeded by no more than a tenth over only a two-year period then the Notice will still apply because of the provisions of Article 8.

The turnover figure is that of the 'participating undertakings'. This phrase is defined in Article 9 and includes companies which are parties to the restrictive agreements, as would be expected. It also applies to subsidiaries of the parties to the agreement, where they exercise indirect or direct control over them, own half the capital or have powers to exercise more than half the voting rights or power to appoint more than half the board of directors or have a right to manage the affairs of that other company. Also regarded as one for the purposes of calculation of turnover are companies able to exercise those same powers of control in respect of the companies which are parties to the agreement. This would include parent companies. The definition extends to other subsidiaries of that parent company.

The effect of Article 9 is that, even if a company is a small enterprise with a very small turnover and the other party to the agreement is in the same position and notwithstanding that they hold only a 2 per cent market share, they may fail to be able to take advantage of the provisions of the Notice. Their parent company's turnover and that of their subsidiaries and other subsidiaries of their parent would be added together to calculate whether or not the 200m ECU limit was exceeded.

As has been considered above one of the difficulties of relying upon the Notice is that it is not always clear what the relevant market is. The Notice itself gives some assistance on this point and defines the relevant product and the relevant geographic markets.

Article 11 provides that the relevant product market includes besides the contract products any other products which are identical or equivalent to them. Some products are sold as components, i.e. they are used for incorporation into other products before the finished product offered to ultimate customers is made. Where these components are offered to third parties and not all used by the manufacturer of the components for incorporation into his own products then the market for those components is the relevant product market. However, if the components are used only by the manufacturer, where they comprise a significant part of the finished product, the relevant market is that for the finished product (Article 12).

The relevant geographical market is also defined, in Article 13, as the area within the Community in which the agreement produces its effects:

> This area will be the whole common market where the contract products are regularly bought and sold in all Member States. Where the contract products cannot be bought and sold in a part of the common market, or are bought and sold only in limited quantities or at irregular intervals in such a part, that part should be disregarded.

The geographic market will not necessarily be the whole of the EC. A company again has difficulties in ascertaining whether it falls within the *de minimis* limits of the Notice. It may have a very large market share in Spain, but this may be very small and well within the limits of the Notice if the geographic market is taken as the EC as a whole.

Article 13, as seen above, makes it clear that the geographic market could be the whole of the EC where goods are bought and sold in all the Member States. Parts of the EC will be disregarded where there are no sales and purchases. A product may not have penetrated the whole of the EC because of high transport costs, or because it is a product which only appeals to the tastes of one nationality within the EC. This will have the effect of making the market definition narrower and companies in those circumstances are more likely to exceed the limits of the Notice. This will also be the case where goods cannot penetrate markets because of barriers to entry caused by State intervention, 'such as quantitive restrictions, severe taxation differentials and non-tariff barriers', for example type approvals or safety standard certifications. Where there are such barriers to entry, a national market itself may be the relevant geographic market, making it more likely that the limits will be exceeded. The Notice, in Article 14, however, goes on to say that 'this will only be justified if the existing barriers to entry cannot be overcome by reasonable effort and at an acceptable cost.'

Despite the seemingly comprehensive definition of the relevant market, it remains difficult, even within the guidelines given, accurately to assess what a market is in any particular case. Regard should be had to the terms of the Notice and it is not without utility. Where there is any doubt as to whether a proposed agreement containing restrictions is in relation to products where the market is unclear, the safer course is either to amend the draft agreement or notify it to the Commission.

In many cases it will be quite clear that an agreement is so insubstantial that it would not have any effect on trade between Member States and clearly involves, on any definition, a miniscule proportion of the market and companies with a very small turnover. For such agreements the Notice is a useful indicator of the views of the Commission, although even in such cases it is not binding.

Other *de minimis* limits appear in the Merger Control Regulation discussed in Chapter 4, where only those mergers with a Community dimension are required to be notified in advance to the Commission. There is a Community dimension where the worldwide turnover of all the companies involved exceeds ECU 5,000 million and the total Community-wide turnover of at least two of the companies involved exceeds ECU 250 million. There will be no Community dimension where a merger falls within those limits, but each of the companies involved achieves more than two-thirds of its Community-wide turnover in one and the same Member State.

From an EC competition law standpoint, therefore, the statement that an agreement is too small or insignificant to invoke the wrath of the competition authorities may or may not be correct; a full analysis of it in the context of either the *de minimis* Notice or the definition of 'Community dimension' under the Merger Regulation will be necessary in order to come to any decision. Agreements may be caught even where the market is small if a narrow market definition is used or where the agreement appears very insignificant, but the parties to it are large corporations with a huge turnover.

12 Commission Regulation (EEC) No.1983/83 of 22 June 1983 on the application of Article 85(3) of the Treaty to categories of exclusive distribution agreements, published in the Official Journal at L173/1, 30 June 1983
13 Commission Regulation (EEC) No.1984/83 of 22 June 1983 on the application of Article 85(3) of the Treaty to categories of exclusive purchasing agreements, published in the Official Journal at L173/5, 30 June 1983
14 Commission Regulation (EEC) No.2349/84 of 23 July 1984 on the application of Article 85(3) of the Treaty to categories of patent licensing agreements, published in the Official Journal at L219/15, 16 August 1984
15 Commission Regulation (EEC) No.123/85 of 12 December 1984 on the application of Article 85(3) of the Treaty to categories of motor vehicle distribution and servicing agreements, published in the Official Journal at L15/16, 18 January 1985
16 Commission Regulation (EEC) No.418/85 of 19 December 1984 on the application of Article 85(3) of the Treaty to categories of research and development agreements, published in the Official Journal at L53/5, 22 February 1985
17 Commission Regulation (EEC) No.417/85 of 19 December 1984 on the application of Article 85(3) of the Treaty to categories of specialisation agreements, published in the Official Journal at L53/1, 22 February 1985
18 Commission Regulation (EEC) No.556/89 of 30 November 1988 on the application of Article 85(3) of the Treaty to categories of know-how licensing agreements, published in the Official Journal at L61/1, 4 March 1989
19 Commission Regulation (EEC) No.4087/88 of 30 November 1988 on the application of Article 85(3) of the Treaty to categories of franchising agreements, published in the Official Journal at L359/46, 28 December 1988
20 Commission Notice of 29 July 1968 on Co-operation Agreements
21 Commission 'Announcement on exclusive agency contracts made with commercial agents', 14th December 1962

Options for restrictive agreements

Companies or individuals wishing to enter into restrictive agreements or arrangements have three alternatives. First it may be possible to amend the agreement so that the restrictions are removed. This may be commercially difficult, particularly if the negotiations have reached an advanced stage. Secondly, there may be general or 'block' exemptions issued by the European Commission which apply to the agreement. Thirdly, the agreement may be notified individually to the Commission for an exemption.

Block exemptions

The Commission has laid down, by way of Regulations having direct effect in the Member States, general exemptions in relation to agreements of certain common varieties. These so called block exemptions have the effect that any agreement falling within their scope will be exempted from Article 85(1) and the parties will not need to obtain an individual exemption for the agreement from the Commission.

There are block exemptions for agreements relating to:

exclusive distribution[12]
exclusive purchasing[13]
patent licensing[14]
motor vehicle distribution and servicing[15]
research and development[16]
specialisation[17]
know-how licensing[18] and
franchising.[19]

The block exemptions list provisions which will not infringe Article 85(1), those which would otherwise infringe but are exempted by the Regulation, and those which are forbidden. Agreements which contain restrictions other than those expressly permitted by the exemption Regulation, but which do not contain any forbidden or 'black-listed' provisions, may benefit from what is known as the 'opposition procedure'. Some of the block exemptions contain a procedure whereby an agreement of this sort may be sent to the European Commission and if no adverse reaction or response is forthcoming from the Commission within six months then the agreement is exempted.

To bring an agreement within such an exemption will involve careful consideration of the terms of the exemption and it is prudent to follow the wording of the exemption in drafting the agreement, to the extent that this is commercially acceptable.

The Commission has also issued Notices, which are not legally binding in the same way as the block exemptions. Such Notices set out, in categories such as co-operation agreements[20] and agency[21] agreements, the Commission's views on the compatibility of typical provisions in such agreements with Article 85(1). Although not legally binding on the European Court, Notices are a useful tool offering guidance in areas where there is no block exemption as to which provisions are likely to infringe Article 85(1).

The provisions of the individual block exemptions and Notices will be considered in more detail in Part 2.

Article 85(3)

Where an agreement falls outside the terms of a block exemption or is in an area where there is no block exemption, such as a joint venture[22] or a restrictive computer software licence or software distribution arrangement,[23] application for individual exemption under Article 85(3) can be made. Parties to an agreement may also notify it to the Commission to obtain a determination as to whether or not the agreement infringed Article 85 *per se*. Such a notification is for 'negative clearance' of the agreement. Often in practice application will be made with respect to one agreement both for negative clearance or as an alternative, if the Commission view the agreement as being *prima facie* contrary to Article 85, for an exemption under Article 85(3).

Article 85(3) provides:

3. The provisions of paragraph 1 may, however, be declared inapplicable in the case of :

– any agreement or category of agreements between undertakings;
– any decision or category of decisions by associations of undertakings;
– any concerted practice or category of concerted practices;

which contributes to improving the production or distribution of goods or to promoting technical or economic progress, while allowing consumers a fair share of the resulting benefit, and which does not:

(a)   impose on the undertakings concerned restrictions which are not indispensable to the attainment of these objectives;
(b)   afford such undertakings the possibility of eliminating competition in respect of a substantial part of the products in question.

Notification procedure

Regulation 17,[24] Article 27 describes the procedure for notification of agreements for specific exemption under Article 85(3). Notification is made on Form A/B and involves the completion of a detailed annex to the form setting out in respect of the agreement and the parties all the relevant details, the justification for the restrictions within the categories of Article 85(3), the parties' turnover, market share and position in relation to their competitors. The provision of such information enables the Commission to evaluate the agreement in its economic context and determine to what extent competition might be affected in the common market or a substantial part of it and conversely what positive benefits the agreement might cause.

Any party to the agreement may notify it to the Commission, but notice must be given to all parties to the agreement who were not party to the notification. The Commission will send a copy of the notification to the competent authorities of the Member States, which in the case of the UK is the Office of Fair Trading. Notifications can be, and often are, made jointly by all the parties to the agreement. The parties are then obliged to appoint a joint representative and supply an authority for him to act when the notification is submitted to the Commission; 13 copies of the notification are supplied, one for each Member State and one for the Commission, with three copies of the agreements and one copy of the supporting documents; copies of

22 Some joint ventures are covered by the Merger Regulation (see Chapters 4 and 10)
23 There is no block exemption for computer software licences (see Chapter 11)

24 Commission Regulation No. 17 of 6 February 1962 implementing Articles 85 and 86 of the Treaty, published in the Official Journal at 204/62, 21 February 1962

the latest Annual Report and Accounts of each of the parties are also submitted.

In drafting the notification regard must be had to the Commission's Complementary Note to Form A/B, which assists with the preparation of the notification and sets out the headings and topics to be covered in the Annex to Form A/B. Form A/B must be completed with an Annex attached.

Where an agreement which is notified to the Commission is also one which falls to be registered under the Restrictive Trade Practices Act then, by virtue of the Registration of Restrictive Trading Agreements (EC Documents) Regulations 1973,[25] a copy of the notification must be sent to the OFT in London.

When submitting a notification it is necessary for the parties to determine whether or not they would be satisifed with a 'comfort letter' from the Commission. This is an alternative to a formal decision. National courts may still apply Article 85 where a comfort letter has been issued and there is no formal decision, but the Commission would be unable to take action in respect of the agreement following the issuing of a comfort letter, unless there had been a material change of circumstance.

Once an agreement has been notified it will be examined by the Commission. Under Article 11 of Regulation 17 the Commission may write to the parties asking for further information.

Finally, a formal decision or comfort letter will be issued, as discussed above. An important consideration in deciding whether or not to notify an agreement is that it is unlikely that the parties will have their decision from the Commission for a period of at least two years. During that interim period, pending a decision, they will not know whether the restrictions in the agreement are void as being contrary to Article 85(1) or not. However, as soon as an agreement is notified the parties are protected from being fined by the Commission. Given the high level of fines which can be and are levied, notification gives useful protection.

There follows consideration of important terms and restrictions which have been given particular attention by the European Commission.

'Agreement'

Article 85 regulates 'agreements' between undertakings, decisions and concerted practices. Agreements have been held to exist even where they are oral or 'gentlemen's agreements' and not in written form.[26] In *Polypropylene*[27] the Commission stated:

> It is not necessary in order for a restriction to constitute an agreement within the meaning of Article 85(1) for the agreement to be intended as legally binding by the parties. An agreement exists if the parties reach a consensus on a plan which limits or is likely to limit their commercial freedom by determining the lines of their mutual action or abstention from action in the market. No contractual sanctions or enforcement procedures are required. Nor is it necessary for such an agreement to be made in writing.

A decision by an association of undertakings may also be caught by Article 85(1). This would include where competitors act together in concert through a trade association. Concerted practices are even less formal than agreements

25 S.I. 1973 No. 950.

26 *ACF Chemiefarma* v *Commission* [1970] ECR 661
27 OJ 1986 L230/1

and decisions by associations of undertakings. They would include co-operation between undertakings falling short of an agreement, which coordination is achieved through contact between the parties to the practice and which has the effect that they are not operating competitively, i.e. they remove in advance any uncertainty concerning their future conduct (see *Dyestuffs*[28] and *European Sugar Industry*[29]).

It can therefore be seen that it is not just formal written agreements between companies which are regulated by Article 85 and it is not possible to avoid its ambit by ensuring no formal agreement is reached.

'Undertaking'

Article 85(1) regulates 'undertakings'. An undertaking would include a company and one single individual, although there is no definition of the term in the Treaty of Rome. Even state owned enterprises have been held to be undertakings. In *Aluminium Imports from Eastern Europe*[30] Eastern European foreign trade organisations which imported and exported goods were held to be 'undertakings' for this purpose. In *Shearson Lehman Hutton Inc* v *Maclaine Watson & Co Ltd*,[31] Article 85 was held to apply to the conduct of a regulatory body.

Restrictions

Restrictions come in many forms. Arguably an agreement for J to supply K with carrots is restrictive. J has earmarked carrots for K which he cannot now supply to anyone else. Also, if the quantity of carrots ordered in practice amounts to the entire actual and potential output of J the sale could be even more restrictive. Competition law rarely goes so far as to be concerned with such agreements.

The holding of intellectual property rights is *per se* restrictive. A patent is a monopoly right and prevents anyone else, even someone independently discovering an invention for himself, from competing by using the same technology. EC law has come close on occasion to challenging such rights as will be considered later, particularly in the context of Article 30 (the free movement of goods provision of the Treaty of Rome). Refusal to grant a licence may in certain cases amount to an abuse of a dominant position, but generally the holding of an intellectual property right, rather than its exercise in a restrictive way, is not challenged.

There are therefore limits to be drawn by competition law as to the types of restrictive provision in an agreement which are acceptable. Generally, under EC law, the length, scope, economic effect and effect on competition will be relevant in assessing a restriction. There are few restrictions upon which a judgment can readily be made without reference to the economic context of the agreement and the position in the market place of the companies accepting the restrictions.

Non-competition restrictions

An agreement by a company or individual not to compete with another company is the clearest restriction of all. Not all such restrictions will be void. Where there is a sale of a business it is usual to have a clause to the effect that

28 OJ 1969 L195/11
29 OJ 1973 L140/17

30 OJ 1985 L92/1

31 [1989] 3 CMLR 429

the vendor will not compete with the purchaser after completion for a fixed period and within a certain area of business and a particular geographical area. Article 85(1) will not always apply to such restrictions. In *Reuter* v *BASF AG*[32] a Dr Reuter sold his interest in certain manufacturing companies to BASF. He agreed for a period of eight years to refrain from engaging in activities in the field of the business sold. He also agreed to keep confidential certain know-how relating to the same field of business. The Commission held that as a general rule it was not essential to have the protection of such clauses agreeing not to compete. However, where goodwill and know-how are also disposed of as part of the arrangements, then non-competition clauses are allowed provided that they are for no longer a period of time than would be needed by a third party, having none of the know-how or inside knowledge which an ex-proprietor would have, to set up a similar business to that of the disposed enterprise. Also the restriction must be limited to the area of business in which the company competed prior to its disposal or in areas into which it might have expanded its business.

32 [1976] 2 CMLR D44

The Commission will look at the type of know-how transferred, the more complex it is the longer the period of protection allowed. In *Remia and Nutricia* v *Commission*[33] the Commission looked to how long it would take an independent third party to be in the same position as the vendor. A four year restriction where the sale involved both goodwill and know-how was allowed but only a two year restriction was allowed when just goodwill was involved. Generally, a period of five years is the maximum that is likely to be permitted and the shorter the period the less likely it is that the non-competition restriction would successfully be challenged in the courts under Article 85.

33 [1984] CMLR 165

In Part 2 there is consideration of agreements not to compete in the context of joint venture and co-operation agreements, exclusive distribution and purchasing agreements and in relation to patent and other intellectual property licensing arrangements. Certain such restrictions are permissible, but only as a general rule when they fall within the limits of what is permissible under any block exemption Regulation issued by the Commission in relation to agreements of that sort.

Collusive tendering

Many contracts, particularly for large projects, are put out to tender. Companies are required to submit a quotation on the basis of the work described in the tender document. Preparation of such quotations in the form of tenders can be an expensive and time consuming business. There is no guarantee that a company tendering will be successful in winning the work. This has led some companies into oral, secret arrangements to allocate tenders between them as in the *Sugar Cartel*[34] case. Such arrangements would inevitably infringe Article 85(1) and exemption under Article 85(3) would rarely be given.

34 *Suiker Unie and others* v *Commission* [1976] 1 CMLR 295

Pricing restrictions

Under Article 85, as has been seen, price fixing is specifically outlawed. Rarely would it be exempted under Article 85(3). Oral agreements between competitors as to the prices which they will charge would be caught as would concerted practices in the pricing area. Fines for infringement of Article 85 have been very high where the Commission has found restrictive agreements as to price.

There are many variants of pricing restriction and EC competition law would catch not only restrictions in relation to price, but also in relation to discounts and rebates. Pricing restrictions may take many forms from a simple agreement with one competitor as to the prices which the parties will charge to their customers to agreements as to a minimum or maximum price or not to undercut a competitor's prices in his principal territory as was the case in *Re European Glass Manufacturers.*[35]

35 [1974] 2 CMLR D51

Resale price maintenance

Resale price maintenance is contrary to Article 85. Individual resale price maintenance involves a vertical arrangement whereby a supplier requires of a purchaser that he resell the goods sold at a certain price. This is expressly forbidden under the block exemption for distribution agreements and is unlikely to be exempted under Article 85(3). Collective resale price maintenance involves an agreement between suppliers of goods as to the price at which they will resell the goods and is unlikely ever to benefit from exemption under Article 85(3) either.

Information exchange

The Commission has condemned various forms of agreement for the exchange of information. In *Re European Glass Manufacturers,*[36] it was stated quite clearly that it was not lawful under Article 85 to communicate to competitors details of a company's pricing policy, price lists, discount structures and the dates when prices would be increased. Similarly, where companies agree to inform competitors after price rises have taken effect the Commission would regard such behaviour as anti-competitive, unless the notification to the other party was a long time after the price rise had taken effect.

36 [1974] 2 CMLR D51

In *Re Welded Steel Mesh Cartel: The Community* v *Trefilunion SA and other,*[37] the Commission held that the circulation of sales figures among competitors was forbidden and such price agreements were illegal even if non-binding. Fines were imposed.

37 [1991] 4 CMLR 13

Other restrictions

There are many other forms of restrictions which can fall within Article 85(1). The various block exemption Regulations provide some indication of the myriad provisions which have been considered by the European Commission, at least potentially, to be capable of infringing Article 85(1). These include tying the purchase of one product with the purchase of another which the purchaser might not necessarily have chosen to buy; clauses obliging the licensee of intellectual property to assign to the licensor improvements which the licensee has developed; clauses forbidding the licensee of intellectual property challenging the validity of, for example, the licensed patent; clauses which have the effect of preventing parallel imports, i.e. clauses preventing the purchase in one Member State where goods are cheap of goods for export to another Member State where they are more expensive to purchase; and even rules for exhibiting at trade fairs (*Sippa* OJ 1991 L60/19).

THE RESTRICTIVE TRADE PRACTICES ACT 1976

The Restrictive Trade Practices Act 1976 is the principal UK statute regulating anti-competitive agreements and it provides a very different system of competition law to that of Article 85 of the Treaty of Rome. The RTPA applies to agreements between two or more persons carrying on business in the UK where there are certain restrictions on two parties. There are a number of rather artificial tests or criteria which are applied in a formalistic way.

Goods and services

There is a distinction between goods and services. For the RTPA to apply there must be two parties carrying on business in the supply of goods or two parties carrying on business in the supply of services. Those parties do not necessarily have to be those who are restricted by the agreement.

In a straightforward example there might be one party which just supplies goods and another services only. The RTPA would not apply. However, most large companies would carry on business in both goods and services, such that the necessary overlap would be there. If one party had a business which was not a part of or involved in the restrictive arrangements, that business, being part of the same legal entity, would be assessed in determining whether the goods or services pre-conditions applied.

There is a further use of this goods and services distinction in the way the RTPA catches restrictive agreements. Section 6 sets out a list of goods restrictions which are caught by the legislation. Section 11 and the Restrictive Trade Practices (Services) Order[38] set out similar restrictions in relation to services. Where an agreement contains one services restriction on one party and one goods restriction on the other party, notwithstanding that there are two parties restricted by the agreement, it would not fall within the RTPA as there must be two goods or two services restrictions on two parties for the RTPA to apply at all.

38 The Restrictive Trade Practices Services Order 1976, S.I. 1976 No. 98 and Amendment Orders 1985 S.I. No. 2044 and 1986 S.I. No. 2204

The restrictions

Section 6 (1) provides:

> This Act applies to agreements (whenever made) between two or more persons carrying on business within the United Kingdom in the production or supply of goods, or in the application to goods of any process of manufacture, whether with or without other parties, being agreements under which restrictions are accepted by two or more parties in respect of any of the following matters –
>
> (a)   the prices to be charged, quoted or paid for goods supplied, offered or acquired, or for the application of any process of manufacture to goods;
>
> (b)   the prices to be recommended or suggested as the prices to be charged or quoted in respect of the resale of goods supplied;
>
> (c)   the terms or conditions on or subject to which goods are to be supplied or acquired or any such process is to be applied to goods;

(d)   the quantities or descriptions of goods to be produced, supplied or acquired;

(e)   the processes of manufacture to be applied to any goods, or the quantities or descriptions of goods to which any such process is to be applied; or

(f)   the persons or classes of persons to, for or from whom, or the areas or places in or from which, goods are to be supplied or acquired, or any such process applied.

There are broadly similar provisions in relation to services.

Unlike Article 85, the RTPA therefore provides a conclusive definite list of the restrictions which will be caught if all the pre-conditions are met.

Restrictions on two parties

The RTPA will only apply to an agreement where there are restrictions on two parties. If there are two restrictions, or indeed one hundred, on one party only the RTPA will not apply. The two parties accepting the restrictions need not be the same two who are carrying on business in the UK, nor need they be the same two carrying on business in either goods or services.

For the purposes of section 6, section 43(2) provides that any two or more interconnected bodies corporate, or any two or more individuals carrying on business in partnership with each other, are treated as a single person. An interconnected body corporate is defined in section 43(1) and effectively means a group company. Section 17(2) of the Interpretation Act 1978 has the effect that section 144 of the Companies Act 1985, which defines subsidiaries and holding companies, is the relevant definition to be used for this purpose for all agreements entered into after 1st September 1990.

The effect of these definitions is that where there are restrictions on a number of companies within a group for the purposes of calculating whether or not there are restrictions on two or more parties, those companies will be classed as one. The provisions of section 43(2) do not however apply to two separate individuals who are not in partnership. However, parent and subsidiary are not treated as one where two companies agree to accept restrictions on the supply of goods to a third which is a subsidiary of one of them (*Registrar* v *Schweppes No. 2*[39]).

39 [1971] 1 WLR 1148

Following the interconnected body corporate provisions and their interpretation, a number of share purchase agreements involving two or more individual vendors restricted from competing with the company being sold after completion have had to be registered. Two statutory instruments, which came into effect on 30th June 1989, exempt certain such restrictions. These are discussed below.

UK business

Two of the parties to the agreement must carry on business in the UK. There is no definition of carrying on business in the UK, except that section 43(4) provides that a party will not be deemed to be carrying on business here by reason only of the fact that he is represented for the purposes of the business by an agent in the UK. It would therefore seem to be a question of fact in each case as to whether there is sufficient activity in this country to satisfy the test.

Where a foreign corporation with a UK subsidiary enters into an agreement with a UK company, the mere fact of the subsidiary's business activities here may not be sufficient to render such activities those of its parent company. However, where there is any doubt, it is always safer to presume that the RTPA applies.

Schedule 3, paragraph 6 exempts agreements which relate exclusively to the supply of goods by export from the UK. In the case of such agreements, however, under section 25, there is an obligation to furnish particulars, but none of the penalties for failure to register which are discussed below.

Where an agreement is entered into and it would be registrable but for the fact that one of the parties does not carry on business in the UK, the agreement would not fall within the RTPA on the date of its signature, but subsequently would become registrable, i.e. fall within the ambit of the Act, if and when that party begins to carry on business in the UK. To provide for such eventuality it is possible to insert contractual terms in an agreement to the effect that the parties will inform each other when they do begin to carry on business in this country and that the party failing to make such disclosure would indemnify the other parties against any losses, cost and expenses arising from the default.

Registration

When an agreement falls within the RTPA there is a duty to register particulars of it with the OFT under section 24 of the RTPA. Failure to register renders the restrictions void and unenforceable; it is unlawful to enforce the restrictions and is an actionable breach of statutory duty, but not a criminal offence (section 35).

Registration should be made in accordance with the RTPA and the Registration of Restrictive Trading Agreements Regulations.[40] Before the restrictions take effect the agreement must be sent to the OFT for registration. Two copies of the agreement, and any ancillary agreements or documents which make up the whole of the transaction, should be sent, one of which should be signed by the party furnishing particulars of the agreement. Form RTP(C) should be completed.

There are strict time limits for the furnishing of particulars of an agreement. As has been seen, particulars must be furnished before the restrictions take effect. It is usual, where the parties are aware of the need to register, for a clause to be inserted in the agreement suspending the restrictions from taking effect until such time as particulars are furnished to the OFT. The parties do not then have an unlimited time in which to furnish particulars. By Schedule 2 to the RTPA, registration must be made before the restrictions take effect and in any event 'within 3 months from the day on which the agreement is made'.

In practice, registration should be made as soon as possible after signature where there is such a 'suspensory' clause as the parties may wish to enforce the restrictions shortly after the agreement is signed and, without registration, the effect of having the suspensory clause is that such enforcement would not be possible. Registration cannot be made late. If a registrable agreement is discovered which ought to have been registered within the time limits and it

40 Registration of Restrictive Trading Agreements Regulations 1984, S.I. 1984 No.392

was not then in order to ensure its enforceability the parties must terminate it, notify the OFT of its termination, and indeed its existence, and enter into a new agreement, ensuring that it is registered immediately.

Fail-safe registration

It is possible to make 'fail-safe' registration, i.e. furnish particulars of an agreement where there is some uncertainty as to whether or not it is registrable, without having to admit by such furnishing that it is registrable. The OFT will then examine it to see if that is the case.

Public register and business secrets

Once an agreement is registered it will be put on the public register of the OFT, and can then be viewed by any member of the public on application at the OFT's Acton office in North West London. For many companies this is the greatest disadvantage of registration. When a notification is made to the European Commission, parts may be designated as business secrets and omitted from publication of any notice in the Official Journal. For example, turnover figures are regularly blanked out in the published decisions of the Commission to protect the business secrets of the parties to agreements which have been notified. There is no such protection for business secrets of any sort under the RTPA. However, particulars which in the opinion of the Secretary of State ought not in the public interest to be published and information as to a secret process of manufacture and other similar matters can, by section 23(3), be placed on a special, secret section of the register.

This is a very limited category of information to be so protected and is of little practical use, though from January 1991 the DTI appear to have adopted more liberal criteria, with greater exercise of their discretion. It should also be borne in mind that the public register is not readily accessible to the public and is rarely searched.

Evaluation of registered agreements

Once an agreement has been furnished to the OFT, an evaluation will begin as to whether or not it is registrable. The Director General of Fair Trading is charged with the duty of taking proceedings before the Restrictive Practices Court in respect of registered agreements.

In many cases a direction is made under section 21(2) of the RTPA that the restrictions are not of such significance as to merit reference to the Court and the particulars are placed on the register, often after further questions are asked by the OFT of the parties. However, where the restrictions are significant the risk of such a reference remains.

Court proceedings, the gateways and tail-piece

Rarely is an agreement referred to the Court and then defended by the parties under the 'gateways' of section 10. An agreement is deemed to be contrary to the public interest unless the Court is satisfied:

(a)   that the restriction or information provision is reasonably necessary, having regard to the character of the goods to which it applies, to protect the public against injury (whether as to persons or to premises) in connection with the consumption, installation or use of those goods;

(b) that the removal of the restriction or information provision would deny to the public as purchasers, consumers or users of any goods other specific or substantial benefits or advantages enjoyed or likely to be enjoyed by them as such, whether by virtue of the restriction or information provision itself or of any arrangements or operations resulting therefrom;

(c) that the restriction or information provision is reasonably necessary to counteract measures taken by any one person not party to the agreement with a view to preventing or restricting competition in or in relation to the trade or business in which the persons party thereto are engaged;

(d) that the restriction or information provision is reasonably necessary to enable the persons party to the agreement to negotiate fair terms for the supply of goods to, or the acquisition of goods from, any one person not party thereto who controls a preponderant part of the trade or business of acquiring or supplying such goods, or for the supply of goods to any person not party to the agreement and not carrying on such a trade or business who, either alone or in combination with any other such person, controls a preponderant part of the market for such goods;

(e) that, having regard to the conditions actually obtaining or reasonably foreseen at the time of the application, the removal of the restriction or information provision would be likely to have a serious and persistent adverse effect on the general level of unemployment in an area, or in areas taken together, in which a substantial proportion of the trade or industry to which the agreement relates is situated;

(f) that, having regard to the conditions actually obtaining or reasonably foreseen at the time of the application, the removal of the restriction or information provision would be likely to cause a reduction in the volume or earnings of the export business which is substantial either in relation to the whole export business of the United Kingdom or in relation to the whole business (including export business) of the said trade or industry;

(g) that the restriction or information provision is reasonably required for purposes connected with the maintenance of any other restriction accepted or information provision made by the parties, whether under the same agreement or under any other agreement between them, being a restriction or information provision which is found by the Court not to be contrary to the public interest upon grounds other than those specified in this paragraph, or has been so found in previous proceedings before the Court; or

(h) that the restriction or information provision does not directly or indirectly restrict or discourage competition to any material degree in any relevant trade or industry and is not likely to do so.

There then follows the 'tail-piece' of the eight gateways, requiring that the Court be further satisfied that the restriction is not unreasonable having regard to the balance between those circumstances set out in the gateways and

. . . any detriment to the public or to persons not parties to the agreement (being purchasers, consumers or users of goods produced or sold by such parties, or persons engaged or seeking to become engaged in the trade or business of selling such goods or of producing or selling similar goods) resulting or likely to result from the operation of the restriction or the information provision.

The provisions of section 10 relate to goods agreements. There are similar such provisions for services agreements.

In practice, the parties are unlikely to defend agreements before the Court. Under section 2(1) the Court may make an order restraining the parties from giving effect to the restrictions or making any agreement to the 'like effect'.[41] Breach of such an order would put the parties in contempt of court, leaving the company open to fines for contempt. Fines could also be levied against directors and others and jail sentences imposed.

Information agreements

The RTPA not only regulates agreements containing goods and services restrictions as explained above, but also, by section 7, information agreements as to the prices charged or quoted, otherwise than to parties to the agreement, for goods which have been supplied or for the application of any process of manufacture to goods, and as to the terms and conditions on or subject to which goods have been or are to be supplied otherwise than to such party or any such process has been or is to be applied to goods otherwise than for any such party. Section 7 covers a number of other sorts of information agreements, but has been applied by statutory instrument only in those areas mentioned above by The Restrictive Trade Practices (Information Agreements) Order 1969.[42]

The provisions in relation to information agreements, *inter alia*, as to quantities or descriptions of goods or persons to whom goods are to be supplied and in relation to services (section 12) have not yet been brought into force by statutory instrument.

Information exchange agreements relating to prices and terms have been treated seriously by the Restrictive Practices Court. In *Galvanised Tank Manufacturers' Association Agreement*,[43] the court condemned an agreement for the giving of notification of price rises two days after the rises had taken effect.

Trade association agreements and recommendations

There are special provisions in section 8 in relation to trade associations. 'Trade association' is defined in section 43(1) and means a body of persons (whether incorporated or not) which is formed for the purpose of furthering the trade interests of its members, or of persons represented by its members.

Where a trade association enters into an agreement for the purposes of the RTPA, the agreement is deemed to have been made, and any restrictions in it accepted, by all the members. Also, any express or implied specific recommendation by a trade association to its members concerning action to be taken in relation to any class of goods has the effect that the constitution of the trade association has deemed included in it a term that all members accept the recommendation. This applies whether or not members are obliged to accept or abide by the recommendation. Therefore, where a trade association recommends that its members, for example, do not purchase a certain raw material from a particular company, that would amount to a registrable agreement as all the members of the association would be deemed to be bound by such recommendation and it would be necessary to furnish particulars of it to the OFT along with the constitution of the association before it took effect.

---

41 Whether an agreement is to the like effect to another will involve the Restrictive Practices Court assessing whether the new agreement achieves the same commercial effect, for example to fix prices, rather than study the form of the restriction and determine whether it is 'like' the earlier restriction with respect to which the court order was made. See *British Concrete Pipes Association Agreement* [1981] ICR 421

42 S.I. 1969 No. 1842

43 [1965] 1 WLR 1074, [1965] 2 All ER 1003

Section 16 controls services supply associations, which are the services equivalent of trade associations, so that the same effect is achieved.

Section 9(3)

Under section 9(3) certain provisions are disregarded when determining whether or not an agreement is registrable. No account is taken of any term which relates exclusively to the goods supplied under the agreement.

This is an important provision in assessing any agreement in order to judge whether or not it is registrable under the RTPA. Restrictions relating to the goods supplied under the agreement are disregarded. This means the goods actually supplied under the agreement, not similar or competing goods. Therefore a provision restricting Mr A from supplying the particular crate of oranges Mr B sold to him that morning to Mr C would not be a relevant restriction under the RTPA because of section 9(3). On the other hand, a restriction on Mr A supplying oranges obtained from any source to Mr C would not be capable of being disregarded under section 9(3) and would be a restriction rendering the agreement registrable if there were also a restriction on another party and no exemptions applied.

Section 9(3) will not apply, by virtue of section 9(4), where section 6 restrictions are accepted as between :

> two or more persons by whom goods are to be supplied, or the process applied, in pursuance of the agreement.

The rather convoluted wording of section 9(4) has been taken to mean that section 9(3) cannot be used to disregard a restriction in relation to a specific agreement the parties to which are at the same level of trade in connection with that agreement. The law is unclear however as to whether the section would apply where the parties generally are competitors at the same level of trade but just happen, for the purposes of the agreement under consideration, to be, for example, supplier and distributor.

Section 18(2) provides that no account shall 'be taken of any term which relates exclusively to the services supplied in pursuance of the agreement in question.' It is virtually impossible to 'resell' services. Goods can be resold in their original form. Services cannot. A restriction in a contract between Mr D and Mr E on Mr D supplying window cleaning services to Mr F is analagous to the 'oranges from any source' example used above. Section 18(2) would not permit such a restriction to be disregarded.

RTPA exemptions

As with EC competition law there are various exemptions from the RTPA. These are not along the same lines as block exemptions however. There are a considerable number of exemptions from the RTPA – 47 are listed in Annex D of the Government's Green Paper *Review of Restrictive Trade Practices Policy.*[44]

44 Consultative Document, March 1988 Cm 331

Schedule 1 of the RTPA provides for a list of services which are excluded, ranging from legal and medical services to the services of surveyors and architects, education provision and the services of ministers of religion.

Schedule 3 sets out a number of excepted agreements:

agreements for statutory purposes;
exclusive dealing;
know-how about goods;
trade marks;
patents and registered designs;
agreements as to goods with overseas operation;
exclusive supply of services;
know-how about services;
agreements for supplying services with overseas operation;
copyrights and topography rights.

Schedule 3 does not have the effect, however, that any agreement in the category described is automatically exempted. Only the restrictions described and permitted in those exemptions can be so exempted and the Schedules cannot be used cumulatively. Thus, where a complex agreement contains both exclusive dealing provisions and trade mark licensing restrictions, only one exemption can be used and, if there are provisions which would amount to relevant restrictions covered by the RTPA but for the benefit of the other exemption, then the agreement will still be registrable under the RTPA. These exemptions will be considered in more detail in Part 2.

Employment

An important category of exemption is that in relation to employment in section 9(6):

> In determining whether an agreement is an agreement to which this Act applies by virtue of this Part, no account shall be taken of any restriction or information provision which affects or otherwise relates to the workers to be employed or not employed by any person, or as to the remuneration, conditions of employment, hours of work or working conditions of such workers.
>
> In this subsection 'worker' means a person who has entered into or works under a contract with an employer whether the contract be by way of manual labour, clerical work, or otherwise, be express or implied, oral or in writing , and whether it be a contract of service or apprenticeship or a contract personally to execute any work or labour.

Section 18(6), the equivalent services provision, provides:

> . . . no account shall be taken of any restriction which affects or relates to any of the matters mentioned in section 9(6) above (which relates to employment) or of any information provision with respect to any of those matters.

Restrictions within these sections will therefore be exempt. However, the sections are not of universal scope. For example, self-employed workers are not covered.

In *Re Association of British Travel Agents Ltd's Agreement*[45] section 18(6)   45 [1984] ICR 12
was considered. The court held that certain staffing requirements and qualifications for travel agents could not be disregarded under section 18(6). The requirements as to staffing levels and qualifications of staff were essential requirements before any travel agent could become a member of ABTA, the travel agents' trade association. This is one of the rare cases in recent years where the parties have fought the agreement in the Restrictive Practices Court

and attempted to justify under the 'gateways' the restrictions, which included a number of others in addition to those considered in relation to section 18(6).

The restrictions were matters relating to the terms and conditions of employment within the measuring of the RTPA but, as they were part of a number of restrictions on the manner of trading, they would not be disregarded by the court. The staffing standard was too high and the court required that new staff qualifications provisions be introduced.

Also relevant in the employment context is section 20, which defines services as not including 'services rendered to an employer under a contract of employment (that is a contract of service or of apprenticeship, whether it is express or implied, and, if it is express, whether it is oral or in writing)'.

There are various other exemptions too, which are set out in miscellaneous legislation; these are listed in the Annex to the Green Paper referred to above.

Ravenseft

One important principle in the context of intellectual property licensing and agreements relating to land arose from the *Ravenseft* case[46] namely, that a right to use land or intellectual property by an agreement which contains restrictions in relation to that which was licensed will not *per se* be restrictive. The case concerned the grant of a right to use property in relation to which the grantee had no right of use but for the grant. Such a right does not therefore restrict a pre-existing liberty and as such is not restrictive. It is merely a limited licence.

The Government has been convinced of this principle which is indeed referred to in the White Paper *Opening Markets: New Policy on Restrictive Trade Practices*.[47] However, intellectual property licences often carry restrictions on the grantor of the right and, in those circumstances, *Ravenseft* cannot be used if there is a second restriction on the grantee of the right which also falls outside the case. The details of the various Schedule 3 exemptions need to be considered in each case.

Furthermore, *Ravenseft* concerned restrictions in connection with real property. The OFT confirmed that the principle could apply to intellectual property licences generally and also that a restriction on a licensor on his rights to grant further licences or under an obligation imposed by law would not be a restriction within the meaning of the RTPA.[48] There may be problems with know-how which is not a proprietary or property right but a right *in rem* and would not therefore seem to fit so neatly if at all into the *Ravenseft* principles. Additionally, if such licences are excluded it is curious that the legislature saw fit to provide specific exemptions in Schedule 3 for certain narrow categories of such agreements.

'Agreement'

The RTPA regulates 'agreements'. Under the RTPA there is an incomplete and rather unhelpful definition of 'agreement' under section 43(1):

> 'agreement' includes any agreement or arrangement, whether or not it is intended to be enforceable (apart from any provision of this Act) by legal proceedings, and references in this Act to restrictions accepted or information provisions made under an agreement shall be construed accordingly.

46 *Ravenseft Properties* [1978] QB 52

47 July 1989, Cm 727

48 Quoted in OFT's Guide to the RTPA, p.16

In *British Basic Slag Ltd's Application*[49] the court decided that 'agreement' should be given the meaning it has in ordinary usage. It is much harder to define an arrangement.

49 [1963] 1 WLR 727

In *Fisher v Director General of Fair Trading*,[50] the court held that it was an essential requirement of an agreement to which the RTPA applied that there should be some manifestation of the common will of the persons alleged to be engaged in restrictive practices falling within the RTPA to make an agreement or arrangement between them to engage in those practices and mutually to abide by the restrictions. Where Mr Y telephones Mr X and informs him that he is thinking of raising his prices to £50 per unit from next Monday and Mr X raises his prices by the same amount and in six months time reciprocates, it is likely that the court would hold that they had an arrangement subject to registration under the RTPA. They have aroused in each other an expectation that the other will act in a particular way. It is essential that there is in fact an agreement, a meeting of minds and a common intention.

50 [1982] ICR 71

All agreements which are part of the same arrangement will be considered as one. It is not possible, for example, to put a restriction on one party in one agreement and a restriction on a second party in another agreement, in order artificially to avoid the RTPA applying. All agreements entered into as part of the same deal will be looked at as one. This means, for example, that if there is a restriction in a share purchase agreement for the sale of a business on the vendor of the business and no other restrictions on any second party in that agreement, the arrangement may be registrable if there is a restriction on any other party in any other of the ancillary agreements, for example in any distribution agreement, in the service contract of a director or even in any bank guarantee or loan agreement entered into as part of the same transaction.

When agreements are dated on different dates they still may be part of the same arrangement if when the first was signed the second was contemplated and an inevitable part of the transaction as a whole. Where they are at least several months apart and the second was not referred to in the first, and the first agreement would have continued in full force and effect notwithstanding that the second might not have been agreed or entered into subsequently, then there would be a better chance of successfully arguing that they were separate agreements. The important point here, however, is that, notwithstanding the formalistic approach of the RTPA and the fact that it is often possible by a little careful redrafting to remove an agreement from the scope of the RTPA, it is difficult to engineer non-registrability by separating out restrictions because of the very broad definition of arrangement and agreement which has been given by the courts and indeed as appears in section 43.

Restrictions

As has been seen above, section 6 and its services counterpart, section 11, set out exactly which restrictions are caught by the RTPA. However, consideration of some specific restrictions follows.

Non-compete restrictions

An agreement by a company or individual not to compete with another company is the clearest restriction of all. Non-compete restrictions occur in many types of agreement. In share purchase or asset sale agreements, i.e. in connection with the disposal of a business, there are commonly such restrictions on two parties in different business areas. Where in any type of agreement there is a restriction only on one party, as has been seen, the agreement would not be registrable.

Regard must also be had to English restraint of trade law, under which such restrictions on competition can be void for being in restraint of trade if they are unreasonable. There are a series of tests in assessing whether a clause would be void under such common law, which are beyond the scope of this book, but generally the court would look to whether the length of the restriction was unreasonably long to protect the business disposed of and the purchaser's investment and whether the geographical and business scope goes beyond that which was necessary to safeguard such investment. These tests are very similar to those of the Commission under Article 85.

The Restrictive Trade Practices (Sale and Purchase and Share Subscription Agreements) (Goods) Order 1989 and the Restrictive Trade Practices (Services)(Amendment) Order 1989[51] came into force on the 30th June 1990. They exempt certain vendor restrictions. There are equivalent provisions for goods and services. The goods order applies where a vendor sells more than fifty per cent of the nominal value of the issued share capital of his company to one purchaser or its group of companies or transfers the whole of his interest in his business to one or more purchasers. An exemption from the RTPA is available, but not where no purchaser acquired more than 50 per cent of the share capital unless two purchasers were within the same group.

51 S.I. 1989 Nos. 1081 and 1082 and see Singleton – New exemptions to the RTPA 10 Law Society's Gazette 8 Nov 1989 35

It is essential, if the exemption is to apply, that there are no restrictions relating to price in the agreement and that restrictions only fall within the categories set out in the order, i.e. they:

> limit the extent to which the person accepting the restriction may compete with the acquired enterprise or may be engaged or interested in, disclose information to, or otherwise assist any business which so competes.

Restrictions, if they are to be exempted, may only be accepted by vendors or members of the vendor's group or individuals who are not purchasers or members of the purchaser's group.

In determining registrability, the exempt restrictions must last for no longer than the 'permitted period', i.e. not more than five years from the date of the agreement. Where there are restrictions accepted by an individual who 'is to have a contract of employment with, or a contract for the supply of services to, the acquired enterprise, the purchaser' or its group, such restrictions must last for no longer than a period beginning with the date of the agreement and ending two years after the date of expiry or termination of the contract of employment or for the supply of services, if that is longer than the five year period.

If there are any restrictions at all, even if only one (except for restrictions discounted under section 9(3) or permitted under the Orders), the agreement will be registrable.

It is common in sale and purchase agreements to have transitional arrangements providing for the exclusive supply of goods or intellectual property licences. The restrictions inherent in such exclusivity are not exempted in the Orders and such arrangements would preclude the application of the Orders and their grant of exemption.

The registrability of exclusive distribution agreements and intellectual property licences, joint ventures and other such arrangements will be considered in Part 2. Many such agreements contain restrictions on competing with the grantee or grantor of the rights under the agreements; these restrictions may cause such agreement to be registrable under the RTPA.

Collusive tendering

Collusive tendering arrangements which come to the attention of the OFT will inevitably be referred to the Restrictive Practices Court. A section 21(2) direction would not be made with respect to them.

Pricing restrictions

Under the RTPA, where two companies agree the prices at which they will sell their respective goods there will be a registrable agreement. This would never benefit from a section 21(2) direction and indeed is highly likely to be referred to the Restrictive Practices Court, as in *British Paper and Board Makers Association.*[52]

52 (1963) LR 4 RP 29

Resale price maintenance

Collective resale price maintenance involves an agreement between suppliers of goods as to the price at which they will resell the goods and is unlikely ever to benefit from exemption under Article 85(3) either.

Individual resale price maintenance involving a restriction on the purchaser, i.e. requiring him to sell the goods at a certain price, would not be caught by the RTPA as there are not restrictions on two parties. However, under the Resale Prices Act 1976, section 9, any term in a contract for the sale of goods by a supplier is void 'in so far as it purports to establish or provide for the establishment of minimum prices to be charged on the resale of goods in the United Kingdom'. The section also provides that it is unlawful to include such a provision in an agreement.

Collective resale price maintenance is outlawed under sections 1 and 2 of the RPA. By section 1, it is unlawful for two parties who are suppliers to withhold supplies from dealers who resell or have resold goods in breach of any condition as to the price at which those goods may be resold, or to refuse to supply those dealers except on terms less favourable than those offered to other dealers 'carrying on business in similar circumstances'. There are similar provisions in relation to collective resale price maintenance by dealers.

Section 11 makes it unlawful for a supplier to withhold supplies of goods from a dealer on the ground that the dealer has sold goods at a price below the resale price. The resale price is any price notified to the dealer:

> . . . or otherwise published by or on behalf of a supplier of the goods in question (whether lawfully or not) as the price or minimum price which is to be charged on or is recommended as appropriate for a sale of that description or any price prescribed or purporting to be prescribed for that purpose by a contract or agreement between the dealer and any such supplier.

Where there is no resale price then there can be no offence under section 11.

Even where there is an offence under section 11, there is a defence under section 13 in relation to loss leaders. This provides that it is not an offence to withhold supplies if you have reasonable cause to believe that within the previous twelve months the dealer or any other dealer to whom the dealer supplies goods has been using as loss leaders any goods of the same or a similar description, whether obtained from that supplier or not (see *J.J.B. (Sports) Ltd* v *Mibro Sports Limited* and *J.J.B. (Sports) Limited* v *Richard Forshaw & Co. Limited*[53]). Selling goods as a loss leader means that they are not sold with a view to profit, but for the 'purpose of attracting to the establishment at which the goods are sold customers likely to purchase other goods or otherwise for the purpose of advertising the business of the dealer.' There are exceptions for goods sold as part of a genuine clearance sale.

Looking at these provisions as a whole, collective resale price maintenance is unlawful. Under the Resale Prices Act, no criminal proceedings will lie (section 25), but injunctions can be granted and actions for breach of statutory duty may be brought. Individual resale price maintenance is also unlawful and the withholding of supplies from dealers who are not applying the recommended price is unlawful, unless the goods are being sold as loss leaders.

Information exchange

Under the RTPA, as has been seen above, both agreements to exchange information before price rises take effect and after are caught by section 7 of the RTPA and the Restrictive Trade Practices (Information Agreements) Order 1969.

Conclusion

Many types of restriction may fall within Article 85 and the RTPA. Each needs in all cases to be considered against the relevant legislation and case law. There follow summaries of Article 85 and the RTPA.

SUMMARY

In assessing an agreement under Article 85(1) consider:

1. Is there an agreement between undertakings which has as its object or effect the prevention, restriction or distortion of competition within the common market and are there any restrictive provisions of the sort referred to in Article 85(1) or along the lines discussed in this chapter?

2. Is it conceivable that trade between Member States might be affected by the arrangements?

3. Do any of the Commission's block exemptions apply to the agreement and if not could the agreement be modified to ensure that it is covered by a block exemption?

4. Would a notification under Article 85(3) be appropriate?

5. If restrictions not covered by a block exemption are found are they essential to the arrangement or agreement which the parties have negotiated? Could they be dispensed with?

53 [1975] ICR 73 (C.A.)

6. What is the risk of fines being levied by the Commission? Is it likely that a party to the arrangements or an aggrieved third party might complain to the Commission, thereby bringing the existence of the agreement to the attention of the Commission? Would one party be likely to attempt to extricate itself from the suspect provision at a later date by alleging that it is void and unenforceable under Article 85(2)?

When assessing an agreement under the Restrictive Trade Practices Act the following checklist of questions should be considered:

1. Are there two parties carrying on business in the supply of goods in the UK and two parties carrying on business in the supply of services? If not, the agreement will not be registrable, although the provisions of the RTPA in connection with furnishing particulars of certain export agreements may apply.

2. Are there restrictions on two parties in the agreement, looking at all ancillary agreements too including side letters and any informal understanding, even if oral, which have been entered into by the parties as part of the same deal? Are those restrictions of the sort set out in section 6 of the RTPA or are there two services restrictions of the sort set out in section 11 or is there an information agreement or trade association recommendation?

3. Are the two parties interconnected bodies corporate, i.e are they part of the same group?

4. Are any of the exemptions under the RTPA of assistance or can restrictions be disregarded under section 9(3)?

5. Can the agreement be amended to render it not registrable?

6. Has it already been entered into? If not have the parties any qualms about its appearance on the public register?

QUESTION

Better Bricks, a partnership of Frances Jones and James Munroe carry on business as a brickmaking enterprise, with substantial exports to France and a large turnover. They enter into an agreement with Aquaco for the sale to Aquaco of the entire business, including goodwill and technical know-how concerning the manufacture of bricks, of Better Bricks.

By the agreement FJ and JM:

undertake for a period of ten years from the date of this Agreement not to compete with, or be interested in (whether by shareholding or not) any brickmaking business or any similar such business which competes with Better Bricks at the date of this Agreement.

1. Discuss whether this clause is void under Article 85 and/or the RTPA.
2. Should the agreement be notified to the Commission and/or furnished to the Office of Fair Trading and how could this be done?
3. If it would be void, how might the clause be amended under EC and UK competition law to ensure compliance?

FURTHER READING

EC law

BOOKS   Bellamy C.W. and Child G.D. – *Common Market Law of Competition*, 3rd ed., Sweet & Maxwell, 1987
Butterworths Competition Law Handbook, 2nd ed. 1990 (Regulations, statutes, etc.)
Green N. – *Commercial Agreements and Competition Law, Practice and Procedure in the UK and EEC*, Graham & Trotman, 1986
Hawk B.E. – *US, Common Market & International Anti-trust*, Prentice Hall Law & Business, 2nd ed. – 1990 Supplement, Volume II, cpt. 2 – Horizontal Agreements under Article 85
Korah V. – *An Introductory Guide to EEC Competition Law and Practice*, ESC Publishing, 4th ed., 1990
Whish R. – *Competition Law*, 2nd ed., Butterworths, 1989

DECISIONS   *Dyestuffs* OJ 1969 L195/11
European Sugar Industry OJ 1973 L140/17
Louis Erauw-Jacquery v La Hesbignonne [1988] 4 CMLR 576, [1988] ECR 1919
Shearson Lehman Hutton v Maclaine Watson & Co Ltd [1989] 3 CMLR 429
Welded Steel Mesh Cartel: The Community v Trefilunin SA and other [1991] 4 CMLR 13
Wilhelm v Bundeskartellamt [1969] CMLR 100, [1969] ECR 585

PUBLICATION   Annual Reports of the European Commission on Competition Policy of the European Community

UK law

BOOKS   *Butterworths Competition Law Handbook* (see EC law above)
Chitty on Contracts, Volume II, Sweet & Maxwell, 26th ed., 1990
Green N. – *Commercial Agreements and Competition Law, Practice and Procedure in the UK and EEC*, Graham & Trotman, 1986
Whish R. – *Competition Law*, 2nd ed., Butterworths, 1989

CASES   *British Concrete Pipes Association Agreements* [1981] ICR 421
Fisher v Director General of Fair Trading [1982] ICR 71
Galvanised Tank Manufacturers' Association Agreement [1965] 1 WLR 1074
Re Association of British Travel Agents Ltd's Agreement [1984] ICR 12, R.P.Ct (E&W)
Re British Basic Slag Ltd's Application [1963] 1 WLR 727
J.J.B. (Sports) Ltd v Mibro Sports Limited and *J.J.B. (Sports) Limited v Richard Forshaw & Co. Limited* [1975] ICR 73 (C.A.)
Ravenseft Properties Ltd [1978] QB 52
Registrar of Restrictive Trading Agreements v Schweppes Ltd and others (No 2) [1971] 1 WLR 1148

PUBLICATIONS   *Annual Reports of the Director General of Fair Trading*
OFT Guide to the Restrictive Trade Practices Act 1976, 1990 (Office of Fair Trading, Free)

3

Anti-competitive behaviour

UK and EC competition law regulate restrictive agreements between individuals and companies as well as activities, conduct and behaviour by single entities, where no other parties are involved. This chapter considers abusive behaviour by one company, rather than the restrictive agreements discussed in Chapter 2.

ARTICLE 86

Article 86 of the Treaty of Rome is the principal EC law on abuses of a dominant position and provides:

> Any abuse by one or more undertakings of a dominant position within the common market or in a substantial part of it shall be prohibited as incompatible with the common market in so far as it may affect trade between Member States. Such abuse may, in particular, consist in:
>
> (a)   directly or indirectly imposing unfair purchase or selling prices or unfair trading conditions;
>
> (b)   limiting production, markets or technical development to the prejudice of consumers;
>
> (c)   applying dissimilar conditions to equivalent transactions with other trading parties, thereby placing them at a competitive disadvantage;
>
> (d)   making the conclusion of contracts subject to acceptance by the other parties of supplementary obligations which, by their nature or according to commercial usage, have no connection with the subject of such contracts.

Whereas Article 85 regulates agreements between undertakings, Article 86 is usually concerned with the activities of companies acting alone.[1] The legislation prohibits abuses of a dominant position, which may affect trade between Member States.[2] The effect of the provision is that undertakings in a dominant position are required to be particularly careful to be fair to all those with whom they contract and compete and to whom they sell goods or provide services. There is a greater obligation put upon them by the legislation, a price to be paid for their success in building up a strong position in a particular market.

In *Europemballage Corporation and Continental Can Company* v *Commission*[3] the European Court emphasised that:

> Article 85 concerns agreements between undertakings, decisions of associations of undertakings and concerted practices, while Article 86 concerns unilateral activity of one or more undertakings.

1 Collective abuse may occur, see *Flat Glass* [1990] 4 CMLR 535, OJ 1984 L212, ALSATEL [1990] 4 CMLR 434 – collective abuse only where within the same group (Court of Justice decision) and *Magill TV Guide* [1989] 4 CMLR 757, OJ 1991 L201/13
2 For effect on trade between Member States see Chapter 2

3 [1973] ECR 215

Dominant position

Article 86 will apply only where an undertaking has a dominant position. There is no statutory definition of the term. There is no offence in being dominant. The offence lies in the abuse of that dominant position. However, it is essential to show dominance before the question of whether or not there has been an abuse can be established.

A company will be dominant when it has such economic strength that it is able to act largely without having to take account of its competitors and customers. An important factor in determining dominance is market share, although this is not the only relevant consideration. In *United Brands* v *Commission*[4] a market share of 40 to 45 per cent was held to amount to a dominant position as there was other evidence of the strong position the company held in the market. The market share was greater than that of competitors. It is highly unlikely that a market share of less than 30 per cent would be held by the court to be sufficient to amount to a dominant position, but market shares over that percentage could show dominance and certainly where a figure of 40 per cent and more is involved then dominance becomes increasingly likely. The greater the share of the market which a company holds, the less likely it is in practice that it will need to take close account of its competitors or indeed its customers.

[1978] ECR 207

Where in a particular market there is one large company with a 70 per cent market share that company would clearly be in a dominant position. However, it is also necessary to look at the geographical market. Where a company has a high market share throughout the EC there is likely to be a dominant position in the common market. Article 86 will also apply where there is a dominant position in a substantial part of the common market. Single Member States have been held by the Commission to amount to substantial parts of the common market. In the *Napier Brown – British Sugar*[5] case, the Commission held that Great Britain 'is a significant part of the common market.' Where a market is smaller than one Member State it would only be in unusual circumstances that it could be held to be a substantial part of the common market.

[1988] OJ L284/41

Other factors will be looked at as well as market shares. In *Hoffman-La Roche* v *Commission*[6] market shares of the order of 70 to 80 per cent over a number of years were in themselves sufficient to prove dominance. Competing companies had much smaller market shares, in relation to some markets, under 10 per cent. However, in looking at the question of dominance, the court also held relevant the fact that the company held technology which was not available to its competitors and which put the company in a much stronger position than its competitors.

[1979] ECR 461

The court will also look at how easy it is for potential competitors to break into the market, looking at the so-called barriers to entry.

The market

In order to ascertain whether a company is dominant, whether it has a high market share or is generally in a position to take little account of its competitors, it is essential to define the market itself. A company supplying a new strain of organically produced turnips may have a miniscule market share of the vegetable market in the UK. There would be a number of potentially relevant markets – the vegetable market generally, perhaps including frozen and tinned vegetables as well as fresh vegetables, or a market solely consisting of fresh vegetables, or the fresh turnip market, the market for organic, fresh vegetables, or the market for fresh organic turnips similar to that produced by the company in question. At the narrowest definition, the turnip produced by this company may be a market of its own, in which the company has a 100 per cent market share, perhaps by virtue of its ownership of intellectual property rights in its discovery of the technology. There may be plant breeders' rights to protect the strain.

The Commission will look at whether products can be substituted for those which are sold by the offending enterprise. Would purchasers consider certain other products by their nature, use, physical appearance or other factors to be a substitute for those in question? If they would then both products are likely to be seen as part of the same market. In *United Brands*, the court held that the banana market was a separate market from that of the fruit market generally. Had the fruit market been taken then the market share would have been correspondingly lower. In *Hugin* v *Commission*[7] the market was that of Hugin-made spare parts required by companies independent of Hugin companies, where those spare parts were needed for maintaining and repairing cash registers. Hugin made the cash registers and itself undertook maintenance work. It refused to supply spare parts to such competing independent companies. This was an abuse of its dominant position in this very narrow market, although interstate trade was not affected. One manufacurer's products could therefore comprise a separate market. In *Magill TV Guide/ITP, BBC and RTE*[8] the products were 'the advance weekly listings of ITP and BBC regional programme services and those of RTE and also the TV guides in which' the listings were published (or broadcast). It was held that 'the TV guide markets referred to above are separate from the market(s) for broadcasting services although the former derive their existence from and may be considered as ancillary to the latter.' Weekly listing of TV programmes was distinguished from the daily listing which is generally made available. It was held that the fact that people were prepared to buy the existing weekly guides showed that daily and weekly listings were not interchangeable, as the daily listings were available in newspapers and yet there was still a large market for the purchase of weekly guides. Substitutability will therefore be an essential factor in determining the relevant market in any particular case.

Abuse

A company holding even 100 per cent of a market will not fall foul of Article 86 unless it abuses that dominant position. By reason of its large market share it would, however, have to be vigilant to ensure that no abuses took place.

In the *Hoffman-La Roche* case, the Court of Justice defined abuse as:

> an objective concept relating to the behaviour of an undertaking in a dominant position which is such as to influence the structure of a market where, as a result of the very presence of the undertaking in question, the degree of competition is weakened and which, through recourse to methods different from those which

7 [1979] ECR 1869 and see European Intelligence June 1991, Commission to draw up Reference Market Paper to assist in determining the market

8 [1989] 4 CMLR 757, upheld in CFI, OJ 1991 L 201/13

condition normal competition in products or services on the basis of the transactions of commercial operators, has the effect of hindering the maintenance of the degree of competition still existing in the market or the growth of that competition.

Article 86 sets out four particular examples of abuses, but these do not comprise an exhaustive list (*Continental Can*). The Commission will look to whether the particular abuses are objectively justifiable or not.

Imposing unfair prices or conditions

Charging an excessive price unrelated to the economic value of goods supplied could amount to an abuse falling within this first category of Article 86 (*United Brands*). In *General Motors* v *Commission*,[9] it was held that General Motors abused its dominant position, by applying unfair prices within the meaning of paragraph (a), by reason of its excessive pricing to applicants for the issue of certificates of conformity and type shields for new Opel vehicles. Also, the excessive price acted as a detriment to, and unfairly discriminated against, dealers who wished to act as parallel importers, i.e. who wished to import goods from one territory where they could be purchased cheaply into another where their selling price was higher.

Low pricing may also amount to an abuse. Predatory pricing occurs where prices are cut by a dominant undertaking with the aim of driving out existing or new competitors. The dominant undertaking because of its position of relative strength is able to bear economic losses engendered by such behaviour, expecting that the loss of the potential competition will more than compensate it for the losses it has borne.

In *ECS/AKZO*[10] it was held that:

Any unfair commercial practices on the part of a dominant undertaking intended to eliminate, discipline or deter smaller competitors would thus fall within the scope of the prohibition of Article 86 if the other conditions for its application were fulfilled.

The Commission went on, in that case, to hold that there can be an anti-competitive object in price cutting whether or not the aggressor sets its prices above or below its own costs. The Commission found what it regarded as convincing documentation of a detailed plan made by AKZO to eliminate ECS as a competitor in the plastics sector. A dominant firm is entitled to compete on merit and large producers may lawfully compete vigorously with smaller competitors or new entrants to the market. In the *ECS/AKZO* case direct threats were found to have been made against ECS by AKZO and selective low price quotations were made to ECS customers, where similar customers of AKZO to whom ECS did not supply were paying up to sixty per cent more.

Limiting production, markets or technical development

Paragraph (b) of Article 86 gives as an example of an abuse the limitation of production, markets or technical development to the prejudice of customers. In *United Brands*, forbidding one's distributor from reselling the relevant product in certain circumstances (while bananas were green in this case) limited markets to the prejudice of customers within paragraph (b). Ceasing to supply a long-standing customer who conforms with market practice and

[1975] 1 CMLR D20 and *Tetra Pak* July 1991 decision prohibitions on modifying machines, reductions in maintenance charges for loyal customers and obligatory long machine leases and restrictive contracts – all abuses), £52m fine (FT 25 July 1991)

[1986] 3 CMLR 273, upheld by CFI OJ 1991 C201/8

places orders which are ordinary in nature similarly limits markets and was held to amount to an abuse.

In *British Telecommunications,*[11] the Commission held that a provision whereby BT insisted that, where an agency or some other third party sent a telex, that third party may not charge less than BT was prejudicial to customers in Europe. It was also held that the maintenance of obsolete systems limited technical development.

11 [1973] 1 CMLR 457

Applying dissimilar conditions to equivalent transactions

Article 86(c) prohibits the application of dissimilar conditions to equivalent transactions with other trading parties, thereby placing them at a competitive disadvantage. This paragraph therefore places an obligation upon dominant undertakings to treat companies with whom they have a trading relationship fairly. Clearly, where there is a large volume order, it is likely that the dominant undertaking would be able to justify giving a large discount, unless there were in fact no economies of scale, or reduced transport costs associated with a large volume order.

The transaction must be equivalent. Price discrimination may come within this heading; the Commission will look to see whether there is any objective justification for any discrimination whether as to price or as to trading conditions generally. In the July 1991 *Tetra Pak* decision (see note 9 above) discriminatory and predatory pricing of cartons and liquid packaging machinery were held to be abuses.

A rigid partitioning of national markets by differential prices may in itself amount to an abuse, as it did in *United Brands*. Dominant undertakings therefore need to be careful to ensure that they can justify a differential pricing system throughout the EC where prices are determined by what the markets in those territories can individually bear rather than by the cost of the goods and other objective factors. With the greater movement of goods throughout the EC and the increases in parallel importing, common market wide pricing policies will increasingly be introduced.

Tying

Article 86(d) prohibits making the conclusion of contracts subject to acceptance by the other parties of supplementary obligations which, by their nature or according to commercial usage, have no connection with the subject of such contracts. Thus, in *Michelin* v *Commission*[12] the linking of Michelin dealers through a refund system amounted to an abuse of a dominant position. It limited dealers' choice of supplier and prevented their being able to pick the most favourable offers and change supplier without economic disadvantage. In *Hoffman-La Roche* it was held that tying 20 buyers amounted to unequal treatment (paragraph (c)), limitation of markets (paragraph(b)) and made the conclusion of contracts subject to the acceptance of supplementary obligations (paragraph (d)). In the *BT* case an obligation not to charge lower prices than BT amounted to an abuse within paragraph (d).

12 [1985] 1 CMLR 282

Refusal to supply

Whereas in the absence of an anti-competitive agreement a non-dominant company may under EC law refuse to supply any customer or potential customer without risk of infringement, a dominant undertaking could by such conduct be held to have abused its dominant position. Dominant undertakings may only refuse to supply such customers where there is an objectively justifiable reason for such a refusal, for example that it cannot produce such a quantity as has been ordered or in some other way the order is out of the ordinary and could not easily be satisfied.

Undertakings in a dominant position cannot suddenly cease to supply a long-standing customer which continues to place the same type of orders as have been satisfied in the past. In *Eurofix-Bauco* v *Hilti*,[13] Hilti refused to supply cartridges for nail guns to those customers whom it suspected would resell them to independent nail manufacturers. The refusal to supply was held to be an abuse. In *Napier Brown – British Sugar*[14] an established customer (Napier Brown) was refused supplies. There was no objective justification, such as the system of sugar quotas unsuccessfully argued in the case or poor quality argued unsuccessfully in *Hilti*.

Acquisition and exercise of intellectual property rights

Intellectual property rights, such as patents protecting inventions, copyright, trade marks, technical know-how and plant breeders' rights, give their owners protection from competition. A patent holder may sue a company which attempts to manufacture goods using the same technology without permission from the owner of the patent. A copyright owner can sue a company for infringement where its copyright work, for example a computer program, has been copied without the consent of the owner of the copyright. The ownership of an intellectual property right will often place the owner of that right in a monopoly position. If only certain technology, which is protected by the patent of company X, can be used to manufacture a certain product, others will not be able to compete with company X unless they are granted a licence of the patent.

EC competition law draws a distinction between the ownership of intellectual property rights and their exercise. Article 30 of the Treaty of Rome provides that quantitative restrictions on imports and all measures having equivalent effect shall be prohibited between Member States. In relation to intellectual property rights, referred to as industrial property rights in the Treaty but meaning the same sort of right, Article 36 provides that Article 30 will not prevent the protection of industrial property rights. Article 222 of the Treaty provides that the Treaty shall in no way prejudice the rules in Member States governing the system of property ownership.

There is no EC law infringement in owning an intellectual property right, notwithstanding that that right confers a near monopoly on its owner. Owners of such rights must, however, as will be seen in Part 2, exercise those rights with care and in accordance with the provisions of the Treaty. Companies in a dominant position must take account of both Article 85 and the various EC block exemptions for licensing of intellectual property rights when they wish to license those rights, and also Article 86.

In *Tetra Pak Rausing S.A.* v *Commission*[15] Tetra Pak Rausing (TPR) acquired the Liquipak Group in August 1981. Novus Corp. was a company in

3 OJ 1988 L65/19

4 OJ 1988 L284/41

5 [1991] 4 CMLR 334

the Liquipak group which had been granted an exclusive patent licence by the National Research and Development Council (now British Technology Group). TPR obtained by the acquisition *de facto* exclusive rights to the patent and the Commission held that TPR was in breach of Article 86 from the date of the acquisition until the end of the exclusivity period of the patent licence. An exclusive licence means that the owner of a patent has granted rights to use the patent to a third party, which can use those rights to the exclusion not only of other third parties, but also to the exclusion of the owner of the patent. The patent owner will agree by such exclusive grant to grant no further licences to other third parties for the duration of the exclusivity. Having such exclusive rights within the group put TPR in a similar position as that which would have obtained had it acquired the patent by purchasing it and thereby becoming the owner of it in the place of British Technology Group. The case was appealed to the European Court of First Instance where the decision was upheld. This court stated:

> Turning to the specific nature of the conduct whose compatibility with Article 86 is considered in the Decision, this Court holds that the mere fact that an undertaking in a dominant position acquired an exclusive licence does not *per se* constitute abuse within the meaning of Article 86. For the purpose of applying Article 86, the circumstances surrounding the acquisition, and in particular its effects on the structure of competition in the relevant market, must be taken into account.

TPR co-ordinates the policy of a group of companies involved in the manufacture of packaging for milk cartons. Packaging was divided into that suitable for fresh milk and that which was adequate for treated or UHT milk, known as asceptic packaging. In the asceptic packaging market TPR had a 90 per cent market share in the EC in 1985 and a 50 per cent share of the market in the EC for fresh milk packaging. These were high market shares and it was clear that dominance had been established.

The Commission found that the acquisition of the exclusivity of the licence strengthened TPR's considerable dominance and prevented or delayed new companies from coming into the market, where there was very little competition existing at the time at all. The right to use the patented technology 'was alone capable of giving an undertaking the means of competing effectively with the TPR in the field of asceptic packaging of milk'.

An interesting point, which was the principal ground of the appeal from the Commission's original decision, was that the terms of the exclusive licence fell within the terms of the patent licensing block exemption. The effect of that block exemption is that notwithstanding that a licence might infringe Article 85 it will be exempted automatically by the terms of the general exemption without any need to notify the Commission of the licence or its terms. TPR argued that if the licence were exempt by the patent licensing Regulation the Court could not then hold that it was contrary to Article 86. The Court rejected this argument and drew on case law in *Hoffman-La Roche* and *Continental Can* to support its position that Article 86 may apply even where an agreement had been exempted. The block exemptions would not always apply in all circumstances and in any event were of limited duration. Article 86 is a separate article which may apply in any event.

16 [1989] 4 CMLR 122

17 [1990] 4 CMLR 265

18 [1990] 3 CMLR 466

In *Volvo AB* v *Erick Veng (U.K.) Ltd*[16] and *Consorzio Italiano della Componentistica di Ricambio per Autoveicoli* and *Maxicar* v *Regie Nationale des Usines Renault,*[17] cases involving automobile body panels, the Court held that Article 86 could not normally be used to force the owner of intellectual property rights such as design rights to grant a licence to third parties, since this would amount to depriving the owner of the specific subject matter of his rights. The court left open the possibility that there might be an abuse where, for example, there was an arbitrary refusal to supply spare parts to independent repairers, the manufacturer was setting prices for spare parts at an unfair level or the manufacturer had decided no longer to produce spare parts of a particular model even though many cars of that model were still in circulation.

In *Pitney Bowes Inc.* v *Francotyp-postalia GmbH and another*[18] the English High Court held that the refusal to grant a patent licence on reasonable terms was not an abuse of a dominant position in that particular case.

It will therefore depend on all the circumstances of a particular case concerning a dominant undertaking as to whether, by the acquisition of intellectual property rights as in *Tetra Pak* or the failure to license such rights as in *Volvo/Veng* and *Renault*, the undertaking concerned has abused its dominant position.

In the TV listings case, *Magill*, the failure to license copyright in lists of weekly TV programmes was an abuse of a dominant position. Here the owners of the copyright had a complete monopoly on the information. The CFI held that the copyright owners used copyright as an instrument of abuse, in a manner which 'falls outside the scope of the specific subject-matter of that intellectual property right'.

In many cases, particularly where patents for technology are concerned, there will be other methods to manufacture a particular product available from other sources so that it will be less likely that there would be found to be an abuse of a dominant position in the refusal to license.

Mergers

In *Continental Can,* a merger or acquisition was held to amount to an abuse of a dominant position. At that time there was no EC merger regulation and the only way in which the Commission could exercise control over mergers at first was by utilising Article 86. The application of Article 86 and possibly Article 85(1) to mergers and acquisitions is considered in the next chapter.

Article 86 procedures

There is no procedure or legislation permitting a specific exemption to be given for abuses of a dominant position by the Commission along the lines of Article 85(3). Regulation 17, which implements Articles 85 and 86, provides in Article 2 that the Commission may certify that, on the basis of the facts in its possession, there are no grounds under Article 86 of the Treaty for action on its part in respect of an agreement, decision or practice.

Notification can therefore be made in the same way as for restrictive agreements under Article 85(1) (see Chapter 2) for negative clearance, i.e. a decision by the Commission that the potential 'abuse' notified did not amount to an infringement of Article 86. There can, however, be no simultaneous application for specific exemption as would usually be made under Article 85(3). The Commission will examine the details submitted and come to a decision as to whether the practice or procedure so notified amounts to an abuse of a dominant position. The company so notifying can submit arguments as to why it is not dominant and why the notified 'abuse' is not such as to amount to an abuse at all. That company will be protected from fines after such notification.

In practice it is much rarer for a company to apply for a negative clearance in respect of conduct which may amount to an abuse than for negative clearance with respect to action which might amount to an infringement of Article 85(1). If a company wishes to stop supplying another it would not be commercially viable to wait over two years for the Commission to decide if the conduct were lawful or not. There would not normally be two parties to an agreement who might be keen to ensure its enforceability *ab initio* as there would be in Article 85 cases.

The powers of the Commission to levy fines under Article 15 of Regulation 17 apply equally to Articles 85 and 86 as do provisions relating to investigation by the Commission of abuses, considered in more detail in Chapter 5.

UK COMPETITION LAW

In the UK, unilateral anti-competitive activity is governed by the Competition Act 1980 and the sectoral monopoly provisions of the Fair Trading Act 1973. The Competition Act provides for investigations of anti-competitive practices and the relevant part of the Fair Trading Act provides for Monopolies and Mergers Commission investigations into monopolies where 25 per cent of a market is controlled by one company or group.

The Competition Act 1980

Under the Competition Act 1980, section 2(1) a person engages in an anti-competitive practice if, in the course of business, he pursues a course of conduct which has the effect of 'restricting, distorting or preventing competition in connection with the production, supply or acquisition of goods in the United Kingdom'. Section 3 provides that the Director General of Fair Trading may carry out an investigation with a view to establishing whether a person has been or is pursuing a course of conduct which does amount to an anti-competitive practice.

The legislation is therefore of less immediate effect than the Restrictive Trade Practices Act. Breach of the RTPA renders restrictions in an agreement void. The parties must take the positive step of notifying the agreement to the Office of Fair Trading if they wish to ensure the enforceability of restrictions in it. If they do not they are at risk of the other party to the agreement not abiding by the restrictions in the future with a defence that such restrictions were void under the RTPA.

The Competition Act is of general application, but there is no list of anti-competitive practices and the risk is of an investigation. Few investigations are carried out although there are a large number of complaints or other enquiries investigated without a formal investigation being initiated.

An anti-competitive practice will not fall within the Act where it arises from a restriction in an agreement which causes it to be registrable under the RTPA.

Exemptions

Where a firm has an annual turnover of less than £5 million, has less than a 25 per cent share of a relevant market and is not a member of a group with either an annual turnover of £5 million or more or which has a 25 per cent share or more of a relevant market, the Act will not apply. There are also certain exempted sectors, for example, international civil aviation other than charter flights; international shipping; and practices pursued by a parish or community council.

Anti-competitive practices

It is the effect on competition rather than the form of the practice that determines whether it is judged anti-competitive. In this way the legislaton is similar to that of Articles 85 and 86 rather than the form based legislation of the RTPA.

The OFT has identified three categories of anti-competitive practice:

1. Practices which do or could *eliminate* the competition a firm faces in a market in which it is engaged.
2. Practices which do or could *prevent* the emergence of new competitors or *restrict* competition in a market in which a firm is engaged by making it difficult for existing competitors to expand in the market.
3. Practices which have such an effect upon the terms and conditions of supply in some market, not necessarily a market in which the firm itself is engaged, that they *distort* competition between firms engaged in that market.

Elimination. Competition may be eliminated by predatory pricing where a large group is able to sustain losses over a period in order to drive competitors out of the market.

Preventing and restricting competition. Where there is a harmful effect on competition the following may, depending on all the circumstances of the case, amount to anti-competitive practices:

1. exclusive dealing arrangements, where a supplier agrees only to supply one customer and the cutomer agrees not to sell competing goods;
2. exclusive purchasing contracts, where a customer agrees to buy all its requirements of a particular product from one supplier only;
3. long term supply contracts with onerous termination provisions to the detriment of the customer;
4. restrictive terms generally, for example, a clause in an agreement preventing a customer from dealing with competitors of the supplier or

loyalty rebates and discounts which inhibit a customer from dealing with a supplier's competitors;

5. selective distribution systems, where a supplier will sell only to certain distributors who meet criteria set by him;

6. tie-ins, where a purchaser is required to purchase additional goods to those which he wants from the supplier as a condition of his obtaining the goods in which he is interested; where a purchaser is obliged to carry a full range of goods this is known as 'full line' forcing and may restrict competition;

7. restrictions on the supply of parts required by competitors, where competitors are only able to obtain raw materials for the manufacture of a finished product and the supplier is engaged in all stages of the production process;

8. restrictive licensing policies; where a refusal to license occurs or there are restrictive terms in an intellectual property licence and one party enjoys a strong position in the market, the effect of such restrictions or refusal can be anti-competitive.

Distortion of competition. Where for legal or tax reasons firms cannot compete fairly or subsidies are available to some, then competition can be distorted. Discriminatory treatment of customers may lead to a distortion of competition.

As there is no list of anti-competitive practices in the Act any practice which has the required effects may fall within this term. Most abuses of a dominant position under Article 86, such as refusals to supply, could potentially also warrant a Competition Act reference.

Investigations

The first investigation which was completed under the Act was *T I Raleigh Industries Ltd*[19] in 1981, which concerned the supply of bicycles from the manufacturer to retailers. T I Raleigh refused to supply retailers whom it expected would sell bicycles at a discount. The Director refused to accept undertakings offered and a reference to the MMC was made. T I Raleigh's criteria for selecting distibutors was held to be anti-competitive and operating against the public interest. It was required to widen its distribution policy to include those discount stores who observed the same standards of pre-sale inspection and other services as comparable outlets and should supply them with bicyles, although it was not required to supply bicycles marked with the trade name 'Raleigh'.

There have been many other investigations since then. In *BBC and Independent Television Publishers Ltd*[20] by casting vote the MMC determined that refusal to license TV listings was an anti-competitive practice, but that it did not operate against the public interest. Compulsory licensing would have had an adverse economic and employment effect.

In the Competition Act investigation of *Black and Decker*[21] Black and Decker's policy of refusing to supply retailers who sold its products below a particular price was held to be anti-competitive. Black and Decker was dominant in the UK as a supplier of power tools and workbenches. Black and Decker refused to supply those products to retailers whom it believed to be

19 27 February 1981 (DGFT Report) and 16 December 1981 (MMC Report HC 67)

20 13 December 1984 (DGFT Report) and September 1985 (MMC Report Cm 9614)

21 8 March 1989 Report

loss leading, i.e. selling the products at a level insufficient to make a profit. The effect of the refusal to supply to such retailers was that Black and Decker products were priced higher than they might have been. Under the Resale Prices Act 1976, as has been seen in Chapter 2, refusal to supply is lawful where loss leading has taken place. However, the OFT held that such refusal could still amount to an anti-competitive practice.

22 22 September 1989 (DGFT Report) and July 1990 (MMC Report Cm 1129)

Finally, in *Highland Scottish Omnibuses Ltd*[22] the Director refused to accept undertakings and referred to the MMC the practice of Highland Scottish Omnibuses Ltd, which operated bus services in Inverness. HSO had run buses on routes of a new rival despite incurring substantial losses and held fares below those of the new market entrant, ITL, running a 'grossly excessive volume of service whilst incurring substantial losses' to drive ITL out of business. This was held to be an anti-competitive practice operating against the public interest.

Procedure under the Competition Act 1980

Most investigations arise from letters from interested individuals to the OFT. Section 3(1) of the Act provides:

> If it appears to the Director that any person has been or is pursuing a course of conduct which may amount to an anti-competitive practice, the Director may in accordance with this section carry out an investigation with a view to establishing whether that person has been or is pursuing a course of conduct which does amount to such a practice.

Before the investigation is carried out notice is given to the persons whose conduct is to come under scrutiny and a notice is also published and sent to the Secretary of State. Once the Secretary of State has received notice he has a period of two weeks in which to instruct the Director General of Fair Trading not to proceed. This veto has never yet been exercised.

23 HMSO March 1986

The investigation involves correspondence with relevant individuals and interviews. The OFT's booklet *Anti-competitive Practices, a Guide to the Provisions of the Competition Act 1980*[23] describes how such an investigation might take place and states that the individuals likely to be interviewed would include people supplying or being supplied by the firm, people in the same line of business, trade associations, consumer bodies or users of the goods or services or those who have responded to the advertisements.

Once an investigation is under way, there is no time limit for its completion. The Highland Scottish Omnibuses Ltd investigation began on 22nd March 1989 and the Director's Report was published on 22nd September 1989. On 15th December 1989 the Director referred the matter to the MMC, which produced its report in July 1990.

The Director's Report will seek to avoid publishing information which might affect the interests of those under investigation. If the conclusion is that the practice is not anti-competitive then no further action will be taken. Where, however, there is an anti-competitive practice and the matter is deemed appropriate to be referred, a reference can be made to the MMC.

The companies involved in the anti-competitive practices may make representations as to what action should be taken on the findings in the Report (section 4). The Director is entitled to accept undertakings from those companies making the representations, such as that they will not engage in the conduct complained of again or will take some positive course of action to remedy the anti-competitive situation complained of in the Report. If no undertakings are offered or are accepted by the Director within eight weeks, the Director may at that stage refer the matter to the MMC. Undertakings are kept generally under review. If an undertaking is given but not kept the Director may at a later stage refer the matter to the MMC, in any event, even though the original period for so doing has passed.

The Director, by section 6(1), must specify the persons to be investigated under the reference, the goods or services to which the investigation is to extend and the course or courses of conduct to be investigated. He may not extend the reference to any person not referred to in his Report.

The Monopolies and Mergers Commission's role

Once a matter is referred, the Monopolies and Mergers Commission will investigate and report within a period of six months, although the Secretary of State may extend this period by up to three months.

The MMC can call for the production of documents and other information and can require people to attend to give information and take evidence on oath. In making its report, as with the Report of the Director, the MMC will bear in mind the need to avoid publication of any information which might damage the business or affairs of any company or individual. The Report is laid before Parliament by the Secretary of State and sent to the Director. The Director may then seek an undertaking from the parties. Where the Director is unable to obtain undertakings from the companies involved or the undertakings offered are not suitable, the Secretary of State can make an order. Orders can also be made immediately after the Report has been made or if the Director thinks it is unlikely that he will obtain suitable undertakings or if an undertaking has been broken.

Orders

By section 10(2), an order may prohibit a person from engaging in any anti-competitive practice which was specified in the report; or from pursuing any other course of conduct which is similar to the practice, and, for the purpose of remedying or preventing any adverse effects and which are specified in the report and which operate against the public interest, may exercise one or more of the powers specified in Part 1 of Schedule 8 to the Fair Trading Act 1973.

The Schedule 8 powers referred to above include powers:

(a) to require that an agreement be ended;
(b) to make it unlawful to make or carry out an agreement;
(c) to make it unlawful to withhold supplies from a specific company or individual;
(d) to make it unlawful to require additional goods to be bought at the same time and as a condition of the purchase of other goods, i.e. a tie;
(e) to make it unlawful to discriminate between persons as to the prices which they are charged for goods or services;

(f) to make it unlawful to give any preference in the supply of goods or services;

(g) to make it unlawful to charge prices for goods or services different from those in any published list;

(h) to require the publication of a list of prices;

(i) to regulate prices to be charged for any goods or services;

(j) to make it unlawful to notify recommended or suggested prices; and

(k) to prohibit or restrict the acquisition of a business or the assets of another business.

Orders can therefore be very broad in scope and, in assessing what is and what is not in the public interest, the MMC will have regard under section 84(1) of the Fair Trading Act 1973:

to the desirability–

(a) of maintaining and promoting effective competition between persons supplying goods and services in the United Kingdom;

(b) of promoting the interest of consumers, purchasers and other users of goods and services in the United Kingdom in respect of the prices charged for them and in respect of their quality and in the variety of goods and services supplied;

(c) of promoting, through competition, the reduction of costs and the development and use of new techniques and new products, and of facilitating the entry of new competitors into existing markets;

(d) of maintaining and promoting the balanced distribution of industry and employment in the United Kingdom; and

(e) of maintaining and promoting competitive activity in markets outside the United Kingdom on the part of producers of goods, and of suppliers of goods and services, in the United Kingdom.

24 Published 17 May 1989

In 1989 the MMC published two Reports under section 8 of the Act. In *Unichem Ltd's Share Allotment Scheme*[24] the MMC found that Unichem's share scheme distorted competition and was against the public interest. They recommended that any share issued by Unichem after the date of the Report's publication should not relate to purchases from the company. *The Unichem Limited (Allotment of Shares) Order 1989*[25] prohibited Unichem from operating its share scheme whereby shares were allocated to members by reference to their purchases from the company. The Unichem investigation was completed within five months.

25 S.I. 1989 No. 1061

The other MMC Report under the Competition Act in 1989 concerned the *Black and Decker* investigation discussed above. The MMC completed its investigations within four months. These examples give some indication of the likely time scale of an MMC investigation.

Conclusion

Many anti-competitive activities which may involve a dominant company in an abuse of its dominant position under Article 86 may also amount to anti-competitive practices under the Competition Act where the company concerned has an annual UK turnover of £5 million or more or 25 per cent or more of a particular market in the UK or where its group fulfils either of those turnover or market share criteria. However, few references are made and there is no immediate or direct impact upon an agreement when one is made.

Resale Prices Act 1976

Action by one company or person in stipulating a minimum resale price for goods can lead that company into breach of the provisions concerning individual resale price maintenance in the Resale Prices Act 1976 as has been considered in more detail in Chapter 2. Section 9 of that Act makes any term in a contract for the supply of goods which establishes a minimum resale price for those goods void and it is unlawful to insert such a clause into an agreement.

Section 11(1) prohibits refusals to supply in circumstances where the refusal to supply is because the dealer has sold the goods at less than a resale price stipulated in a price list or published by other means. There is a defence where the goods have been sold as loss leaders, i.e. where the goods are sold not for profit but to attract to the establishment where they are to be sold customers likely to purchase other goods or otherwise for the purpose of advertising the business of the dealer. Goods are not sold as loss leaders where they are sold as part of a genuine clearance sale.

In *J.J.B. (Sports) Ltd* v *Milbro Sports Ltd*[26] an interlocutory injunction was refused to a price cutter as the supplier had made out a sufficient case that he had reasonable cause to believe that use had been made of the goods as loss leaders in the last twelve months.

26 [1975] ICR 73

Monopolies and Mergers Commission investigations into monopolies

The Director General of Fair Trading is charged by section 2 of the Fair Trading act to keep under review commercial activities so as to detect monopoly situations and uncompetitive practices. Where a monopoly situation appears to exist, the Director may refer it to the Monopolies and Mergers Commission for investigation. There is no presumption that a monopoly will operate against the public interest or that monopoly situations when found will inevitably be referred to the MMC. The MMC will determine whether or not a monopoly situation exists and, if so, whether or not it operates against the public interest or may be expected to operate against the public interest.

A monopoly situation exists in relation to goods where (a) 'at least one-quarter of all goods of that description which are supplied in the United Kingdom are supplied by one and the same person, or are supplied to one and the same person'; (b) one-quarter of goods of that description are supplied by or to one group of companies; (c) one-quarter of goods are supplied by or to two or more persons who adopt uncompetitive practices as defined in section 137(2); (d) 'one or more agreements are in operation, the result or collective result of which is that goods of that description are not supplied in the United Kingdom at all' (section 6(1)).

Paragraphs (a) and (b) relate to factual situations based on market share and paragraphs (c) and (d) to behavioural situations. By section 11(1), these behavioural situations are referred to as 'complex monopoly situations'.

There are provisions in section 7 concerning monopoly situations in relation to services which are slightly different to those in section 6.

The Director has powers to obtain information under section 44, where he has reason to believe that a monopoly situation exists. When a monopoly has been referred to the Commission by section 81(1) the MMC must take into consideration representations by interested parties. Witnesses can be compelled to attend. The MMC in its reference can be asked to determine the effect on the public interest of the monopoly situation to be investigated. Section 84(1) sets out the relevant criteria, including the maintenance of effective competition and the promotion of consumer interests. The latter applies only in the case of a full reference under section 49 but references can be limited to particular facts, in which case no public interest considerations will be considered.

As with the Competition Act, a Report is prepared. This must be laid before Parliament. Undertakings can be obtained and orders made, which can be far-ranging in their scope. Where the monopoly has been found to operate against the public interest and adverse effects have been found, under section 73, orders can be made using the powers in Schedule 8, Parts 1 and 2, which include making it unlawful to carry out an agreement to enforce tying obligations and requiring businesses to be divided.

Some examples of MMC investigations under these provisions are useful as an indicator of the breadth and scope of the investigations and their consequences.

In their report on *Cross-Channel Car Ferry Services*[27] the MMC determined that a proposal by P&O and Sealink to provide a joint car ferry service would be expected to operate against the public interest. The proposal was not permitted. The MMC had been asked to investigate cross-Channel car ferry services between the ports of Dover, Folkestone or Ramsgate and Boulogne, Calais or Dunkirk, and to consider the effect on the public interest of the proposal by P&O and Sealink to enter into agreements for the joint or co-ordinated supply of services on those routes. Arguments by the companies involved that it would be necessary to have such co-operation in order for the ferry services to compete with the Channel Tunnel were rejected by the MMC.

In *The Supply of Beer* Report[28] the MMC found that a complex monopoly in the supply of beer operated against the public interest. The Commission recommended structural changes in the brewing industry. *The Supply of Beer (Tied Estate) Order 1989*[29] required brewers owning more than 2,000 licensed premises, by 1st November 1992, to cease to be brewers or reduce the number of their licensed premises below 2,000 or release from all product ties (i.e. permit tenants of the licensed premises to purchase whatever beer they chose and not that produced by their landlord brewer) that number of their tied houses amounting to half the excess over 2,000 premises which they owned. The Order also required that, by 1st May 1990, all tied tenants should be entitled to choose at least one cask-conditioned beer from another supplier, i.e. a supplier other than their landlord brewer, and that, by 1st May 1990, all ties on wines, spirits, ciders, soft drinks and low-alcohol and alcohol-free beers be ended. There was another Order which permitted recipients of loans from brewers to terminate them on no more than three

27 Published 20 December 1989

28 Published 21 March 1989

29 S.I. 1989 No. 2390

months' notice and without penalty and required brewers to publish wholesale price lists for their beer showing the maximum prices for different categories of customer (*The Supply of Beer (Loan Ties, Licensed Premises and Wholesale Prices) Order 1989*[30]).

30 S.I. 1989 No. 2258

Such Orders have considerable impact upon the running of businesses, requiring licensed premises to be sold and agreements to be amended, and illustrate the wide powers of the MMC when reporting, investigating and making orders in relation to monopolies and complex monopolies under the Fair Trading Act 1973. The parallel monopoly provision under EC law is Article 86, which works rather differently; it first finds a company in a dominant position and then discerns whether or not there has been an abuse of that position.

DUMPING AND STATE AIDS

Other actions which can have anti-competitive effects are those of dumping and state aid, both areas of which are regulated by EC law.

Dumping involves the import of goods into the EC from outside it and the placing upon the EC market of goods at a low price. Such goods become more competitive than those of EC companies, which are not then able fairly to compete against this form of extra-community predatory pricing. State aids are economic assistance granted to EC companies by their governments, the writing off of loans or straight cash receipts, which therefore put those in receipt of such assistance in a better position than those with no such aid. Fair competition cannot thrive when such aids are permitted.

Dumping

Regulation 2176/84, *On Protection against Dumped or Subsidized Imports from Countries not Members of the European Economic Community*,[31] as amended, is the principal legislation concerning dumping. Its essential effect is set out in Article 2.A:

31 OJ 1984 L201/1, amended by Regulation 1761/87, OJ 1987 L167/9

1. An anti-dumping duty may be applied to any dumped product whose release for free circulation in the Community causes injury.
2. A product shall be considered to have been dumped if its export price to the Community is less than the normal value of the like product.

Individual rights

The legislation is therefore designed to penalise by way of the imposition of duties, a form of fine or penalty which is related to the 'dumping margin' to be levied, rather than render agreements void or give rights to private individuals to bring proceedings. This does not mean that companies are powerless to intervene when goods are imported into the EC and dumped.

Article 5 of the Regulation provides that any person acting on behalf of a Community industry which considers itself injured or threatened by dumped or subsidised imports may lodge a written complaint. The complaint must contain evidence of the dumping and the injury caused by it and may be submitted to the Commission, or to a Member State for forwarding to the Commission. Member States are sent copies of complaints which are received.

Complaints may be withdrawn after they have been submitted, in which case the proceedings are terminated unless this would not be in the interests of the Community. Where a complaint does not show sufficient evidence to justify an investigation the complainant is notified.

Member States are charged in Article 6 of the Regulation with bringing to the attention of the Commission any evidence in their possession of dumping even where a complaint has not been made.

Normal value

'Normal value' is a key phrase in Regulation 2176/84. Dumping only takes place where a product's export price is less than the normal value of a like product. Normal value is defined in Article 2.3 in rather complicated form and includes comparable prices paid for like products intended for consumption in the exporting country. In ascertaining whether or not dumping has taken place, the basic idea is to see what the goods would have been sold for in their country of origin, i.e. the country outside the EC from which they were exported. In the normal course of events, there will be products of the sort being exported which are sold in the country of origin. Dumping will have taken place where the export price is less than the normal value. Article 3 takes that normal value to be the price paid for the goods in their country of origin.

There may be circumstances where there are no sales in the country of origin and the second part of Article 3 addresses the problem of there being no such sales or where such sales would not permit a proper comparison. Where that is the case, it is possible to take the price of like goods exported to another country or a constructed value can be taken. A constructed value is a way of constructing or building up what might be a normal value by looking at the cost of production and adding a reasonable margin for profit.

There may be an ascertainable normal value of goods sold in the home market, but also evidence that goods are sold in their home market at less than the cost of production of those goods. Where this is the case, Article 3.4 provides that normal value shall be taken as either (i) the sale price for goods on the home market where this is not less than the cost of production, (ii) the price of exports to third countries, (iii) a constructed value, or (iv) an amount calculated by adjusting the sub-production-cost price to eliminate loss and provide for a reasonable profit.

There may be imports from non-market economies. If the price paid in the ordinary course of trade in the country of origin were used as the normal value, then, where the goods were very cheap and heavily subsidised, it would be difficult to show that dumping had taken place. Article 3.5 therefore permits a choice of alternative bases in those circumstances. The price at which like products are sold in a third country's market economy can be taken, or a constructed value of a like product in a market economy, or, if neither of those two alternatives can be utilised, then the price paid in the EC for a like product, adjusted to include a reasonable profit margin if necessary, will be used.

Export price

Once normal value has been established the export price against which it is compared should be calculated under Article 2.8.

Article 2.8 of Regulation 2176/84 provides a definition of export price which is the price actually paid or payable for the product sold for export to the Community. Where there is no export price, the export price may be constructed on the basis of the price at which the imported product is first resold to an independent buyer. Essentially, the export price is therefore the price paid for the product in the EC, except that the export price can be constructed in the circumstances set out in Article 8 where necessary.

Comparison

Once the normal value and the export price have been established their comparison is undertaken. This comparison must be at the same level of trade and must be between products which have the same physical characteristics, quantities, conditions and terms of sale. If it is not possible to have so exact a comparison, then, by Article 2.10, allowances can be made for the difference, bearing in mind certain guidelines set out in that paragraph in making the comparison.

Where the export price is less than the normal value, dumping will have been established.

Subsidies

The Regulation also permits duties to be imposed 'for the purpose of offsetting any subsidy bestowed, directly or indirectly, in the country of origin or export, upon the manufacture, production, export or transport of any product whose release for free circulation in the Community causes injury.' There is an illustrative list of 12 export subsidies in an Annex to the Regulation, which includes direct government subsidies for companies contingent upon export performance and reductions of taxes for exports.

Injury

Duties may only be imposed in relation to dumping and subsidised imports where injury can be established. The products must be causing, or threatening to cause, injury to an established EC industry or materially retarding the establishment of such an industry. In examining the injury, regard will be had to the volume of the products dumped, whether there has been an increase in that volume, and whether there has been significant price undercutting compared to the prices at which other like products have been sold in the EC. The impact on the industry concerned will also be examined by looking at production, utilisation of capacity, stocks, sales, market share, prices, profits, return on investment, cash flow and employment.

Procedure

Once the Commission has consulted an advisory committee and established that there is sufficient evidence upon which to initiate dumping proceedings, then a notice will be published in the Official Journal, indicating the product and the countries concerned, giving a summary of the information received and providing that all relevant information is to be sent to the Commission. The notice will also give the period within which interested parties may pass on their views in writing to the Commission and apply to be heard orally by the Commission. All relevant parties are also notified personally. An investigation is then begun.

The Commission may carry out investigations in third countries where their governments consent and the firms themselves have no objections.

Under Article 7.5, parties applying in writing may be heard orally by the Commission.

Confidentiality

Where a supplier requests confidential treatment of information passed to the Commission, then, by Article 8.2(a), it must be kept confidential. The Court may order disclosure of confidential information if this is necessary for a fair trial (see the complaint of Al-Jubail Fertiliser Company (Financial Times 9th February 1991)). In certain circumstances, the Commission is entitled to disregard information from the enquiry entirely.

Undertakings

The Commission may accept undertakings from companies during the course of an investigation and, on the basis of those undertakings being satisfactory and acceptable to the Commission, the investigation can be terminated.

Duties

Where a preliminary investigation shows that dumping or a subsidy exist and the interests of the Community call for immediate intervention, then, by Article 11 of Regulation 2176/84, the Commission shall impose a provisional anti-dumping duty or countervailing duty. For subsidies, the duty is called a countervailing duty, and for dumping cases, an anti-dumping duty. The goods will not be released for free circulation within the EC unless security is given for the amount of the provisional duty. Such provisional duties have a maximum duration of four months. Where exporters do not object, this period may be extended for a period of two months.

Where the investigation shows that there has been dumping or subsidisation and the interests of the Community call for Community intervention, then a definitive duty can be imposed. It is essential for the imposition of both provisional and definitive duties that the interests of the Community call for the imposition of the duty.

Duties are imposed by Regulation (Article 13). The amount of the duty must not exceed the dumping margin[32] or the amount of the subsidy and 'it should be less if such lesser duty would be adequate to remove the injury'. In a straightforward case goods might sell for £200 per item in the country from which they were exported, which would be their normal value. They might be sold in the UK at £150, which would be their export price. The dumping margin would be the difference between the two figures, i.e. £50. The duty could not exceed £50. However, it may well be less if such lesser figure would be sufficient to remove the injury.

32 Defined in Art 2.13

No product can be the subject of both anti-dumping duty and countervailing duty in respect of the same situation.

Duties are kept under review and in any event will expire after five years from the date when they entered into force or were last modified. A notice is published in the Official Journal six months before they are due to expire.

Competition policy within the EC is the reponsibility of DG1V (Directorate-General 1V of the Commission). However, in relation to dumping and subsidies DG1 (the External Relations Directorate) has responsibility.

Intra-community dumping

Dumping generally concerns the placing of goods on the common market of the EC from a territory outside the EC. Where a British company wishing to penetrate the market in Italy 'dumps' goods on that market there will be no risk of proceedings under Regulation 2176/84 being taken. That company may be abusing its dominant position, or may be guilty of no infringements of EC competition law at all, depending on all the surrounding circumstances. However, in relation to Spain and Portugal, which joined the EC most recently, there is a separate dumping Regulation (812/86), which contains transitional anti-dumping provisions within the EC for industrial goods until 1st January 1993 (and in relation to agricultural goods until 1st January 1996). This regulation is the responsibility of DG1V, rather than DG1, which is responsible for the rest of dumping policy. After that time, those countries are expected to be fully integrated into the common market so that anti-dumping measures would be unnecessary and inappropriate.

State aids

For a level playing field of free competition to exist across the common market, companies in all the Member States must be able to compete fairly. Where their governments are making over to them large aid packages, thereby placing them in a stronger position as against others of their competitiors in Member States where the governments are not giving such aid, free competition cannot flourish.

Articles 92 to 94 of the Treaty of Rome therefore regulate the giving of aids to companies in Member States. Article 92 provides:

> 1. Save as otherwise provided in the Treaty, any aid granted by a Member State or through State resources in any form whatsoever which distorts or threatens to distort competition by favouring certain undertakings or the production of certain goods shall, in so far as it affects trade between Member States, be incompatible with the common market.

The Article then provides that non-discriminatory aid of a social character, aids to make good natural disasters and aid concerning the division of Germany are compatible with the common market and aid to assist areas with a low standard of living or with serious unemployment and important projects of common European interest or to remedy a serious disturbance in the economy of a Member State may be compatible with the common market.

Article 93 provides that where, after the parties have submitted comments, the Commission finds that the aid is not compatible with the common market, the Member State must abolish the aid within a time period specified by the Commission and, if the Member State still does not comply, then the Commission has the right to refer the matter to the Court of Justice.

There are many different forms of state aid, from capital contributions to loans at a lower rate of interest than the market rate. Companies who are aware that they are unable freely to compete with competitors from other Member States, or indeed in the same Member State, because of state aids granted to their competitors can notify the Commission of that fact. Over 100 such notifications are made each year, although only between a tenth and a fifth of those will result in a decision declaring such aid to be incompatible with the common market in any one year. The Commission has powers to require that aid be repaid.

Article 92 has been held not to have direct effect and cannot be invoked in national courts (in *Ignelli* v *Meroni*[33]). However, an individual can seek a declaration that a proposed aid, if implemented, would be contrary to Article 92.[34]

33 [1977] ECR 557

34 *R v A-G, ex parte ICI* [1987] 1 CMLR 72, see further Bellamy & Child, *Common Market Law of Competition*, Chapter 14

35 Industry Act 1972, amended by the Industry Act 1976 and the Industry Act 1982, see further Green, *Commercial Agreements and Competition Law*, p.660 *et seq*

THE INDUSTRY ACTS

Under the Industry Acts[35] the UK Government can make state aid available to industry for modernisation, to improve efficiency and reconstruction. Section 93(3) of the Treaty of Rome requires that all aid must be notified to the Commission. Where consent for the aid is not sought, the Commission may order repayment and those suffering damage may bring an action against the Government for breach of the Treaty.

SUMMARY

Competition law can be infringed by single entities as well as by restrictive agreements between companies and individuals.

1. *Abusing a dominant position.* Companies enjoying a large share of a market, for example over 30 or 40 per cent, and which are therefore in a dominant position in the EC, must not abuse that dominant position contrary to Article 86 of the Treaty of Rome or else they lay themselves open to fines from the Commission. Activities such as refusing to supply products and applying discriminatory prices and conditions to equivalent transactions can be abuses of a dominant position.

2. *Anti-competitive practices.* Any unilateral anti-competitive practice could be the subject of a UK Competition Act 1980 investigation by the Monopolies and Mergers Commission, which has strong powers to forbid companies to continue with such practices. The Act will apply only where turnover exceeds £5 million or market share exceeds 25 per cent.

3. *Individual resale price maintenance.* Requiring a purchaser to sell goods at a specified minimum resale price is unlawful under the Resale Prices Act 1976, as is refusing to supply to a customer on the grounds that goods would be resold at a price less than the published or notified resale price.

4. *Monopolies.* Under UK competition law as set out in the Fair Trading Act 1973, the MMC can investigate UK monopolies where a company

supplies more than 25 per cent of any particular market and require, either by the extraction of undertakings or by the making of an order, that conduct be modified, property be disposed of or products be supplied or that such other action as may be specified is carried out.

5. *Dumping.* Under EC dumping regulation 2176/84, DG1V will investigate cases of products exported from outside the EC being placed on the market in the EC at low prices, i.e. dumped, and the placing of products subsidised abroad and sold in the EC. Anti-dumping and countervailing duties can be imposed.

6. *State aids.* Companies in receipt of aid from a State in the EC may be required to repay the aid where it has been paid in breach of Articles 92–94 of the Treaty of Rome.

QUESTION

Company 1 manufactures and sells children's tricycles. It supplies 30 per cent of the market for children's bicycles and tricycles and 60 per cent of the children's tricycle market in the UK. It also supplies into France and Italy and, over the whole of the EC including the UK, it has 21 per cent of the children's tricycle market and 10 per cent of the children's bicycle and tricycle market.

Company 2 is the leading bicycle manufacturer in the EC and UK and sells both adults' and children's bicycles and tricycles. Company 1 has for many years supplied Company 2 with components for its tricycles and with tricycles themselves.

Company 2 has begun an aggressive marketing campaign for tricycles and is beginning to encroach into areas previously only supplied by Company 1 and take market share away from it.

Company 1 wishes to refuse to supply Company 2 with either components or finished tricycles. Company 2 wishes to sell bicycles at below cost price in some areas in order to make inroads into Company 1's areas of the market.

Are they entitled legally under EC and UK competition law to do as they wish? What further information might assist in assessing such action and what risks do they run if they both pursue their proposed course of conduct?

FURTHER READING

EC

ARTICLES

Daltrop J. and Ferry J. – *The Relationship between Articles 85 and 86: Tetra Pak* [1991] 1 EIPR 31

Harden I.J. – *The Approach of English Law to State Aids to Enterprises* [1990] 3 ECLR 100

Horovitz D. – *Dealing with Dumping in the EEC-EFTA Trade Areas* [1989] ECLR 540

Lasok P. – *The Commission's Power over Illegal State Aids* [1990] 3 ECLR 125

Schodermeier M. – *Collective Dominance Revisited* [1990] 1 ECLR 28

Tollemache M. – *Tetra Pak: Exemption and Abuse of Dominant Position* [1990] 6 ECLR 268

BOOKS

Bellamy C. and Child G.D. – *Common Market Law of Competition*, Sweet & Maxwell, 3rd ed., 1987, cpts. 8, 13 & 14

Davy W.J. – *Anti-dumping Laws: a time for reconsideration*, chapt. 8 of Hawk B.E. (ed.) Matthew Bender 1989, Fordham Corporate Law Institute, annual proceedings

Green N. – *Commercial Agreements and Competition Law, Practice and Procedure in the UK and EEC*, Graham & Trotman, 1986, cpt. 6(H), p. 250

Hawk B.E. – *US, Common Market & International Anti-trust*, Prentice Hall Law & Business, 2nd ed. – 1990 Supplement, Volume II, p. 739

Schina D. – *State Aids under the EEC Treaty, Articles 92–94*, ESC Publishing Ltd, 1987

Van Bael I. and Bellis J-F – *Anti-Dumping and Other Trade Protection Laws in the EEC*, CCH Editions Ltd, 2nd ed. 1990

Van Bael I. and Bellis J-F – *Competition Law of the EEC*, CCH Editions Ltd, 2nd ed. 1990, cpt.2 p.57 *et seq* & cpt 9

CASES

ALSATEL [1990] 4 CMLR 434

Consorzio Italiano della Componentistica di Ricambio per Autoveicoli and *Maxicar* v *Regie Nationale des Usines Renault* [1990] 4 CMLR 26

Eurofix-Bauco v *Hilti* OJ 1988 L65/19

Europemballage Corporation and Continental Can Company v *Commission* [1973] ECR 215

Hoffman-La Roche v *Commission* [1979] ECR 461

Hugin v *Commission* [1979] ECR 1869

Magill TV Guide/ITP, BBC and RTE [1989] 4 CMLR 757

Michelin v *Commission* [1985] 1 CMLR 282

Napier Brown/British Sugar [1988] OJ L284/41

Tetra Pak July 1991 decision (FT 25 July 1991)

Tetra Pak Rausing S.A. v *Commission* [1991] 4 CMLR 334

United Brands v *Commission* [1978] ECR 207

Volvo AB v *Erick Veng (U.K.) Ltd* [1989] 4 CMLR 122

PUBLICATION

Annual European Commission Reports on Competition Policy

UK

BOOKS

Chitty on Contracts, Vol. II, Sweet & Maxwell, 26th ed., 1990, *Monopolies, Mergers and Anti-competitive Practices*, para. 4514 *et seq* and *Resale Price Maintenance*, para. 4542 *et seq*

Cunningham – *The Fair Trading Act 1973*, Sweet & Maxwell, 1974 and Supplement, 1978, Part II, Monopolies p.127 and Part VI, Resale Price Maintenance p.383

Green N. – *Commercial Agreements and Competition Law, Practice and Procedure in the UK and EEC*, Graham & Trotman, 1986, cpt. 3

CASE

J.J.B. (Sports) Ltd v *Milbro Sports Ltd* [1975] ICR 73

COMPETITION ACT REPORTS

BBC and Independent Television Publishers Ltd, DGFT – 13th December 1984, MMC – September 1985 (Cm 9614)

Black and Decker, Report 8 March 1989

Highland Scottish Omnibuses, DGFT – 22nd September 1989, MMC – July 1990 (Cm 1129)

T I Raleigh Industries Ltd, DGFT – 27th February 1981, MMC – 16 December 1981 (HC 67)

Unichem Ltd's Share Allotment Scheme, published 17th May 1989

MMC REPORTS

Cross-Channel Car Ferry Services, published 20th December 1989

The Supply of Beer, published 21st March 1989

PUBLICATION

Anti-competitive Practices – A Guide to the Provisions of the Competition Act 1980, OFT, March 1986 (Free)

4

Mergers: marriage and divorce

A merger is the coming together of what were two or more separate enterprises, businesses or undertakings. For example, a company purchases the share capital of another or acquires the business, assets, goodwill or properties of another, with the consequence that one company thereafter continues the business which was previously carried on by two.

Where the companies concerned operated in the same market, and particularly where they were competitors and had a large market share, there can be substantial implications for consumers arising from such concentrations of power. Clearly, in an extreme case, if two companies previously dominated a particular market segment with 50 per cent of the market each and one takes over the other, there will result one company with 100 per cent of the market. There will be no competition. The company could increase its prices as far as the market could bear. It would have none of the effective checks on its behaviour which a company operating in a competitive market place would have.

Competition law intervenes as regards the behaviour of such dominant companies generally, as has been seen in Chapter 3 as regards companies in a dominant position. Excessive pricing itself can be an abuse of a dominant position. However, not only will there be regulation of the behaviour of entities in such a strong market position, but competition law seeks to control the merging process itself. Both UK and EC competition law contain the power to order the divestiture of assets acquired by virtue of a merger, the effective unscrambling of a merger, in extreme cases.

The Merger Control Regulation No. 4064/89,[1] which came into force on 21st September 1990, requires prior notification of large EC mergers having a community dimension. Prior to such Regulation coming into force, mergers had been regulated at an EC level by the application of the blunt weapon of Article 86 and, to a certain extent, Article 85. The Fair Trading Act, as amended by the Companies Act 1989, regulates UK mergers, although it contains no obligation to notify a merger in advance of it taking place.

1 Published in the Official Journal at L257/13, 21 September 1990 in corrected form

THE MERGER CONTROL REGULATION

Council Regulation (EEC) No. 4064/89 of 21st December 1989 on the control of concentrations between undertakings made notification to the Commission of large mergers compulsory for the first time; in practice, prior to the Regulation coming into effect, many large companies, as a matter of course, consulted with the Commission prior to entering into a large merger. The Regulation was first proposed in 1973 and was the subject of much controversy prior to its adoption.

Concentrations

The Regulation will only apply where there is a 'concentration'. Article 3 provides that a concentration is deemed to arise where two or more previously independent undertakings merge, or one or more persons already controlling at least one undertaking acquire, 'whether by purchase of securities or assets, by contract or by any other means, direct or indirect control of' one or more other undertakings. Operations, including the creation of joint ventures, which have as their object or effect the co-ordination of the competitive behaviour of companies which remain independent are not 'concentrations' within the meaning of the Regulation. The creation of a joint venture 'performing on a lasting basis all the functions of an autonomous economic entity, which does not give rise to coordination of the competitive behaviour of the parties amongst themselves' and the joint venture is a 'concentration'. Common control was considered in *Renault/Volvo* (see Further Reading).

In many cases there will be no doubt that a concentration has taken place. In the most straightforward case a company will acquire the entire share capital of another. That would be a concentration within the meaning of the Regulation. 'Control' would have been obtained by one undertaking of another by virtue of the acquisition of the entire share capital. There will however be circumstances where it is not clear if there is a 'merger' as such, for example where a minority shareholding is acquired. The Regulation defines 'control' so as to make it clear whether a particular deal comprises a regulated concentration.

Article 3.3 provides that control shall be constituted by rights, contracts or any other means which:

> confer the possibility of exercising decisive influence on an undertaking, in particular by:
> (a) ownership or the right to use all or part of the assets of an undertaking;
> (b) rights or contracts which confer decisive influence on the composition, voting or decisions of the organs of the undertaking.

Control therefore would include the ability decisively to influence the Board of Directors of a company or the shareholders, by virtue of having a majority on the Board or of the shares; but it would also cover minority interests where there was a 'possibility' of the exercise of decisive influence, notwithstanding the minority position.

In *Arjomari-Prioux/Wiggins Teape Appleton*,[2] the Commission considered which companies' turnover should be aggregated. The *de facto* position at Arjomari's last general meeting, at which its largest shareholder GSL had exercised only 45 per cent of the voting rights was not sufficient for it to be said that GSL 'controlled' Arjomari.

Some concentrative joint ventures, where parties come together and set up a separate and long-lasting company may be caught by the Regulation. Joint ventures are considered in Chapter 11 in more detail. The Commission has issued a Notice[3] regarding such concentrative joint ventures, setting out where they would be caught as concentrations within Article 3 and where they would fall to be considered under Article 85 as restrictive agreements in the usual way. To fall within the Regulation joint ventures must be separate

2 Case IV/M025, unreported to date

3 Commission notice regarding the concentrative and cooperative operations under Council Regulation (EEC) No. 4064/89 of 21 December 1989 on the control of concentrations between undertakings, published in the Official Journal at C203/10, 14 August 1990, paragraphs 37, 38 and 39

undertakings. The joint venture must operate as an independent supplier and buyer on the market. It must exist on a lasting basis and it must not have as its object or effect the coordination of the competitive behaviour of undertakings that remain independent of each other.

The Regulation may also catch exchanges of shareholdings or reciprocal directorships. These will be evaluated in accordance with 'their foreseeable effects in each case' (para. 40 of the Notice). Paragraph 45 states:

> Personal connections not accompanied by shareholdings are to be judged according to the same criteria as shareholding relationships between undertakings. A majority of seats on the managing or supervisory board of an undertaking will normally imply control of the latter; a minority of seats at least a degree of influence over its commercial policy, which may entail a coordination of behaviour. Reciprocal connections justify a presumption that the undertakings concerned are coordinating their business conduct. A very wide communality of membership of the respective decision-making bodies – that is, up to half of the members or more – may be an indication of a concentration.

Community dimension

Once it has been established that there is a concentration within the definition in the Regulation, the next consideration is whether that concentration falls within the 'scope' of the Regulation. Article 1 contains the criteria and limits of this 'scope' and essentially excludes small mergers from the Regulation, providing that only concentrations with a community dimension will be caught. The concept of a community dimension is central to the Regulation. It is defined in Article 1.2:

> 2. For the purposes of this Regulation, a concentration has a Community dimension where;
>   (a)   the aggregate worldwide turnover of all the undertakings concerned is more than ECU 5,000 million, and
>   (b)   the aggregate Community-wide turnover of each of at least two of the undertakings concerned is more than ECU 250 million,
>
> unless each of the undertakings concerned achieves more than two-thirds of its aggregate Community-wide turnover within one and the same Member State.

This should be read in conjunction with Recital 15 of the Regulation which provides that, where the market share of the undertakings concerned does not exceed 25 per cent either in the common market or in a substantial part of it, it may be presumed that the merger is compatible with the common market.

Thus, a merger between two very small companies would not be caught as the worldwide turnover of all the undertakings involved must exceed ECU 5,000 million (£3,500 million). Similarly, a merger between two companies with a huge non-EC turnover and no EC turnover would not be caught as there must be two parties to the merger with a turnover in the EC of more than ECU 250 million (£175 million).

Even if both these requirements are met, a merger will not have a Community dimension where each of the companies involved achieves two-thirds of its total EC turnover in one Member State, i.e. the same Member State. Guidance Note 4, appended to the ancillary Regulation (No.2367/90),[4] which sets out the detail for notifications of mergers,

4 On the notifications, time limits and hearings provided for in Council Regulation (EEC) No. 4064/89 on the control of concentrations between undertakings, published in the Official Journal at L219/5, 14 August 1990

illustrates the application of the two-thirds rule. Where two companies A and B are to merge and A achieves 75 per cent of its Community-wide turnover in Member State X and B achieves only 50 per cent of its Community-wide turnover in that Member State, the Note provides:

> In this case, although undertaking A achieves more than two-thirds of its Community-wide turnover in Member State X, the proposed concentration would fall within the scope of the Regulation due to the fact that undertaking B achieves less than two-thirds of its Community-wide turnover in Member State X.

The thresholds in Article 1 will be reviewed, and may be altered by majority on a proposal by the Commission before 21st September 1994.

The criteria in Article 1 relate solely to the size of turnover. There may be a merger involving big EC companies where both are involved throughout the EC, and which therefore fall within the thresholds in Article 1, yet possess very small market shares so that the merger is unlikely to have any impact whatsoever on competition. Recital 15 gives a non-binding 'indication' that, where the market shares of the parties do not exceed 25 per cent in the EC or a substantial part of it, then merger is unlikely to impede effective competition. However, the merger would still fall within the scope of the Regulation and need to be notified to ensure compliance.

Turnover

Turnover is the measure used to determine whether or not a concentration falls within the scope of the Regulation. There is a definition of turnover in Article 5. Turnover comprises sums derived in the preceding financial year from the sale of products or the provision of services which fall within the ordinary activities of the companies concerned. A deduction is made for value added tax and for sales to group companies, but group companies' turnover is aggregated in calculating total turnover. Article 5.2 is important in calculating turnover. It provides that where the concentration consists of the acquisition of parts of an undertaking 'only the turnover relating to the parts which are the subject of the transaction shall be taken into account with regard to the seller'.

5 See note 4 above

Regulation 2367/90[5] on the notifications, time limits and hearings provided for in the merger control Regulation has appended to it the form for notification of mergers and Guidance Notes. Guidance Note 1 sets out notes to assist in the calculation of turnover for credit and other financial institutions. Guidance Note 2 does the same for insurance undertakings and Guidance Note 3 provides for joint undertakings.

Notification

Concentrations with a Community dimension must be notified to the Commission not more than one week after the conclusion of the agreement, or the announcement of the public bid, or the acquisition of the controlling interest (Article 4). The week begins when the first of those events occurs.

There is therefore an obligation to notify the Commission of a merger prior to its taking effect. There are penalties for failure to notify; these are discussed below. Where two undertakings merge or joint control is acquired the notification should be joint. In other circumstances the person acquiring control makes the notification. Unlike the UK system for pre-notification of mergers, which is discussed below, there is no fee payable to the Commission on submission of a notification.

After notification, the Commission will evaluate whether the merger falls within the scope of the Regulation. Where it determines that it does, it will publish the fact of the notification with the names of the parties, the nature of the merger and the economic sectors involved. The Commission is charged, by Article 4.3, to 'take account of the legitimate interest of undertakings in the protection of their business secrets'.

Regulation 2367/90 sets out the detail of what should be included in the notification and the form (CO) which must be completed. The immense amount of detail which is required on submitting a notification was the subject of much heated debate and lobbying prior to the adoption of the Regulation. The form was greatly simplified so that only information relevant to the merger need be supplied. The Commission has a discretion to permit companies to supply less information than is required by the form. There still remains a large amount of information which will need to be submitted in making a proper notification on form CO. The Commission's discretion in determining what information it needs is exercised according to each individual case.

A representative of the undertakings notifying the merger must sign the notification and produce written proof that he is authorised to act, as with notification under Article 85(3). Twenty copies of the notification have to be submitted, with fifteen copies of the supporting documents. Where copies of supporting documents are sent rather than originals, the parties making the notification must certify that they are true and complete copies. The parties must submit the documents and notification in one official Community language, which will then become the language of the subsequent proceedings (Article 2.4).

Parties making a notification have to be extremely careful that they supply all the information which is required. There is an obligation under the Regulation that the information supplied is correct and complete and incorrect or misleading information is deemed to be incomplete information. A notification will not be effective until the date when complete information is given to the Commission. As parties to a merger usually work to very tight time-scales and are keen to complete a merger in the shortest possible time, it is important that complete information is supplied.

Each party completing the notification is responsible for the accuracy of the information he supplies.

Supporting documentation

Notification must be accompanied by:

(a) copies of the final or most recent versions of all documents bringing about the concentration, whether by agreement between the parties concerned, acquisition of a controlling interest or a public bid;
(b) in a public bid, a copy of the offer document; if unavailable on notification it should be submitted as soon as possible and not later than when it is posted to shareholders;

(c) copies of the most recent annual reports and accounts of all the parties to the concentration;

(d) copies of reports or analyses which have been prepared for the purposes of the concentration and from which information has been taken in order to provide the information requested in sections 5 and 6 (information on, and general conditions in, affected markets);

(e) a list and short description of the contents of all other analyses, reports, studies and surveys prepared by or for any of the notifying parties for the purpose of assessing or analysing the proposed concentration with respect to competitive conditions, competitors (actual or potential), and market conditions. Each item in the list must include the name and position held of the author.

The form itself sets out these requirements. The sections and paragraph numbers used in the form must be utilised in completing the notification by supplying the information requested by the form. There are detailed provisions concerning the counting of days for the various time limits in the Regulation which are given in ancillary Regulation 2367/90, to which reference should be made in making a notification using form CO.

Business secrets

Where there are parts of the information supplied which the parties regard as legitimate business secrets, each page of those secrets must be marked as such and reasons must be given as to why that information should not be divulged by the Commission. Separate parties to a merger may supply their business secrets independently to the Commission and the information may be kept secret from the other party.

The information

The information to be supplied includes:

1. Information on the notifying party.
2. Details of the concentration, including what type of merger it is, what economic sectors are involved, whether the parties enjoy any form of public support, the economic and financial details of the concentration, details of turnover for each of the parties for the last three financial years worldwide, Community-wide, in each Member State and in the Member State in which more than two-thirds of Community-wide turnover is achieved, profits before tax worldwide and the number of employees worldwide.
3. Ownership and control details, lists of undertakings in the same group and acquisitions made in the last three years.
4. Personal and financial links.
5. Information on affected markets, including an explanation of the affected relevant product markets, market data on affected markets and market data on conglomerate aspects. The form defines the relevant product market as a market 'comprising all those products and/or services which are regarded as interchangeable or substitutable by the consumer, by reason of the products' characteristics, their prices and their intended use'.

A relevant product market may be composed of a number of individual product groups. An individual product group is a product or small group of products which present largely identical physical or technical characteristics and are fully interchangeable. The Form states 'The difference between products within the group will be small and usually only a matter of brand and/or image. The product market will usually be the classification used by the undertaking in its marketing operations'. This is very similar to the market tests which have been applied in connection with Article 86, discussed in Chapter 3.

The definition of geographic market is also instructive and states that the relevant geographic market comprises the area in which the undertakings concerned are involved in the supply of products or services 'in which the conditions of competition are sufficiently homogeneous and which can be distinguished from neighbouring areas because, in particular, conditions of competition are appreciably different in those areas'. Factors relevant to the assessment of the relevant geographic market include the nature and characteristics of the products or services concerned, the existence of entry barriers or consumer preferences, appreciable differences of the undertakings' market shares between neighbouring areas or substantial price differences. The EC Commission is drawing up market definition guidelines – the Reference Market Paper.

Further information is required as to:

6. General conditions in affected markets, whether there has been any significant market entry over the last five years and whether there is likely to be any in the next five years, factors influencing market entry, the relevance of research and development to the parties' ability to compete in the future, an explanation of the distribution channels and service networks that exist on the affected markets, details of the competitive environment, main competitors etc., details of co-operative agreements which exist in the affected markets, a list of the trade associations representing the interests of companies operating in the relevant market and a description of the worldwide context of the proposed concentration.

7. General matters, how consumers will be affected and the development of technical progress.

A declaration is required to be signed at the end of form CO.

Officials

The Commission has set up a task force of thirty officials within the Competition Directorate DG1V to police and operate the Merger Regulation. The officials operate in three groups dealing with different areas. Form CO can be delivered by hand to their offices at:

> Commission of the European Communities,
> Directorate General for Competition (DG1V),
> Merger Task Force,
> 150, avenue de Cortenberg,
> B–1040 Brussels.

Postal notifications are sent to the Commission address at 200, rue de la Loi, B–1049 Brussels (where notifications under Articles 85 and 86 are sent) addressed to 'Merger Task Force (Cort. 150)'.

Proceedings

When a notification is received it will be examined by the Commission which will either declare that it does not fall within the scope of the Regulation and publish a decision to that effect, declare that it is compatible with the common market or, where there are serious doubts about the compatibility of the merger with the common market, initiate proceedings.

Parties are not entitled to put in a notification and then proceed with their merger, as they might proceed with an agreement notified under Article 85(3). The concentration, by Article 7 of Regulation 4064/89, must not be put into effect for three weeks from the notification being made. The Commission may extend the period during which the merger may not be put into effect until it takes its final decision.

The notification will have stressed the factors showing that the concentration was compatible with the common market. Compatibility with the common market is the crucial criteria in the Commission's assessment of a merger.

Compatibility with the common market

Article 2 of Regulation 4064/89 provides that concentrations will be appraised to establish their compatibility with the common market, taking account of the need to preserve and develop effective competition within the common market and the market position of the undertakings concerned and their economic and financial power, the opportunities available to suppliers and users, their access to supplies or markets, any legal or other barriers to entry, supply and demand trends for the relevant goods and services, the interests of the intermediate and ultimate consumers, and the development of technical and economic progress provided that it is to consumers' advantage and does not form an obstacle to competition. These are the factors which the Commission will examine in determining whether a concentration will be authorised or not.

Ancillary restrictions

Recital 25 of the Merger Regulation provides that the Regulation is not disapplied where the undertakings concerned accept restrictions which are directly related and necessary to the implementation of the concentration. The Commission has issued a Notice regarding restrictions ancillary to concentrations,[6] which is not legally binding on the Court of Justice but which, as with all Commission Notices, is a useful indication of the likely views of the competition authorities, in this case, on aspects of restrictions ancillary to concentrations.

The sorts of restriction that parties to a merger regularly contemplate are that one of the parties will not carry on business in competition with the enterprise of which it has disposed for a certain period after the disposal. The restrictions must be ancillary to the deal. They cannot restrict third parties or

6 Published in the Official Journal at C203/5, 14 August 1990

be 'wholly different in nature from those which result from the concentration itself'. Such restrictions must be necessray to the implementation of the concentration. The nature of the restriction will be looked at, as will its duration, subject matter and geographic field of application. The Notice examines a number of the more typical restrictions that are found in mergers.

1. Non-competition clauses

Restrictions on the vendor are permitted as they guarantee the transfer to the acquirer of the full value of the assets transferred. This sort of protection is not considered necessary when *de facto* the transfer is 'limited to physical assets (such as land, buildings or machinery) or to exclusive industrial and commercial property rights (the holders of which could immediately take action against infringements by the transferor of such rights)'.

Restrictions on the purchaser are not permitted. Often parties to a merger will want some form of reciprocal protection from competition. If they want to achieve this and ensure that the restrictions are enforceable, it may be necessary to ensure that they are of small geographic scope, short in time and notified to the Commission on form A/B for specific exemption under Article 85(3).

Period

A period of five years is regarded under the Notice as a reasonable period for such non-competition restrictions when the transfer includes goodwill and know-how and two years when it includes only goodwill. This is similar to the 'rules' which have grown up under case law in connection with non-competition restrictions where there is a disposal of a business, discussed in Chapter 2. It is particularly stated in the Notice that these are not absolute rules and longer peiods may be allowed in particular circumstances, where customer loyalty is likely to last beyond two years or 'the economic life-cycle of the products concerned is longer than five years and should be taken into account'.

Geographic scope

The geographic scope of the restriction, i.e. the areas of the EC in which the vendor will not be able to operate in competition after the merger, 'must be limited to the area where the vendor had established the products or services before the transfer'.

Products and services

Paragraph 3.A.4 of the Notice provides that the non-competition clause must be limited to products and services which form the economic activity of the undertaking transferred. Where there has been a partial transfer of assets only, it is the view of the Commission that the acquirer does not need to be 'protected from the competition of the vendor in the products or services which constitute the activities which the vendor retains after the transfer'. The parties therefore cannot go further and provide that the vendor will not compete in areas in which the acquired enterprise may later begin to operate.

Restrictions may be binding on the vendor and its subsidiaries and commercial agents. Other restrictions would not be classed as ancillary restrictions and would fall to be considered under normal competition rules. Restrictions on distributors of the vendor or on the parent company of the vendor would not therefore be able to be counted as ancillary restrictions.

2. Licences of industrial and commercial property rights and of know-how

Where an enterprise is disposed of, there may be patent or trade mark or other intellectual property rights which are part of that business. They may be owned by the company being sold and the vendor may not be interested in using them after the merger is effected. Where that is the case there will be no additional issue to consider. However, often the vendor will wish to retain ownership of those rights so that they can be used within the vendor's retained business after completion of the merger. In such a case, the vendor grants a licence, i.e. permission to use, to the purchaser by way of a licensing agreement. Simple or exclusive licences of patents, similar rights or existing know-how are allowed in the merger context where necessary for the completion of the transaction. Restrictions in such agreements may restrict the use of the technology to certain feilds of use, to the extent that they correspond to the activities of the undertaking transferred. Normally it will not be necessary for such licences to include territorial limitations on manufacturer which reflect the territory of the activity transferred. Licences may be granted for the whole duration of the patent or similar right or the duration of the normal economic life of the know-how. As such licences are economically equivalent to the partial transfer of rights, they need not be limited in time.

Were it not for the provisions of the Notice, normal intellectual property licences which are part of many mergers would fall to be considered under Article 85 and possibly Article 86. Where there are licences which go beyond the scope set out above, they may still fall within the terms of the patent licence or know-how block exemptions. If not they would need to be notified on Form A/B and it is conceivable that notification on both Forms CO and A/B would need to be made simultaneously where a particular merger contains restrictions which go beyond the scope of the ancillary restrictions Notice.

It may be necessary to have agreements concerning the use of trade marks and trade names after completion of a merger so as to avoid confusion between trade marks. The Notice goes on to provide that the same principles apply to licences of trade marks, business names or similar rights as to licences of patents.

3. Purchase and supply agreements

Undertakings transferred as part of a merger will often have existing agreements whereby the vendor of the company sold goods, perhaps raw materials for manufacture, to the transferred company. To make the transfer operate smoothly it will often be necessary to continue those supply lines for a transitional period. They may lead to restrictions on competition which are ancillary to the deal. The Notice permits such agreements in favour of both the vendor and the acquirer.

The Notice provides:

> The legitimate aim of such obligations may be to ensure the continuity of supply to one or other of the parties of products necessary to the activities retained (for the vendor) or taken over (for the acquirer). Thus, there are grounds for recognizing, for a transitional period, the need for supply obligations aimed at guaranteeing the quantities previously supplied within the vendor's integrated business or enabling their adjustment in accordance with the development of the market.

Obligations providing for fixed quantities of goods to be supplied may be permitted.

Only where there is no market for goods or where there are special specifications will exclusive supply or purchase obligations be permitted under the Notice. The Commission does not regard such exclusivity as 'objectively necessary to permit the implementation of a concentration in the form of a transfer of an undertaking or part of an undertaking'. The duration of the supply or procurement obligations must be limited to the 'period necessary for the replacement of the relationship of dependency by autonomy in the market. The duration of such a period must be objectively justified.' The notification on Form CO will therefore set out the justification for all ancillary restrictions in an effort to bring them within the scope of the Notice.

Ancillary restrictions for concentrative joint ventures

The Notice also considers the evaluation of ancillary restrictions in the case of a joint acquisition and where there is a concentrative joint venture, as discussed above.

Where there is a restriction on a parent company of a concentrative joint venture (i.e. a joint venture which is a separate entity of lasting duration) from competing with the joint venture company, that restriction will be permitted where it 'aims at expressing the reality of the lasting withdrawal of the parents from the market assigned to the joint venture'. Exclusive licences to the concentrative joint venture company may be granted by the parent companies which wish to retain their ownership of intellectual property rights, as they 'serve only as a substitute for the transfer of property rights'. They must therefore be considered necessary to the implementation of the concentration. To grant a company exclusive rights means that the owner of those rights agrees not to grant licences to third parties and also agrees not himself to use those rights in the territory in relation to which exclusive rights have been granted. The effect is therefore almost the same economically as the assignment or absolute transfer of rights and the Commission appreciates this similarity.

In this context purchase and supply agreements will be examined 'in accordance with the principles applicable in the case of the transfer of an undertaking.'

The Commission, therefore, will examine all agreements sent with the Form CO and, in particular, will look at the ancillary restrictions in the light of the Notice and representations made by the parties in connection with such restrictions on Form CO. It will determine whether or not the merger is compatible with the common market.

Procedure

By Article 18 of the Merger Regulation (and Article 11 of ancillary Regulation 2367/90), the Commission will give the concerned parties an opportunity to make their views known before any decision is taken as to whether or not the merger is incompatible with the common market. A time limit will be fixed within which the parties must make their views known.

The parties may request an oral hearing under Article 13 of Regulation 2367/90. The competent authorities of the Member States, in the case of the UK, the MMC or OFT, may appoint an official to take part in the hearing. Copies of notifications are sent to all the competent authorities in the Member States within three working days and there is constant liaison with those competent authorities. Hearings are not in public and persons are heard separately or with others, having regard to the need to protect business secrets. Third parties also have the opportunity to make their views known orally.

Before any decisions are taken, the Advisory Committee on concentrations is consulted and, by Article 19.4, that Committee consists of representatives of all the Member States. The Advisory Committee delivers an opinion on the draft decision of the Commission. The Committee can recommend publication of its opinion, having regard to the need to keep business secrets confidential. However, although the Commission has to take 'utmost account' of the opinion, it could disagree with it and come to an opposite decision.

Time limits and powers of the Commission

The Commission must make its decision as to whether or not to initiate proceedings within one month from the date of notification (Article 10.1).

A decision of incompatibility must be made not more than four months after the date on which the proceedings are initiated (Article 10.3).

Unscrambling

Where a concentration has already been implemented, the Commission may, by Article 8.4 of Regulation 4064/89, require the undertakings or assets brought together to be separated or the cessation of joint control or any other action that may be appropriate in order to restore conditions of effective competition.

Conditions

Even where the Commission finds that a concentration is compatible with the common market under Article 8.2, they may impose conditions and obligations intended to ensure that the undertakings concerned comply with the commitments they have entered into with the Commission with a view to modifying the original concentration plan.[6a]

Where it appears to the parties that the Commission may be coming to a decision of incompatibility, they may wish to make representations of possible conditions that might be attached which would make the merger acceptable.

Fines and periodic penalty payments

Where a decision requiring such separation or cessation is made, the

6a See *Alcatel/Telettra* OJ 1991 L122/48 for an approved merger with attached obligations

Commission has powers to impose fines of a sum not exceeding ten per cent of the aggregate turnover of the undertakings concerned. 'In setting the amount of the fine, regard shall be had to the nature and gravity of the infringement.'

It follows that a company considering not notifying a merger which falls within the Regulation should be aware that the Commission can come to a decision declaring that merger incompatible with the common market even though a notification has not been put in. The Commission keeps a close watch on press announcements and the trade press and also there is always the possibility that a disgruntled competitor or customer finding out about a confidential deal would make a complaint to the Commission. The Commission could then, under Article 8.4, issue a decision effectively unscrambling the merger. If the decision is not obeyed fines of up to ten per cent of aggregate turnover can be imposed. Fines of between ECU 1,000 and 50,000 may be levied for a failure to notify a concentration or for supplying incorrect or misleading information.

The Commission envisages that between 30 and 50 mergers will be scrutinised each year, given the current turnover levels. The number of mergers to be examined is set to rise when turnover levels are reduced after the 1994 review. It is likely that any merger within the Regulation would come to the Commission's attention by some means or another. Notification before a merger goes ahead is the safer method of proceeding.

There are other powers to fine and levy periodic penalty payments under the Regulation. Penalty payments can be levied where the Commission is awaiting full information. These may amount to ECU 25,000 per day of default.

Requests for information

The Commission may, under Article 11, make requests for information to undertakings, stating the legal basis for making the request and the penalties for supplying incorrect information. Where information is not supplied within the time period set by the Commission, the Commission may make a decision requiring that the information be provided (Article 11.5).

Investigative powers of the Commission

Commission officials are empowered, by Article 13.1:

(a) to examine the books and other business records;
(b) to take or demand copies of or extracts from the books and business records;
(c) to ask for oral explanations on the spot;
(d) to enter premises, land and means of transport of undertakings.

These are similar to the powers which the Commission can exercise under Articles 85 and 86 in carrying out 'dawn raids' of premises. Officials from the competent authorities of the Member States may accompany and assist Commission officials in carrying out their duties.

Member State requests

Some Member States do not have effective national competition law for the regulation of mergers. A Member State may request that the Commission intervene, under Article 22.3 of the Regulation, in a merger which does not have a Community dimension, but which would affect trade between Member States, provided that the merger creates or strengthens a dominant position as a result of which effective competition would be significantly impeded in the Member State concerned. The Commission may then reach a decision either that the concentration is compatible with the common market, with conditions attached if necessary, or that it is incompatible and, if the merger has already taken place, may require that it be unscrambled.

If a UK company merges with a company from a Member State which has little national merger legislation there will therefore be a risk that the national authorities of that other Member State may ask the Commission to intervene, particularly where the UK competition authorities have taken, or appear to be taking, no action.

National legislation

Article 21.2 provides that no Member State shall apply its national legislation on competition to any concentration that has a Community dimension.

This area of EC and national law overlap was hotly contested in the negotiations leading to the final settlement of the wording of the Regulation. It is advantageous to companies to know that only one set of rules will apply to their merger and that they will not have to have it vetted in Brussels and a number of Member States as well. However, by Article 9.2, a Member State may inform the Commission that a proposed merger relates to a market 'having all the characteristics of a distinct market'. The Commission can then deal with the merger itself, or it may refer it to the Member State to apply its own national competition law. By the EEC Merger Control (Distinct Market Investigations) Regulations 1990,[7] the Director General of Fair Trading in the UK may require the production of relevant documents or estimates by any person. Article 9.2, along with the threshold limits, will be reviewed before the end of September 1994. Member States, under Article 9.8, may only take 'the measures strictly necessary to safeguard or restore effective competition on the market concerned.'

There is a second derogation from the general principle of 'one stop shopping' in Article 21.3, which provides that Member States may take appropriate measures to protect legitimate interests other than those taken into consideration by the Regulation and compatible with the general principles and other provisions of Community law. It provides that 'public security, plurality of the media and prudential rules shall be regarded as legitimate interests'. Any other public interest must be communicated to the Commission by the Member State concerned and will be recognised by the Commission after an assessment of its compatibility with the general principles and other provisions of Community law before the measures referred to above may be taken. The Commission will inform the Member State concerned of its decision within one month of that communication.

7 S.I. 1990 No. 1715

The effect of Article 21 is that a merger may be cleared by the Commission and then scrutinised under national legislation in Member States and forbidden from going ahead, for example where it involves an issue of public security, which might include a company manufacturing weapons, or a newspaper monopoly.

Articles 85 and 86

Regulation 17, as has been seen in Chapter 2, implemented Articles 85 and 86, setting out the procedures for notification, levying of fines etc. Article 22 of the Merger Regulation provides that Regulation 17 shall not apply to 'concentrations as defined in Article 3'. This wording is important as it does not say concentrations having a community dimension. Article 3 merely defines mergers and applies to all mergers, big or small, whether the thresholds in Article 1 are met or not.

Regulation 17 is therefore disapplied from all mergers. However, it is not within the *vires* of a regulation to amend the Treaty of Rome itself and therefore the Commission was not able in the Merger Regulation to provide that Articles 85 and 86 would not apply to mergers at all. As will be seen below, Article 86 in particular has been applied where a merger has amounted to an abuse of a dominant position and, historically, that was the legislation used by the Commission in connection with mergers so it could have some jurisdiction over mergers at an EC level. Therefore, since 21st September 1990, when the Regulation came into effect, the Commission has had no power to apply Articles 85 and 86 in the usual way to any 'concentration' as defined in Article 3.

This does not, however, mean that those Articles will no longer have any relevance to mergers. Before the implementation of those Articles by Regulation they were still binding Articles of the Treaty and it is possible that they could have been applied, although in practice it would have been difficult to do so. Secondly, as will be seen in Chapter 5, there is scope for individuals to bring proceedings, particularly in national courts, which may have some application in a merger context. It is therefore necessary to look briefly at the application of Articles 85 and 86 to mergers.

ARTICLE 86

Europemballage Corporation and Continental Can Company v *Commission,*[8] a decision of the Court of Justice, established that Article 86 could apply to mergers, which might amount to an abuse of a dominant position.

By virtue of the Merger Control Regulation, Regulation 17, which implements Article 86, does not apply to most mergers and it is unlikely that the Commission will exercise any vestiges of power to use Article 86 now that the Regulation is in place and it is clear that a merger falls within Article 3 of the Regulation.

In *Continental Can*, the Court held that the acquisition of a competitor could amount to an abuse of a dominant position, if the degree of dominance achieved by the acquisition substantially fettered competition. In that case there already was pre-merger dominance. On the facts of the case the Court

8 [1973] ECR 215. See also *Re Metaleurop SA* [1991] 4 CMLR 222 where neither party in dominant position so *Continental Can* not applied and negative clearance granted

found that the Commission had not sufficiently well defined the market and overturned the Commission's decision.

There would therefore be a risk of Article 86 applying only where a company was in a dominant position before the acquisition and the acquisition amounted to an abuse of that dominant position within the meaning of *Continental Can* and where the Commission or a third party attempted to utilise Article 86 notwithstanding Article 22.1 of Regulation 4064/89.

ARTICLE 85

The Commission traditionally held that Article 85 did not apply to mergers as Article 85(3) exemption was inappropriate in this context and, following a merger, there are not two parties who compete. Restrictions on competition are therefore irrelevant. Its 1966 *Memorandum on the Problem of Concentrations in the Common Market* stated quite clearly that 'it is not possible to apply Article 85 to agreements whose purpose is the acquisition of total or partial ownership of enterprises or the reorganisation of ownership of enterprises'.

In *British American Tobacco Company Limited* v *Commission*[9] the European Court of Justice held that Article 85(1) could apply to mergers. It is arguable from the case that in fact this only applied to partial mergers, but the consequences could have been far-reaching had the Merger Regulation not been agreed. Mergers falling foul of Article 85(1) could be void *ab initio*. This case is referred to in a footnote to the Notice on concentrative joint ventures in the context of the acquisition of minority interests. Where a set of circumstances is not such as to amount to a merger, Articles 85 and 86 may apply in the usual way. Paragraph 38 of the Notice says:

> As long as the threshold of individual or joint decisive influence has not been reached, the Regulation is not in any event applicable. Accordingly, the assessment under competition law will be made only in relation to the criteria laid down in Articles 85 and 86 of the EC Treaty and on the basis of the usual procedural rules for restrictive practices and abuses of dominant position.

In *Irish Distillers Group* v *GC&C Brands Limited,*[10] the Commission threatened to prohibit a consortium made up of various UK spirit manufacturers from bidding for Irish Distillers, where the various parties had already agreed how they would divide up various brand names after the acquisition was completed.

Now the Merger Regulation has been agreed, it seems highly unlikely that any of this case law would be applied, and the risk of a concentration, even one not within the scope of the Regulation through failure to satisfy the threshold criteria, being held to be void under Article 85(1) is very small. Large companies may, however, feel it prudent to approach the Commission for advice generally where a merger of some significance is proposed, but which is not one with a Community dimension falling to be considered under the Regulation.

9 [1988] 4 CMLR 24

10 [1988] 4 CMLR 841

UK MERGER LAW

Although Article 21 of the Merger Control Regulation provides that national competition legislation cannot be applied to any merger having a Community dimension, other mergers, not within the thresholds laid down in the Regulation, are regulated by their own Member States' legislation. Member States may also intervene to protect legitimate interests, for example, on public security grounds or where a 'distinct market' is involved. For most purposes EC law will apply above the thresholds and UK below.

Part V of the Fair Trading Act 1973 (FTA) sets out UK law in relation to mergers and comprises a system whereby mergers are at risk of investigation by the Monopolies and Mergers Commission when certain criteria are satisfied. There is no obligation to notify a merger to the MMC, but there is a formal procedure for pre-notifying a merger on payment of a fee.

There are different systems for newspaper and other mergers.

Merger situation

For non-newspaper references the legislation will apply where there is a 'merger situation'. Section 64(1) of the FTA defines a merger situation qualifying for investigation and provides that a merger reference may be made to the Commission by the Secretary of State where two or more enterprises, of which one at least was carried on in the United Kingdom or by or under the control of a body corporate incorporated in the United Kingdom, have ceased to be distinct enterprises and one of two alternative tests are satisfied.

The two tests are the assets test and the market share test. The assets test is that the value of the assets taken over exceeds £30 million. Section 64(2) specifies the market share test, which provides that in relation to the supply of goods of any description at least one quarter of all the goods of that description which are supplied in the United Kingdom, or in a substantial part of the United Kingdom, either–

(a) are supplied by one and the same person or are supplied to one and the same person, or

(b) are supplied by the persons by whom the relevant enterprises (so far as they continue to be carried on) are carried on, or are supplied to those persons.

In *R v MMC, ex parte South Yorkshire Transport Ltd and Another* ([1991] BCC 347), South Yorkshire, Bolsover, Chesterfield, Derbyshire Dales, High Peak, North-East Derbyshire and Bassetlaw were held in the High Court not to be a 'substantial part' of the UK, applying the words of the section in their ordinary sense. Section 64(3) gives the equivalent provisions for services. The market share test applies by examining whether the merger has resulted in 25 per cent of the UK market for goods being held, or supplied by or to, one person. If company X had twenty per cent of the UK market for filing cabinets before a merger and, after the merger, had forty per cent, then, irrespective of whether the value of the assets taken over exceeded £30 million, the merger would be a qualifying one under the FTA. Where a company already has over 25 per cent of a market and a merger has the effect that its market share is larger, again the merger will be caught.

The market share and assets tests are alternatives. It is sufficient if one applies. Hence, tiny acquisitions in terms of assets can be caught where the participants are involved in small specialist markets where they have large market shares. Mergers involving companies with very small market shares, but comprising large deals in terms of the value of assets, are caught too.

There are many forms of acquisition and not all will fall within the legislation. The legislation applies when two enterprises cease to be distinct, which by section 65 applies where any two enterprises either–

   (a) are brought under common ownership or common control (whether or not the business to which either of them formerly belonged continues to be carried on under the same or different ownership or control), or

   (b) either of the enterprises ceases to be carried on at all and does so in consequence of any arrangements or transaction entered into to prevent competition between enterprises.

A company purchasing the share capital of another or all the business of another would be brought under common control of the acquiring enterprise. It would be a qualifying merger. Common control is defined in section 65(2):

> For the purposes of the preceding subsection enterprises shall (without prejudice to the generality of the words "common control" in that subsection) be regarded as being under common control if they are –
>
>   (a)   enterprises of interconnected bodies corporate, or
>
>   (b)   enterprises carried on by two or more bodies corporate of which one and the same person or group of persons has control, or
>
>   (c)   an enterprise carried on by a body corporate and an enterprise carried on by a person or group of persons having control of that body corporate.

Interconnected bodies corporate effectively means companies within the same corporate group.

The usual merger situation is therefore common control. However, where a company ceases to carry on business at all, that may in certain circumstances amount to a qualifying merger under the FTA. The enterprise must cease to be carried on at all and must so cease because of arrangements entered into to prevent competition between enterprises. Where, for example, company A wishes to close down part of its business or a subsidiary company of it and knows that one of its competitors would be one of the most likely potential buyers, and it decides that rather than putting the business on the open market to be sold to the highest bidder it will be cheaper and simpler to offer the company to its rival, any agreement between those parties to that effect could have the effect that the shutting down of the business amounts to a qualifying merger as the arrangements were entered into to prevent competition. However, it is not clear either from the legislation or case law whether the companies must intend to prevent competition or whether it is enough that the effect of the arrangements is that in practice competition is prevented. The former is the better view on a reading of the legislation, though, in practice, the competition authorities may take the wider interpretation.

The legislation refers to 'enterprises'. This is partially defined in section 63(2) to mean 'the activities, or part of the activities, of a business'. It covers companies, partnerships, sole traders, and sales of shares and it is possible that the sale of assets alone without the goodwill of the business and without customer lists and other business type assets could fall within the legislation where the sale of those assets was coupled with the shutting down of a business and a competitor purchased the assets. The enterprises must have ceased to be distinct within the last six months for a merger reference to be made. If the MMC do not make a reference in that time they cannot do so later (section 64(4)), unless by reason of the EEC Merger Control Regulation.[11]

11 The EEC Merger Control (Consequential Provisions) Regulations 1990, S.I. No. 1563, Reg.3

Valuation of assets

Section 67 provides that the assets to be valued for the purposes of deciding whether the £30 million threshold is reached are the total value of the assets employed in the enterprises which ceased to be distinct, except for any that remained under the same ownership or control. Where Company B acquires the entire share capital of Company C then only the assets of Company C will be calculated as Company B stays under the same ownership and control.

Merger references

Within six months of a merger it may be referred to the Monopolies and Mergers Commission. By section 69, the MMC will look at whether there is a merger situation qualifying for investigation and/or 'whether the creation of that situation operates, or may be expected to operate, against the public interest'. References to the MMC must specify a time limit within which the Report must be produced.

By no means all qualifying mergers are referred to the MMC. Increasingly more mergers have been referred. In 1987 1.9 per cent of all mergers considered by the Office of Fair Trading were referred, in 1988 3.6 per cent and in 1989 5 per cent. The OFT considered 427 mergers in 1989.

In July 1984, Norman Tebbit, then Secretary of State, announced the results of a review of mergers policy.[12] His statement, often referred to as the 'Tebbit Guidelines', effectively made it clear that mergers would be referred primarily on competition grounds. This has been the case throughout the 1980s. Peter Lilley, Secretary of State from July 1990, has, however, also referred mergers on the grounds that the proposed acquirer is state owned where a large company or high market shares are involved. The MMC has not upheld this approach, which may be abandoned.

12 House of Commons written answer by the Secretary of State for Trade and Industry, 5 July 1984

In *British Aerospace PLC and Thomson-CSF SA,*[13] a reference was made on competition grounds and also because Thomson's parent company was owned by the French Government. The merger concerned the proposed merger of BAe's and Thomson-CSF's guided weapons businesses into a joint company, Eurodynamics, to be owned equally by them. The MMC concluded that the merger would 'introduce a new competitive element into the market. Competition will be stimulated'.[14] It was noted that the French Government had not used its interest to intervene in the management of Thomson-CSF.

13 MMC Report January 1991, Cm 1416

14 Cm 1416, p.59, para. 6.53 and see EC Commission 5 June 1991 probing letter to UK Government on the Lilley doctrine

Newspaper mergers

Sections 57 to 62 of the FTA set out the provisions for the regulation of newspaper mergers. Consent is needed from the Secretary of State for certain acquisitions of newspapers with a large circulation.

Notification of mergers

There is no obligation to notify the UK competition authorities of a qualifying merger before it takes place, unlike under EC merger law. However, as the consequences of a subsequent reference can result in extreme cases in orders for the divestiture of the assets acquired, it is important that a purchaser has some certainty that it will be allowed to retain the business or company puchased from the vendor. Many purchasers therefore, when faced with a qualifying merger, will wish to pre-notify it to the Office of Fair Trading. The sale and purchase agreement may well contain a condition that the merger is 'cleared' by the OFT before the vendor is obliged to sell the company to the purchaser.

There are two methods of obtaining such clearance. Either the parties can apply for confidential guidance or formal pre-notification can be made.

Confidential guidance

The parties to a merger may make a confidential guidance submission to the OFT setting out a description of the proposed transaction, details of the parties and reasons why the parties believe that the merger is not one falling within the FTA. The parties will set out their description of the relevant market. The question of what comprises this market is important as in a narrowly defined market the parties may have over 25 per cent of the market, but if a broader definition is used then the merger may not be a qualifying one as the market share is below 25 per cent. The parties will also describe the economic context of their merger and any positive bencfits which may flow from it, for consumers and others.

There is no legislation concerning confidential guidance. It is an informal procedure to assist companies. However, as it is confidential there are no opportunities for third parties to make their views known and the OFT and MMC are not bound by the guidance given. The OFT will, however, give its views on whether or not a merger is likely to be referred to the MMC once it has had an opportunity to consider the documentation submitted. This is at the least a strong indication of the risks involved in going ahead with the proposed merger and a useful procedure. There are no time limits attached to the procedure and parties requiring a decision within a certain time and needing a binding decision will make a formal pre-notification under section 75A of the Fair Trading Act. This section was introduced by section 146 of the Companies Act 1989 and came into force on 1st April 1990.

Formal pre-notification of mergers

Companies wishing to utilise the procedure make a notification to the OFT on the Merger Notice form obtainable from the OFT. This form requires full details of the merger to be given and there are detailed guidance notes with the form describing how the information should be given. The information must include details of the merger situation itself, financial information, and the likely time scale of the proposed transaction, a statement as to whether the deal is subject to the City Code on Takeovers and Mergers, the reasons for the merger and plans in connection with it and a description of the markets involved, with market share estimates. The form ends with a declaration and draws the signatory's attention to the fact that under section 93B it is an offence knowingly or recklessly to give false or misleading information to the Director General of Fair Trading. The penalty for breach is a fine of up to £2,000 or a term of up to two years imprisonment, or both. The verification of all information submitted on the form is therefore important.

The Merger (Prenotification) Regulations 1990[15] give further detail concerning the submission of a merger notice. The form must be accompanied by the relevant fee.

15 S.I. 1990 No. 501

Fees

The Merger (Fees) Regulations 1990,[16] which came into force on 1st October 1990, set out the fees payable. The fee for a merger notice is (under paragraph 4(b) of the Regulations) £5,000, where the value of the assets which have been or are to be taken over, does not exceed £30 million, and increases thereafter up to £15,000.[17] The fee is £5,000 where there is a merger which is caught by the market share criteria alone and the value of the assets is low. The person giving the merger notice is liable for the fee.

16 S.I. 1990 No. 1660

17 Where the value of the assets exceeds £30m but not £100m, the fee is £10,000 and where the asset value is over £100m, the fee is £15,000

Under paragraph 8, the fee is repayable if the situation notified does not in fact amount to a merger situation. Where the parties are not sure, for example, what the proper definition of the market is and put in a merger notice to protect themselves, and the conclusion of the OFT is that there is not a merger situation, then the fee is repaid. A merger notice may be rejected where it is of a merger with a Community dimension which would fall for consideration under the EEC Merger Regulation (see the EEC Merger Control (Consequential Provisions) Regulations 1990[18]). Where it is rejected on those grounds the fee is repayable.

18 S.I. 1990 No. 1563, Reg.2

There are no other grounds for repayment of the fee, so if the parties decide not to go ahead with the deal or the negotiations break down the fee is not repayable. The fee may be demanded whether or not voluntary clearance is sought.

Time limits

The procedure can be used only for mergers which have not yet taken place. Details of the proposed merger will be published so, if there is a highly confidential deal which is the subject of confidential negotiations, the parties may wish to postpone their application until details have been made public. In the interim they could submit a confidential guidance submission to give the OFT an opportunity to study the details of the proposal earlier and ensure a prompter response when the formal pre-notification is put in. Alternatively, the merger notice information could be submitted in advance of publication and the OFT asked to hold it until the parties wish to formalise the notification. Neither alternative is laid down in the legislation, however.

Either alternative may ensure a prompter response from the OFT. Many mergers are very urgent. Particularly where the fate of employees and contracts with third parties are concerned, the longer the period of deliberation and indecision the worse the effect on the businesses of the parties. Applying for a merger clearance, whether from the European

Commission or the OFT, will inevitably exacerbate these problems and cause delay in finalising the arrangements.

Under the pre-notification procedure, if 20 working days have expired without a reference being made to the MMC, no reference can subsequently be made. The Director General of Fair Trading may, however, extend this period by a further 10 days and may extend the extended period by a further 15 days. If the merger does not go ahead within six months of the end of the period for considering the notification, the merger may be referred if it subsequently goes ahead.

Undertakings in lieu of reference

Where the Director has recommended that a merger reference be made and has specified certain effects adverse to the public interest, the Secretary of State may accept undertakings from the parties which will have the effect of preventing those adverse effects, instead of making a reference. The undertakings must provide for one of three actions: the division of a business by the sale of any part of the undertaking or assets or otherwise, the division of a group of connected companies or the separation (by the sale of assets or other means) of companies which are under common control otherwise than by reason of their being connected companies.

In addition to the mandatory requirement, undertakings may be required to safeguard assets or for the carrying on of activities until the division or separation is effected, or to ensure any other matters necessary to effect or take account of the division or separation, and to enable the Secretary of State to ascertain whether the undertakings are being fulfilled. Details of the undertakings will be published and kept under review. Individuals may bring civil proceedings where there is a failure or 'apprehended failure' of the 'responsible person to fulfill the undertaking'.

The Director's advice to the Secretary of State specifying effects adverse to the public interest attracts absolute privilege for the purposes of defamation law.

OFT consideration and merger reference

The OFT in considering a merger will first determine whether it is a qualifying merger under the FTA. It will look to whether the merger is 'horizontal' (a merger between companies producing similar goods or services), 'vertical' (a takeover of a potential supplier or customer) or 'conglomerate' (a merger of companies supplying unrelated goods or services). The OFT will consider any improvements to efficiency from the merger, any employment and regional considerations, and whether it would promote exports, as well as other relevant facts about the merger, the markets and the parties.

Prior to a reference to the MMC, the OFT may call a meeting of the parties to allow them to expand upon the information which they have supplied. A written report is then prepared and the Secretary of State determines whether or not the merger should be referred to the MMC, having considered the advice of the Director.

The MMC will be given a period in which to consider the merger within the terms of the reference. Section 84 of the FTA sets out the criteria for determining whether a merger operates against the public interest, including such factors as the desirability of maintaining competition and promoting consumer interests. Section 84 is set out in Chapter 3 because of its relevance under the Competition Act.

The parties are invited to submit a written statement concerning the merger to the MMC and are invited to attend hearings of the MMC. Witnesses are invited to give evidence in person. Other interested parties are contacted for their views.

A merger report will then be submitted to the Secretary of State.

Orders

There are wide-ranging powers in s.73 of the FTA, where a merger has been found to operate against the public interest and specific adverse effects have been identified, to make orders. Schedule 8 of the FTA sets out the orders which can be made and these are wide and varied, including making it unlawful to withhold supplies, to tie the purchase of goods with the purchase of others, to discriminate in the prices charged for goods, prohibiting the acquisition of a business and, under Part 2 of the Schedule, requiring the disposal of assets (such as divestiture of the business acquired by the merger).

In *Tate & Lyle PLC and British Sugar PLC,*[19] the proposed merger in the sugar industry was held to be expected to operate against the public interest. The views of users are always sought by the MMC. In this case, users feared the merger would mean a loss of competition. The MMC did not accept that imports from abroad would check prices charged in the UK if the merger went ahead. The merger was not allowed to proceed.

In *Caldaire Holdings Ltd and Bluebird Security Ltd,*[20] a merger which had already taken place was held to operate against the public interest in the South East Durham area. The merger related to companies in the bus services sector; the MMC found a 'removal of choice and competition on a number of routes', but held that 'divestment of the Bluebird assets acquired would be a disproportionate remedy to the adverse effects' identified. Instead undertakings were sought, including an undertaking that for two years a bus route would not be deregistered without consent and there would only be one annual price increase limited to increases in the Retail Prices Index.

There are many other MMC reports which illustrate well the workings of UK merger law in practice and to which reference should be made.

19 MMC Report, February 1991, Cm 1435

20 MMC Report, January 1991, Cm 1403

SUMMARY

EC Law

1. A merger must be notified to the European Commission on form CO where it comprises a concentration with a Community dimension, i.e. the total worldwide turnover of the parties exceeds ECU 5,000 million and the total Community-wide turnover of two or more of the undertakings involved is more than ECU 250 million. There will not be a Community dimension where each undertaking achieves more than two-thirds of its Community-wide turnover in one and the same Member State.

2. The Merger Control Regulation No. 4064/89 and ancillary Regulation No. 2367/90, with the Notices on ancillary restrictions and concentrative joint ventures of 14th August 1990 set out the EEC Merger Regulation regime.

3. The concentration will be appraised by the Commission to ascertain whether it is compatible with the common market. Where the market share of the parties does not exceed 25 per cent in the EC or a substantial part of it then there is a rebuttable presumption that the merger will be compatible.

4. The Commission will reach a decision as to the compatibility of the concentration with the common market and has powers to prohibit the merger from going ahead and to impose fines. The Commission has a period of one month to decide whether or not to initiate proceedings and a further period of four months to determine that the concentration is incompatible with the common market. Where a merger has proceeded without consent having first been obtained the Commission has powers to order that companies dispose of assets or undertakings acquired.

5. Articles 85 and 86 have been applied to some mergers. Regulation 17 has been disapplied from mergers falling within the Merger Control Regulation No. 4064/89, whether they be mergers with a community dimension or not. The scope of Articles 85 and 86 in the merger context is therefore now severely restricted.

UK law

1. Mergers will be regulated where the value of the assets acquired exceeds £30 million or one party increases its market share over 25 per cent.

2. Mergers which do not have a Community dimension will be considered under the Fair Trading Act 1973, The Merger (Prenotification) Regulations 1990 and the Merger (Fees) Regulations 1990.

3. Parties to a merger are at risk of its being referred to the MMC, which will investigate the merger and has powers to make orders, such as requiring the purchaser to divest itself of assets.

4. The parties may notify their merger in advance if they so wish, although there is no obligation to do so. Notification will give the parties assurance that the merger will not subsequently be referred to the MMC provided that it goes ahead within six months, or will result in their being informed that the merger will be referred to the MMC. The OFT has 20 working days to determine whether a reference should be made or if undertakings are to be requested from the parties. Fees of £5,000, £10,000 and £15,000 are payable on such a notification depending on the value of the transaction. The transaction is made public.

5. Companies wishing to maintain confidentiality may apply for informal guidance from the OFT. Such guidance will give the parties an indication of whether it is likely the merger will be referred to the MMC, but is not legally binding on the OFT. Confidential guidance is free, but there are no time limits attaching to it.

QUESTION

Company UK is considering making two acquisitions as part of its corporate strategy for 1992 and the single European market. It proposes to purchase the entire share capital of Company England, which holds 40 per cent of the market in the UK for the manufacture of personal computers. Company UK has a large market share in that field too. Secondly, it is negotiating for the purchase of its biggest competitor in Europe, Franco/Deutsch GmbH, a German company dominating the EC market for personal computers.

1. Company UK seeks advice on the impact of EC and UK competition law on its proposed mergers. List the further information which is needed in order to advise whether there is a concentration with a Community dimension and/or a qualifying merger under the Fair Trading Act.
2. Company UK is paranoid about secrecy. How is it best able to proceed with its plans with the minimum of publicity?
3. Assuming a proposed merger is caught by EC law, what procedures should be followed to inform the EC Commission, if this is necessary?
4. Assuming a proposed merger does not have a Community dimension, but is a qualifying merger under the FTA, what risks will Company UK take as purchaser if it decides not to involve the OFT at all?

FURTHER READING

Mergers – EC law

Canenbley C. & Weitbrech A. – *EEC Merger Control Regulation: a Preliminary Analysis* (1990) 18 IBL 104   **ARTICLES**
Elland W. – *Merger Control Regulation (EEC) No 4064/89* [1990] 3 ECLR
Pathak A.S. – *EEC Concentration Control* [1990] 3 ECLR
Ridyard D. – *An economic perspective on the EC merger regulation* [1990] 6 ECLR 247

Hawk B.E. – *US, Common Market & International Anti-trust*, Prentice Hall Law & Business,   **BOOKS**
  2nd ed. – 1990 Supplement, Volume II, Mergers & Acquisitions – p.909
Jacquemin A. – *Merger and Competition Policy in the European Community*, Blackwell, 1990
Van Bael I. & Bellis J-F – *Competition Law of the EEC*, CCH Editions, 2nd ed., 1990, cpt. 6

Alcatel/Telettra, OJ 1991 L122/48   **CASES**
British American Tobacco Company Limited v *Commission* [1988] 4 CMLR 24
Europemballage Corporation and Continental Can Company v *Commission* [1973] ECR 215
Irish Distillers Group v *GC&C Brands Limited* [1988] 4 CMLR 841
Re Metaleurop SA [1991] 4 CMLR 222
Re the Mergers between Carnaud and Metal Box and between Pechiney and American Can
  [1990] 4 CMLR 285 (Press Release)
Renault/Volvo (Re the Concentration between) [1991] 4 CMLR 297

Mergers – UK law

Howe M. – *UK Merger Control : How does the System Reach Decisions?* [1990] 1 ECLR 1   **ARTICLES**
Polito S. – *UK Merger Control – a review of current policy* [1988] CMLR 461
Soames T. – *Merger Policy: As Clear as Mud?* [1991] 2 ECLR 53

All MMC Merger Reports. Comparatively recent reports include: **MMC MERGER REPORTS**
British Aerospace PLC and Thomson-CSF SA, January 1991, Cm 1416
Caldaire Holdings Ltd and Bluebird Securities Ltd, January 1991, Cm 1403
Tate & Lyle PLC and British Sugar PLC, February 1991, Cm 1435

Mergers – Office of Fair Trading Guide to Procedure under the Fair Trading Act 1973 (OFT)   **PUBLICATION**

5

Consequences and penalties

In this chapter consideration will be given to the consequences of infringement of competition legislation, the penalties which flow from such infringement and, finally, the extent to which competition law can be applied in relation to companies outside the EC/UK respectively, so-called 'extra-territoriality'. Competition law can be used both as a shield and a sword and the use of the courts by private companies rather than competition enforcement bodies will also be addressed.

The consequences of infringement of competition law can be disastrous for companies and individuals, who ignore such legislation at their peril. Fines of many millions of pounds have been levied by the European Commission for the most flagrant price-fixing cartels which they have discovered. In the UK, companies subject to a court order under the Restrictive Trade Practices Act can be fined for contempt of court. Six figure sums have been imposed by way of fine, and individuals involved in such arrangements could themselves be held to have aided and abetted contempt and be fined or jailed.

Agreements may be void if they infringe Article 85 of the Treaty of Rome, or where such agreements have not been registered at the Office of Fair Trading, where they fall within the RTPA.

EC COMPETITION LAW

By Article 85(2) of the Treaty of Rome, agreements infringing Article 85(1), the provision prohibiting restrictive agreements, will be void. This is also the case where a company abuses its dominant position, thereby infringing Article 86. Thus an agreement by a group of manufacturers as to the prices that they will charge to the distributors of their products would be unenforceable. If one manufacturer did not abide by the agreement and the others sought to sue him for breach of contract, he could raise in his defence the fact that the agreement was void in any event. The agreement could not be relied upon.

This is an extreme case. Agreements of that sort are more likely to be covert and action for breach of contract unlikely to be pursued. A more likely scenario would be where two companies enter into an agreement which contains restrictions on their competing with each other for a period of ten years, in the context of a larger agreement between them, perhaps for the supply of raw materials for manufacture or for joint research and development. Where one party acts in breach of the agreement the other may be prevented from successfully suing for breach of contract. However, the entire agreement will not necessarily be void. The courts will look to the law of the individual EC Member State in which the litigation is brought as to whether or not the entire contract will fall or whether the void provision can be 'severed' from the rest of the contract.

This doctrine of severance is known in English law and would be applied in such circumstances. If the agreement in question was principally a non-competition agreement, the provision within it which would be void under EC law was the non-competition provision and there were very few other provisions of any substance to the agreement, then it is likely that the entire agreement, would be unenforceable. If, however, as in the example used above, the non-competition provisions were a small part of the agreement and there were provisions which could stand alone, for example dealing with research work which the parties would carry out and the licensing of technology discovered through the research work, it may be possible to sever the void provisions and find that the rest of the agreement has not lost its commercial purpose and is capable of standing alone. This rule is often known as the 'blue pencil' rule. The courts will look to whether the contract which is left after void provisions have been removed from it is the same sort of contract which the parties intended to enter into.

Void *ab initio*

The restrictive provisions or the whole agreement, as the case may be, will be void *ab initio*. Where parties believe when entering into such an agreement that there is a risk of its infringing Article 85 or 86, they may choose to notify the agreement to the Commission as has been seen in Chapter 2. They may apply for negative clearance in relation to Articles 85 and 86, i.e. a decision that the agreement does not infringe those articles, or, where there is a potential Article 85(1) problem apply for a specific exemption under Article 85(3).

The Commission will deliberate and investigate the matter for some considerable time, at least two years, possibly longer. During that period the parties do not know whether their agreement is enforceable or not. Where there is an adverse finding, the parties may be required to alter their agreements by the Commission, for example by agreeing a lesser period for a restriction. It is unlikely, however, that one party would be entitled to sue the other in connection with goods which have been supplied or royalties paid under the agreement as the contract is not only void but also 'prohibited'. Parties to an illegal contract cannot recover damages in connection with any such contract through the courts.

Defences

EC competition law can be used as a shield or defence to actions for breach of contract as has been seen above. It may also be used as a defence to other actions. Where a company or individual uses the intellectual property rights of another, for example a patent, without consent from the owner of such rights, then, in the normal course of events, he can be sued for infringement of those rights and may be liable for damages to compensate the owner of such rights for the loss which he has suffered by reason of the infringement. Also, an injunction can be applied for through the courts for an order restraining the infringing party from continuing with the infringement. EC law can be invoked as a defence to such infringement actions, for example where it can be shown that the use of the patent rights by the alleged infringer was consistent with the free movement of goods provisions of the Treaty of Rome in Article 30.

In considering the use of EC competition law as a sword and a shield, the cases of *R* v *Dearlove* and *R* v *Druker*[1] illustrate an attempt to use EC competition law in a novel way.

1 [1988] Crim L R 323, 88 Cr App Rep 279

The case involved the Theft Act offence of obtaining goods by deception. The accused, Messrs Dearlove and Druker were convicted of conspiring together to obtain from Brooke Bond Exports Limited (BBEL) 3,334 cases of Oxo cubes with the intention of permanently depriving BBEL 'thereof by deception namely by falsely representing that the goods (i) were intended for export to Bulgaria, and (ii) were being exported to Bulgaria'. The price at which Brooke Bond Oxo Limited sold Oxo cubes for the home market was substantially greater than the price which its export arm, BBEL, charged for sales for export purposes. The defendants wished to take advantage of this price differential and purchase Oxo cubes for sale in the UK, representing that they were being purchased for export.

It was accepted on behalf of the Crown that the restriction on ultimate sale destination infringed Article 85. The European Commission seeks to encourage 'parallel imports', i.e. the purchase of goods within the EC in areas where prices are low and their import into areas where their purchase cost is high, leading to a true single market, unhindered by export or import restrictions. It was accepted by the court that if BBEL had sought a civil injunction such action would not succeed as they would need to rely on restrictions which offended against Article 85(1). The court, however, held that, unlike civil proceedings which would have relied upon the term in the contract between the parties which stated that the goods were for sale in Bulgaria, the criminal proceedings were based on the defendants' dishonest deception. The Theft Act was not statutorily supporting the offending pricing policy of BBEL, it was concerned with protecting the public. The prosecution was not regarded by the courts as in any way undermining the effectiveness of Article 85 or favouring or reinforcing the breach of Article 85.

The case shows that in criminal proceedings breach of Article 85 will not necessarily be a defence, although in parallel civil proceedings it may well be.

Damages and injunctions

EC competition law can also be used as a sword through an action in the national courts for damages. In *Garden Cottage Foods Limited* v *Milk Marketing Board*,[2] the House of Lords held that an infringement of Article 86 is similar to a breach of direct UK legislation and that it would be possible to bring an action for damages for breach of statutory duty.

2 [1983] 3 CMLR 43

In that case, the Milk Marketing Board (MMB) refused to supply Garden Cottage Foods Limited (GCFL) with bulk butter, which, prior to the refusal to supply, they had been purchasing from the MMB and reselling in the Netherlands. An injunction applied for by GCFL was refused in the circumstances of the case. The Court, however, held:

> A breach of the duty imposed by Article 86 not to abuse a dominant position in the Common Market or in a substantial part of it, can thus be categorised in English law as a breach of a statutory duty that is imposed not only for the purpose of

promoting the general economic prosperity of the Common Market but also for the benefit of private individuals to whom loss or damage is caused by a breach of that duty.

Even Lord Wilberforce, dissenting, said:

> It can I think be accepted that a private person can sue in this country to prevent an infraction of Article 86. This follows from the fact, which is indisputable, that this Article is directly applicable in Member States. The European Court of Justice has moreover decided in Case 123/73 (SABAM), in connection with Article 86, that it is for the national courts of the Member States to safeguard the rights of individuals.

In *Argyll Group PLC* v *The Distillers Company PLC*,[3] the judge refused to grant an interim inderdict, the Scottish equivalent of an injunction, to prevent a proposed takeover which was alleged to amount to an abuse of a dominant position under Article 86. Both Argyll and Guinness were bidding for the Distillers company. Argyll objected to the Guinness proposal and sought to use EC competition law to prevent the takeover by its rival taking place. The judge stated:

3 [1986] 1 CMLR 764

> It is probable that Argyll could recover any loss which they could quantify as a result of the merger if this was ultimately held to be an abuse, by way of an action for damages.

He expressly referred to the *Garden Cottage Foods* case in support of this principle.

In *Cutsforth* v *Mansfield Inns Limited*,[4] the plaintiffs supplied coin-operated amusement machines to pubs in Humberside. The defendants were the owners of 57 tied pubs, i.e. they owned the freehold of those premises and granted tenancies to publicans for their use. The defendants instituted a new policy whereby they replaced their existing list of approved suppliers of such coin-operated machines by another list which did not include the plaintiffs.

4 [1986] 1 All ER 577

The court held that the defendants did not hold a dominant position in the common market or a substantial part of it. South Humberside was not a sufficiently large area to amount to a 'substantial part'. The court considered the application of Article 85 and took note of the fact that the block or general exemption for beer supply agreements of the sort the defendants had with their tenants, Regulation 1984/83, expressly precluded the inclusion of such a restrictive term as that considered by the court. That being so the agreement, part of which comprised the new list of approved suppliers, would infringe Article 85 to the detriment of the plaintiffs. The relief by way of injunction sought by the plaintiffs was granted. The judge stated that:

> Damages would not be an adequate remedy for the plaintiffs because the denial of interim relief would virtually put an end to a business which has operated with a degree of success over a period of fifteen years or more.

In another case, in 1989, three operators of chatline services alleged abuse of a dominant position in the national courts against British Telecom in suspending their services. They sought a writ preventing disconnection of the chatlines. The application was however refused.

Actions in the UK courts based on EC competition law have not generally been successful, although in principle there is nothing to prevent such actions where the relevant breach of EC competition law can be shown.

It can be seen therefore that EC competition law can be used both as a sword and a shield, although cases before the UK courts for damages or injunctions in relation to infringements of Articles 85 and 86 have been rare.

EC competition law, as has been seen, can result in agreements being void and unenforceable. Parties to such agreements may find themselves unable to rely upon them in suing for breach of contract. Articles 85 and 86 can be a defence to such actions and to actions for infringement of intellectual property rights. They are unlikely, however, to be of use as a defence in criminal cases. Competition law can also be used before the English courts to recover damages for breach of Articles 85 and 86.

Fines

Article 15 of Regulation 17 provides for the fines which can be levied by the Commission; they may be between ECU 1,000 and 100,000 or up to ten per cent of:

> the turnover in the preceding business year of each of the undertakings participating in the infringement where, either intentionally or negligently:
> (a)   they infringe Articles 85(1) or Article 86 of the Treaty.

The Regulation goes on to provide that in fixing the amount of the fine 'regard shall be had both to the gravity and to the duration of the infringement'. Companies can be held to have intentionally infringed even where they were unaware of the provisions of Article 85 and 86. The relevant infringing entity must be aware that its activities would restrict competition. The longer the period that the infringement was operated and the greater the degree of anti-competitive effects of the arrangement the greater the fine will be.

Fines for covert price fixing cartels in major industries involving large companies will be the largest. In 1986 the Commission imposed fines of ECU 57.85m (£41m) on 15 petrochemical producers, mainly multinational companies, who operated a market sharing and price fixing cartel in the polypropylene market in contravention of Article 85(1). Officials carried out surprise visits in 1983, and the Commission discovered that the cartel had been operating since 1977, when seven new producers of polypropylene entered the market. In consideration of the new entrants agreeing to join a price cartel, the existing producers were willing to make room for them in the market. The participants held regular meetings at a number of different levels within their organisations and generally operated a tightly controlled arrangement. Commissioner Sutherland, then the Competition Commissioner, commented (quoted in *EEC Bulletin 4 – 1986*, p.43):

> Market sharing and price fixing are particularly serious violations of the competition rules of the Treaty. Producers and consumers can only reap the benefits of the internal market if competition in the market is not distorted. The need to safeguard competition is particularly important in the case of key industrial products such as polypropylene.
> The Commission on several occasions last year made clear its policy of imposing fines at a level sufficient to deter serious violations of the competition rules. Under

Regulation 17 firms participating in an infringement may be fined up to 10% of their total turnover in the preceding financial year. In line with this policy, the Commission has decided to impose on each undertaking participating in the polypropylene cartel fines which reflect the serious and deliberate nature of this infringement.

Fines can be heavy for serious violations of this sort. In the soda-ash cases, *ICI and Solvay*[5] in December 1990, the Commission fined ICI and Solvay a total of £36m. ICI was fined £12.07m and Solvay £21m (a record for an individual fine) for rigging the market for soda ash. A record fine of £52m was levied in July 1991 against Tetra Pak.[5a]

5 OJ 1991 L152/1

5a *Tetra Pak* FT 25 July 1991

On the other hand, if a patent licence agreement does not technically fall within the relevant block exemption and contains restrictions which are not particularly anti-competitive and over which perhaps there is some doubt as to whether Article 85 would apply at all, or if the Commission finds that Article 85 applies to some arrangement in a novel way which no one previously would have said was a serious violation of the Treaty, then it is highly unlikely that a fine would be levied at all. The parties might however find their agreement was void.

Fines are levied on each of the parties to an agreement separately. One may be guilty of a greater infringement than another. Many competition infringements will involve groups of companies. The Commission will look at the activity of the undertaking responsible for the infringement, so that, if a parent company effectively determined the behaviour of its subsidiary and exercised very tight control over its activities, it is likely that the parent and/or the subsidiary would be fined. Where however, the subsidiary exercised quite a high degree of autonomy then the subsidiary alone may be subject to a fine.

Successor undertakings may be liable for fines in relation to activities carried out by 'third parties'. Where a company acquires another, including the rights and liabilities of another, then liability for a fine could also be inherited. Where, however, only assets are acquired from a company, it is unlikely that the Commission would be able to levy fines against the company which had acquired the assets, had played no part in the infringement and not sought to acquire the liabilities of the infringing entity. It is wise in agreements for the purchase of a company to provide for a warranty that there are no infringements of Article 85 or 86 (or the RTPA under English competition law).

Regulation 17 expressly provides that fines are not criminal penalties (Article 15.4).

In its Thirteenth Report on Competition Policy the Commission made a general statement concerning its policy on fines. The Commission seeks to levy fines at a high level to deter infringements. In particular, where companies have refused to co-operate with Commission investigations, the Commission is likely to levy higher fines. Fines of up to 10 per cent of turnover have been levied.

Notification and fines

Article 15.5 of Regulation 17 provides:

> The fines provided in paragraph 2(a) shall not be imposed in respect of acts taking place:

(a)   after notification to the Commission and before its decision in application of Article 85(3) of the Treaty, provided they fall within the limits of the activity described in the notification.

One of the more important reasons for notifying an agreement to the Commission is the protection from fines which this involves. The parties know that once they have submitted their notification they are protected from fines no matter how seriously the Commission regards the anti-competitive arrangements in the agreements so notified. There will, however, be no protection from fines for the period before the agreement was notified and therefore it is important to put in a notification as soon as possible after entry into the agreement.

Periodic penalty payments

The Commission may impose periodic penalty payments, effectively daily fines, in respect of continuing infringements or failures to supply information, by Article 16 of Regulation 17.

Investigations and procedural steps

Before any decision is taken under Regulation 17, an Advisory Committee on Restrictive Practices and Monopolies is consulted. Each Member State appoints an official to serve on this body. The Advisory Committee reaches an Opinion, which is annexed to the draft decision, but which is not made public.

Infringements of competition law can lead to investigations by the European Commission. Regulation 17 sets out the detailed provisions for such investigations. Under Article 11, the Commission is empowered to make requests for information from undertakings and associations of undertakings as well as from Member States themselves. There is an obligation to supply the information which has been requested.

By Article 11.5, where an undertaking does not supply the information requested within the time limit fixed by the Commission, or supplies incomplete information, the Commission may by decision require the information to be supplied. The decision specifies what information is required, fixes an appropriate time limit within which it is to be supplied and indicates the penalties provided for in Articles 15(1)(b) and 16(1)(c) and the right to have the decision reviewed by the Court of Justice. The penalties in Articles 15 and 16 are fines and periodic penalty payments.

In *Solvay & Cie v Commission*[6] and *Orkem v Commission*,[7] requests for information under Article 11 were resisted. The European Court annulled parts of the original decision which required the parties to admit infringements of the competition rules. As there are rights to produce arguments in defence of the undertakings under investigations after the statement of objections has been issued, the preliminary stage of the proceedings should not have the effect of prejudicing those rights.

Regulation 17 contains no right to remain silent and imposes a duty of active collaboration upon undertakings. There is no right to protection against self-incrimination, but the Commission must not prejudice at an early stage the right to a fair hearing later on in the proceedings.

6 [1991] 4 CMLR 502
7 [1991] 4 CMLR 502

As well as powers to request information backed up with the right to fine for failure to supply such information, the Commission has wide-ranging powers of investigation, which enable them to carry out what are commonly known as 'dawn raids'. These powers are set out in Article 14 of Regulation 17. The Commission may undertake 'all necessary investigations into undertakings and associations of undertakings'. To this end, the officials authorised by the Commission are empowered:

(a) to examine the books and other business records;
(b) to take copies of or extracts from the books and business records;
(c) to ask for oral explanations on the spot;
(d) to enter any premises, land and means of transport of undertakings.

Consultation with the competent authority in the relevant Member State takes place before an investigation is made and officials from that authority may attend to assist at the investigation. In the UK, the competent authority is the OFT.

In *Hoechst AG v Commission*[8] and *Dow Benelux NV v Commission*,[9] companies challenged the Commission's investigation, refusing to submit to investigations under Article 14.3 of Regulation 17. The applicants sought to argue that the powers of the Commission under these provisions of Regulation 17 violated fundamental rights or violated rights of fairness or non-discrimination.

In *Hoechst* the company resisted the entrance of Commission officials on to their premises even after the Commission adopted a decision imposing periodic penalty payments of ECU 1,000 for every day of delay in allowing entrance by the officials. Hoechst began an action before the German courts to prevent the competent authority in Germany, the Bundeskartellamt, from carrying out the investigation on behalf of the Commission. They succeeded in resisting a search warrant which the Bundeskartellamt obtained in connection with the premises of Hoechst. The matter was taken to the European Court which decided that interim measures, i.e. the periodic penalty payments, should be suspended pending a final decision as the Commission had not shown that there was any urgency in having the measures imposed pending the final resolution of the matter through the courts.

The Bundeskartellamt then succeeded in obtaining a search warrant and the investigation took place. However, one of the greatest assets which the Commission is able to exercise is that of surprise. It is empowered to arrive to investigate without notice and for serious infringements of the competition rules no notice may be given; in practice, for less serious cases, two days notice may be given. In this case, Hoechst may have been able to benefit from the delay as the Commission lost the element of surprise.

Hoechst was partially successful when the matter went for final consideration before the European Court. The Court held that where an undertaking refuses to collaborate with Commission officials undertaking an investigation under Article 14.3 of Regulation 17, it is bound to observe the procedural guarantees laid down by the relevant national legislation. It was for national law to lay down the appropriate procedural mechanisms in order to guarantee the observance of the rights of undertakings. The role of national courts, however, was restricted. It was held the national authority cannot

8 [1989] ECR 2859, OJ 1989 C266/7, [1991] 4 CMLR 410
9 OJ 1989 C288/4, [1991] 4 CMLR 410

substitute its own assessment of the need for the investigations ordered by the Commission. The Commission's assessments are open to review only by the European Court of Justice. The Court went on to say:

> On the other hand, the national authorities are entitled to consider, once the authenticity of the decision ordering the investigation has been seen, whether the restrictive measures envisaged are arbitrary or excessive in relation to the purpose of the investigation and to ensure that the rules of national law are complied with in the application of those measures.

In *Dow* much the same decision was reached; also, the Commission had used information which it had gleaned from an earlier investigation and this was challenged. It was held that the Commission could use information obtained in an earlier investigation in order to initiate a fresh investigation, although it could not use the information obtained from the earlier investigation other than for those purposes indicated in the authorisation or decision ordering the investigation.

The Commission, however, has wide-ranging powers of investigation which have been used to great effect. Although many covert restrictive arrangements will never be reduced to writing, there may be correspondence of the parties which gives at least some evidence of the practices which the parties have been operating and the Commission will go through filing cabinets and ask employees to make copies for them of relevant documentation. Generally Commission officials arrive in the afternoon after a flight from Brussels in the morning and may spend up to several days at the premises of companies suspected of operating restrictive agreements.

Appeals

Appeals against all Commission decisions can be made whether on procedural grounds or on matters of law following decisions under Article 85 or 86.

The Court of First Instance, which was established by Council Decision of 24 October 1988,[10] is the first court of appeal. It was instituted to assist with the large volume of cases coming before the Court of Justice. The Court consists of twelve members and sits in a chamber of three or five judges. It acts as a court of first instance and exercises the jurisdiction conferred on the Court of Justice by the Treaties establishing the EC.

An appeal can be made to the Court of Justice from the Court of First Instance within two months of the notification of the decision against which the appeal is made. Any party which has been unsuccessful either in whole or in part in respect of its submissions may bring an appeal, provided that the decision affects the party appealing. Where a Member State or a Community institution is appealing they do not need to be affected by the decision in order to appeal; the requirement applies only in relation to individuals.

Appeals to the Court of Justice are limited to appeals on points of law. An appeal may lie on the grounds of lack of competence of the Court of First Instance, a breach of procedure before it which adversely affects the interest of the appellant, or the infringement of Community law by the Court of First Instance. No appeals may be made in relation only to the amount of costs or the party ordered to pay them, although this could be part of an appeal on other grounds.

10 OJ 1988 L319/1 and see Chapt. 1

The Court of Justice is able to refer cases back to the Court of First Instance or reach a decision itself. Where a case is referred back, the Court of First Instance is bound by any decision of the Court of Justice on points of law.

Article 177 references

Under Article 177 of the Treaty of Rome, where questions of EC law arise in domestic litigation, the national court may request the European Court to give a ruling on the issue. The Court will give a ruling on the interpretation, for example, of Article 85 in a particular context. Many EC cases arise from Article 177 references.

Conclusion

The consequences of infringement of Articles 85 and 86 include agreements being void, parties being sued for damages and fines being levied by the Commission. Interim measures may be ordered and investigations undertaken by the Commission. Appeals against decisions of the Commission may be made to the Court of First Instance and the Court of Justice and national courts may refer points concerning the interpretation of the competition provisions of the Treaty of Rome to the Court for a decision to be reached.

The consequences and penalties which arise from breach of merger control legislation are addressed in Chapter 4.

UK COMPETITION LAW

English competition law also has methods of enforcement and policing of its rules. These have not always been as effective as the weapons available to the equivalent regulatory authorities in the EC.

Under UK law, fines may only be imposed for breach of competition law where the party in default was already subject to an order of the Restrictive Practices Court and has acted in breach of that order, putting itself in contempt of court. There is therefore no power to fine for a first offence. Agreements may be void for want of registration, which in relation to commercial agreements between companies can be a heavy sanction where enforcement of the provisions of the agreement is essential.

By section 35(1) of the RTPA, if particulars of an agreement which is subject to registration are not duly furnished within the time required by section 24, or within such further time as the Director General of Fair Trading may allow:

(a) the agreement is void in respect of all restrictions accepted or information provisions made thereunder; and
(b) it is unlawful for any person to the agreement who carries on business within the UK to give effect to, or enforce or purport to enforce, the agreement in respect of any such restrictions or information provisions.

The UK system of registration of agreements has been looked at in Chapter 2. Essentially, where an agreement between two parties carrying on business in the UK in the supply of goods or services contains two restrictions of the sort listed in section 6 or 11 of the RTPA which are accepted by two parties, the agreement will be registrable under the RTPA. The agreement must be sent to the OFT before it is put into effect. The OFT may refer it to the Restrictive Practices Court or merely put it upon the public register.

If this procedure is not followed the restrictions are void. It can be seen from section 35 (above) that it is not the entire agreement that is void for want of registration. However, if the restrictive clause is incapable of severance from the rest of the agreement under the general English law of severance, the entire agreement may founder. It is therefore wise to place restictions in separate clauses which could if necessary be deleted from the agreement without affecting the rest of the provisions. Splitting the restrictions up into separate parts, some of which could be more easily severed by a court using the judicial 'blue pencil', could again be advantageous. This applies equally in the EC context.

It is not clear whether all restrictions in the agreement are void if the agreement is not registered in accordance with the RTPA. Section 35 refers to restrictions being void. Not all 'restrictions' amount to relevant restrictions under the RTPA, i.e. restrictions of the sort which would be assessed and counted for the purpose of determining whether or not the agreement were registrable and whether or not there were restrictions on two parties in the agreement. The better view is that only restrictions which would have made the agreement subject to registration under the RTPA would be void. There are many other sorts of provision which might amount to 'restrictions', but which are either not within the wording of the restrictions contained in the exhaustive lists of sections 6 and 11 or which are disregarded under section 9(3). It seems unlikely that the legislators intended that any such provision, whether a restriction under the RTPA or not, would be void, given the very wide meaning which could be given to 'restriction'.

For example, where the parties to an agreement have entered into mutual non-competition restrictions, these are likely to amount to a registrable agreement. If they failed to register the agreement before the restrictions came into effect, the restrictions will be void but other provisions in the agreement between them may well be enforceable. It is not possible to register an agreement late, and the only alternative on discovering a registrable, but unregistered, agreement is to terminate it and enter into another, ensuring that it is registered at the OFT.

The second consequence of non-registration set out in section 35(1) is that it is unlawful to give effect to the agreement or its restrictions. It is not however a criminal offence to give effect to such agreements.

The third consequence therefore of entering into such agreements is that actions for breach of statutory duty may be brought by any person affected by the contravention of the law. The Resale Prices Act 1976, in section 25(2), contains a similar provision and in the Government's White Paper on Restrictive Trade Practices it is envisaged that any new legislation would encourage private actions in the courts for damages.[11]

Companies operating an agreement, for example, to drive a competitor out of the market place by predatory pricing, i.e. charging very low prices in areas where the competitor is operating or seeking to operate, could be sued in the High Court by that aggrieved competitor for damages arising from the operation of the restrictive agreement, provided that the agreement had not been registered with the OFT. The damages awarded, if the case were

11 White Paper – *Opening Markets: New Policy on Restrictive Trade Practices*, July 1989, Cm 727, paras. 5.15 – 5.19, p.27

successful, would be likely to amount to the losses suffered by the competitor by virtue of the operation of the agreement, as may be the case in actions brought in the UK courts for breach of EC competition law discussed earlier in this chapter. However, attractive though this section may appear to those who have suffered loss at the hands of anti-competitive operators, there have been no reported cases which have reached the courts.

Investigatory powers

There are powers to investigate anti-competitive practices (which were examined in Chapter 3) and, under the RTPA, the Director has powers to obtain information.

By section 36, if the Director has reasonable cause to believe that a person is or may be party to an agreement subject to registration under the RTPA, he may serve a notice on that person. Investigations may thus be made where there is 'reasonable cause to believe' that a person is or may be party to a registrable agreement. There must be evidence of some form, perhaps a complaint from a customer of the parties to the alleged agreement or an ex-employee, before the Director can investigate at all; 'fishing expeditions' are not permitted.

The Director has commented that this leaves him in a difficult position or 'catch 22' situation; he cannot investigate until he has evidence and he cannot obtain evidence by investigation unless there is evidence already in his possession. This makes investigation difficult and the White Paper proposals discussed later seek to improve on this position.[12]

12 White Paper, *op cit*, para. 5.1, p.24

Investigations may be made only in relation to companies operating in the United Kingdom and only where there 'is' an agreement. It would seem, although there is no case law on the point, that investigations under section 36 in relation to restrictive arrangements or agreements which have ceased before the date the OFT begins its investigation would not be possible under the literal wording of this section.

The Director's notice may require any person to notify the Director (within such time as may be specified in the notice) as to whether he is party to any registrable agreement, and if so to furnish to the Director such particulars of the agreement as may be specified in the notice.

Powers to examine on oath

Section 37 permits the Director to apply to the Restrictive Practices Court for an order that persons to whom section 36 notices have been given attend and be examined on oath concerning the matters in respect of which the Director has given notice. The Director will take part in such examination and may be represented by a solicitor or counsel.

The person examined must answer all questions relevant to the notice as the Court may put or allow to be put to him, but may at his own cost employ a solicitor, with or without counsel, who is at liberty to put to him such questions as the Court may deem just for the purpose of enabling him to explain or qualify any answers given by him. There appears to be no privilege against self-incrimination in the legislation, i.e. an individual subject to such an examination under oath may not refuse to answer questions on the grounds that it might incriminate him to do so, even if there is a risk that he might be sent to jail for aiding and abetting contempt of court. Persons so examined may be required by the Court to produce particulars, documents or information in their possession or control.

In many instances companies will be potential infringers of the legislation. Clearly their only presence before a court can be through their employees. Section 37(3) provides that an order may be made for the attendance and examination:

(a) of any director, manager, secretary or other officer of that body corporate; or
(b) of any other person who is employed by the body corporate and appears to the Court to be likely to have particular knowledge of any of the matters in respect of which the notice was given.

The section would appear to preclude the calling of ex-directors or ex-employees.

There is protection for privileged communications in section 37(6), where it is provided that nothing 'shall be taken to compel the disclosure by a barrister, advocate or solicitor of any privileged communication made by him or to him in that capacity, or the production by him of any document containing any such communication'. Advice given by solicitors employed by a company, or given by independent solicitors, could be protected under this section from disclosure in such proceedings.

Penalties under section 38

Failure to comply with a section 36 notice without reasonable excuse brings with it a fine not exceeding £100.

Where information is furnished, whether under section 36 or generally in making a registration under the Act, and a person (i) makes a statement or furnishes a document which he knows to be false, or (ii) recklessly makes such a statement or furnishes any document, which is false in a material particular, or (iii) wilfully 'alters, suppresses or destroys any document which he is required to furnish', an offence will be committed under section 38(2). A jail sentence of up to three months can be imposed and/or a fine of up to £100.

There are no similar provisions to those in Regulation 17, discussed above under EC competition law, which would permit 'dawn raids' or their equivalents to be carried out under the RTPA. The OFT has found its lack of effective investigatory powers frustrating, hence the proposals in the White Paper. Where, for example, a price fixing cartel is uncovered, the OFT has no powers to fine or imprison individuals involved in those arrangements unless this was effectively a second offence for the company.

Orders

There are two sorts of orders which can be made under the RTPA. The bringing of proceedings has been considered in Chapter 2, with a description of the section 10 'gateways' or justificatory defences which defendants in such proceedings can use.

Where restrictive agreements are found to operate against the public interest, then by section 2(2) of the RTPA the Restrictive Practices Court can make an order restraining the parties to the agreement:

(a) from giving effect to, or enforcing or purporting to enforce the agreement in respect of those restrictions or those information provisions;

(b) from making any other agreement (whether with the same parties or with other parties) to the like effect; or

(c) where such agreement as is mentioned in paragraph (b) above has already been made, from giving effect to that agreement or enforcing or purporting to enforce it.

The parties are clearly forbidden from operating the agreement itself. A section 2 order also forbids making any other agreement to the like effect. The 'like effect' is interpreted as meaning a similar result rather than requiring that a subsequent arrangement be in the same form as the earlier. The parties would not be entitled to apply a different method of entering into the same arrangement, for example having an oral rather than a written agreement, and thus be able to avoid breach of the order.

Such orders do not have the result that companies entering into different, but registrable, agreements are in breach of the order. The agreements entered into subsequently would have to be to the like effect to the earlier agreement for there to be any breach of the order.

By section 35(3), the Court may make such order as appears to it to be proper for restraining the parties to the registrable agreements from giving effect to, or enforcing or purporting to enforce the agreement in respect of, any restriction or information provisions and other unregistered but registrable agreements.

Section 35 orders are made in respect of unregistered agreements. Section 2 orders follow from the registration of agreements.

Once a company has an order made against it, particularly a section 35 order, it needs to ensure that all agreements which it enters into are carefully vetted before they come into effect in order to determine whether or not they are registrable agreements, which would put the company in contempt of court. Such orders are therefore an administrative burden for companies and require a large compliance effort. The consequences of breach of such an order are that the company will be in contempt of court.

Those companies which are subject to court orders need to exercise particular caution in their membership of trade associations. As has been seen in Chapter 2, any specific recommendation by a trade association is deemed to be a restriction accepted by all the members of that association and to amount to a registrable agreement. Companies subject to orders could therefore find themselves in contempt of court for failing to register particulars of trade association recommendations of which perhaps they were unaware.

Contempt of court

Companies subject to orders under sections 2 and 35 which act in breach of those orders are liable to fines for contempt of court. Also, individuals who have aided and abetted the contempt could personally be liable to fines and possibly jail sentences for such aiding and abetting.

Companies are able to produce in mitigation the fact that they took legal advice concerning how they could best comply with the orders and by showing that they had a comprehensive compliance programme in operation to attempt to prevent restrictive arrangements being entered into by employees.

13 [1991] ICR 52 (RPC)

In *Re Ready Mixed Concrete,*[13] proceedings relating to contempt of court arising from restrictive arrangements entered into in the Oxfordshire area by companies already subject to orders, the Court rejected the argument by one of the parties that, as a separate corporate entity, it could not have been in contempt through the actions of an employee who was acting outside the terms of his employment and in breach of clear company policy. However, the Court of Appeal overturned the lower Court and accepted that argument

13a CA decision, TLR 26 July 1991

in *DGFT v Smiths Concrete Ltd.*[13a] The DGFT may appeal to the House of Lords as the decision makes it much harder to bring contempt proceedings against companies with comprehensive compliance programmes.

In *Re Ready Mixed Concrete* the judge took into account in mitigation the fact that the arrangements applied only in relation to a small geographical area, but not that they had had very little commercial effect. Also relevant to mitigation was the fact that some of the companies concerned had good compliance programmes to ensure that the orders were adhered to by their staff. The fact that some companies involved had apologised promptly and unequivocally to the court and not raised arguments as to whether or not they were party to the arrangements was a relevant factor in mitigation, as was the fact that senior management had been involved in trying to enforce the companies' procedures for compliance with the RTPA. Early co-operation with the OFT was also relevant in setting the amount of the fines. Interestingly, the parties' legal fees, including those fees payable by the two individuals who were personally brought before the court for aiding and abetting the contempt of their employers, were relevant to the setting of fines in the case, as was the turnover of the companies and the financial position of the individuals involved. The fines against the companies for contempt ranged from £16,000 to £25,000.

When Somerville Nails Limited breached an undertaking given to the Restrictive Practices Court and sought to fix prices and discounts it was fined £100,000. Six figure fines are not out of the ordinary, particularly where companies have breached orders in a particularly flagrant fashion and had very little by way of a compliance programme.

Personal liability of directors and officers

Employees of companies in contempt can be found guilty of aiding and abetting their employer's contempt. To date no individuals have been jailed, although the OFT has brought proceedings against individuals in a number of cases.

14 [1990] 2 All ER 216

In *A-G for Tuvalu and another* v *Philatelic Distribution Corp. Ltd and others*[14] (a general case of contempt of court), the Court of Appeal held that where a company was ordered not to do certain acts and a director of the company was aware of the order or the undertaking given, the director was under a duty to take reasonable steps to ensure that the order was obeyed. If the director wilfully failed to take those steps and the order or undertaking was breached he could be punished for contempt, unless he reasonably believed that some other director or officer of the company was taking the

necessary steps. The judge quoted from *Re Galvanised Tank Manufacturers'*
Association's Agreement[15] where Megaw J had said that a company which   15 [1965] 2 All ER 1003
had given an undertaking to the court must be treated as having:

> failed lamentably and inexcusably in its elementary duty if it fails to take adequate
> and continuing steps to ensure, through its responsible officers, that those officers
> themselves, and anyone to whom they may delegate the handling of matters which
> fall within the scope of the undertaking, do no forget or misunderstand or overlook
> the obligations imposed by such undertakings.

In *Tuvalu* the judge decided, as to sentencing, that for the appellant
individual, who was a married man of 49 with a family and, apart from the
matters revealed by the case, had a perfectly good record and character, a
sentence of imprisonment was a very grave punishment indeed. In the
circumstances, the court did not consider it necessary to impose a sentence of
imprisonment. The earlier court's fine of £3,000 stood, but the three month
prison sentence was overturned.

The Rules of the Supreme Court, Order 45, Rule 5(1)(b) provide:

(i)   Where... a person disobeys a judgement or order requiring him to abstain from
      doing an act then, subject to the provisions of these rules, the judgement or
      order may be enforced by one of the following means, that is to say...
(ii) where that person is a body corporate, with the leave of the Court, a writ of
      sequestration against the property of any director or other officer of the body;
(iii) subject to the provisions of the Debtors Act 1869 and 1878, an order of
      committal against that person or, where that person is a body corporate,
      against any such officer.

An order of committal cannot be made by Order 45, Rule 7(3):

> unless –
> (a)   a copy of the order has also been served personally on the officer against
>   whose property leave is sought to issue the writ of sequestration or against
>   whom an order for committal is sought.

Also there must be a penal notice endorsed on the order:

> If the body corporate disobeys this order you [a director or officer of the body
> corporate] will be liable to process of execution for the purpose of compelling the
> said [body corporate] to obey the same.

In *Tuvalu* the appellant himself had given an undertaking and it was accepted
in any event that the requirements for service did not apply. It was sufficient if
a director was aware of the undertaking.

The Director has expressed his belief that prison sentences for involved
individuals would prove a useful disincentive to directors and managers
operating restrictive agreements. *Director General of Fair Trading* v *Buckland*
and another[16] was a contempt of court case concerning breach of section 35   16 [1990] 1 All ER 545
orders. The Director applied for orders committing directors to prison for
breach of the orders. The judge decided that 'Ord 45, r 5 does not render an
officer of the company liable in contempt by virtue of his office and his mere
knowledge that the order sought to be enforced was made. Resort can be had
to r 5 only if he can otherwise be shown to be in contempt under the general
law of contempt.' The issues of service under Order 45 were not therefore

decided upon and in particular arguments by the Director that the need for service upon the directors could be dispensed with under Order 45, Rule 7 were not judicially considered.

In *Re Ready Mixed Concrete*, two employees, who were not directors but were involved in the day-to-day operation of restrictive arrangements, were brought before the court for aiding and abetting the contempt of their employer companies. The judge said that they 'stood a real chance of being sent to prison'. However, as there were others who had been involved in the arrangements who had not been brought before the court and the individuals had made no personal gain from the arrangement which related only to a limited area they were only fined £1,200 and £1,000. The fines were payable over two years. The judge said:

> He has, we are told, incurred legal costs in the region of £10,000. He will be indemnifying the Director for his costs, a further financial burden. He is a man of limited financial means. Any four figure sum will create serious difficulties for him. But the fact remains that his offence is a serious one. He is fined £1,200 payable over two years, a figure that would have been higher but for his heavy liability in costs.

The position concerning the liability of directors and other officers and managers of companies subject to orders is that they are at risk of being fined for contempt under Order 45, Rule 5, provided their individual conduct was culpable, particularly if they were personally involved in the contempt, for example, by entering into the restrictive arrangement complained of on behalf of their employer. It is unlikely that an individual would be penalised for aiding and abetting the contempt of his employer company by reason merely of his office, or even through a failure in ensuring effective compliance with the order.

The inheritance of orders

As has been seen in connection with Article 85, where a company acquires the liabilities of another it may become liable for fines levied by the Commission in relation to past infringements of the acquired undertaking. Under the RTPA, it is possible that where assets and liabilities are acquired there may be some level of inheritance of orders of the Restrictive Practices Court too, but only where one company aids and abets the contempt of another or where one acquires the liabilities of another by a vesting order of the state.

Declarations

Under section 26 of the RTPA, any person 'aggrieved' may apply to the Restrictive Practices Court for the Register to be rectified 'by the variation or removal of particulars included in the Register in respect of any agreement'.

The Court also has power to declare that an agreement is one subject to registration under the RTPA either on the application of one of the parties to an agreement, or on the application of the Director in respect of an agreement of which particulars have been furnished under the RTPA. This procedure can be of use where one party to an agreement wishes subsequently to avoid the terms of the agreement and to raise the fact that it is a registrable agreement of which particulars should have been furnished to the OFT. For want of registration the agreement is void and so the party is no longer bound by the restriction. A declaration of non-registration has been used in cases of this type with success.

Conclusion

Breach of the provisions of the RTPA can lead to agreements being void and third parties can sue for damages for breach of statutory duty. Where one of the parties is subject to RTPA court orders and then enters into a registrable agreement without first registering it, that party would be in breach of those orders and in contempt of court.

The penalty for contempt of court against companies is a fine and, increasingly, six figure sums have been awarded for the more flagrant of contempts in this field. Individuals employed by companies in contempt may be liable for aiding and abetting the contempt and could be fined. Although there is power to jail individuals none has yet served a term in jail.

The investigatory powers and the penalties available to the OFT for 'first offenders' are weak and ineffective. The White Paper proposes powers similar to those of the European Commission discussed above.

EC AND UK COMPLAINTS

Generally, under both EC and UK competition law, companies infringing competition legislation are at risk that those aggrieved may make a complaint to the Commission or the OFT. Companies refused supplies may make an Article 86 complaint. Competitors left out of a price fixing cartel, or against whom a campaign is being operated to drive them out of business, may make an Article 85 complaint or a complaint to the OFT alleging breach of the RTPA, or a complaint under the Competition Act. Ex-employees with a grievance, perhaps having been dismissed by the company, may choose for personal reasons to 'spill the beans' to the competition authorities. Customers who feel their suppliers have 'got the market stitched up' may bring a complaint.

There is no formal procedure in EC or UK legislation for making such complaints. Complaints may be made by way of letter to the relevant competition authorities, perhaps accompanied by any independent evidence which the complainant has to back up his arguments. Not all complaints will be investigated. Some will be groundless and others not of sufficient importance compared to other cases with which the competition authorities are busy, but complaints are one of the principle means available to those authorities in uncovering covert cartels and similar such arrangements.

EXTRA-TERRITORIALITY

International law and the subject of the conflict of laws is beyond the scope of this book and there are many excellent text books on that subject. However, in considering competition law regard must be had to the question of the scope and application of the laws of both the EC and the UK.

As to conflict between those two laws, the position is comparatively straightforward. EC law applies directly in the UK and will prevail over UK law. However, agreements which are exempt under Article 85 may still be caught by the RTPA. It is not sufficient for a defendant to allege that because the agreement would have been exempt under Article 85, national competition legislation will not apply. The two systems operate in tandem and it is only in the merger control field, considered in Chapter 4, that the competition law of the UK and EC have a more clearly defined scope. Even in that area, the principle of one-stop shopping has not been achieved in some cases.

In *R v Secretary of State for Transport, ex parte Factortame Limited and other*[17] (the fishing vessels case), the House of Lords reaffirmed the supremacy of EC law over UK law and that it could restrain the UK courts from enforcing an Act of Parliament pending a decision by the European Court as to its legality under EC law, if, taking all circumstances including the public interest into account, the balance of convenience favours such a measure, in particular where there appear to be strong grounds for challenging the validity of legislation. The ECJ in July 1991 affirmed this supremacy.

International agreements will often have to be drafted with a number of competition authorities in mind. Not only will there be EC and UK competition law to consider, but frequently other national legislation in, say, Germany.

Extra-territoriality and the EC

For EC law to apply, clearly, there must be some link with the EC. An agreement in Australia of purely domestic effect is unlikely to have the necessary effect on trade between Member States for the issue of the Treaty of Rome to arise at all. However, purely domestic agreements may have potential anti-competitive effects in the EC, depending on their terms. They may be in terms, for example, that the parties agree not to export to the EC or to supply certain areas of the EC market exclusively.

The European Commission will look to where the agreement is implemented rather than to where it is made. The leading decision in this area is *Re Wood Pulp Cartel: A. Aglstrom Oy v Commission.*[18] The Commission found that infringements of Article 85 had occurred, whereby producers of wood pulp acted together in the announcement of prices for each quarter and in the actual prices charged to customers. A number of the parties involved, all having their registered offices outside the EC, appealed to the European Court of Justice. In the context that Article 85 prohibits all agreements between undertakings affecting trade between Member States and which have as their object or effect the restriction of competition in the common market, the Court noted that the main sources of supply of wood pulp are outside the EC, in Canada, the US, Sweden and Finland and that the market had global dimensions because of that fact. The Court went on to say:

> Where wood pulp producers established in those countries sell directly to purchasers established in the Community and engage in price competition in order to win orders from those customers, that constitutes competition in the Common Market.

This is quite a far reaching statement and the appealing wood pulp producers argued that it was contrary to public international law as the conduct

17 [1990] 3 CMLR 375 (HL), [1990] 3 CMLR 1 (ECJ), see also the Advocate General's opinion of 13 March 1991 (Cases C-221/89 and C-246/89) and ECJ final decision of July 1991, *Independent* Law Reports 26 July 1991

18 [1988] 4 CMLR 901

complained of was adopted outside the Community. However, the Court took a practical approach and said:

> If the applicability of prohibitions laid down under competition law were made to depend on the place where the agreement, decision or concerted practice was formed, the result would obviously be to give undertakings an easy means of evading those prohibitions. The decisive factor is therefore the place where it is implemented.

In this case the agreement was held to have been implemented in the EC. 'It is immaterial in that respect whether or not they had recourse to subsidiaries, agents, sub-agents, or branches within the Community in order to make their contracts with purchasers within the Community,' it was stated in the judgment.

One therefore has a situation where companies which do not themselves as separate legal entities operate in the EC can be held to have infringed Article 85 as they supply to subsidiaries or agents in the EC and that is where their restrictive agreement is implemented. It would seem, however, that the companies against whom the Commission takes action under Article 85 must in one sense be 'implementing' an agreement. They must have some influence or control over those agents or subsidiaries or it would not be the case that their implementation took place in the EC. The question of the degree of presence required within the EC, if indeed any presence is required at all, is far from being beyond doubt after the *Wood Pulp* case. The Court referred to the earlier case of *Imperial Chemical Industries Ltd* v *Commission*.[19] In that case it was held that the activities of a subsidiary within the EC could be deemed those of the parent company operating outside the EC, and the issues of extra-territoriality were discussed at some length.

Enforcement of EC competition law against non-EC entities was considered in *Aluminium Imports from Eastern Europe*,[20] a case concerning state trading companies. The Commission made it clear that there was no provision of international law precluding the application of EC law to non-EC companies. The Commission did stress that it would look to the balance of interests, such as whether EC law would affect the interests of other territories or whether non-EC national law was contrary to EC law.

The Merger Regulation

Considerable discussion concerning the issues of territorial scope was undertaken in the process of agreeing the Merger Control Regulation,[21] which came into force on 21st September 1990. There were two issues in this area. The first area was conflict between EC and Member States' merger laws. This was settled, as has been seen in Chapter 4, by Article 21 precluding member states from applying their national merger laws to mergers with a Community dimension, with exceptions on public security and other grounds.

The second area was that of overlapping jurisdictions with non-EC territories. The scope of the Merger Regulation has been considered in Chapter 4. If the merger is one with a Community dimension then it is quite possible that the Regulation would apply even though the parties to it were, for example, US companies. It is believed that the Commission in practice will only seek to regulate those parts of a large international merger which relate

19 [1972] CMLR 557

20 OJ 1985 L92/1

21 Regulation No. 4064/89, published in corrected form OJ 1990 L257/13

to the EC. It has been proposed by Sir Leon Brittan, the Competition Commissioner in charge of the Commission's competition directorate, DG1V, that a US/EC Treaty be negotiated, not only in the field of merger control, but in relation to all anti-trust disputes where there are potentially overlapping jurisdictions.

The Regulation, in Article 24, states that Member States must inform the Commission of any general difficulties encountered by their undertakings with concentrations in a non-member country. The Commission will regularly draw up a report examining the treatment accorded to Community undertakings regularly as regards concentrations in non-member countries. The Commission will submit those reports to the Council, together with any recommendations.

Whenever it appears to the Commission, either on the basis of the reports referred to above or on the basis of other information, that a non-member country does not grant Community undertakings treatment comparable to that granted by the Community to undertakings from that non-member country:

> the Commission may submit proposals to the Council for an appropriate mandate for negotiation with a view to obtaining comparable treatment for Community undertakings.

This so-called 'reciprocity clause' merely permits the Commission to send proposals to the Council to obtain approval for its entering into negotiations to obtain comparable treatment, where other jurisdictions do not offer comparable treatment. It would not necessarily be the case that any substantive results would flow from that mandate and it is likely that the provision will be little used.

Extra-territoriality and UK competition law

The Restrictive Trade Practices Act

The RTPA applies only where there are two parties to an agreement carrying on business in the supply of goods or services in the UK. Two Australian companies, no matter how restrictive their price fixing arrangement relating, for example, to the supply of a product within Australia, would not therefore find that they had entered into an agreement which would have to be registered under the RTPA (see Chapter 2). The business must be carried on in the UK but the RTPA does not define this phrase. Section 43(4) provides that a person will not be deemed to carry on a business within the UK by reason only of the fact that 'he is represented for the purposes of that business by an agent within the United Kingdom'.

The law is not clear.[22] However, it is likely that having an office and premises in this country from which business is done by a foreign corporation would amount to carrying on business here. Appointing an agent in this country, however, would not be sufficient. If the agent does more than procure orders for its principal, perhaps begins manufacturing products here, then that may be sufficient. It will be a question of fact in each case.

Foreign corporations with subsidiaries in this country are treated as separate legal entities and the activities of the subsidiary are unlikely to be

22 See *Chitty on Contracts*, Vol. II, 26th ed., Sweet & Maxwell, 1989, para. 4372, Green *Commercial Agreements and Competition Law*, Graham & Trotman, 1986, p.13, *The OFT's Guide to Restrictive Trade Practices*, 1990 ed., r. p.11 – 12 and Cunningham *The Fair Trading Act*, Sweet & Maxwell 1973, para. 13–40 (1956 RTPA)

deemed those of the parent in assessing whether or not the parent is carrying on business in this country. This is not the case under EC law, where whether a subsidiary's activities are deemed those of its parent for the purposes of infringements of EC competition law will depend on the degree of control which the parent exercises over the subsidiary and the extent to which the subsidiary carries on its own business without reference to its parent company. However, it is by no means certain as to when a parent company's activities in this country, notwithstanding the fact that it is a foreign corporation, could amount to carrying on business here. In determining whether or not to register an agreement a cautious view is recommended in order to ensure the enforceability of restrictions by registering the agreement with the OFT.

In some circumstances, an agreement can become registrable where one party begins to carry on business in this country after the agreement has been in operation for some time, as has been seen in Chapter 2. In those circumstances, on the occurrence of the first business activity in this country, the agreement comes within the scope of the UK legislation, i.e. within its territorial scope, and should be registered before that occurrence.

Where only one party to an agreement carries on business in the UK, the agreement will not be registrable under the RTPA. It is essential that two parties carry on business in this country for the RTPA to be applicable.

This formalistic approach is in keeping with the general operation of this legislation, which, as has been seen in Chapter 2, looks to whether the agreement in form falls within the series of requirements of the RTPA and does not as part of that exercise require any regard to be had to the commercial or anti-competitive effect of the legislation.

In the context of territorial scope the provisions of Schedule 3, paragraph 6 are relevant.[23] This is an exemption which applies where there is an agreement between two parties carrying on business in the UK which would otherwise be registrable. The RTPA will not apply where the restrictions relate exclusively:

(a) to the supply of goods by export from the United Kingdom;
(b) to the production of goods, or the application of any process of manufacture to goods, outside the United Kingdom;
(c) to the acquisition of goods to be delivered outside the United Kingdom and not imported into the United Kingdom for entry for home use; or
(d) to the supply of goods to be delivered outside the United Kingdom otherwise than by export from the United Kingdom.

23 See Chitty, *op cit*, paras. 4411 – 4413, Green, *op cit*, pp. 92 – 93 and Cunningham, *op cit*, paras. 14–62, 63 (1956 RTPA)

As with all Schedule 3 exemptions, the wording of the exemption will not fit all forms of export deal. For example, there may be some doubt as to whether the exemption would apply where there is an agreement for export but before export, there will be a supply of the goods to be exported between two UK companies whereby title to the goods will pass in this country. In cases of doubt registration is advisable. In any event, under section 25(a) of the RTPA, particulars of export agreements of the sort covered by the exemption must be sent to the OFT. Export agreements of this kind are treated for registration purposes as if they are agreements which fall to be registered in the normal way under the RTPA. However, the penalties for failure to register do not apply.

The Competition Act

Competition Act investigations have been considered in Chapter 3. The Act permits investigations of anti-competitive practices where the company concerned has over 25 per cent of a market or a turnover of £5m. By section 2(1) of the Act, an anti-competitive practice is one which, *inter alia*, distorts competition in the production, supply or acquisition of goods in the UK. There could not be an investigation into activities which had effects only in relation to the supply of goods in Canada, for example, even if the companies concerned were operating in this country. The reverse situation would apply too, however. In theory foreign corporations' anti-competitive practices which had the necessary effect in this country of distorting or restricting competition could be investigated. However, to have practical effect and properly to be in a postion to carry out an investigation, those corporations would need some type of presence in this country or else agree to co-operate fully.

The Fair Trading Act

UK merger law is discussed in Chapter 4. A merger under section 64 occurs where two enterprises cease to be distinct. By section 64(1), one at least of these enterprises must have been carried on in the UK 'or by or under the control of a body corporate incorporated in the UK'. Where the merger qualifies for investigation because of high market share, rather than the £30m assets test, then a further jurisdictional point arises from section 64(2); 25 per cent of goods in a particular market must be supplied in the UK or a substantial part of the UK by one of the parties, where the assets test limit is not achieved.

Where a merger takes place between two US corporations and no UK entities are involved then there would be no qualifying merger on the assumption that the US companies did not carry on business in this country. If a US company takes over a UK company or business the first part of the jurisdictional test will have been satisfied as there is one company carrying on business in this country. However, if the value of the assets is under £30m, it will only be a qualifying merger if there is more than a 25 per cent market share held by one of the parties in this country. If neither has that share, even if both hold together 99 per cent of the world market, it would not be a qualifying merger.

The Schedule 8 orders which may be made both in connection with the Fair Trading Act and the RTPA can be made against both UK and foreign companies. Where one party has no assets or business in this country the enforcement of such orders may be difficult, however.

QUESTIONS

1. Mr X has been appointed Managing Director of Euroco. Within two days of taking up the position he receives a telephone call from his opposite number in Italy asking him if he will be attending the 'usual meeting', which on this occasion is in Rome, with his counterpart from a rival company in the next large city. Mr X has good reason to suspect that a price fixing arrangement is in place and was told by his predecessor that he should do nothing to 'upset the apple cart' and the business could not operate if 'things were changed'. Mr X has come from a huge multinational company with a tough compliance programme.

He seeks your advice on behalf of Euroco.

(a) If he continues with the arrangement what 'is the worst that could happen'? He tells you that Euroco is subject to a section 35 order under the RTPA.

(b) Could any penalties be applied against him personally?

(c) Should he drop out of the arrangement quietly or complain to the European Commission and/or the Office of Fair Trading?

(d) If he wished to continue could he sue the Italians, who operate in this country too, for breach of the arrangement?

2. WodgeUK makes wodges, a form of door wedge which can be used without infringing fire regulations. It wishes to enter into an agreement with the Fire Authority whereby the Authority will exclusively recommend the products of WodgeUK and WodgeUK will not compete with the Fire Authority in the manufacture of any products which the Authority currently makes, such as fire hoses and protective suits.

WodgeUK's Managing Director suspects there may be competition law problems. Assuming both parties to the agreement operate in the UK is he safe to assume he has no Article 85(1) problem, ignoring any relevant EC block exemptions?

His arrangement works very well for a year. With 1992 on the horizon, he has lunch in Paris with the Paris Fire Authority Chief and hopes to come to a similar such arrangement, exporting the wodges to France.

What advice would you give him concerning whether his agreement is likely to affect trade between Member States? What information would you need from him before making an assessment? Draw up a list of questions to which you would seek answers in order properly to advise him.

FURTHER READING

EC

ARTICLES

Brealey M. – *Remedies in domestic courts for breach of EC law*, Law Society's Gazette, 42, 21 November 1990 p.24 & 45, 12 December 1990 p.26
Ferry J.E. – *Towards Completing the Chain: The* Woodpulp *Judgement*, [1989] 1 ECLR 58

BOOKS

Bellamy & Child – *Common Market Law of Competition*, Sweet & Maxwell, 3rd ed., 1986, chapt. 10 (civil remedies)
Butterworths Guide to European Court Practice, 1990
Green N. – *Commercial Agreements and Competition Law*, Graham & Trotman, 1986, chapt. 7 & chapt. 12 (enforcement & procedure)
Hawk B.E. – *US, Common Market & International Anti-trust*, Prentice Hall Law & Business, 1990 Supplement, Vol. II, chapt. 7 (policing & enforcement)
Joliet R. (Judge) – *National Anti-competition Legislation and Community law*, chapter 16, in Hawk B.E. Ed., Matthew Bender 1989, Fordham Corporate Law Institute
Kerse – *EEC Anti-trust Procedure*, European Law Centre Ltd, 2nd ed., 1988
Lasok K.P.E. – *The European Court of Justice, Practice and Procedure*, Butterworths, 1984
Van Bael & Bellis, *Competition Law of the EEC*, CCH Editions Ltd., 2nd ed., 1990, p.78 (scope, procedure and extra-territorial reach) & Part II (procedure p. 469)
Waude, Jones & Lewis – *EEC Competition Law Handbook 1989/90*, Part XXIX, Procedure & Remedies, p.262 *et seq*, Sweet & Maxwell 1990

CASES

Aluminium Imports from Eastern Europe OJ 1985 L92/1
Argyll Group PLC v The Distillers Company PLC [1986] 1 CMLR 764
Cutsforth v Mansfield Inns Ltd [1986] 1 All ER 577
Dow Benelux NV v Commission [1991] 4 CMLR 410 OJ 1989 C288/4
Garden Cottage Foods Ltd v Milk Marketing Board [1983] 3 CMLR 43
Hoechst AG v Commission [1991] 4 CMLR 410 [1989] ECR 2859, OJ 1989 C266/7

Imperial Chemical Industries Ltd v *Commission* [1972] CMLR 557
R v *Dearlove* and *R* v *Druker* [1988] Crim.L.R. 323, 88 Cr.App.Rep. 279
R v *Secretary of State for Transport, ex parte Factortame Limited and other* [1990] 3 CMLR 375
(HL) and 3 CMLR 1 (ECJ) and ECJ final decision July 1991 (*Independent* Law Reports 26
July 1991)
Solvay & Cie v *Commission* and *Orkem* v *Commission* OJ 1989 C288/5
Wood Pulp Cartel : *Re A. Aglstrom* v *Commission* [1988] 4 CMLR 901

UK

ARTICLE Walker-Smith A. – *Collusion: Its Detection and Investigation* [1991] 2 ECLR 71 (OFT employee
describes stages of investigation)

BOOKS *Chitty on Contracts*, Sweet & Maxwell, 26th ed., 1989, Vol II, para. 4411 (export agreements),
para. 4485 (s. 36 Notices) and para. 4507 (contempt)
Cunningham – *The Fair Trading Act 1973*, Sweet & Maxwell, 1974, p.144 (monopolies), p.161
(mergers)
Green (*op cit*), p.113 (Competition Act), p.140 (RTPA) & chapt.5 (Restrictive Practices Court)

CASES *AG for Tuvalu and another* v *Philatelic Distribution Corp. Ltd and others* [1990] 2 All ER 216
Director General of Fair Trading v *Buckland and another* [1990] 1 All ER 545
Re Galvanised Tank Manufacturers' Association's Agreement [1965] 2 All ER 1003
Re Ready Mixed Concrete [1991] ICR 52 (RPC decision) and *DGFT* v *Smiths Concrete Ltd*
TLR 26 July 1991 (CA decision)

6

The proposed new UK system and competition law in EC and non-EC countries

This chapter first considers proposals for reform of UK competition law and goes on to explore conpetition law in other jurisdictions.

PROPOSALS FOR CHANGE IN THE UK

The Government has proposed widespread changes to the UK legislation governing restrictive trade practices described in Chapter 2. Proposals for legislative change are important notwithstanding the fact that they are not at present implemented and are therefore subject to the vagaries of the legislative process, i.e. changes of Government and demands on Parliamentary time and the overriding caveat that any legislation following on from proposals may not survive to the statute book in the same or even similar form.

The legislation proposed in the White Paper 'Opening Markets: New Policy on Restrictive Trade Practices',[1] would involve the repeal of the Restrictive Trade Practices Act 1976 and the form based legislation currently in place and its substitution with restrictive practices legislation based on the EC model of Article 85 (discussed in Chapter 2), which the Government believes 'will have advantages in the Single European Market which will be operating by 1992'.[2] When enacted, the legislation will have effects on agreements entered into before it came into force and therefore regard should be had to the proposals prior to their becoming enshrined in legislation.

The formalistic operation of the RTPA has been shown in Chapter 2. The RTPA will apply provided a series of hurdles or pre-conditions are met, for example there must be two parties to the agreement carrying on business in the supply of goods or in the supply of services. If one carries on business in the supply of goods and the other only in the supply of services, then the RTPA will not apply at all, even though the agreement may have substantial anti-competitive effects. The RTPA will only apply where there are restrictions on two parties to the agreement. If one party is restricted by 20 clauses the RTPA will not apply unless there is also a restriction on the other party. There are complicated exemptions and an agreement must be examined against the pre-conditions. Whether. it is in practice anti-competitive is irrelevant to the analysis.

The Government concluded:[3]

> that the present system incorporated in the RTPA is inflexible and slow; is too often concerned with harmless agreements. One result of this inflexibility was noted to be

1 July 1989, Cm 727

2 White Paper, *op cit*, para.1.2

3 Para.2.1

the large and growing number of exceptions to the legislation and the absence of procedures for reviewing these against consistent criteria.

The prohibition

The nub of the new law will be a general prohibition of restrictive agreements, as with Article 85(1). The prohibition will be closely 'aligned' to Article 85(1) and is likely to comprise a prohibition on agreements or concerted practices which have the object or effect of restricting or distorting competition in the UK or in a part of the UK.

There will be an illustrative list of agreements which would be regarded as anti-competitive and which will be supplemented by guidance issued by the Government to help in interpretation of the legislation. It is proposed[4] that the list will proscribe agreements and concerted practices, including:

(i)   those fixing prices and charges including any terms or conditions (e.g. resale prices, discounts, credit terms) which determine effective net prices;
(ii) those which may be expected to lead to the fixing of prices, such as price information exchange agreements and recommendations on fees;
(iii) collusive tendering;
(iv) those sharing or allocating markets, customers, raw materials or other inputs, production or capacity;
(v)   collective refusals to supply or to deal with suppliers, collective discrimination in the terms on which different customers or classes of customer are supplied and collective anti-competitive conditions of supply such as tie-ins, aggregated or loyalty rebates and 'no competition' clauses.

This list contains few surprises and summarises most of the provisions likely to fall under scrutiny in any analysis under the existing EC legislation of Article 85(1).

Resale price maintenance is currently proscribed under the Resale Prices Act 1976. The new legislation will encompass this area too as well as that covered by the RTPA. Indeed price fixing is singled out by the Government[5] as being one of the most pernicious forms of anti-competitive activity and will not be subject to *de minimis* limits proposed for other forms of restriction which are deemed insignificant and to which the legislation would therefore not apply. No matter how insignificant a price fixing agreement the law will apply to it and it will fall within the prohibition.

The list will not be exhaustive. There may be other forms of anti-competitive agreements or structures which would be covered by the general prohibition. Agreements falling within the list would not necessarily be impossible to effect. Exemptions will be available even for agreements within this list.

As under Article 85(1) and the RTPA the new legislation would apply to concerted practices as well as formal written agreements and oral arrangements.[6]

> Proof of a concerted practice entails more than simply parallel behaviour by competitors but could, for example, include substantially simultaneous and identical price changes following a meeting at which all parties were present.

It is not clear upon whom would fall the burden of proof in such a case, whether the anti-trust authorities would be able to draw an inference from the

4 Para.2.10

5 Para.2.18

6 Para.2.14

action of the parties after the meeting which those parties would have to rebut or whether the authorities would need to be able to show that the parties really had acted in concert. Reference is made to EC case law in the area.

De minimis

Under the RTPA, the legislation applies even to an agreement between two ice-cream vendors as to the persons to whom they will sell ice creams on various parts of a housing estate. One seeking to enforce the agreement against the other in a court could be presented with an argument by the other that the agreement was void and unenforceable for want of registration under the RTPA. A reference to the Restrictive Practices Court would be unlikely. The new legislation will follow the EC mould and provide for *de minimis* limits to apply.[7] The Commission's Notice on Agreements of Minor Importance[8] was considered in Chapter 2. The principle it embodies, that the legislation will not apply to agreements which do not have appreciable effects, will be incorporated into the legislation.

7 Para.2.16

8 OJ 1986 C231/2

It is proposed that where the total turnover of the parties to the agreement does not exceed £5 million then the legislation will not apply. The figure will be 'fixed by statutory instrument and may be raised or lowered in the light of experience'. This will not apply where the Director General of Fair Trading has investigated the effects of the agreement individually and as a result 'it has been declared anti-competitive and ordered to be abandoned'.[9]

9 White Paper, para.2.17

Even where an agreement involves parties falling outside the limit and there is no price fixing involved, although the powers to levy fines proposed in the legislation will not apply, it is proposed that there will be no immunity from private actions which the government hope will be an important method of ensuring compliance with the new legislation. However, in such cases, it will be for the plaintiff to demonstrate how such an agreement could adversely affect competition in the relevant market taken as a whole and the parties would be able, if they wished, to apply for individual exemption.

The Government have proposed a *de minimis* criterion based on turnover rather than market share or a combination of the two. This is an easier test to apply as most companies are able to state their turnover. Defining market shares is not as easy or precise, it involves a decision as to what is the relevant market in each case. The effect of this route is that an agreement may have insignificant effects but because of the large turnover of the parties it would be caught by the legislation. The White Paper recognises this risk and proposes that the Guidance issued by the Director will 'indicate a level of market power which will normally be present before an agreement could reasonably be thought to affect competition in the relevant market'.[10] Where, in an exceptional case, the general prohibition was infringed even though the market share was less than that specified in the Guidance, the Director would not seek the imposition of penalties. This brings an element of doubt into the analysis and seems to be incorporating a market share limb to the turnover test, although that part of the test would merely be set out in the Guidance and not be part of the statute. Under the EEC Notice on Agreements of Minor Importance there is a similar principle in so far as the Notice itself is not binding, as the Guidance would not be, and it is stated in the Notice that

10 Para.2.19

penalties would not be imposed where there is an agreement which falls within the limits of the Notice but which, notwithstanding that fact and because of the particular circumstances of the case, infringes Article 85(1).

11 Para.2.20

There is a different *de minimis* limit for vertical agreements.[11] Vertical agreements are those which are between companies or individuals at different levels of supply, such as those between a supplier and a manufacturer, who are not therefore competing with each other in connection with the particular transaction. These agreements will not be caught by the general prohibition unless one of the parties has an annual turnover in excess of £30 million 'or such amount as may be fixed by secondary legislation'. Again this limit will not apply where there is resale price maintenance.

A number of special areas are addressed in the White Paper. It is proposed that the legislation will apply in a particular way, in relation to agreements on standards, trade associations and intellectual property rights.

Standards

12 See Notice on
Co-operation Agreements OJ
1968 C75/3
13 White Paper, para.2.23

There is an exemption from the RTPA for agreements to apply British Standards. This exemption does not apply to agreements in connection with any other standards, such as quality specifications agreed by the parties. The Government proposes to follow the EC approach,[12] where, under Article 85, the view is taken by the Commission that if a standard is objectively justified or does not significantly restrict competition then it will not infringe EC law.[13] The new legislation will not have as many exemptions for specific sectors as does the present law and many sets of professional rules or standards will fall to be considered against the general prohibition. Some rules will need to be examined to consider whether their effect is to restrict entry to a profession or industry unreasonably. Stipulations about the type of premises from which a business may be conducted are quoted as an example of this. Exemption may be possible where such stipulations gave rise to benefits:

14 Para.2.25

> It may also be that some standards of conduct essential in one profession or service industry would not be necessary, or even desirable, in another.[14]

The position will therefore be more complicated after the new legislation comes into effect as the rules of bodies, and standards as a whole, will need to be examined in the light of these criteria. Looking at the example of rules governing the type of premises from which a business may be run, this immediately catches many forms of franchising arrangements, which may, however, be the subject of a separate block exemption under the legislation. In each case all the relevant facts need to be examined.

Trade associations

15 Para.2.29

In Chapter 2 consideration was given to trade associations. The RTPA treats any specific recommendation by a trade association as a restriction within the Act whether or not the members of the association are bound to follow the recommendation. Under the new law there will be no automatic prohibition of recommendations by trade associations, but they will all be assessed in order to discern whether or not they distort competition.[15]

It is envisaged that the Guidance which the Government will issue to assist in determining whether or not an agreement falls within the prohibition will also give some indication both to trade associations and to professional bodies as to 'which types of rules and recommendations do or do not distort competition'.

Intellectual property rights

The issue of restrictions in connection with intellectual property rights merits some detailed consideration. Intellectual property rights, such as patents, copyrights and trade marks, are in some cases monopoly rights. A patent entitles the owner of the patent to sue anyone for infringement whether or not that person read or had access to the published patent. With copyright there will only be infringement where there has been copying, but even copyright is a form of monopoly right to the extent that the work produced by the owner may not be used by anyone else without consent. Competition law has to determine the limits of such rights, whilst acknowledging and indeed supporting their existence.

In the White Paper, the Government quotes from the *Ravenseft Properties Ltd*[16] case, which was discussed in Chapter 2, and suggests[17] that the proposed prohibition should follow the doctrine established in *Ravenseft Properties* that the restrictions in the grant of a right to use property do not restrict competition, since in the absence of the licence there would be none. The prohibition will not therefore be intended to 'encompass agreements to grant licences in areas such as patents, know-how, plant variety rights and other intellectual property, so long as the restrictions they contain do not go wider than the subject matter of the licence, for example by tying-in the supply of other goods or services'.

It is likely that this method of dealing with intellectual property licences under the legislation may be modified substantially in the legislation as many find the treatment of it in the White Paper unsatisfactory. It has the effect that English legislation would be out of step with that of the EC and therefore undermines one of the advantages of the proposed new system. Also, it will not always be clear when a term in a licence merely relates to the subject matter of the licence and when it goes further.

The Green Paper[18] which preceded the White Paper set out areas in which there could be general or block exemptions along EC lines from the prohibition. Intellectual property licences were one category.[19] If the new legislation is merely silent as to the treatment of such licences except for whatever general effect the prohibition will have on those agreements, it will be more difficult to advise on such agreements. If block exemptions are proposed, then issues such as exclusivity, restrictions on dealing in competing goods and tying would clearly be addressed. *Ravenseft* concerned restrictions in a lease. Although the case has been used to cover licences of intellectual property under the RTPA it is by no means certain that that is a correct interpretation of the law and statute, although the Office of Fair Trading has publicly supported it (see Chapter 9). There are specific exemptions for certain types of intellectual property licences in Schedule 3 of the RTPA. If those licences are not restrictive *ab initio* then it is difficult to fathom why Parliament felt the need for exemptions in those fields. Also, *Ravenseft* applied in relation to intellectual property. Know-how or technical

16 [1978] QB 52
17 White Paper, para.2.30

18 Review of Restrictive Practices Policy: A Consultative Document, Green Paper, March 1988, Cm 331
19 Green Paper, para.5.12

information, which is often licensed in conjunction with patents and is often more important than the patent part of any licence to manufacture, is not classed as property and is not covered by *Ravenseft* at all.

The detail of the legislation will have to be examined in this area very carefully. If there is merely a reliance on *Ravenseft* and no block exemptions then the issue of whether restrictions go further than the subject matter of the intellectual property right will be very important and no doubt case law will be built up to assist in the analysis. The Guidance to be issued may also make this clear.

Exemptions

It is proposed that agreements which may fall within the prohibition would be capable of exemption, either a specific exemption following a notification of the agreements to the competition authorities or by use of a general exemption for particular categories of agreements.

The specific exemption test will be based closely on Article 85(3), considered in Chapter 2, adapted as necessary to make it clear that the legislation applies to services as much as to goods and also to ensure that rights of access to land are also included. The improvement which an agreement brings about will be measured against the situation which would develop in the absence of the agreements and not necessarily that which held prior to the agreement. An exemption will not be available if an agreement eliminates competition, that is where there is no competition between the parties or from other suppliers.

Again the EC route is being followed. Agreements will be considered and will qualify for exemption where they improve the supply of goods or services or produce economic or technical improvement. Competition will be the principal criterion and the Government has decided against the public interest being a ground for exemption.[20] However, issues such as health and safety will be relevant factors and will be brought into any assessment of an agreement.

The general view in the White Paper is that there should not be many exemptions from the legislation other than in connection with notified agreements which can be justified looking at the factors considered above. The vast array of exemptions for particular industries and professions, which have grown up in piecemeal fashion under the RTPA, will be abolished.

There will be a general exemption in connection with monopoly and other restrictive rights which are enshrined in statute; some of these already have a separate regime for the consideration of competition issues, for example financial services are regulated by the Financial Services Act 1986. There will be a similar exemption in connection with areas where EC law has the same effect.

Coal and steel and other special sectors being covered by international treaty obligations will be exempted from the legislation.[21] The other areas of competition law which are not proposed to be amended may overlap with the new legislation in a number of areas. The Fair Trading Act will remain, and the interface between that and the new legislation will be addressed in the new legislation and may involve exemptions in necessary cases to avoid an agreement being covered by both pieces of legislation.

20 White Paper, para.3.2

21 Para.3.11

There will be exemptions to honour existing commitments:[22]   22 Para.3.12

1. agreements involving the Bank of England and/or the Treasury for the purpose of conducting monetary policy and related operations;
2. agreements between petroleum suppliers in a fuel emergency;
3. existing agreements relating to the supply of gas won under a petroleum production licence;
4. the Concession Agreement for the Channel Tunnel and certain related agreements;
5. and any agreements within the electricity supply industry which have been granted temporary exemption from the RTPA under the relevant provision of the Electricity Act.

Agreements relating to the advertising and marketing of tobacco products, which are approved by the Secretary of State for Health, will also be excluded from the prohibition. There will also be an exemption for agreements regulating employer/employee agreements. This follows the RTPA, which provides a similar such exemption.

Block exemptions

Block exemptions are familiar territory to those accustomed to EC competition law. Provision will be made 'for agreements which are exempt under Article 85(3), whether individually or falling within a block exemption, to be exempt under the new legislation without the need for the parties to make separate application to the DGFT. The law will also enable agreements which would fall within the terms of an EC block exemption, but for the fact that they do not affect trade between Member States, to be exempted in the UK'.[23]   23 Para.3.16

This helpful proposal means that agreements can be analysed as against the existing EC block exemptions both in order to discern whether they infringe EC competition law and to check whether they infringe the prohibition under UK law. If an agreement falls under a block exemption but would not affect trade between Member States, then, under the new law, that EC block exemption could be used. If that is the case, UK block exemptions would not be needed. However, the Government, although intending to follow EC block exemptions as far as possible in its own exemptions, has said that it would not necessarily follow their wording in all cases.

Exclusive distribution and purchasing agreements

These are summarised in the Green Paper[24] as covering the situation where a   24 Green Paper, para.5.10
supplier or manufacturer grants a dealer or retailer an exclusive territory, whether or not the retailer agrees to buy solely from him (exclusive distribution), and agreements where a retailer agrees to purchase from a sole supplier but is not necessarily granted an exclusive territory (exclusive purchasing). The exemptions are likely to follow those under EC law. Agreements which restrict entry and limit inter-brand competition would not be exempted. Clearly, therefore, the block exemption is unlikely to be applicable where there are, for example, only two suppliers and purchasers in a particular market and inter-brand competition is seriously impeded by the proposed arrangement.

Provided the exemptions are similar to the EC block exemptions, the proposals will make simpler the task of assessing such agreements under competition law as companies will have one coherent set of rules with similar tests instead of having to bear in mind two very different systems and wrestle with the detail of Schedule 3 of the RTPA, which often does not apply to the types of agreements in respect of which it was instituted to exempt. If the EC block exemptions and the UK exemptions can both be relied upon, it may be possible for companies to choose between the two rather in the way that it is currently possible to choose between the know-how and patent block exemptions, depending on which is most advantageous in the context of the particular deal proposed.

Patent licensing, intellectual property and know-how agreements

These have been considered above in this chapter in the context of the *Ravenseft* case. It may well be that there will be no exemptions in this area as the Government does not regard restrictions which go no further than the subject matter of the intellectual property right to be restrictive of competition at all, as they are agreements giving permission to a licensee who, but for the licence, would have had no rights at all.

If block exemptions are introduced in this field then they may be along the lines of the existing EC block exemptions for patent and know-how licences respectively. They would particularly preclude the tying of the licence rights to the purchase of other unrelated goods.

Research and development agreements

These agreements provide for joint research and development between companies and the joint exploitation of the results. There is an existing EC block exemption in this field. Some research and development agreements would not infringe the general prohibition at all. The example of these given in the Green Paper is those which stop short of industrial application or those where each party exploits the results independently.

The Government considers that it would be necessary to ensure that the block exemption covered only agreements where the potential for any reduction in competition is limited. For example, vertical agreements between one party which provides the technology and the other which manufactures the product, or where the parties have distinct complementary skills and resources. In these circumstances, where neither has the potential to enter the market on his own, competition is unlikely to be restricted. Where agreements are horizontal between competing manufacturers, there would be a case for making the exemption conditional on the parties' share of the market for the new product not exceeding a certain level. Where there are such horizontal agreements between competitor manufacturers it seems unlikely that the block exemption would apply.

Franchising agreements

Franchising agreements are the subject of an EC block exemption. They are described in the Green Paper[26] as agreements where an undertaking, the franchisor, grants another, the franchisee, in exchange for financial

25 Para.5.12
26 Para.5.16

consideration, the right to exploit a franchise for the purpose of manufacturing or marketing particular goods and services. They consist of licences of intangible property rights concerning trade marks, trade names or know-how, which can be combined with restrictions relating to supply or purchase.

Franchise agreements notified to the OFT will invariably receive 'section 21(2) treatment', i.e. they will be placed upon the Register if they are registrable, but not referred to the Restrictive Practices Court as they are not sufficiently significant in terms of anti-competitive effect. The new legislation would follow the EC method and many agreements would no longer need to be notified at all if they fell within the wording of the block exemption.

'Every effort' will be made to ensure that the block exemptions come into force at the same time as the legislation.[27] This leaves open the possibility that despite these efforts the Government does not achieve this coordination; this would lead to the unsatisfactory situation of there being the prohibition in place but no block exemption, with the consequence that many agreements would have to be sent for specific notification.

There may well be block exemptions other than those proposed above and indeed in the White Paper the Government refers to exemptions in the fields of development of the North Sea gas fields and of money transmission systems.

The block exemptions will list in some detail provisions in agreements which are acceptable and those which would bar an agreement from exemption or necessitate its consideration on an individual basis:

> A prerequisite for drafting workable block exemptions will be for the DGFT to have received and had an opportunity to analyse a sample of relevant agreements. Other candidates for block exemption may therefore become apparent once the legislation is in full operation.[28]

In the fields in which there are already EC block exemptions this experience will presumably not be needed prior to the promulgation of the block exemptions or else they would not succeed in being in place when the prohibition begins to take effect.

Effects of an exemption

Agreements which are exempted will not be void and the parties will be immune from private suits and penalties generally. For individual exemptions these can be back-dated to when the agreement was lodged but not before.[29] This follows EC law where the notification only protects the parties from the day when it is lodged and encourages them to lodge agreements as soon as possible after signature and preferably before they come into effect.

Exemptions will be for a specific duration and not for all time. Exemptions may be for five, ten or fifteen years, or possibly for shorter periods where appropriate; the parties to an agreement which has had the benefit of an exemption would need to negotiate further exemptions. Similarly, the block exemptions would, as under EC law, be for a limited duration and would be renewed, possibly in modified form, at a later stage.

Exemptions would also be capable of being revoked:

27 White Paper, para.3.17

28 Para.3.17

29 Para.3.18

if material changes of circumstance result in the operation of the agreements no longer being beneficial or if new facts come to light which call into question the benefits of the agreements. Revocation will follow a period of notice and there will be an opportunity for appeal.[30]

Individual exemptions may be conditional and failure to meet the conditions would lead to the withdrawal of the benefit of the exemption.

Guidance may also be issued on the general policy underlying certain exemption decisions. The Guidance will not be very specific and companies should therefore look to the published decisions which emerge once case law is available. The Guidance will, however, provide those subject to the legislation with some indication of the restrictive effects which are most or least likely to be exemptible, and under what circumstances. General Guidance would be supplemented and amended from time to time, as decisions are made covering types of agreements not previously considered.[31]

Enforcement and penalties

The Director is often in a 'catch 22' situation under the existing legislation. He has no powers to investigate unless he receives a complaint or other evidence of an infringement of the existing legislation, but cannot obtain that evidence without having some powers to initiate investigations, which powers he does not have. One of the aims of the Government is to strengthen those powers. At present, there is no power to levy fines at all for a first offence and it is only where a company has already been caught out once and is subject to an order of the Court that fines can be levied, and then only for contempt of court. The new legislation will very much follow the model of the EC where there are wide investigatory powers and there are fines for infringements of Article 85(1).

Powers of investigation

Powers to investigate will be granted to the Director 'on reasonable suspicion of a breach'.[32] Whether this would ensure that 'fishing expeditions' would not be permissible where the Director has no suspicions at all and is merely wishing to discover if there is anything within a company which could be investigated is debatable. A reasonable suspicion is not a difficult test to satisfy.

The powers would be similar to those of the Monopolies and Mergers Commission under the Competition Act 1980 and the Fair Trading Act 1973. The parties would be given notice of an investigation into their affairs being initiated. However, if the notice is not complied with or there are grounds to suspect that evidence might be interfered with if notice is given, a magistrate's or sheriff's warrant may be obtained to enter business premises, without warning and using reasonable force if necessary, to search for, examine and remove business records and take copies of them. It will be a criminal offence to obstruct the Director or deliberately or recklessly to supply false or misleading information.[33]

This proposal is more reminiscent of the Commission's powers in carrying out 'dawn raids' than the existing UK system and will substantially assist the UK competition authorities in their policing of anti-competitive agreements.

30 Para.3.21

31 Para.3.23

32 Para.5.3

33 Para.5.3

These wide-ranging powers should ensure that more covert restrictive agreements come to light.

Confidentiality

Under the RTPA, agreements which are registrable are placed upon the Register to which the public has access on the payment of a small fee. There are no rights to keep off the Register any parts of an agreement which are confidential to the parties, who will often be reluctant to register knowing that the consequence may be a valid agreement to which their competitors would have access, albeit technical access. In practice the Register is rarely searched and difficult to search. There is a special section of the Register for agreements which relate to mineral deposits or information as to secret processes of manufacture and agreements important to the national interests.[34] This section of the Register is confidential, but few agreements fall within its terms.

34 RTPA s.23(3)

Under EC law, parts of a notification can be identified by the parties as confidential and in its published decisions the Commission will often leave blanks, particularly where there are figures which the parties regard as confidential.[35]

35 Regulation 17, Art.21(2) OJ 1962 13/204 and amended and Complementary Note to Form A/B, VIII Secrecy

Under the proposed new UK system, the normal requirements of commercial confidentiality will apply to all information supplied to, or obtained by, the Director under the legislation. There will be rights, however, to use the information gleaned under the new legislation for purposes connected with other legislation, under the Fair Trading Act and other national and EC legislation. Communications between legal advisers and businesses will be subject to the usual rules of privilege, whether those legal advisers are employed in-house or are external solicitors or barristers.[36] It will therefore be important, as under EC legislation, to ensure that privileged documents are marked as such and preferably filed separately from other documents so that when the officials arrive unannounced to carry out investigatory work there is less chance of disputes arising over what is and what is not a privileged communication.

36 White Paper, para.5.4

As has been seen above, professional rules will be subject to the new legislation and therefore solicitors and other professionals could find themselves on the receiving end of an investigation involving a search of their offices. The White Paper makes it clear that client files would not be searched as part of such an investigation, only the management files of the business.

An interesting additional power that is proposed would enable the Director to obtain information from businesses which were not party to an agreement. This power would be exercisable by warrant only and examples are given of the persons from whom such information might be sought including suppliers, customers and even competitors where they have declined an invitation to participate. This is in line with the Government's stated intention of ensuring that the legislation is capable of better enforcement than the RTPA.

Penalties

Under the RTPA the penalties for failure to register an agreement are that it will be void at least as to its restrictions and the parties may be made subject

37 RTPA s.35(1)
38 RTPA s.35(2)

to orders of the Restrictive Practices Court.[37] There are also rights for third parties to pursue actions for damages for breach of the duty to register.[38] It is only where a company has already had an order made against it that the rights to fine for contempt of court apply against both the company and individuals, with the risk of jail sentences for individuals.

39 White Paper, para.5.7

Penalties under the new legislation would include a right to impose a fine for infringement of the law of up to 10 per cent of the total UK turnover of a business, or £250,000 if this is higher.[39] This very much increases the likely effectiveness of the legislation and brings it into line with EC law. The directors and managers of a business who are responsible for negotiating or implementing a prohibited agreement may be liable to penalties of up to £100,000.

Parties to *de minimis* agreements would not be subject to these penalties unless there had been a finding against the agreement concerned. It is not clear what is meant by 'a finding against the agreement concerned' in the light of the statement that agreements falling within the *de minimis* limit which are held still to infringe the prohibition would not be the subject of fines. Perhaps it is intended that fines would be levied in such circumstances where an agreement within the limits has been investigated and the parties still continue with it notwithstanding an adverse decision of the competition authority.

The penalties against individuals involved in prohibited arrangements will make enforcement easier. The proposal departs from EC law in this respect; there only companies can be fined.

A Restrictive Trade Practices Tribunal will determine the fines that will be levied in cases brought under the new legislation. To start with the Tribunal will not have power to award fines of over £1 million. This does not, however, mean that companies will only have potential liabilities under the legislation of £1 million. Application will be able to be made to the High Court 'which will consider the imposition of a penalty of any amount up to 10 per cent of the turnover of the business'.[40] Where penalties are sought to be imposed on directors or managers then application will have to be made to the High Court. There will be a right to appeal from the High Court to the Court of Appeal.

40 Para.5.8

The Government may include a non-exhaustive list of factors which the Tribunal or the High Court should take into account in setting the penalty in each case. This would provide guidance both to the authorities and to the business community without, the Government believes, constituting a mechanistic approach to penalties. The factors could include:[41]

41 Para.5.9

> seriousness of the offence (by reference to the core list of prohibited practices); duration, including continued operation of an agreement after advice that it is prohibited; secrecy/openness; and co-operation during the investigation.

The tribunal will be able to distinguish between minor breaches and serious infringements and it is unlikely that penalties will be imposed with any great frquency. It is those who persist in practices such as price fixing and market sharing who would expect harsh treatment.

The list of relevant penalties is very similar to the factors which the European Commission has regard to under EC competition legislation. Where in rare cases fines have been levied for RTPA infringements in the UK (which can only be where the parties are in contempt of court) the relevant factors are very much the same.

One major issue which arises from the proposals is the protection which a notification would confer. As has been seen, under EC competition law, the parties are protected from the risk of fines being levied against them in respect of agreements notified to the Commission from the date when the notification is made. There is no protection in relation to acts committed before the notification was submitted, however. The Government proposed in the White Paper that that position would not be followed, despite the general aim to emulate EC competition legislation. The view was taken that such protection would effectively sanitise infringements and the law would be sufficiently clear for companies to know when they are at risk of infringing the legislation. If they wish to take the risk of entering into a registrable agreement then they must run the risk of fines whether or not the protection of a notification was sought.[42]

It has been strenuously argued that this would act as a disincentive to notification and, given the criticism which has been levied at the proposal, the proposal may well be modified in any legislation. The Government argues, however, that this involves an issue of principle and also one of practicality:

> First, it is possible that firms whose motive is to share markets in order to 'stabilise' an industry would submit an application for exemption for an agreement which was *prima facie* a pro-competitive joint venture arrangement but was later found to be unacceptable. The Government do not believe such an arrangement should be operated without penalty. Even if an accelerated procedure were available with a lower level of proof for a temporary order against the agreement, the Government remain of the opinion that a provision which allowed such a practice would undermine the prohibition. In the case of price-fixing, for which there is to be no *de minimis* provision, the situation would be even more anomalous.[43]

This is the argument of principle. There do not appear to be many examples of this sort of difficulty experienced under EC legislation. Parties to price fixing cartels, except where they believe that they have very strong justifications and economic benefits arising from their arrangements, would never sensibly notify such arrangements, as the cost of notification can be high and most arrangements of this sort are covert.

In theory at least there is a risk that companies who are contemplating entering into a price fixing arrangement, knowing that it would take a number of years for a decision to be reached by the UK competition authorities and that there were by that stage greater investigatory powers which might uncover any secret such arrangement, would go ahead with a notification. Their reason for so doing would be the protection from fines which a notification would bring. However, it would be clear that that protection would be likely to last only for as long as it took the authorities to examine the notified agreement, and their activities would effectively have come into the public domain in a manner which would not necessarily enhance their business reputation.

It seems that the principles upon which the Government's position are based founder when the practicalities of such notifications are examined, particularly in the light of EC experience. The practicalities are, however, one

42 Para.5.10

43 Para.5.11

of the issues which is pleaded in defence of the proposal in the White Paper where it is stated[44] that the restrictive elements of a prohibited agreement will be void and unenforceable and the parties liable to third party action if an agreement has been operated without exemption. If an exemption application were refused, the parties might have to unravel the commercial arrangements entered into under the agreement. These are likely to be significant considerations and the Government regards it as difficult to see that the possibility of being fined would be the most compelling factor in persuading the parties not to operate the agreement without exemption. The theoretical possibility of a penalty would also be less of a threat to those applying in good faith for an exemption if guidance on the factors relevant to penalties were to be introduced.

The logic of this argument defies practical experience under EC law. Taken to its logical conclusion, no one would ever notify an agreement as the effect may well be a decision that it is void and unenforceable under EC law and in those circumstances agreements do have to be unravelled as best the parties are able. In practice, parties negotiating an agreement seek to ensure that it does not infringe the legislation in the first place so as to avoid the need for an expensive and time consuming notification. However, often it is impossible to achieve such a position whilst retaining commercial terms which the parties regard as essential to the deal. The fact that a decision may be adverse is a relevant factor as is the protection from fines which an EC notification brings, but neither factor is conclusive in any case.

The Government seeks to emphasise the proposed differences in this context between the EC regime and that proposed in the White Paper. It hopes that there will not be the back-log of cases which the Commission has accumulated because of transitional arrangements which have been proposed and which will be discussed later in this chapter. The legislation is intended to be efficient and the risk of fines whether or not a notification is made, argues the Government, would ensure that fewer such restrictive arrangements were entered into in the first place.

The issue of agreements being declared void after a notification has been made is considered in the proposals. Exemption after a notification will have the same effect as under EC law, i.e. that the agreement is valid from when it was entered into. If an exemption is refused, however, the courts would be wrong to order performance of the agreement or award damages for its non-performance. The Government thinks that it would be undesirable in many cases to allow one party to benefit from an unwarranted windfall gain. The legislation would permit the courts to order one party to make restitution to the other if, as a result of a partially performed agreement, it has received value which it would not otherwise have received.

This clarification of the position in such circumstances is useful. Under general law, *quantam meruit* claims are permitted, i.e. one party could bring an action for payment for work partially performed or goods had and received, although without the statutory provisions for such a right one party to the agreement may have been able to argue that as the agreement was prohibited and therefore unlawful there may be public policy grounds for refusing such applications. It is likely that the legislation would still permit the courts some discretion in the worst of cases.

Private actions

Businesses infringing the law will suffer the risk of both penalties and damages as third parties damaged by the infringing agreement will have the right to bring claims for damages against the parties to the agreement.[45] Over time the Government hopes that the role of private actions in enforcement of the legislation will grow and become a significant part of enforcement in this area.

45 Para.5.15

The Government's consideration of which measures to take to promote private actions under restrictive trade practices legislation, such as making provisions for class actions or the introduction of contingency fees, will be complete in the context of other decisions yet to be taken, for instance, on aspects of reform of the legal profession. However, it is likely that, where a litigant has incurred costs to establish that an agreement is anti-competitive, the legislation will permit these to be included in any damages claim.

Class actions are not provided for under English law although they are widely used in the United States. They permit one set of proceedings to be used by a class of potential litigants which has suffered under the same facts, for example where they have been harmed by a particular drug. The other litigants are not then required to prove again all those elements of the case which the first has done. In the context of restrictive trade practices legislation an example would be where two large suppliers of products to wholesalers had operated a covert anti-competitive agreement for years whereby they agreed to sell products at a certain high price. They supply a considerable number of companies who have lost large sums of money over the years because of this pricing policy. Those who have suffered would be able to bring a class action rather than many individual sets of proceedings; the substantial benefit is that action would be cheaper and involve less court time.

Contingency fees are also permitted under US law and allow lawyers to be paid by results. If they win they are paid a percentage of the damages awarded in favour of their client; if they lose they either receive no fees or reduced fees. The Government feel that such arrangements, which must be seen in the context of reform of the legal profession in this country, may have the effect of encouraging more individuals, who otherwise would have been put off by the cost of litigation in such a specialised and expensive field of the law, to bring actions in the courts for damages for infringements of competition legislation.

Transitional arrangements

Changes of competition law of this order will necessarily involve review of agreements and reconsideration of companies' corporate policies. Compliance policies will have to be amended and other measures taken to allow for changes in the law. There is therefore considerable detail given in the White Paper to transitional arrangements which might apply whilst the changeover from one system to the other occurs. Complex phased repeals are not envisaged, however, and the Government wants the benefits of the new law to take effect as soon as possible after enactment. The Government anticipates that many agreements would be furnished for registration on a 'fail-safe' basis.[46]

46 See White Paper, Chapt.6

The Government will allow sufficient time between Royal Assent and the prohibition coming into force for block exemptions to be drawn up. The OFT will recruit more staff to deal with the new legislation in that period and the proposed new RTP Tribunal will be set up. It is expected that the Guidance which will be issued will give such a strong indication to legal advisers as to whether or not an agreement needs to be notified and whether it falls within the legislation at all that there will not need to be much time for transitional arrangements.

After Royal Assent there will be a period of about six months before the prohibition comes into force during which the RPTA will remain in force. Once this six month period is over there will be a further period of one year during which agreements which have been made before introduction of the new legislation into Parliament will remain fully enforceable and the parties to them will not be liable to penalties or third party action.

In the case of an agreement entered into before the introduction of the Bill, for example, in May 1991, which did not fall within the RTPA because, for example, it had five restrictions on one party and none on the other, but which would infringe the new prohibition if it is assumed that the new legislation receives Royal Assent on 1st December 1992, the following will apply. From the date of the agreement until six months after Royal Assent, the RTPA continues to apply. From 1st June, the prohibition applies generally but this agreement will not be subject to it for a further twelve month period has expired, i.e. until June 1994. The company will have until that date to re-evaluate the agreement and negotiate with the other side to vary it or make a decision to register it. They will need to put in any application for a specific exemption at least three months before the end of the year, although the Director will have the power to extend the benefit of the transitional arrangements on a case by case basis for six months at a time up to a maximum of a further two years. After that time, only the RTP Tribunal will have further powers to extend, though it 'would normally do so if they were still considering a case, or it had gone to appeal'. So, using our example, the parties will need to notify the agreement before March 1994 unless they can gain an extension of time in accordance with the above procedure.

Many agreements have been registered at the OFT and put on the Register, having been given section 21(2) treatment, i.e. deemed of insufficient significance to merit reference to the Restrictive Practices Court. The Government believes that most of these will qualify for exemption.[47] However, prior registration under the RTPA will not render an agreement automatically exempt under the new legislation and therefore companies will need to examine all agreements which they have registered over the years as against the new prohibition. Such agreements will have a longer transitional period of five years rather than the one year described above, although this only applies where agreements were properly furnished. Before the expiry of the five year period the parties will need to make an assessment, in the light of Guidance issued and case law which by that time is likely to be available, as to whether their agreement needs to be exempted. Many agreements will have expired during that period in any event.

There are many agreements which have not been furnished to the OFT, either through ignorance of the law, particularly where there is an agreement

47 White Paper, para.6.8

which is not apparently anti-competitive but, because of the formalistic nature of the RTPA, which falls within the Act, or because they were obviously and significantly restrictive and were kept secret by the parties. Agreements in either category, whenever they were registrable but unregistered, will immediately fall foul of the prohibition and the parties would have no right to benefit from any transitional provisions.

Companies subject to orders of the Restrictive Trade Practices Court will be pleased that it is proposed that the orders will simply lapse.[48] Such orders have the effect that breach of them is contempt of court, leaving the company open to fines for contempt, which may be high, and directors and managers involved in the infringing agreements open to fines and the risk of being jailed. Such orders mean that companies the subject of them must ensure that they do not enter into agreements which infringe the RTPA, which involves a rigorous, time consuming and expensive effort. However, if it should later come to the notice of the Director that a court order had been breached prior to repeal of the RTPA, an action for contempt would be possible, in addition to any penalties which could be imposed under the new law.

There will also be agreements which have been furnished to the OFT when the prohibition comes into effect (six months after Royal Assent) but which have been made since the introduction of the Bill.

The Government is already taking measures to minimise the number of outstanding cases. Outstanding cases will not qualify for interim validity and immunity from penalties which the transitional arrangements entail and they will be evaluated against the new statutory criteria. In some cases this may result in informal advice that the agreements are not caught by the prohibition but in others information necessary to complete an application for exemption will be requested. It will be possible to backdate any exemption granted in these circumstances to the time when the prohibition came into force.

The provision for informal advice is welcomed; it seems that, in all cases, the parties will be able to remedy the situation by applying for exemption.

There will be an overriding power for the Director to evaluate an agreement notwithstanding the fact that it is apparently protected under the transitional arrangements, as the Government is concerned that otherwise seriously anti-competitive agreements would be outside the scope of the legislation for the deferred transitional period. If the investigation results in a finding that the agreement is anti-competitive and does not warrant exemption, the parties will be required to amend or abandon it after a short period of notice. They will not, however, be liable to sanctions or third party action up to that point.[49] There will therefore be no power to levy fines in such circumstances.

The transitional arrangements are complicated but in practice appear to be a workable solution to the two aims of ensuring quick application of the new law and ensuring that the stretched resources of the OFT are able to deal with the potentially increased workload. The White Paper summarises them on the lines of Table 6.1.

Table 6.1

Position under RTPA	Position under new law
Not registrable	
Specifically excluded	
Not caught by registration requirements	*1 year transitional period (Director may extend up to a further two years)
Registrable	
Upheld by Court	
Made before Bill introduced	
Not significant (Section 21(2))	*5 year transitional period
Made after Bill introduced	Considered under new law
Unfurnished by date required in RTPA	Void

*The Director will be able to investigate agreements within the transitional period if they appear to be anti-competitive.

Conclusion

The proposed changes seek to bring UK competition legislation into line with that obtaining in the EC. The legislation will be more logical than the RTPA which catches agreements because of their form even if they have no anti-competitive effects. There are, of course, difficulties with the EC effects based approach which are not apparent with the RTPA. Under the RTPA, if the various requirements of it are understood, it is possible to undertake an analysis and at the end of the exercise be able to reach a decision as to whether or not it is necessary to register an agreement. Also, drafting changes can often be made which remove the application of the Act at all.

The effects based approach will inevitably involve market analysis. What is the market? How large are the parties' respective shares of that market? What will be the effect on the market of the proposed agreement? Often a definite answer under effects based legislation cannot be given because of the subjective nature of such analyses, which might not coincide with the interpretation given by the anti-trust authorities looking at the agreement in question. Economics as well as law come into play, and the lawyer will have to put on his economist hat as well as liaising closely with the client to obtain full details of the relevant market.

However, such an approach is already necessary under EC law and many agreements have potential effects on trade between Member States, so that notwithstanding that they relate only to the UK, it is necessary to consider EC competition law too. In future, only one type of analysis will be required.

To illustrate how the law is expected to work the DTI issued a leaflet setting out its likely operation. Part of this document sets out a table of the various stages in an investigation. This is set out in Fig. 6.1.

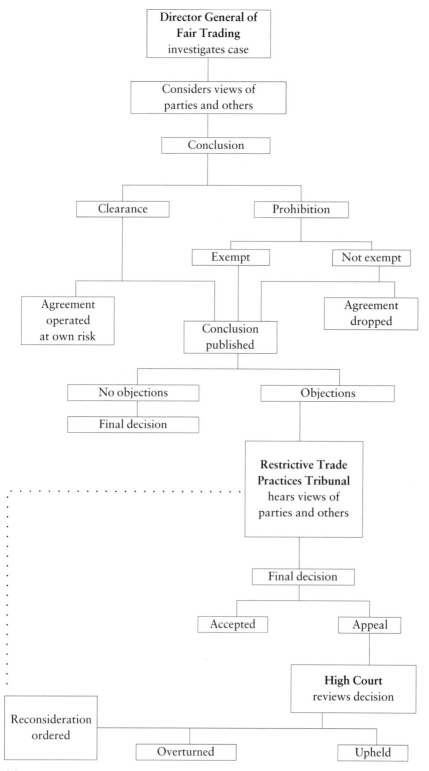

Fig. 6.1

It seems likely that this proposed legislation will be enacted by 1995 at the latest, subject to changes in Government. Agreements drafted now will need to reflect potential changes in the law. In effect, an analysis under Article 85 should perhaps be given to all agreements even if they are purely domestic. However, given the slippage in time since the White Paper was published in July 1989, it is clearly important that the RTPA be considered carefully in all cases. For the moment, at least, the form and effects based systems must continue to coexist side by side.

COMPETITION LAW IN EC AND NON-EC COUNTRIES

In this country, both UK and EC law are of universal applicability in the competition field. However, many agreements involve non-UK parties and in such cases, or where an agreement may have commercial effects abroad or involve sales into other jurisdictions, the competition law in that other jurisdiction needs to be examined.

It is beyond the scope of this work to consider in detail other territories' competition laws. In many cases the safest advice is to instruct local lawyers to vet a proposed agreement before it is entered into or to approach the relevant competition authority within the other jurisdiction for prior clearance of a merger. For example, the consent of the Bundeskartellampt in Germany may be sought before a merger goes ahead.

Some indication of the laws of some other jurisdictions is however useful, and there follows below a brief summary in connection with some other jurisdictions, beginning with the EC. EC states are, of course, bound by EC competition law as well as their national legislation.

EC

Belgium

The Law of 1960 on Abuse of Economic Power prohibits abuse of economic power where prejudice is caused by practices which distort competition or hinder economic freedom. Fines may be levied under this legislation.

Price fixing agreements may be valid under Belgian law where their objective is to ensure a fair profit, or maintain the quality of a product or protect the market against price cutting. All parties must be bound by the price fixing agreement. If one party acts in breach of the agreement the others cease to be bound by it. The 1971 Law on Commercial Practices prohibits sales at below cost, subject to certain exceptions.

Denmark

On 1st January 1990, a new Competition Act (Konkurrenceloven) came into force replacing the Monopoly and Control Act 1955. Restraints of trade are regulated. Within 14 days of an agreement being concluded where a dominant influence is exerted, the Competition Council, consisting of 15 members, must be notified. Agreements will not be valid unless notified to the Competition Council. The Competition Council can demand, for up to two years after notification, the submission of information on prices and profits. It can undertake investigations.

France

The Competition Law of 1977 permits prosecution of anti-competitive acts. The Commission de la Concurrence enforces competition matters. It has power to initiate investigations into anti-competitive practices of its own volition. Fines may be levied against companies infringing the legislation.

All agreements restricting competition are prohibited where they distort the normal functioning of the market as are abuses of a dominant position. This is similar to EC law except that there are no provisions for specific notification. If an exemption is required, infringers are obliged to admit their infringement as part of the proceedings.

Joint price lists have been held to be illegal, as have exclusive dealing agreements where the exclusivity cannot be justified. Refusals to supply, joint selling and some activities by trade associations have been held contrary to the law in some circumstances. Mergers can be investigated following notification by the parties concerned or on the application of a Minister. Market shares of 25 per cent each (or 40 per cent between the parties) are required. There are powers in extreme cases to order divestiture as under EC and UK merger law. Abuses of a dominant position are forbidden, but not the mere holding of a dominant position.

Germany

Germany has one of the toughest, most strictly enforced and sophisticated anti-trust regimes in Europe. There is control of mergers. The Federal Cartel Office will prohibit a merger where a merger will result in or reinforce a market dominating position. There are market share and turnover criteria. Mergers must in certain circumstances be pre-notified and there are powers to levy heavy fines. There are powers to prohibit practices which amount to an abuse of a dominant position. Profits made by the abusive practices may be confiscated. There is control of restrictive agreements too.

Greece

Law 703/77 protects free competition and controls monopolies. It is effectively a translation of Articles 85 and 86, without the provisions requiring there to be an effect on trade between Member States. The law expressly states that refusal to deal may be an anti-trust infringement. There is automatic invalidity for restrictions or conduct falling within the legislation. The Minister of Commerce decides whether to grant the Greek equivalent of negative clearance where an appropriate notification has been made.

There are penalties of prison sentences and fines for infringements of the legislation. Mergers do not fall within the legislation, but if they are above certain limits they must be notified.

Ireland

The Competition Bill will void all anti-competitive practices and imports in total Articles 85 and 86.

Italy

Italy has new laws governing anti-trust which were introduced in 1988. Its provisions are designed to dovetail with those of Articles 85 and 86 and to regulate mergers. Where there is an abuse of a dominant position companies can be fined up to 3 per cent of turnover. There is a compulsory system for pre-notification of mergers. The Competition Guarantee Authority is responsible for administering the law.

Netherlands

The Dutch Economic Competition Act regulates cartels and provides for interference where competition will be affected by a cartel, rather than outright prohibition of the cartel. The public interest is the sole criterion for assessing cartels. There are penal and civil sanctions under the legislation. Refusals to deal and excessive prices could come within the relevant provisions of the Act.

Spain

With its entrance into the EC, Spain has enacted new anti-trust legislation, which came into force on the 17th July 1989. Abuses of dominant positions and unfair practices are covered and there is a system for individual and group exemptions. The Court of Defence of Competition has the principle enforcement role under the legislation.

Non-EC

Australia

The Trade Practice Act 1974 of the Commonwealth regulates restrictive trade practices. A trade practice which inhibits competition in commercial dealings is proscribed and there are provisions in connection with price fixing. By section 46, action by dominant undertakings to eliminate or inhibit a competitor or potential competitior is forbidden. The Trade Practice Commission enforces the laws governing market dominance. Refusal to supply, as under Article 86, amounts to an abuse of market power.

Exclusive intellectual property licences may be granted under Australian law, except that tying-in the purchase of other goods is forbidden. There should be no restriction as to the price at which the licensee sells the finished products which he manufactures using the technology. Export bans would be enforceable and there is an exemption under the Trade Practices Act for agreements in relation to exports, provided it is notified to the Trade Practices Commission within 14 days of the agreement.

Austria

Cartels are encouraged in Austria where much of industry is nationalised. Application for authorisation of price rises has to be made before they can be put into effect. Despite this, Austria is an associate member of the EC and a member of EFTA – the European Free Trade Association. EFTA is a free trade agreement[50] to which the UK and others were party prior to entry into the EC. The remaining members today are Austria, Finland, Iceland, Norway, Sweden and Switzerland. Liechtenstein is an associate member. The EC has entered into free trade agreements with separate EFTA member countries[51] and is reaching agreement on extending the single market to EFTA countries;

50 Established by Convention in 1959
51 Austria Cm 5159 (1.1.73), Finland OJ 1973 L328/1, Iceland Cm 5182 (1.4.73), Norway OJ 1973 L171/1, Sweden Cm 5180 (1.1.73) and Switzerland Cm 5181 (1.1.73)

these contain provisions prohibiting restrictive agreements, abuses of dominant positions and public aid which distorts competition.[52]

The Cartel Act 1972 requires the registration of cartels. There are approximately seventy registered cartels. The Cartel Court deals with the registration of cartels, which must, unless they are below *de minimis* limits, be economically justified. Abuses of a cartel are subject to criminal penalties, which extend not only to the undertakings themselves but also employees, of up to three years in jail or heavy fines.

Foreign cartels which have an effect on the Austrian market will be regulated, but, in practice, the Cartel Act has little extra-territorial effect due to difficulties of enforcement abroad. Where an Austrian cartel only concerns foreign markets then registration is not required, unless it impairs trade under the agreement for Austria's associate membership of the EC.

A cartel may be economically justified in the interests of the end-user or consumer or because of jobs or the smooth distribution of goods.

The Cartel Act also regulates abuses of dominant positions. The Cartel Court can order that an abuse cease and profits be forfeited which were obtained through that abuse. Again registration is required, but the legislation is not strictly enforced and only about 300 companies have registered under the Act.

Mergers involving market shares of over 5 per cent must be registered within a month with the Cartel Office. Licences of intellectual property will fall outside the Cartel Act provided they provide no more protection in any restrictions which they contain than the legal protection granted by the patent or other right.

Bulgaria

From 20 May 1991 the law protects against monopoly abuse actions leading to restraints of competition and unfair competition.

Canada

Anti-trust laws began in 1889. The Competition Act 1986 and recent Abuse of Dominance Provisions apply. Fines of $5m have been levied.

Czechoslovakia

The Law on Protection of Economic Competition came into effect on 1 March 1991. This *inter alia* regulates acquisitions where the assets of an existing state enterprise are transferred to a new joint stock company where the new company will have at least 30 per cent of the relevant market, or a merger where a 30 per cent threshold is exceeded.

A notification to the Competition Office is necessary. The Office considers the merits of the merger. Agreements leading to an influence over production or circulation of goods to the exclusion of economic competition may require permits from the Competition Office, where market shares exceed 5 per cent

52 See Schmitthoff C.M. – *The Law and Practice of International Trade*, Stevens, 1990, 9th ed., p.361

of a national market or 30 per cent of a local market. Exemption is possible by application to the Competition Office on public interest grounds or grounds of technical development. A register of permitted cartels is kept. Breach of the legislation carries penalties of 5 per cent of revenues from the previous year.

Japan

In September 1989 Japan's Fair Trade Commission announced a review of its trade practice laws. In 36 years of the existing definition of unfair trade practices only one conviction was recorded, against a Japanese oil cartel over a decade ago. In the year to March 1991, 175 companies were fined a total of £51m.

The Anti-Monopoly Law governs anti-competitive practices and cartel law. Cartels are expressly forbidden. The Fair Trade Commission may require that businesses be sold off and that illegal cartels cease operating; it may levy substantial fines up to 6 per cent of sales. Criminal action is possible. In July 1991, the FTC issued rules allowing it to order linked companies involved in unfair practices to divest equity stakes.

New Zealand

In New Zealand, the Commerce Act 1986 and Fair Trading Act 1986 set out the competition law of New Zealand. The Commerce Act prohibits anti-competitive practices, such as price fixing, collusive arrangements and tying.[53]
The Fair Trading Act proscribes deceptive conduct in trade, including false representations about goods and unfair practices such as those typified by trading stamp schemes.

The Commerce Commission enforces the legislation. With effect from 1 July 1990 fines have been increased substantially, up to a maximum of $5 million for companies and $500,000 for individuals. Actions for damages are possible and injunctions may be sought in appropriate cases.

Sweden

The Restrictive Business Practices Act prohibits certain types of restrictive business practice, resale price maintenance and collusive tendering. A breach of the relevant provision is a criminal offence, subject to fines and imprisonment for serious cases. Exemptions from this absolute ban can be sought from the Market Court, on the grounds that there are benefits such as lower costs arising from the restrictive provisions.

In June 1982 the Competition Act made some changes to the Restrictive Business Practices Act and introduced a formal system for the regulation of mergers. This applies in connection with dominant positions. Acquisitions can be prohibited and orders for divestiture can be made within six months of the merger taking place.

Switzerland

The Swiss Cartel Act 1985, Price Control Act 1985 and Uniform Competition Act 1956[54] regulate competition in Switzerland. Vertical arrangements are regulated only in limited circumstances. Cartels and dominant positions are allowed and their abuse is outlawed only if a decision to that effect is made. There is no automatic penalty of agreements being unenforceable as in the EC and UK.

54 See Jakobs-Siebert article (Further reading)

United States of America

The United States has a long and effective anti-trust tradition.[55] The Sherman Act makes contracts and combinations in restraint of trade illegal, with the potential for large fines to be levied and three years in jail for individuals. The Clayton Act prohibits certain anti-trust violations, such as tying and exclusive dealing arrangements where competition is lessened; mergers are also covered by it. The Robinson-Patman Act amended the Clayton Act and prohibits discrimination in price to different purchasers.

55 See generally Hawk (Further reading)

The Federal Trade Commission Act established the Federal Trade Commission as the independent anti-trust enforcement body and proscribed unfair methods of competition affecting commerce. The other competition body is the Anti-trust department of the US Department of Justice. Mergers, joint ventures and other arrangements may all fall foul of the various pieces of legislation which are generally vigorously enforced.

Conclusion

Only a flavour of some selected international competition laws has been given here. Such laws alter regularly and there are many other jurisdictions than those considered here. However, there are common threads within many of the countries considered. Many EC territories have introduced or intend to introduce anti-trust legislation along the lines of Articles 85 and 86. Common outlawed practices are non-competition restrictions, tying clauses, abuses of dominant positions and refusals to supply. In many places mergers involving a high market share or large turnover may be caught.

Local legal advice should be sought in the jurisdictions to which parties to an agreement operate or belong or in which the agreement will have effect, to ensure enforceability and that the appropriate competition law notifications are made.

QUESTION

Worldwide plc is a huge multi-national corporation whose headquarters are in the UK. It has been fined heavily by the European Commission in the past and is the subject of orders of the Restrictive Practices Court not to enter into agreements subject to registration under the RTPA without first registering them.

Joe Bloggs, the managing director, comes to see you, having read about the White Paper. He is very aware of competition issues and has a comprehensive in-house compliance programme. He asks you what he should be doing to prepare for the legislation and what its effects will be on his business. Will he have more or fewer lawyers' fees to pay?

Answer his questions and give him a brief overview of the proposals. He is particularly interested in transitional arrangements.

FURTHER READING

ARTICLES

Assant G. – *Anti-trust Intracorporate Conspiracies* [1990] 2 ECLR 65

Burke-Gaffney M. – *Restrictive Trade Practices Policy*, Law Society's Gazette, 22 June 1988, p. 23

Burnett-Hall R. – *A New UK Competition Law and Its Application to Intellectual Property* [1988] 11 EIPR 1331

Eccles R. – *Transposing EEC Competition Law into UK Restrictive Trading Agreements Legislation*; the Government's Green Paper, [1988] ECLR 227

Hill J.C. – *The Spanish Defence of Competition Law*, Supplement I, [1990] 4 ECLR 1

International Bar Association Report, *Constraints on Cross-Border Takeovers and Mergers – A Catalogue of Disharmony*, (1991) 19 IBL 51

Jakob-Siebert T. – *Competition Rules in the EEC and Switzerland – a comparison of law and practice* [1990] 6 ECLR 255

Maitland-Walker J. – *Proposals for New UK Restrictive Practices Law* [1989] ECLR 469

Rowley J.W. – *Canadian Competition Law: Past Surprises Future Predictability* (1991) 19 IBL 162

Singleton E.S. – *The White Paper: will it make you blush red?*, (1989) 133 S.J. 1354

Tollemache M. – *Exclusive Dealing and the Law: of Fridges and Franchising* [1990] 6 ECLR 264 (New Zealand)

Weatherhill S. – *Regulating Competition in an Expanded Germany* NLJ (141) 1 March 1991 278

BOOKS

Gijlstron and Murphy (eds.) – *Competition Law in Western Europe and the USA*

Hawk B.E. – *US, Common Market and International Anti-trust: a Comparative Guide*, Prentice Hall Law & Business, looseleaf 1990 Supp.

Raybould D.M. – *Comparative Law of Monopolies*, 1988

Schmitthoff C.M. – *The Law and Practice of International Trade*, 9th ed., Stevens 1990, p. 372 (UK Proposals) and p. 361 and p. 371 (EFTA)

PUBLICATIONS

Opening Markets: New Policy on Restrictive Trade Practices, White Paper, July 1989, Cm 727

Review of Restrictive Trade Practices – a Consultative Document, March 1988, Cm 331

7

Compliance procedures

Compliance procedures are invoked to ensure that companies, partnerships and other entities comply with competition law, whether it be national or that of the EC. Many individuals are unaware of competition law, often these are the very people within an organisation who will be negotiating the agreements or selling products or otherwise involved in the business of the company. They will regularly come into contact with competitors and education is needed to show them what is and what is not permitted under competition legislation. This chapter describes such procedures to provide insight into the practical day-to-day working of competition law in businesses.

Companies are unlikely to be successful before the courts or the European Commission in arguing that they are not vicariously liable for the acts of their employees who have infringed competition law because all such infringements were expressly forbidden. Compliance procedures, often in the form of a compliance programme, are therefore necessary to ensure that infringement of the law does not take place at all. Even if it is infringed the programme may be of some use.

In *National Panasonic (UK) Ltd,*[1] the European Commission emphasised that the level of fine imposed took into account the constructive attitude of management and the fact that an audit of legal practices in the EC had been carried out and a code of conduct issued by the company. In *Hilti*[2] one of the undertakings required of the parties as part of the adverse decision by the Commission was that they initiated a compliance programme along *National Panasonic* lines.

In the English courts, the penalties for contempt of court (arising from infringement of a Restrictive Practices Court order not to enter into agreements registrable with the Office of Fair Trading without first registering them) have been less because of comprehensive compliance programmes being in place (as in *Re Ready Mixed Concrete*[3]). A programme shows a court that the company is committed to ensuring that it complies with the law and that it takes it seriously.

Compliance programmes are not just relevant to the field of competition law. There could be such programmes for environmental compliance or in the area of health and safety or financial services legislation. Such programmes are common in the United States, where there is a longer history of effective anti-trust law, infringement of which has resulted in the imposition of stiff penalties.

In a one man business there would clearly be no need for any form of programme at all, except that the proprietor would need to know something about competition law to ensure that he did not enter into any restrictive arrangements. With large multi-national corporations formal compliance programmes are an accepted part of corporate life. Their cost is small

1 [1983] 1 CMLR 497, OJ 1982 L354/28 and *John Deere* [1985] 2 CMLR 554, OJ 1985 L35/58
2 *Eurofix-Bauco* v *Hilti* OJ 1988 L65/19

3 [1991] ICR 52 and see *DGFT* v *Smiths Concrete Ltd* (CA) July 1991

compared to the cost of fines levied by the European Commission for infringement of Articles 85 and 86, the bad publicity resulting from such cases, lawyers' fees and management time spent fighting competition cases in court.

COMPLIANCE PROGRAMMES

The elements of a compliance programme can be many and varied and form a method of educating staff. Most employees will be aware that agreeing prices with a competitor or dividing jobs between companies is illegal. However, there are many other forms of restrictive agreement which are not so obvious, even to the lawyers.

The most basic compliance effort would be a term in contracts of employment that staff must ensure that they do not infringe competition law. This would not tell them anything about what forms of activity might amount to infringement and most programmes go much further. They are often instituted after the company has been fined or otherwise involved in competition law matters.

An example will assist. Splodgit plc makes splodgits. It is an international concern and operates in most of the countries of the EC as well as being based in the UK. Its managing director, M.D. Splodgit, thinks they have had a 'terrible run of bad luck' in the competition law field.

Six years ago Mr Fixit, then an employee, was caught selling products without putting them through the books. He was interviewed and said everyone else was taking part in this fraudulent activity so he had not thought that he was doing anything wrong. M.D. Splodgit dismissed him on the spot and said Mr Fixit was lucky he had not called the police. He undertook an internal investigation and found that a number of other employees were involved in the same activities. They were not dismissed, but merely given written warnings. Mr Fixit found out about this disparity and felt very hard done by.

Wanting his revenge he sent two letters. The first was to the OFT. He described regular meetings that took place every month between the sales people of Splodgit and its two competitors in the UK. They knew each other well and met as much socially as for any other purpose. However, an important part of those meetings was to discuss how business was, whether there were any new competitors in the market and what prices were doing. They agreed the prices they would charge for different types of splodgits and ensured in that way that good profit margins were achieved. Mr Fixit sent all his written notes of the meetings to the OFT and hoped to embarrass the Company as much as possible.

He then sent a letter to the European Commission. At an international level he had been less involved personally. However, he was a sociable man and knew one international salesman extremely well. Mr Brown sold splodgits around the EC. One night, after a few drinks, he had told Mr Fixit how he had the EC 'stitched up'. 'They're all doing it over there. It's the civilised way to do things. I'd look a fool if I wouldn't play ball', he said.

'How do you organise things, Bill?', his friend enquired.

'Well, we all know our patch and the people we sell to. We keep away from each other's customers. We're very careful and have nothing in writing. The French lot have agreed not to sell into this country at all if I do not sell into France and we are working towards having fixed prices too. We've had so much trouble from these parallel importers, something had to be done'.

What Bill Brown also told Mr Fixit was the names of the individuals involved and their companies throughout Europe. Mr Fixit sent this information to the Commission and sat back, a smile of satisfaction on his face, before leaving for the Job Centre.

The OFT had had suspicions for some time about this particular industry as several customers had over the years complained that they suspected that some covert arrangements were affecting the market for splodgits. They seized on this information and all the companies involved were brought before the Restrictive Trade Practices Court.

M.D. Splodgit found it was necessary to engage specialist lawyers, who explained that the order made against the company under the Restrictive Trade Practices Act meant that he would have to be very careful in the future not to enter into restrictive agreements.

'I am laying it on the line to you as a friend, M.D.,' the partner concerned told him. 'If this sort of thing happens again there are going to be very large fines for a company of your size and international reputation. I've interviewed the men on the ground. You know that quite a number believed, rightly or wrongly, that you encouraged them. If you are personally involved then you could be up before the court yourself for contempt of court. The Director General of Fair Trading knows that jailing directors and employees is going to keep companies from breaking these laws much more effectively than fining their companies. You need to do something about it, take it seriously or you could go to jail or be fined, and the company could suffer huge fines, probably over £100,000.'

'You've convinced me.' Said M.D., 'Tell me what to do and I'll do it'.

Meanwhile the European Commission had arrived at Splodgit's premises to carry out a dawn raid. The door man had no instructions about what to do in such circumstances and rang upstairs to M.D. Splodgit. M.D. came down, saying 'No one is looking through my filing cabinet or any other in this building. Get out before I kick you out. We're not criminals here.'

He was persuaded to telephone his lawyer, who suggested it might be wise to be co-operative in the circumstances. M.D. had a file of papers in his room of distribution agreements, patent licences and other agreements, which he had drawn up himself. They almost all infringed Article 85. The officials asked for copies. In another part of the building they had come to the office of Bill Brown. He had been tipped off by a colleague and had already been down to the shredder twice. Despite telling his ex-colleague that nothing was kept in writing, he had kept files on each of his competitor companies and did not know what might be incriminating in each one. Four had been destroyed. The Commission asked for copies of those that remained.

They had simultaneously raided the premises of all the other parties named by Mr Fixit and in at least one the corresponding copy of each letter was available even if the original had been destroyed by one of the other parties. They were able to piece together the full picture and found a Europe-wide cartel. Proceedings were brought and the Commission fined the companies ECU8 million in total.

M.D. Splodgit sat down with his solicitor and two more board directors and discussed how to proceed. That year's profits had all but been extinguished by the Commission fines and they had no desire for events to be repeated.

'I had no idea they could even be interested in my distribution agreements. Are they likely to do us for those too?' M.D. asked.

'They may.' replied his solicitor. 'You have explicit export bans in those agreements. All the agreements carve up the European Market and do not follow the various "block exemptions" which I discussed in my recent letter to you M.D. You should have put them through your in-house lawyers, if not me.'

'They only look for problems. They aren't on my side . . .'

'That sort of attitude has to change now, M.D. We've known each other for years. I am on your side. What we need to do now is administer a dose of compliance medicine. Prevention is better than cure. I'm sure you don't want to be paying fines every year. This is what we must do.'

The solicitor then described his proposals, which after much argument, were grudgingly accepted by Splodgits and which helped to ensure that although there was the occasional infringement there were no more big anti-trust actions brought against the company. A positive corporate attitude of proper compliance with competition legislation was encouraged. It became known within the industry that anti-competitive practices were not the sort of thing which Splodgits indulged in. Competitors dared not approach them as they knew it would mean an inevitable rebuff and the matter would be taken up with their superior. New employees soon realised that 'that sort of thing' was not done there. Surprisingly, M.D. Splodgit did not find that the business suffered at all. The secret restrictive arrangements had never worked very well and had not been capable of being enforced in the courts.

His solicitor proposed:

1. A written note summarising the law in easy terms, which would not only be sent to all employees, but which would be discussed with them.
2. Regular seminars on the subject of competion law run by the in-house legal department and attended by all staff.
3. Giving one senior person overall responsibility for anti-trust enforcement within the company, with a chain of responsibility down to the lowest level of employees.
4. Vetting of all agreements by the legal department.
5. Restrictions on meetings with competitors and requiring employees to fill out a form each time a meeting with them took place.
6. The insertion of a clause in employment contracts that there would be instant dismissal for infringers of competition laws and that new employees be informed both in writing and orally about the Company's policy in this area.
7. A document retention policy.
8. Instructions be set out on how to react to subsequent competition investigations.

The Note

Written notes or other documents will form an important part of any compliance programme. The law is complicated and full of jargon. The document will be prepared for staff at all levels. It may be necessary to have two versions of it, one for senior managers and another for others within the organisation. There may be such significant differences between areas of the business that different documents need to be prepared for different parts of the business.

In the case of Splodgits they had the same programmes for everyone in each country, with slight differences to reflect local competition law. They required employees to sign and return a form every year and on joining the company or being moved to a different country. The form contained an acknowledgement that they had read and understood the note and been through it with their superior. They were required to acknowledge not only that they had completed a contact reporting form each time they had met with competitors, but also that they had not acted in breach of the company's policy in this area on any occasion and were not aware that anyone else within the organisation had broken the rules in any way.

The Note briefly and readably described EC and UK competition law and the various penalties. It made it clear that under UK law the individuals themselves could go to jail for contempt of court and therefore, if in doubt, that the views of the legal department should be sought. There was then a list of the sorts of activities to be avoided and areas in which caution should be exercised. Splodgits found it difficult to ensure that the document was comprehensive on the one hand, but on the other not so long that it would not be read or understood by the individuals to whom it was addressed. The list included price fixing and job allocation, as well as collusive tendering, various forms of restriction on competition, exclusivity and other similar areas. General guidelines on meetings with competitors were given.

Seminars

Many employees will not always fully understand a written note about competition law and explaining the practical effects of the policy to them face to face and being able to answer any particular questions which they might have is essential. At Splodgits, the company's own solicitors went round all the divisions and subsidiaries in both this country and abroad and undertook a rolling programme of visits. These visits took place every year and attendance at seminars was compulsory.

Responsibility

To show that competition law was taken seriously by Splodgits, the Managing Director's second in command, a main board director who happened to have a legal background before going into industry, took control and ultimate responsibility for competition law compliance. The notes which were circulated emanated from him.

His job was to make quarterly reports to the Board on competition law matters and problems. He had individuals within the various subsidiaries and divisions of Splodgits regularly reporting to him direct on competition enforcement matters. They were responsible for others below them through a chain of responsibility.

Vetting of agreements

Competition law is complicated and it is comparatively easy to enter into agreements which infringe the legislation, without knowing that this has occurred in cases where a difficult point of law is involved or the infringement is technical.

Where solicitors familiar with competition law have had an opportunity to look at agreements then there is less of a chance that the rules will be broken. At Splodgits, Mr Splodgit found that he had to engage an additional solicitor in his legal department to assist with the vetting of agreements and to undertake the rolling programme of seminars. However, he also found that generally agreements were tighter and better drafted than they had been when he had drafted many of them himself and when relationships broke down his company's position was better protected. The cost of the extra lawyer was more than covered by his peace of mind. There had been some very unpleasant questions raised at the last meeting of shareholders in this area. He was not looking forward to a repeat performance.

Competitors and contact reporting

Meetings with competitors are dangerous. At the least, information is in danger of being exchanged which is sufficient to amount to a registrable information exchange agreement under the RTPA, i.e. where information about prices charged in the past or terms and conditions is passed between the parties on a reciprocal basis.

The compliance programme would therefore seek to discourage meetings with competitors generally. Where they took place there would be strict guidelines, particularly in the area of trade association meetings. Minutes should be taken and, where the conversation veers towards any of the areas set out in the compliance programme Note, the individual representative of the company should be instructed to leave the room.

In many industries contact with competitors will be frequent. They may even be the best customers of a company. In many cases they will buy parts from each other for incorporation into finished products. Any overriding rule never to meet with competitors therefore would be unworkable. In some industries where individuals frequently change jobs, they will know their ex-colleagues on a personal basis and keep up their friendships. UK and EC competition law have not yet reached the position which can apply in America where some companies forbid any form of contact with competitors at all, even on the golf course, because of the view which others may take as to what the parties were discussing.

Splodgits decided that in their business there was not much necessary contact with competitors except on rare occasions when they supplied each other or entered into joint venture agreements or other forms of co-operation, which would now be throroughly vetted from a competition law point of view. In their case it was practical to institute what they called the 'contact reporting system' and which meant that every time they had contact with their competitors they completed a short form and sent it off quickly to their superior who was responsible for competition law enforcement. If he thought there might be any problem with the meeting from the competition law standpoint then he would refer the matter upwards.

Anyone meeting secretly with competitors would not fill in a form and such a system is by no means fool-proof, but it can cause those meeting with competitors to be reminded of the company's policy on restrictive trade practices.

Employees

Companies operate only through employees. The purpose of a compliance programme is to educate employees so that restrictive agreements and infringements of competition law are avoided. Employees often enter into restrictive arrangements where there is no personal gain to them. They may often have the best interests of their company foremost in their minds and believe that they are acting only for the good of the company. They may erroneously presume that they have at least tacit approval from on high.

The compliance programme, if effective, would overturn such assumptions. There can be advantages to employees in carrying out secret meetings for the purposes of price fixing and the like. They may have bonuses linked to their performance or the high prices which they are able to charge for their company's products. They may be given target market shares which must be achieved by their superiors or minimum prices to which they must adhere.

In circumstances where there is a price war between competitors achieving such corporate aims may be very difficult. The principal advantage to employees in running an arrangement or 'price ring' in those circumstances would be that it would make easier the working life of those involved. Instead of fighting all week to wrest potential orders from competitors they can sort the orders out on a 'fair' basis over lunch every Monday. Even though in the main individuals receive little material gain from these arrangements, they do take place. The ultimate, and often the most effective, sanction is to make breach of the company's policy on restrictive trade practices a disciplinary offence, perhaps punishable by instant dismissal. This is the case in some large corporations who take seriously their compliance programmes and obligations under the law in the competition field.

Only where the company is already the subject of an order of the Restrictive Practices Court is there any risk of a jail sentence or fine for an individual where there has been contempt of court. In all other cases, and always under EC competition law, this prospect is not faced by employees. They may feel that they have nothing to lose by operating agreements of this type. However, if they know that their job is at risk then clearly that is a very strong incentive to ensure compliance with the company's policy in this area.

When first amending disciplinary rules to provide that in future it will be a 'sackable' offence for individuals to infringe competition law it may be necessary to offer some form of amnesty for past infringements, particularly if the company wishes to investigate fully its potential existing exposure. The other important element of this part of any compliance programme is that the threat is in fact carried out and that others become aware of the fact that it is carried out. If it becomes generally known that Mr X was found out but then quietly allowed to carry on in his job as before, then the threat becomes hollow.

Document retention policies

Many companies operate so-called 'document retention' policies as a legitimate part of their compliance programme and for other purposes too. In fact such policies are really document destruction programmes. Their aim is to ensure that documents are not retained indefinitely.

There is no general rule of law that documents must be retained. Once European Commission officials arrive to carry out a 'dawn raid' then documents cannot be shredded or otherwise disposed of. However, prior to such investigation, it is perfectly legitimate to destroy documents, say every three years as a matter of policy, principally because the storage costs for papers are so high. To sift through files and take out and destroy any letters or agreements which would be of interest to competition investigators would probably be counter productive. It would often be the case that copies of the letters would be held by another company which would be disclosed elsewhere. The company which had systematically destroyed all incriminating evidence would appear in a particularly bad light in the eyes of the Commission.

General policies for destruction of documents are a good idea, however, and may have the advantage of removing embarrassing anti-trust infringements from the files along with other documents but there may in many cases be commercial advantages in retaining documents for a reasonable period of years. Even in the context of an anti-trust investigation, if all the documents from, say five years ago, have been destroyed and the Commission has access to them from the other parties who have retained the papers, the company being advised could find itself at a disadvantage not knowing what those letters, papers or agreements said.

Instructions

Instructions to senior managers, receptionists and security officers should be readily available for reference purposes when investigators arrive at a company's premises.

Bringing in a compliance programme

Companies bringing into force a compliance programme for the first time clearly need to draft the relevant documents for signature and the rules to which adherence will in future be sought.

Involvement by individuals at all levels of the company is useful and, in particular, high level involvement is important to ensure that the matter is taken seriously at Board level. The programme will need to be brought in over a period of months, depending on the size of the company. If it has offices in many towns or indeed countries then the necessary communication will need to take place and the establishment of chains of responsibility will need to be put into place.

Conclusion

It is difficult for a company to know if it is infringing competition law if it has no effective method of checking and no policy in the area. Regular reminders to staff are necessary to ensure that they do not forget what they have been told and they are conscious in all their business dealings of the potential competition law aspects.

A compliance programme is one method of ensuring compliance with legislation. If no checks are made or policy issued then the cost of operating such a policy is avoided, but the company runs the risk that it will infringe legislation. A view may be taken that those who are determined within the company to enter into these types of arrangements on a covert basis are not going to be put off by dictats from the company, as long as the company continues to be pleased with the good results which their area of the business is producing. However, the courts have regarded it as relevant that competition law is taken seriously by companies when looking to the level of fine to be meted out to infringers. The compliance programme may well pay for itself. Also, the programme should at least ensure that those operating such agreements are well aware that they are acting in breach of company policy and that their jobs are at risk. This may deter some.

Difficult areas where it is not clear to the lay-man that there may be agreements which infringe competition legislation can at least be drawn to the attention of employees as sectors in which they should exercise caution and seek more detailed advice.

COMPETITION AUDIT

Allied to compliance programmes are so-called 'competition audits'. Companies are familiar with audits for accounting purposes of their books and records. Other corporate 'health checks' are increasingly becoming common. As mentioned above, these may be in the field of environmental law, health and safety, financial services, or racial or sexual discrimination in the field of employment law. Companies may feel a need from a public relations point of view to undertake such checks, perhaps for the purpose of using them in publicity material – 'none of our products damage the environment' or 'we are an equal opportunities employer'.

Alternatively, there may be a potential disposal of the company on the horizon. The acquiring company may not wish to rely on warranties and traditional disclosure against the warranties, but may wish to undertake a full US style 'due diligence' exercise in relation to the target company to ascertain whether it has any potentially damaging restrictive trading agreements in operation. There may be a need in those circumstances for warranties in the agreement of purchase, stating whether or not the company is subject to orders of the Restrictive Practices Court and requiring that a list of all agreements which it has registered with the OFT be disclosed, as well as disclosure of all proceedings or investigations by the European Commission.

In all cases where an audit is required, a major part of that task will be to examine agreements to which the company is a party to determine whether or not they infringe competition law. This will not just be important to discover whether there is a risk that the company will be brought before the various competition authorities, but also for enforcement purposes. For example, the principal supply agreement upon which most of the business of a company depends for raw materials, which are obtained from the only acceptable supplier in the market (perhaps because that supplier is the only one with the capacity to supply the company with the quantities of product which it needs), may be void as to its restrictions. If the contract is important enough to the business, the competition law issue may be sufficiently serious to undermine the worth of the business.

As well as an examination of agreements, enquiries can be conducted about the general ethos within the organisation, whether there appear to be any concerted practices and whether the activities of any trade association of which the company is a member are likely to have led it into any infringement of competition law.

All these measures should ensure that the fullest possible investigation of the company is undertaken.

Splodgit plc
Competition Law Compliance Programme

EMPLOYEE ACKNOWLEDGEMENT FORM

I acknowledge by my signature below that I have read and fully understood the Competition Law Rules attached to the copy of this form for my retention and that I have complied with the Company's Rules in this area in all respects during the previous year.

I also confirm that all those individuals for whom I am responsible, listed below, have complied with the Rules and I am not aware of anyone else within the Company who has broken the Rules in any way.

I am aware that breach of these Rules is regarded as a serious disciplinary offence by the Company which would result in instant dismissal, as well leaving the company open to fines by UK and EC authorities. Breach may result in my being ordered to pay fines and be committed to jail.

Signed   ....

Name   ....

Job title   ....

Date   ....

Individuals for whom responsible   ....

....

....

I attended the annual seminar on competition law on 199

Please send this form to   ....

Fig. 7.1

A COMPLIANCE PROGRAMME

Splodgit Company took seriously its compliance effort, being anxious to avoid fines and perhaps more important, the bad publicity which it had had for past infringements. Instead of being a laughing stock of the industry, or so it had seemed to M.D. Splodgit on his worst days in court, their new policy was held up as being a model in their field. They required individuals to sign a form each year, and on joining the company or moving to another position in the company abroad. The form ran along the lines of Fig. 7.1, adapted according to the circumstances.

Individuals were required to sign a 'contact reporting form' whenever they met with competitors in terms similar to those shown in Fig 7.2.

Splodgit plc

COMPETITOR CONTACT REPORTING FORM

Every time you meet in person or speak on the telephone to a competitor this form should be completed and sent within three days to your Competition Law Reporting Officer. If you are in any doubt as to whether a form should be completed in any particular circumstance refer the matter to the Officer or a member of the Company's legal department.

The completion of this form is required by the Company's Competition Law Rules and is a term of your contract of employment. Any breach of those Rules is regarded as a serious disciplinary offence.

Where you find you are required to complete this form more than once a week please refer to your Reporting Officer for advice.

Your name and job title: ....

Name of competitor and individual: ....

Form of contact: ....

Who initiated contact?:   ....

Purpose of contact: ....

What was said and done: ....

Any follow up: ....

....

Date of completion of this form: ....

Fig. 7.2

The principal document, however, was the compliance programme itself, the written notes or rules, which appeared in different formats for different territories. In the UK, Splodgits was subject to an order of the Restrictive Practices Court so had to be particularly careful not to enter into agreements subject to registration under the RTPA. The rules were kept deliberately short to make them digestible even to the lower grades of employee and were as follows:

Splodgit plc
Competition Law Compliance Programme

RULES

You are required to read these rules carefully and follow them exactly. If you need any help or are unclear about any point then please speak to your Competition Law Reporting Officer, who is Mr/s ... or a member of Splodgit plc's legal department, telephone...

Breaking these rules is a serious disciplinary offence which will lead to instant dismissal.

The rules are designed to make sure that Splodgit plc keeps within the law – competition law, both of this country and the Common Market. If Splodgit breaks those laws it can suffer heavy fines of millions of pounds. Splodgit is subject to a special court order in the UK. If it breaks that order it will be in 'contempt of court'. As well as the company being liable to large fines, individuals could be fined or even jailed for contempt of court, so not only your job, but your assets and personal freedom could be at risk.

Competition law forbids certain types of agreements and behaviour which you may not even think is in any way wrong. That is why you must read these rules carefully.

Once a year you will be required to attend a seminar on competition law organised by Splodgit plc's legal department. Attendance is compulsory, but if for any reason you are unable to attend on the designated day it is your responsibility and that of your Reporting Officer to arrange your attendance on an alternative day.

You must submit a Contact Reporting Form every time you have contact with competitor companies. If you are in any doubt as to whether a particular company is a competitor company refer the matter to your Reporting Officer or the legal department or complete a form anyway. Copies of the form are attached to these Rules.

Each year you must complete an Acknowledgement Form which requires you to confirm that you have kept the Rules and reported any infringements to your Reporting Officer. You are responsible for Mr/s... and ... You must ensure that they complete all necessary forms and that they understand the Rules. You must also report any breach of the Rules by anyone within the Company, whether or not you are responsible for them.

Finally, all commercial agreements which the company proposes to enter into should be vetted by the legal department to check whether they comply with competition law. You may send documents direct to the legal department by fax (No...), but should send details to your Reporting Officer too.

There follows a brief description of competition law which seeks to highlight some of the danger areas. It is not comprehensive as the law is complicated in this area, so if in doubt refer matters to the legal department.

Mr/s..., who is a main Board Director of Splodgit plc, has overall responsibility for compliance with competition law. If you feel a matter could not appropriately be raised with anyone else then please contact him at the Company's head office.

Thank you for your co-operation.

Competition law

EC competition law forbids agreements which have as their object or effect the prevention, restriction or distortion of competition. It also prohibits company's occupying a strong market position, such as that occupied by Splodgit plc, from abusing that dominant position.

UK competition law requires that agreements containing restrictions be registered at the Office of Fair Trading, which can refer them to the Restrictive Practices Court. Anti-competitive practices can be investigated by the Monopolies and Mergers Commission.

These Rules are designed to minimise potential infringement by the Company.

Competition law applies to written agreements, arrangements, concerted practices and oral understandings, even gentlemen's agreements. They do not have to be legally binding. There are strong powers of investigation, particularly those given to European Commission officials. As a general matter of course follow the Company's Document Retention Policy, details of which should have been given to you when you joined the Company. Further copies are available from the legal department. Senior management and those manning Reception must familiarise themselves with the Company Procedures for Investigations (attached for such employees).

The following list sets out what you must not do:

1. Never agree with other companies a price at which you will each sell your products, or the terms or conditions on which you will sell products. For example, never agree with C Co what Splodgits and C Co will each charge for their competing products. Do not even discuss pricing policy or when price rises may be announced.
2. Do not agree with another company that you will not operate in one country or market if they agree not to operate in another. If you wish to enter into agreements restricting competition refer the matter to the legal department. This applies to joint venture arrangements, agency, distribution and licensing, research and development ventures and other commercial agreements in particular, but also to general contact with competitors or suppliers or customers. For example, you may be approached by an individual from another company to arrange a meeting to discuss the market. Report all approaches on a Contact Reporting Form and do not attend such meetings.
3. Do not agree how you and another company will submit tenders for work nor divide potential contracts between you and another company or companies. It is dangerous even to discuss what contracts are available and the state of the market for splodgits.
4. Exchanges of information with competitors may infringe competition law. Do not exchange any information without legal advice.
5. Avoid contact with competitors. If you are required to attend trade association meetings, such as those run by the Splodgit Manufacturers' Association follow the Trade Association Guidelines obtainable from the legal department. Be cautious at social events with competitors and stick to strictly social topics of conversation.
6. Where you propose to refuse to supply a customer or competitor, refer the

matter to the legal department as refusals to supply or refusals to grant licences may in certain circumstances infringe competition law. It may make commercial sense to refuse to supply, but advice must be sought first.

7.   Do not seek to impose a minimum resale price on goods sold or try to dictate the price at which distributors will sell Splodgits.

If you are in any doubt concerning a particular agreement or discussion you have had then seek further advice.

Thank you for your cooperation.

....

[Board Director]
Splodgit plc

The amount of detail which should go into compliance rules very much depends on the individuals to whom the programme is addressed and the extent to which the legal department of the company will be involved. It may be necessary to set out in some considerable detail the circumstances in which an agreement will be registrable under the RTPA or may infringe Articles 85 and 86 if legal advice cannot readily and practically be sought. Much depends on the nature of the company and its size. The above provides an indication of the areas likely to be addressed in an average compliance programme.

In an increasingly regulated corporate environment compliance programmes are becoming more and more common and represent best business practice.

QUESTION

Write a letter to the Chairman of a large international conglomerate setting out why it would be commercially wise to set up a compliance programme and explain briefly what that programme would involve.

FURTHER READING

ARTICLES   Burnside M. – *Violation of antitrust policy*, Les Nouvelles, [1990] vol. 4, p.162
Marks D.H. – *Setting up an anti-trust compliance programme* [1988] ECLR 88
Stanbrook C. & Ratcliff J. – *EEC Anti-trust Audit* [1988] ECLR 334

CASES   *Eurofix-Bauco* v *Hilti* OJ 1988 L65/19
John Deere [1985] 2 CMLR 554, OJ 1985 L35/58
National Panasonic (UK) Ltd [1983] 1 CMLR 497, OJ 1982 L354/29
Re Ready Mixed Concrete [1991] ICR 52 and *DGFT* v *Smiths Concrete Ltd* (CA) July 1991

Part 2

Agreements

8

Distribution, purchasing and agency agreements

Competition law, particularly that of the EC, tends to categorise agreements. Block or general exemptions have been issued for particular categories of agreements which are commonly found and which would often infringe Article 85(1) so as to avoid repetitious specific notifications to the Commission. This makes their analysis in terms of the competition law much easier. However, there can be problems where complex arrangements are involved when the deal being struck does not fit neatly into one particular category.

DISTRIBUTION AGREEMENTS

One category which has had specific treatment under the competition law of both the EC and UK is the exclusive distribution agreement. A distribution agreement is a long-term agreement by a manufacturer or supplier to sell products to a distributor, who would commonly then sell those goods on to wholesalers, or even shopkeepers directly, before they were sold to the public. He is given rights to distribute the goods. As this arrangement is envisaged as lasting over the long term there is a need for a specific agreement rather than relying on the standard terms and conditions of sale or purchase of the parties.

The distributor may be given training in the products or advertising assistance by the supplier and there may be restrictions on the activities of both parties. In a simple case of an exclusive distribution agreement the supplier may agree to give the distributor an exclusive territory, a whole country, such as the UK, or a small part of one nation, such as North West England. The supplier may agree not to appoint other distributors in that region. *Prima facie* there is an anti-competitive situation which has been addressed by the competition law of both the EC and UK. A distributor may not be prepared to take risks in marketing a new product without the 'protection' of an exclusive territory.

EC law

There are many such arrangements in the EC and the block exemption for exclusive distribution agreements carefully sets out what restrictions are permitted in agreements of this sort.

Regulation (EEC) No. 1983/83 on the application of Article 85(3) of the Treaty to categories of exclusive distribution agreements,[1] to give it its full title, is the relevant Regulation in this area. This Regulation replaced the earlier EEC block exemption Regulation 67/67 which dealt with the same subject matter. Agreements of this sort are 'vertical' arrangements, i.e. comprise restrictions down the chain of supply rather than restrictions horizontally between competitors and are not as inherently anti-competitive.

1 Commission Regulation (EEC) No 1983/83 of 22 June 1983 on the application of Article 85(3) of the Treaty to categories of exclusive distribution agreements, published in the Official Journal, 30 June 1983, at No L173/1

However, the Commission in the 1966 decision of *Consten & Grundig* v *Commission*[2] determined that vertical agreements can restrain competition, hence the need for a block exemption in this area. The Commission recognised that exclusive distribution agreements facilitate the promotion of sales of products and ensure continuity of supplies, as well as rationalise distribution. They can also stimulate competition and have positive benefits to consumers.

The Regulation provides that Article 85(1) will not apply to agreements to which only two undertakings are party and under which one party agrees with the other to supply certain goods for resale within the whole or a defined area of the common market only to that other.[3]

Only two undertakings must be party to the agreement, otherwise the benefit of the block exemption will not be available and the agreement would have to be examined on first principles as to whether it infringes Article 85(1) *per se*. The Commission has issued a Notice,[4] *inter alia*, concerning this Regulation, which provides that to be covered by the block exemption the agreement must be between only one supplier and one reseller in each case. Several undertakings forming one economic unit count as one undertaking.[5] Group companies may therefore count for these purposes as one undertaking, depending on the level of control the parent exercises over the subsidiary. It is also stated in the Notice that the seller may delegate his supply obligations to an independent undertaking and the exemption will still apply,[6] but the involvement of undertakings other than the contracting parties must be confined to the execution of deliveries. Most distribution agreements, however, are between one supplier and one dealer and this is not a practical problem.

Restriction on supplier

The only restriction on the supplier must be one not to supply goods for resale to others within a certain area. The following examples illustrate the application of this provision:

1. Company Y agrees to supply grapes only to Company G in France.

The exemption may not apply. It only applies where there is an agreement to supply goods for resale only to the dealer in the territory. The goods must be supplied for resale. The Commission further explained this in the Notice[7] as requiring that the goods are disposed of by the purchaser to others in return for consideration. Agreements where the purchaser transforms or processes the goods into other goods, or uses or consumes them in manufacturing other goods, are not agreements for resale. The same applies to the supply of components which are combined with other components into a different product.

In the example here the grapes may be resold as they were purchased. However, Company G may be a wine manufacturer. The grapes would merely be used in the manufacturing of wine. The exemption could not be used. The criterion is that the goods distributed by the reseller are the same as those the other party has supplied to him for that purpose. The economic identity of the goods is not affected if the reseller merely breaks up and packages the goods in smaller quantities, or repackages them, before resale.

2 *Etablissements Consten SARL and Grundig-Verkaufs-GmbH* v *Commission* [1966] ECR 299

3 Article 1

4 Commission notice concerning Commission Regulations (EEC) No 1983/83 and (EEC) No 1984/83 of 22 June 1983 on the application of Article 85(3) of the Treaty to categories of exclusive distribution and exclusive purchasing agreements, published in the Official Journal 13 April 1984, at No C101/2
5 Notice, *op cit*, Para.13
6 Para.15

7 Para.9

The agreement between Y and G is only legible when the economic identity of the product is not changed. In case the Y and G agreement concerns a certain quantity for resale, the contract will infringe Art 85 when G is using them for making wine

2. Company X grants exclusive rights to Company H to provide rustproofing of metals using Company X's proofing liquids within the UK.

8 Paras.11,12

The exemption would not apply as it only applies to 'goods'. The Notice referred to above describes what is meant by this requirement in some detail.[8] Agreements for the supply of services rather than the resale of goods are not covered by the Regulation. Where the reseller provides customer or after-sales services incidental to the resale of the goods, the agreement would still be covered. Nevertheless, a case where the charge for the service is higher than the price of the goods would fall outside the scope of the Regulation.

This is a different approach to that taken under UK competition law, discussed below in relation to exclusive arrangements of this sort. Under the Restrictive Trade Practices Act there are exemptions for exclusive dealing in relation to goods and also for services.[9]

9 See RTPA Sch.3, para.2

However, where there is an exclusive agreement where the purchasing party hires out or leases to others the goods supplied to him this would be covered by the Regulation. Computer software distribution licences (considered in Chapter 11) are copyright licences and it is unlikely that they would be able to benefit from the exemption.

3. Company I agrees to purchase all its requirements for metal brackets from Company Z. There are no restrictions on Company Z at all.

10 Regulation 1984/83, 1983 OJ L173/5

This would be what is known as an exclusive purchasing agreement and there is a different block exemption for agreements of that sort which will be considered later in this chapter.[10]

4. Company A enters into a distribution agreement with Company B. Company B agrees to purchase minimum quantities of the products as well as a number of other restrictions. However, there is no exclusive supply obligation on the supplier. Can the exemption be used as there are restrictive provisions in the agreement which could have been exempted under the block exemption?

The language of the Regulation appears to be permissive, that the only restriction which is allowed to fall on the supplier is the one set out, not that there must be such a restriction. Although the Notice is not binding as the Regulation is, it is at least indicative of the Commission's attitude and in paragraph 17 it is stated that 'apart from the exclusive supply obligation... which must be present if the block exemption is to apply...'. It may well be dangerous to rely on the block exemption when there is no restriction on the supplier of the sort described in Article 1 of Regulation 1983/83.

Article 2 of the Regulation provides that there must be no other restrictions on the supplier other than an obligation not to supply the goods sold to the distributor to others. If the supplier also manufactures other goods of a different type then there can be no restriction on the supply by the supplier into the territory of those goods.

11 Notice, para.30

The restriction on the supplier, however, need not be absolute.[11] Clauses permitting a supplier to supply certain customers in the territory will not prevent the block exemption applying provided that those customers are not resellers.

Restrictions on distributor

Article 2.2 lists the only restrictions which can be imposed on the distributor. These are described in turn below.

Not to sell or make competing goods. Suppliers hope for an indication of commitment to their product from an exclusive distributor. Such a restriction as is permitted here is common and regarded as justifiable by the Commission. Restrictions on manufacture or sale of goods which do not compete with the contract goods, however, would be regarded as contrary to Article 85 and the parties could not benefit from the block exemption.

Exclusive purchase obligation. The distributor may be restricted from obtaining the contract goods from anyone other than the supplier under the distribution agreement. The supplier can therefore be assured that the distributor will not be able, for example in a distribution agreement for filing cabinets, to purchase filing cabinets for resale from any other company.

Soliciting customers outside territory. The distributor may be prevented from seeking customers outside the territory, but only in relation to the contract goods. Restrictions on establishing a branch or maintaining any distribution depot may also be inserted.

What is clearly not permitted and is regarded as a most heinous crime by the Commission is any explicit export ban such as 'The distributor shall not sell the contract goods outside the Territory'. The only permitted restriction of this sort is that set out in Article 2.2.

In *Bayer Dental,*[12] a price list of Bayer Dental used for the wholesale of dental/medical products in Germany contained a paragraph headed 'Resale'. This required that the seller's packages carrying a trade mark must be resold unopened. Also, it stated that the preparations were intended solely for distribution in Germany:

> Their resale abroad may, in the country concerned, be prohibited because they contravene registration regulations and may lead to claims for damage because they infringe intellectual property rights.

The Commission decided that this meant the preparations were not intended for sale abroad, such sale being prohibited and that this export ban infringed Article 85(1).[13]

Other permitted restrictions. Article 2.3 sets out other provisions which are generally not restrictive of competition and which may be included in agreements of this sort. They must not be formulated or applied in such a way as to take on the character of restrictions of competition that are not permitted.[14]

> Article 2.3 provides that the exclusive distributor may undertake all or any of the following obligations:
>
> (a) to purchase complete ranges of goods or minimum quantities;
> (b) to sell the contract goods under trademarks or packed and presented as specified by the other party;
> (c) to take measures for promotion of sales, in particular:
>   – to advertise,

12 OJ 1990 L351/46. In *Gosme/Martell – DMP* OJ 1991 L185/23 a clause banning exports, even where never enforced infringed Article 85 as there was manipulation of discounts

13 Export bans are virtually never exempted

14 Notice, para.19

– to maintain a sales network or stock of goods,
– to provide customer and guarantee services,
– to employ staff having specialized or technical training.

A supplier may manufacture, say, plastic containers for domestic use. He appoints an exclusive distributor for the UK. He is allowed to insist that the distributor must purchase the full range of his products even if the distributor believes he would have difficulty selling certain sizes or types of container in the particular market.

A supplier who has agreed to a restriction that he will not sell the contract goods in the exclusive territory of the distributor is cutting himself off from a market in which he might otherwise have made a large number of sales. The distributor, although granted exclusive rights to sell in the territory, may choose to do very little. It is therefore accepted by the Commission that the distributor can be obliged to purchase minimum quantities of the contract goods.

This means that even if the distributor does not think he will be able to sell the goods which he wishes to purchase from the supplier he is obliged to purchase them or else will be in breach of contract. Such a provision is within the terms of the block exemption.

The supplier may insist that the goods be sold under a particular trade mark even if the distributor has his own trading name or style under which he would have preferred to sell the goods.

A distributor may be obliged to advertise the goods, keep a full stock of them to satisfy customer demand and retain specialised staff and offer after-sales service or guarantee work.

Selective distribution

After-sales service may be essential for certain forms of goods, such as complicated electrical goods, and the supplier may be concerned to ensure that only specialised distributors are appointed. He would not be prepared to appoint any company as a distributor. This would be the case whether or not he was operating an exclusive appointment system. He would vet potential distributors carefully. This would result in fewer outlets and some companies being refused appointment and therefore the opportunity to sell the goods at all.

Such selective distribution networks are permissible where anyone who meets objective qualitative criteria would be appointed. The proposed company must, for example, have competent and experienced staff and be able to offer an after-sales service. Discrimination by the back door would not however be permitted. A distributor wanting to limit the number of distributors he appoints in his network across Europe where the products concerned are carrots would be hard pressed to show the Commission that his 'objective' criteria of trained staff etc. were necessary for the goods to be distributed properly.

In *Metro* v *Commission*,[15] SABA operated a selective distribution system for electrical goods such as hi-fis. In 1976 it applied for exemption under Article 85(3) for its selective distribution system and a renewal of the exemption was granted in 1983. Metro was a cash and carry firm which was

15 *Metro v Commission (No 1)* [1978] 2 CMLR 1 and Metro-SB-*Grossmarkte GmbH & Co. KG* v *Commission (No 2)* [1987] 1 CMLR 118

refused entry to the selective distribution network and complained to the Commission. The Commission held that the system was justifiable given the qualitative criteria which were applied by SABA.

The Notice allows a restriction on the reseller supplying the contract goods to unsuitable dealers, provided that admission to the distribution network is based on objective criteria of a qualitative nature relating to the professional qualifications of the owner of the busines or his staff or the suitablility of his business premises, the criteria are the same for all potential dealers, and the criteria are actually applied in a non-discriminatory manner. Distribution systems which do not fulfil these conditions are not covered by the block exemption.[16]

Examples of clauses which may preclude the application of the Regulation would therefore include the following:[17]

1. *Terms.* A provision in the distribution agreement requiring the distributor to sell the goods on certain specified terms and conditions. A supplier may want a distributor to exclude liability for defects in the products in a certain way or address the question of suits by third parties for breach of, for example, patent rights in the products, by a form of indemnity or exclusion specified by the supplier. It may be necessary to make an individual notification in such circumstances.

2. *Resale prices.* A supplier may be concerned to ensure that his brand, for example an expensive perfume, is given a high price to maintain the brand image. He cannot insist that the perfume be sold at a specified price. He would be wise to seek specific exemption even where only a minimum price is specified, below which the distributor should not sell the product.

In *Pronuptia*[18] (a case concerning a franchising network for the sale of wedding dresses), prices which were merely advisory and not binding on the party to whom they were stipulated were acceptable under Article 85(1) provided such advisory pricing did not result in a concerted practice to maintain uniform prices in a certain territory. Even advisory pricing is inherently dangerous and better avoided.

A provision requiring the distributor to send information to the supplier, such as the prices at which he has sold the goods, may be acceptable depending on the use to which the supplier puts the information.

3. *Export bans.* As considered above, a restriction on the distributor exporting the goods is not permitted although he may be prevented from advertising and soliciting sales outside the territory.[19] He should remain free to respond to unsolicited requests for sales of the product even when they come from a territory in relation to which the supplier has granted exclusive rights to another distributor.

The Commission seeks to ensure that there is the possibility of parallel imports, i.e. that purchasers within Europe should be able to purchase products from any EC country, importing them from cheaper countries to those territories where they are more expensive, thus helping the creation of a single market. Many large companies are working towards single pricing across the whole of the EC to deal with this problem. The block exemption cannot be used where an agreement gives the exclusive distributor absolute

16 Notice, para.20, *Vichy* OJ 1991 L75/57 discusses such criteria

17 See para. 17 of the Notice

18 *Pronuptia de Paris v Schillgalis* [1986] 1 CMLR 414

19 For consideration of 'export bans', see *Bayer Dental* OJ 1990 L351/46, discussed above

20 Notice, para.31

territorial protection.[20] Article 3 of the Regulation sets out circumstances in which the Regulation will not apply; these include (Article 3(c)) circumstances where users can obtain the contract goods in the contract territory only from the exclusive distributor and have no alternative source of supply outside the contract territory.

Where a supplier is the only manufacturer of certain products in the EC and appoints one distributor on an exclusive basis for the whole of the EC then the agreement would not benefit from the exemption. Those of its provisions which, but for the exemption, fall within Article 85(1) such as the exclusivity provision would be void. Any such agreement, to be enforceable, would need to be notified on an individual basis to the Commission.

The parties must ensure either that the contract goods can be sold in the contract territory by parallel importers or that users have a real possibility of obtaining them from undertakings outside the contract territory, even outside the EC, at the prices and on the terms there prevailing. The supplier can represent an alternative source of supply for the purposes of this provision if he is prepared to supply the contract goods on request to final users located in the contract territory.[21]

21 Para.31

The permitted restriction on the supplier from supplying into the exclusive territory would not restrict sales by the supplier to resellers for export into the exclusive territory and indeed should leave him free to do so.[22]

22 Para.27
23 [1988] 4 CMLR 548

In *The Community* v *Konica UK Limited and Konica Europe GmbH*,[23] export bans in the context of distribution agreements were considered. The prices for Konica brand colour film for cameras differed markedly in the UK and West Germany, where they sold for up to 20 per cent more than in the UK. Practices aimed at preventing the export of Konica colour films from the UK to other EC Member States and the resale of parallel imported Konica colour film in the German market were held contrary to Article 85(1).

In Germany the film was advertised as being available only from specialist dealers, and consumers were more interested in the quality of the film than the price, which was the reverse of the position in the UK market. Konica Europe bought up all parallel imported film which found its way into Germany and committed itself to its German dealers to prevent parallel imports. The Commission held that such a commitment was contrary to Article 85(1).

Dealers in the UK, Northern Ireland and the Channel Islands were told that a large number of parallel imported goods were finding their way on to the German market and that in future no exports would be permitted and if they did not co-operate then supplies to them would cease. They were told that the supplier could tell which goods had been parallel imported as there was a special number on each film. This was not in fact true. Although there was no export ban in the original distribution agreements with the dealers, the subsequent issuing of such an instruction or threat, whether or not expressly acknowledged and accepted by the dealers, was sufficient to amount to an export ban and was held to infringe Article 85(1). The Commission held that such an export ban 'leads to artificial division in the Common Market and impedes the establishment of a single market between Member States'. Konica Europe and Konica UK were each fined 75,000 ECU (£52,500).

Customer restrictions

The distributor should be free to determine the customers which he serves. It would be incompatible with the Regulation for the exclusive distributor to be restricted to supplying only certain categories of customers (e.g. specialist retailers) in his contract territory and prohibited from supplying other categories (e.g. department stores), which are supplied by other resellers appointed by the supplier for that purpose.[24] Although a supplier may have exclusive distributors for particular territories, which may be the whole of the EC or part of it, he may not make divisions according to types of customer.

24 Notice, para.29

Reciprocal agreements

Article 3(a) provides that, even where an agreement falls clearly within all the terms of the block exemption the parties will not be able to benefit from its provisions where they each manufacture identical goods or goods which are considered by users as equivalent in view of their characteristics, price and intended use and enter into reciprocal exclusive purchasing agreements in respect of such goods. It may be difficult in some cases to determine which goods are interchangeable in this way. Goods can form a separate market on the basis of their characteristics, their price or their intended use alone. This is especially true where consumer preferences have developed.[25]

25 Para.21

The provisions apply even where the parties have not yet started to compete in any market inside or outside the Community. Competitors may be able to enter into distribution agreements with each other but not in relation to goods which are identical or equivalent.

Non-reciprocal competitor agreements

Companies which manufacture identical or equivalent goods may not benefit from the block exemption where they enter into non–reciprocal exclusive dealing agreements unless one of them has an annual turnover of no more than 100 million ECU (£70m).[26]

26 Art.3(b) of the Reg.

To illustrate the difference between Article 3(a) and (b), envisage two companies R and S. They both manufacture plastic sink bowls, clearly identical or equivalent goods. One has traditionally operated in the UK and the other in France. They see opportunities for their respective products in the territory of the other and think their products would be better marketed by their rival with knowledge of the local language, customs and business practice. They wish to appoint each other on an exclusive basis for France and UK respectively as distributors of their products.

Under Article 3(a), they cannot enter into such a reciprocal arrangement without notifying their agreement for exemption individually under Article 85(3) or running the risk of a Commission investigation and fines and their agreement being void. If, however, Company R merely decides that it wants to exploit the French market by appointing Company S as its exclusive distributor there, then the exemption may still be used if one of the two companies has a turnover under 100 million ECU (£70m).

These provisions will also apply where the manufacture is done by an undertaking connected with one of the parties.[27] An undertaking is connected with another for these purposes where (i) directly or indirectly it owns more

27 Art.4

than half of the assets, or capital of another, or (ii) it has power to exercise more than half of the voting rights or may appoint more than half the members of the Board of Directors of the other, or (iii) it merely has the right to manage the affairs of the other.

The annual turnover limit is used as a means of assessing the economic strength of the parties. The turnover of the parties in relation to all goods is taken and not just the turnover in relation to the particular contract goods which are the subject matter of the distribution agreement.

The total turnover limit can be exceeded by up to 10 per cent during any period of two successive financial years without loss of the block exemption. The block exemption is lost if, at the end of the second financial year, the total turnover over the preceding two years has been over 220 million ECU (£154m).[28]

28 Art.5.2

Hindering parallel imports

Under Article 3(d) the exemption will not apply where one of the parties makes it difficult for users to obtain the contract goods from other dealers in the common market or, where there are no alternative sources of supply in the EC, from outside of the EC, and in particular:

where one or both of them:

1. exercises industrial property rights so as to prevent dealers or users from obtaining outside, or from selling in, the contract territory properly marked or otherwise properly marketed goods;
2. exercises other rights or takes other measures so as to prevent dealers or users from obtaining outside, or from selling in, the contract territory contract goods.

Trade mark rights, for example, cannot therefore be used to prevent parallel imports because of this provision.

Withdrawal of exemption

The Commission has the right to withdraw the benefit of the exemption under Article 6 where an agreement falling within the terms of the exemption nevertheless has effects which are incompatible with Article 85(3), in particular where:

(a) the contract goods are not subject, in the contract territory, to effective competition from identical goods or goods considered by their users as equivalent in view of their characteristics, price or intended use;
(b) access by other suppliers to the different stages of distribution within the contract territory is made difficult to a significant extent;
(c) where it is not possible for intermediaries or users to obtain supplies of the contract goods from dealers outside the contract territory on terms there customary:
(d) the exclusive distributor:

1. without any objectively justified reason refuses to supply in the contract territory categories of purchasers who cannot obtain contract goods elsewhere on suitable terms or applies to them differing prices or conditions of sale;
2. sells the contract goods at excessively high prices.

Difficulties in obtaining supplies, refusals to supply and high prices therefore can have the effect that the exemption would not apply.

Application

The Regulation does not apply (i) to agreements for the resale of drinks in premises used for the sale and consumption of drinks, or (ii) to agreements for the resale of petroleum products in service stations (Article 8).

The Regulation expires on 31st December 1997, but is likely to be renewed, probably with more detail as in later block exemptions.

Conclusion

The Distribution Block Exemption removes the necessity for individual notification of many distribution agreements. However, its provisions are by no means universally applicable and, where there are export bans, customer restrictions or terms or prices dictated to a distributor, the exemption will not be available. Only those restrictions expressly permitted in the exemption are allowed.

In examining an agreement, questions concerning whether the parties are competitors and whether there are alternative sources of supply must always be asked in order to determine whether or not the exemption applies at all. Where the exemption does not apply it may be the case that the agreement does not contain restrictions which infringe Article 85(1) (discussed in Chapter 2). If there are restrictions which would infringe Article 85(1), notification on an individual basis for exemption under Article 85(3) should be considered or the agreement modified so that it falls within the exemption.

Figure 8.1 illustrates the working of the exemption.

UK law

The RTPA addresses distribution agreements in a very different way from Regulation 1983/83. Even if an agreement falls within the requirements of the EC block exemption and therefore does not infringe EC competition law it may still fall foul of the RTPA and restrictions in it be rendered void. It may be necessary to furnish the agreement to the Office of Fair Trading before the restrictions take effect or, if the agreement has not yet been signed, drafting changes may be possible to ensure that it does not fall within the scope of the Act.

Any number of restrictions may be imposed on one party. The RTPA applies only where there are restrictions on at least two parties. A very one-sided agreement, therefore, would be able to avoid the RTPA entirely. Also, there must be at least two parties to the agreement, though not necessarily those accepting restrictions under it, who carry on business in this country. An agreement to appoint a non-UK distributor, which distributor has no operations in the UK, is unlikely to be caught.

Where those pre-conditions for the application of the RTPA are satisfied, the agreement will have to be registered at the OFT and will be put on the public Register. Such an agreement is at risk of being referred to the Restrictive Practices Court.

**Exclusive Distribution Agreements
under the Block Exemption
Regulation 1983/83**

1. Need
   (a) 2 parties only
   (b) goods
   (c) sold for resale, not to make into other products

2. Acceptable Restrictions
   (a) on supplier – not to supply goods into territory; this is the
       only permitted restriction on supplier.
   (b) on distributor
       – not to make or sell competing goods
       – only to obtain contract goods from supplier
       – not to solicit customers, establish branch or maintain depot
         outside territory
       – to purchase complete range or minimum quantities
       – to sell under trade marks or use packaging
       – to advertise, have sales network, keep stock of goods, provide
         customer and guarantee services, employ trained staff (consider
         selective distribution rules)

3. Exemption will not apply where:
   (a) reciprocal distributorships between competitors
   (b) exclusive distributorship with competitor where both have a turnover
       over 100 million ECU p.a.
   (c) no alternative supply source exists
   (d) parties hinder parallel imports
   (e) restrictions other than those permitted expressly particularly
       – export bans
       – customer restrictions
       – price or terms distributor is to use dictated by supplier

4. Commission may withdraw exemption where incompatibility with Article
   85(3), particularly:
   (a) where no competition with other goods
   (b) access for other suppliers to distributors is made difficult

5. Does not apply to certain drinks and petroleum agreements

Fig. 8.1

The RTPA has been considered in detail in Chapter 2. A restriction on a supplier selling the contract goods into the exclusive territory of the distributor would be a relevant restriction under the Act. It is not a restriction relating to the actual goods sold, which could therefore be discounted under the provisions of section 9(3). It would be a restriction as to the areas within which goods are to be supplied under section 6(1)(f). If there were also a restriction on the distributor from dealing in similar goods purchased from other suppliers, then there would be a corresponding restriction on the distributor rendering the agreement registrable as there would be restrictions on two parties.

The exclusive dealing (goods) exemption

Schedule 3 to the RTPA contains, in paragraphs 2 and 7, exemptions for exclusive dealing agreements in relation to goods and services respectively. Paragraph 2 provides:

> This Act does not apply to an agreement for the supply of goods between two persons, neither of whom is a trade association, being an agreement to which no other person is party and under which no such restrictions as are described in section 6(1) above are accepted or no such information provisions as are described in section 7(1) above are made other than restrictions accepted or provision made for the furnishing of information–
>
> (a) by the party supplying the goods, in respect of the supply of goods of the same description to other persons; or
>
> (b) by the party acquiring the goods, in respect of the sale, or acquisition for sale, of other goods of the same description.

This is a densely worded paragraph which bears close examination.[29] The requirements can usefully be listed:

29 See Green (Further reading) p.465

1. *Agreement for the supply of goods.* The agreement must relate to the supply of goods. There is a parallel exemption for distribution agreements concerning the supply of services, which are not covered under the EC block exemption. However, because of the way these Schedule 3 exemptions work, only one can be used. If an agreement is for both the supply of goods and the supply of services it is not possible to use both exemptions. They cannot be used cumulatively.

Nor would it be possible to put the arrangements in relation to goods in one agreement and those in relation to services in another (if they are part of the same transaction), as the Act looks at all agreements, even if merely oral, as one where they are part of the same transaction. Also, where there are other types of provision, such as arrangements for a licence of trade marks or patents, which also contain restrictions, other Schedule 3 exemptions for agreements of that sort cannot be used.

However, if a distribution agreement contains other peripheral issues, such as a trade mark licence which does not contain any other restrictions within the meaning of the RTPA, and it is clearly principally an agreement for the sale of goods or services, then the exemption may still apply.

2. *Between two persons.* As with the EC block exemption, the exemption only applies where there are two parties only to the agreement. Where an agreement is with three parties, but two of them are interconnected bodies corporate within the definition in section 43 (i.e. they are group companies) or they are two individuals carrying on business in partnership with each other, then those two parties are treated as a single person for this purpose.

Neither of the parties to the agreement must be a trade association. This is defined in section 43(1) as 'a body of persons (whether incorporated or not) which is formed for the purpose of furthering the trade interests of its members, or of persons represented by its members'.

No other restrictions

Schedule 3, paragraph 2, operates by setting out two restrictions which are permitted. If there are any other restrictions the exemption cannot be used. Unlike the provisions of section 9(3), where restrictions can be disregarded when adding up the total to calculate whether there are restrictions on two parties, the Schedule 3 exemption will not be available at all if there are any other restrictions within the meaning of section 6(1) (i.e. not restrictions which do not fall within the RTPA); they must be 'relevant restrictions'.

Supplier restriction

The supplier may only accept a restriction in respect of the supply of goods of the same description to other persons. The supplier may therefore give the distributor an exclusive territory, for example Manchester, and agree not to supply goods of the same description to persons in that area, or even agree to supply those goods to no one at all anywhere in the world. This is an exclusive supply arrangement in its purest sense and is expressly permitted. Any other restrictions may render the agreement void as to its restrictions as the benefit of the exemption would be lost.

Goods of the same description

In distribution agreements it is preferable to use the same words as are used in this exemption (and indeed as are used in the EC block exemption) if these exemptions are needed, in case they later fall to be scrutinised by the competition authorities of either jurisdiction.

In this case the words used are 'goods of the same description'. This would not necessarily have the same meaning as 'competing goods' or 'goods of a similar description', both of which phrases are broader terms. However, it is highly likely that a court would hold that the wider meaning encompassing competing goods would be placed upon the exemption, otherwise its scope would be much more limited and would probably not cover the area intended by the Parliamentary draftsman.

Distributor restriction

The only restriction which may be put upon the party acquiring the goods, i.e. the distributor or dealer, must be 'in respect of the sale, or acquisition for sale, of other goods of the same description'. The restriction may therefore state that the distributor shall not sell goods of the same description as the contract goods, other than those purchased from the supplier, or purchase such goods for sale from anyone other than the supplier. This is the classic exclusive purchase obligation and it is permitted whether or not the parties are competitors of each other and whatever their turnover.

However, such reciprocal arrangements could be looked at as one agreement by the OFT and would contain restrictions on the supplier both as to selling to others and as to acquiring goods for resale. It is not clear whether the Restrictive Practices Court would look at the parties as having dual status as both supplier and dealer. It seems unlikely, particularly if there were anti–competitive effects generated by such a reciprocal arrangement.

Goods for resale

The distributor must purchase the goods for sale. Many distributors acquire goods for incorporation into other goods prior to resale. They are unlikely to be able to benefit from the exemption, which makes it clear that the goods must be acquired for resale. Repackaging alone is unlikely to render the exemption inapplicable, but melting down the goods, crushing grapes for wine or even using them as a part for another finished product would not easily fall within the wording of the exemption. The goods must be acquired for resale rather than manufacture.

Restrictions not exempted

As has been seen above, any restrictions other than those contained in Schedule 3 render the agreement registrable and the exemption inapplicable. Some examples of fairly common restrictions in distribution agreements of this sort which would not be exempted would include:

1. *Manufacturing restrictions.* The exemption would not allow restrictions on either party manufacturing goods even of the same description as the contract goods. The same commercial effect as a restriction on manufacture could possibly be achieved by a restriction on sale of the manufactured goods. Clearly a party would need to be able to sell the goods so such a restriction expressed as a sales restriction would be exempted. This is an example of how careful drafting can avoid the impact of the RTPA.

2. *Imposition of terms on the distributor.* The supplier cannot dictate the terms upon which the distributor will sell products other than the contract goods. This would be a restriction as to the terms or conditions subject to which the goods are to be supplied within section 6(1)(c). However, a restriction in relation to the contract goods would be able to be discounted under section 9(3) as a restriction relating to the goods supplied and would not affect the exemption.

3. *Pricing restrictions.* Any attempt to specify the price at which the distributor will sell goods other than the contract goods would be caught by section 6(1)(b). However, specifying prices at which the goods which were sold to the dealer under the distribution agreement may be resold would be a restriction relating to the goods supplied (section 9(3)) and could therefore be discounted. That, however, is not the end of the matter. The Resale Prices Act 1976 prohibits individual resale price maintenance. In section 9 it provides:

> Any term or condition–
>   (a) of a contract for the sale of goods by a supplier to a dealer, or
>   (b) of an agreement between a supplier and a dealer relating to such a sale,
> is void in so far as it purports to establish or provide for the establishment of minimum prices to be charged on the resale of the goods in the United Kingdom.

It is expressly provided in section 9 that a supplier may notify dealers of 'prices recommended as appropriate for the resale of goods supplied or to be supplied by the supplier'.

The agreement will not become subject to registration under the RTPA but the term which establishes a minimum price will be void and it is unlawful to include such a term in a contract. The Resale Prices Act does not forbid establishing a maximum price.

Any pricing restrictions in a distribution agreement relating to goods other than those which the supplier has sold to the distributor will be restrictions under section 6 of the RTPA and the exclusive dealing exemption cannot then be used.

The exclusive dealing (services) exemption

Schedule 3, paragraph 7 contains an exemption for agreements for the exclusive supply of services along the lines of the Schedule 3, paragraph 2 exemption discussed above.

There must be only two parties to the agreement for the exemption to apply and one must not be a services supply association, which is the services equivalent of a trade association. The only restrictions permitted are in respect of the supply of services of the same description to other people or the obtaining of services of the same description from other persons. This therefore permits an agreement whereby a supplier agrees to supply only the distributor with certain services and no one else and the distributor agrees only to obtain certain services from the supplier.

This exemption is very similar to the provisions which are permitted in respect of the supply of goods. The principal practical difference is that rarely will the equivalent of section 9(3) (disregard of provisions) be available in connection with the supply of services. Section 18(2) only permits restrictions to be disregarded if they relate to the services supplied. A distributor of goods may be restrained from supplying those goods except on certain terms and conditions of sale by the supplier to his own customers because section 9(3) allows restrictions in relation to those goods to be disregarded for the purposes of counting restrictions.

It is difficult to envisage any circumstances in which services would be sold-on in this way. Similar services may be supplied, but not the very same services. For this reason a restriction on the supplier of services as to the terms on which he will supply services to others would not be exempt and would render the agreement subject to registration.

Conclusion

The RTPA is a technical form based statute. In many cases, if sufficient caution is exercised in a timely manner, distribution agreements will not be caught by its terms. However, the detail of the exemptions and the proposed terms and conditions of an agreement need to be examined carefully in all cases.

EXCLUSIVE PURCHASING AGREEMENTS

An exclusive purchase obligation is one in which the dealer agrees only to obtain certain goods from the supplier and from no one else. There is no corresponding restriction on the supplier from supplying into the dealer's territory, as there would be in an exclusive distribution arrangement.

EC law

In *Brasserie de Haecht S.A.* v *Wilkin and Another,*[30] Wilkin agreed to obtain their supplies of beer, drinks and lemonade exclusively from Brasserie de Haecht. This was an exclusive purchase obligation. Wilkin did not adhere to the agreement and used Article 85(1) as a defence to court proceedings. An Article 177 reference was made to the European Court which held:

> Agreements by which one undertaking agrees to obtain supplies from one undertaking only to the exclusion of all others do not *eo ipso* contain elements which constitute incompatibility with the Common Market under Article 85(1) of the Treaty. They may, however, contain them when, either separately or together with others, in the economic and legal context in which they are made and on the basis of a collection of objective legal or factual factors, they are capable of affecting trade between member-States and have as either their object or their effect the prevention, restriction or distortion of competition.

It was therefore clear from as early as 1967 that exclusive purchasing arrangements could cause problems under Article 85(1) and the necessity for a block exemption was apparent. Commission Regulation 1984/83[31] governs exclusive purchasing agreements. The Commission issued its Notice,[32] discussed above, to elaborate the differences between this Regulation and Regulation 1983/83. However, the essential difference is that Regulation 1984/83 applies where the reseller agrees to purchase goods exclusively from the supplier, i.e. an exclusive purchase obligation is included in the agreement, whereas the exclusive distribution Regulation applies where the supplier itself is restricted in the agreement from supplying goods into the exclusive territory.

Where there is no restriction on the supplier then the purchasing block exemption is relevant. The Regulations were conceived to avoid overlap and Article 16 of Regulation 1984/83 provides that the Regulation shall not apply to agreements covered by Regulation 1983/83.

Exclusive purchasing agreements falling within Regulation 1984/83 will leave the supplier free to supply other resellers in the same sales area and at the same level of distribution. Unlike an exclusive distributor, the tied reseller is not protected against competition from other resellers who, like himself, receive the contract goods direct from the supplier. On the other hand, as the Commission state in the Notice, he is free of restrictions as to the area over which he may make his sales effort.

Regulation 1984/83 is divided into three sections named 'Titles'. Titles II and III regulate beer supply agreements and service station agreements which are considered in Chapter 11.

Article 1 provides that Article 85(1) shall not apply:

> to agreements to which only two undertakings are party and whereby one party, the reseller, agrees with the other, the supplier, to purchase certain goods specified in the agreement for resale only from the supplier or from a connected undertaking or from another undertaking which the supplier has entrusted with the sale of his goods.

This permits a restriction on the distributor of the goods to the effect that he will not purchase certain goods from anyone except the supplier. The distributor may be locked into the supplier for the duration of the agreement.

30 [1968] CMLR 26

31 Commission Regulation (EEC) No 1984/83 of 22 June 1983 on the application of Article 85(3) of the Treaty to categories of exclusive purchasing agreements, published in the Official Journal, 30 June 1983, at No L173/5

32 OJ 1984 C101/2

As with the distribution block exemption, the Commission believes that in agreements of this sort there are substantial benefits to consumers which justify the obvious restriction on competition which agreements of this sort contain.

The restriction should be for no longer than five years and there must just be two parties to the agreement. The question of what comprises two parties was discussed in the context of distribution agreements above and is equally relevant here.

Similarly the agreement must be for the sale of goods to the distributor for resale and not for the supply of services or for incorporation of goods into other goods, issues addressed in the Notice and considered above.

Supplier restriction

No restriction may be imposed on the supplier other than the obligation not to distribute the contract goods or goods which compete with the contract goods in the reseller's principal sales area and at the reseller's level of distribution.[33]

There is no exclusive territory given to the distributor hence the reference to the reseller's principal sales area. Any restriction on goods other than the contract goods and those which compete with the contract goods will fall outside the scope of the exemption. In some cases it may be difficult to ascertain whether goods compete with the goods the subject matter of the contract or not. In cases of uncertainty an individual application for exemption under Article 85(3) could be made or the agreement could be modified to ensure that the restriction is removed. The Notice states that the reseller's principal sales area is determined by his normal business activity, which may be more closely defined in the agreement.

The supplier must not be forbidden from supplying dealers who obtain the contract goods outside this area and afterwards resell them to customers inside it, or from appointing other resellers in the area. If the supplier is any further restricted as to selling the goods into an exclusive territory then Regulation 1983/83 would be more likely to be applicable.

Reseller restrictions

By Article 1 the reseller may agree with the supplier, as seen above, to purchase goods for resale only from the supplier.

Not to manufacture or sell competing goods

The reseller may be restricted from manufacturing or distributing goods which compete with the contract goods (Article 2.2). This is the same as the corresponding permitted restriction in Regulation 1983/83, discussed above.

Article 2.3 sets out other permitted 'restrictions', which would not necessarily infringe Article 85(1) but which, for the avoidance of doubt, are included in the Regulation.

Complete ranges of goods

The distributor can be obliged to undertake to purchase complete ranges of goods and not just be able to choose those of the products offered by the supplier which he best feels able or inclined to sell.

33 Art.2.2

Minimum quantities

The distributor may be required to enter into an obligation to purchase a minimum quantity of those goods which are subject to the exclusive purchasing obligation. Where a supplier has agreed not to sell goods into the distributor's territory then minimum quantities are often seen as essential to ensure proper exploitation of the relevant territory. In the context of an exclusive purchasing arrangement, where the supplier may have a considerable number of distributors covering the same territory this restriction is not quite as justified. However, under this Regulation the supplier may, by Article 2.1, be restricted from selling the goods into the principal sales area of the distributor and minimum quanitites would clearly protect the position of the supplier there, where he has to a certain extent locked himself out of exploitation of that principal sales area.

In any event, the supplier may be investing considerable effort in the distributor, by means of spending funds on advertising on his behalf in the territory and perhaps giving him training and other assistance. The minimum quantities obligation ensures that there is some reward for such effort.

There must be no minimum quantities obligations in connection with other goods. An agreement may, for example, provide that a distributor will purchase all his requirements for nails from the supplier. That would be permitted under Regulation 1984/83. The agreement may also provide for the sale of hammers to the distributor, but not on an exclusive basis. If there were minimum quantity obligations in connection with the hammers then the block exemption may not apply. However, that would only be the case if the minimum quantities obligation itself infringes Article 85(1). This would involve an economic analysis. There is at least a risk that, where the minimum quantity specified is so large as to involve the whole output of the distributor, that it amounts in practice to a restriction of competition within Article 85(1).

Trade marks and packaging

As with Regulation 1983/83, the distributor may be obliged to sell the contract goods using certain types of packaging and presentation specified by the supplier and under certain specified trade marks.

Sales promotion

By Article 2.3 the reseller or distributor may be obliged:

> to take measures for the promotion of sales, in particular:
> – to advertise,
> – to maintain a sales network or stock of goods,
> – to provide customer and guarantee services,
> – to employ staff having specialized or technical training.

Some exclusive purchase agreements may also be selective distribution agreements (see p. 163 on 'Selective distribution').

Reciprocal exclusive purchase agreements

Article 3 provides that the block exemption cannot be used where manufacturers of identical goods or goods which are considered by users to be equivalent by reason of their characteristics, price and intended use enter into reciprocal exclusive dealing agreements in relation to those goods. Article 4 ensures that goods manufactured by undertakings connected with the supplier or reseller are counted in this connection as if manufactured by the manufacturer. Thus a company would not be able to render the block exemption applicable where there were reciprocal exclusive dealing arrangements by having manufacture done by another group company.

Such manufacturers could enter into such reciprocal arrangements in relation to other goods however, and the restriction is applicable only in connection with manufacturers. Where the suppliers merely sell goods which they have themselves purchased from a third party, there is no restriction. The block exemption applies to suppliers who do not themselves manufacture goods.

Competitor non-reciprocal exclusive purchase agreements

The Regulation will not apply where manufacturers of identical or competing (equivalent) goods (or undertakings connected with the same) enter into a one way exclusive purchase arrangement in connection with those goods where one of them has a turnover of more than 100 million ECU (£70m).[34]

Non-connected goods

The exemption will not apply where the exclusive purchasing obligation is agreed for more than one type of goods where these are neither by their nature nor according to commercial usage connected to each other. Where the arrangement involves exclusive purchasing of different types of goods then the benefit of the block exemption will be lost because of this provision in Article 3(c).

The products included for exclusive purchase must be thought of as belonging to the same range of goods. The relationship can be founded on technical (e.g., a machine, accessories and spare parts for it) or on commercial grounds (e.g. several products used for the same purpose) or on usage in the trade (different goods that are customarily offered for sale together). In the latter case, regard must be had to the usual practice at the reseller's level of distribution on the relevant market, taking into account all relevant dealers and not only particular forms of distribution.

Exclusive purchasing agreements covering goods which do not belong together can be exempted from the competition rules only by an individual decision. This means that there may be circumstances where the right to oblige the dealer to purchase a complete range of goods is restricted as it would involve the purchase of goods from outside a particular range. In cases of doubt an individual notification should be made.

Duration

The exemption will not apply, by Article 3(d), where 'the agreement is concluded for an indefinite duration or for a period of more than five years'.[35]

Many commercial agreements provide for an automatic renewal unless one of the parties gives notice to terminate the agreement. If the benefit of the block exemption is needed, such terms must not be included. The parties

34 Art. 3(b)

35 By para.39 of the Notice automatically renewable agreements are considered indefinite

should merely provide that the agreement will terminate at the end of the term and can be renegotiated.

Withdrawal of exemption

There are provisions enabling the Commission to withdraw the benefit of the exemption where there are effects which are incompatible with Article 85(3),[36] in particular where the contract goods are not subject to effective competition and access by other suppliers to the different stages of distribution in a substantial part of the common market is made difficult to a significant extent.

The Commission may also exercise its discretion to withdraw the benefit of the block exemption where the supplier without any objectively justified reason:

1. refuses to supply categories of resellers who cannot obtain the contract goods elsewhere on suitable terms or applies to them differing prices or conditions of sale;
2. applies less favourable prices or conditions of sale to resellers bound by an exclusive purchasing obligation as compared with other resellers at the same level of distribution.

A company supplying resellers who are bound by exclusive purchase obligations must therefore exercise caution whenever it proposes to refuse to supply, particularly when it holds a large share of the market and there are few alternative sources of supply. Similar caution should be exercised to ensure that resellers are treated on the same basis and there is no discrimination between them.

Application

By Article 19, the Regulation expires on 31st December 1997.

Conclusion

By Regulation 1984/83, agreements under which a reseller or dealer agrees to purchase goods only from a supplier must follow the wording of the block exemption otherwise they will be subject to individual scrutiny under Article 85(1). The supplier may only be restricted from distributing competing goods in the reseller's principal territory and at his level of distribution. The reseller may be bound to buy only goods of one sort within one range from the supplier and may be restricted from manufacturing or distributing competing goods. The agreement must last for no longer than five years.

By Article 16 of this Regulation, the Regulation will not apply where the supplier undertakes with the reseller to supply only to the reseller certain goods for resale within a certain part of the EC and the reseller agrees only to purchase these goods from the supplier. Agreements of that sort are dealt with under Regulation 1983/83, the exclusive distribution block exemption.

Figure 8.2 summarises how the block exemption operates.

UK law

There is no specific exemption for agreements containing a restriction on a purchaser requiring him to purchase all his requirements for a certain product

---

**Exclusive Purchasing Agreements under the Block Exemption Regulation
1984/83
(other than beer and petrol)**

1. Need
   (a) 2 parties only
   (b) goods
   (c) sold for resale, not to make into other products
   (d) duration 5 years or less
2. Acceptable Restrictions
   (a) on supplier
      − not to sell competing goods in reseller's principal sales area at the
        reseller's level of distribution
   (b) on reseller
      − only to purchase specified goods from supplier
      − not to make or sell competing goods
      − to purchase a complete range or minimum quantity of goods to
        which the exclusive purchase obligation relates
      − to sell under trade marks or use packaging
      − to advertise, have sales network, keep stock of goods, provide
        customer and guarantee services, employ trained staff (consider
        selective distribution rules)
3. Exemption will not apply where:
   (a) reciprocal arrangement between competitors
   (b) exclusive purchase agreement with competitor where both have a
       turnover over 100 million ECU p.a.
   (c) exclusive purchasing obligation is agreed for more than one type of
       goods which are not connected
   (d) duration longer than five years or indefinite
   (e) restrictions other than those permitted included
   (f) there is a restriction on supplier selling into defined sales area of
       reseller
4. Commission may withdraw exemption where:
   (a) no competition from similar goods
   (b) access of other suppliers to stages of distribution network is made
       difficult to significant extent
   (c) supplier refuses to supply resellers who cannot obtain goods
       elsewhere or supplier imposes differing terms on them
   (d) supplier imposes less favourable conditions on those bound by
       exclusive purchase obligations compared to those at the same level
       of distribution

Fig. 8.2

37 See Green, *op cit*, p.492 for
exclusive purchasing under UK
law generally

from one supplier, unlike the exclusive distribution exemption in Schedule 3,
paragraph 2 of the RTPA.[37] However, any agreements containing just this
restriction would not fall within the RTPA at all as the necessary precondition
of restrictions on two parties would not be present. An agreement with a
restriction on only one party would not be registrable. Nor would registration
be necessary if there were other restrictions on the distributor, such as a
restriction on selling competing goods. Again there would be no restriction on
a second party.

There may be circumstances where an exclusive purchasing agreement is registrable. The essential restriction of exclusive purchase would be a relevant restriction under the RTPA. It is a restriction as to the persons from whom goods could be acquired. It would not be a restriction which would be capable of being discounted under section 9(3) as relating only to the goods supplied. The restriction seeks to prevent the reseller from buying from other suppliers.

Any restriction on a reseller from manufacturing competing goods would also be a relevant restriction.

Where there is a restriction on the supplier, such as that within Article 2 of Regulation 1984/83 discussed above, that the supplier will not sell competing goods into the principal sales area of the reseller, the provisions of Schedule 3 paragraphs 2 or 7 may apply if the restriction on the supplier is one relating to the supply of goods of the same description to other persons. For RTPA purposes the agreement is then capable of being treated as an exclusive distribution agreement.

Other restrictions, perhaps tying the parties to certain goods or requiring that the reseller sell goods other than the contract goods at fixed prices or on certain terms and conditions, are also likely to render such agreements registrable provided there is a restriction on the supplier.

AGENCY AGREEMENTS

There is much confusion in industry as to the distinction between an agency agreement and a distribution agreement and often the term 'agency agreement' is used loosely to mean a distribution agreement and the term 'distribution agreement' is used to mean some form of commission agreement. The essential distinction, which must be made in order to undertake a proper competition law analysis of agreements of this sort, is that an agency agreement appoints a company or individual as agent to make sales on behalf of the supplier. The agent does not trade on his own account. The contracts which he arranges are contracts between the supplier and the customer procured by the agent.[38]

From a general competition law perspective, terms of an agreement between an agent and his principal are unlikely to be as restrictive of competition as those between a distributor and his supplier as the acts of an agent from a legal point of view are deemed to be those of his principal. Anti-competitive effects are unlikely to flow from such arrangements.

EC law

Agency agreements may be caught by Article 85(1) notwithstanding the comments above, and the position was clarified by the Commission to a certain extent in a Notice it issued in 1962. The Notice of 24 December 1962 on Exclusive Agency Contracts made with Commercial Agents[39] is merely a notice rather than a regulation so does not have legal force and is not binding upon the Commission, as the block exemptions, being Regulations, are. However, it is a useful indication of the likely views of the Commission in various cases. Clearly, as a starting point, it is necessary to address the issue

38 See agency law generally, Bowstead on Agency, Sweet & Maxwell, 1985

39 Published in the Official Journal, 1962 at page 2921

of whether the Notice applies at all where there are restrictions on competition in an agreement, which would perhaps be the case where the agreement is an exclusive agency contract.

The Notice has been in existence since 1962 and begins, in paragraph I:

> The Commission considers that contracts made with commercial agents, in which those agents undertake, for a specified part of the territory of the Common Market:
> – to negotiate transactions on behalf of an enterprise, or
> – to conclude transactions in the name and on behalf of an enterprise, or
> – to conclude transactions in their own name and on behalf of this enterprise,
> are not covered by the prohibition laid down in Article 85, paragraph (1) of the Treaty.

This sets out the basic idea behind the Notice, but there then follow details concerning what a commercial agent is. The Notice is now considerably old and a new draft Notice[40] is in circulation, which is likely soon to supplant the old. The new Notice takes account of case law in this area since the original Notice was issued.

In *Suiker Unie and others* v *Commission,*[41] the Commission held that where an agent for the supply of sugar carries out business for third parties in the same field and was an economic entity of some substance and power the Agency Notice did not apply at all. In *Belgian Travel Agents,*[42] the Court held that Belgian travel agents were independent undertakings as they deal with a large number of tour operators, even though they may have assumed no risk under the contracts they effected for their various principals. Again the Notice did not therefore apply.

Agent

The draft Notice provides that a 'commercial agent' means:

> a self-employed intermediary who has continuing authority to negotiate or to negotiate and conclude – either in his own name or in the name of the principal – the sale or the purchase ('the transaction') of goods or services ('the product') on behalf of another person ('the principal').

In some cases it may not be clear whether an individual is acting on his own behalf or as an agent. In those circumstances the Commission will not be bound by whatever term is used to describe the individual in the contract.

Continuing relationship

It is intended that the draft Notice would only apply where the agent has a continuing relationship with the principal and not where he is engaged for a 'one-off' transaction or a 'very limited number of transactions which is set in advance'.

Express or implied

The agency can be oral or written and express or implied. The parties would therefore be able to use the Notice even where there was no formal written agreement.

40 Unpublished – Version used here 1V/484/90 – EN

41 [1976] 1 CMLR 295

42 [1989] 4 CMLR 213

Risk

In assessing whether an individual or company is an agent of another for the general purposes of English law of agency, whether the agent accepts risk in relation to his transactions can often be a decisive factor. The Commission in the draft Notice states[43] that it will disregard the general financial risk resulting from the conduct of the intermediary's undertaking such as whether he is responsible for personnel or professional liability. It will instead take into account the risk connected with the performance of the transactions negotiated by the agent, though the Commission considers that a commercial agent must not, *vis-à-vis* the customers or suppliers he is dealing with, assume primary responsibility for the performance of the transactions by his principal; conversely, profit or loss resulting from the performance of these transactions by the customers or suppliers must in the first place accrue to the principal.

43 Notice, para.4

Agency and principal activities

Some agents are agents in some parts of their business life and also act on their own account. Where an agent acts for one company both as an agent and also on his own account for other products then, by paragraph 5 of the Notice, it seems that the Commission would regard him as an independent trader for all the activity on behalf of that principal unless the independent activity were merely ancillary. Such ancillary activity may occur where the commercial agent keeps a small stock of the product covered by the agreement as his own property for demonstration purposes or for immediate delivery, but deliveries are normally made by the principal out of his own stock.

The Notice is very restrictive as to what criteria must be satisfied before the full benefits of agency status from a competition point of view are granted.

No determination of marketing strategy

The agent will not be classed as an agent for these purposes where he determines the principal's 'product and marketing strategy in respect of the product distributed under the agency agreement, thereby relegating the principal to the position of a subcontractor'.[44]

44 Para.6

Duty of loyalty

Where the agent owes a duty of loyalty not only to his principal but also to the party with whom he is negotiating on behalf of a principal, then the Notice will not apply.

Oligopolistic markets

Where the market concerned is oligopolistic and all principals deal through commercial agents, as there is a risk that systematic recourse to commercial agents may contribute to the elimination of price competition, the Notice would not apply.[45]

45 Para.6

Permitted activities under the draft Notice

Once it has been established in any particular case that an individual or company is a 'commercial agent' within the restrictive definition of the Commission's draft Notice, the agency agreement must be examined in conjunction with the Notice to ascertain whether the restrictions contained in the agreement fall within the terms of the Notice.

Stipulating prices and terms

There is no restriction on the principal giving the agent instructions such as obliging the agent to negotiate or conclude transactions on behalf of his principal only at prices and on terms and conditions provided by the principal, or subject to approval by the principal.

Any attempt by a supplier to stipulate the prices at which an independent distributor will sell the contract goods would be an infringement of Article 85(1). For an agent, however, the provision is perfectly acceptable as the contract negotiated will be between the principal and the customer.

Restrictions on transactions

The agent may be restricted as to the contents of transactions which he carries out on behalf of the principal. Restrictions as to the manner in which the agent finds customers or suppliers for the principal are acceptable too.

These restrictions are only acceptable under the Notice where the agent is integrated into the principal's distribution system. 'Integration' means where the agent has a particularly intensive link with the principal and has to dedicate himself in the field of the relevant product to this principal. Customers must not expect autonomous behaviour from such an agent.

Integration

Paragraph 10 looks at integration in more detail and this is an important element of the Notice. The Notice is divided into two sections which set out restrictions which are allowed where the agent is integrated and then those which are allowed when the necessary integration cannot be shown.

The agent may conduct activities for other principals or on his own account in other areas, but these must not interfere with the subject matter of the agency agreement. The business of the agent under the agency agreement must account for at least one third of his business activity although, where the agent is a particularly large undertaking, this share may be lower.

There will not be the necessary integration where the agent has outside interests which conflict with his duty of loyalty to the principal. This will be the case where the commercial agent carries competing product ranges, regardless of whether he does so as a commercial agent or as an independent trader. Product ranges are deemed to compete when most products, from the vantage point of the customer or supplier with whom the agent deals – taking the characteristices, price and intended use of the products together – are equivalent. Slight overlap between product ranges does not preclude the conclusion that the product ranges seen as a whole do not compete.

This may cause substantial problems for agents. It is common in many industries for agents to handle a number of clearly competing brands. Such agents would not be able to claim that they were integrated within the Notice.

This requirement of integration applies where the principal restricts the agent as to the contents of transactions to be negotiated and the manner in which he finds customers. Where integration is not present, such 'restrictions' would need to be assessed as against Article 85(1) to see if they were restrictive of competition outside of the 'protection' of the Notice. The definition of agent does not require integration in this sense. All that is required is that the agent must not deal with that principal as an independent purchaser unless such dealings are merely ancillary to the agency activities.

Where there is no integration, the agent may still be restricted as to the terms and conditions on, and prices at, which the goods may be sold-on.

Integration – restrictions

Competing goods. The Notice permits a restriction on the agent handling competing products. This does not infringe Article 85(1) and indeed fosters integration.

Exclusive appointments. The principal may be restricted from appointing another agent for the designated territory or from dealing directly with certain customers or suppliers without paying compensation to the agent. This applies only where the agent is integrated with the principal.[46]

46 Para.12

An integrated agent may be restricted from pursuing an active policy of negotiating or concluding transactions outside the designated territory. This again leads to further integration. Where the agent is not 'integrated' such restrictions are not allowed.

Absolute ban. Even where there is integration the agent must not be restricted by an absolute ban on negotiating or concluding transactions outside his territory, provided he has not pursued an active policy of soliciting such sales there.

Where the agent is only allowed to enter into transactions approved by the principal, the principal should not refuse to conclude or confirm transactions negotiated by the agent on the grounds that they originate outside the designated territory, if the agent has not actively promoted these. The conditions imposed on the agent must not have the effect of making transactions outside the designated territory impossible or unpractical.

The agent can be obliged to deliver goods only in the territory, so those seeking to parallel import would need to arrange to have the goods collected in the agent's territory if such a restriction was in place on the agent.

Where the transaction is in relation to services, prices and terms and conditions may be less favourable than those offered to customers within the designated territory 'to the extent that these differences are attributable to higher costs incurred by the principal....solely because they are located outside the designated territory.'

The agent may be paid less by his principal in connection with an unsolicited sale, for example one which has come from outside the designated territory, as the agent has not put in the same amount of effort in obtaining the sale as with a solicited sale. The reduction in compensation paid to the agent must reflect the lesser cost of the transaction, however.

Post-termination restrictions. The agent may be restricted for a period of two years after the expiry of his agreement from competing with his principal or the agent who succeeds him in the territory of the agreement.[47]

Non-integration – restrictions

An agent who is allowed to carry competing goods may act for several competing principals, and the Commission believes that there is therefore greater danger that concerted practices as to prices, territories, customers or suppliers may arise.

Commercial agency agreements with unintegrated agents will be assessed by the Commission as if the agents were independent traders. The agent may, as has been seen above, be lawfully obliged to sell the goods at prices and on terms stipulated by the principal.

Conclusion

The draft agency Notice provides useful protection for common restrictions in agency agreements where the agent is 'integrated' with the principal. For agents who carry competing goods they would be better placed entering into pure distribution arragements as then they would at least have the benefit of the distribution or purchasing block exemptions if restrictions are contemplated. Otherwise they will be caught without the benefit of any exemption and agreements will have to be specifically notified to the Commission.

The draft Notice closely follows recent case law in this area. Notwithstanding that it is still very much a draft for initial discussion, it is probably a better exposition of the Commission's views on agency agreements than the existing Notice, particularly given that Notices are not in any event binding.

Figure 8.3 illustrates the working of the draft Notice.

Council Directive of 18 December 1986 on the coordination of the laws of Member States relating to self-employed commercial agents[48] requires English law to be changed by 1 January 1994 to accord with the provisions of the general commercial law of agency contained in the Directive. This very much follows German agency law and will require compensation to be paid to agents in various cases of early termination and require certain provisions to be laid down in agency agreements.

UK law

The RTPA applies to restrictions in agreements between undertakings where there are two parties engaged in the production or supply of goods. In legal terms, often agents will not themselves supply goods as they merely procure contracts on behalf of their principal. Some agents who also supply goods on their own account may be caught, but, in relation to the agency agreement, most restrictions are likely to relate to the goods which the principal is legally supplying to his own customers, albeit procured through the agent.

The agent may be restricted as to dealing in competing goods and there may be circumstances where the principal agrees to refrain from selling goods which the agent sells on his own account. Such arrangements would fall

---

**Agency Agreements
under the Draft EC Agency Notice**

The Notice:

1. Applies to commercial agents where the following apply:
   (a) is a self-employed intermediary
   (b) has continuing authority
   (c) can make purchases on behalf of principal
   (d) doesn't carry risk
   (e) does not 'for same product' deal as agent and independent trader,
       unless is ancillary
   (f) does not decide marketing strategy or have loyalty conflict

2. Integration means
   (a) limited outside interests (no more than ⅔ of activity)
   (b) outside interests do not conflict (no competing ranges to be carried
       as agent or independant)

3. If integrated
   (a) restriction on agent handling competing goods is permitted
   (b) restriction on principal appointing agents or dealing direct in the
       exclusive territory permitted
   (c) restriction on agent from negotiating or concluding transactions
       outside the territory is permitted
   (d) agent must be free to sell outside territory where a sale is unsolicited
       – terms may vary
   (e) non-competition clause for two years after expiry of agency
       agreement is acceptable
   (f) principal may stipulate terms and prices at which agent may deal on
       his behalf

4. If not integrated
   (a) principal may stipulate terms and prices at which agent may deal on
       his behalf
   (b) other restrictions under paragraph 3 above would be examined
       under Article 85(1) and notification may be necessary

Fig. 8.3

within the RTPA. If the parties agree mutual exclusive dealing obligations then restrictions on competition would not be capable of exemption under paragraph 2 of Schedule 3 to the RTPA as an exclusive dealing agreement, because the parties in this particular contract are not selling goods to each other. In those circumstances it would be better to enter into a distributorship where the exemption is clearly available.

Investigations under the Competition Act 1980 have been initiated into the activities of agency arrangements.

CONCLUSION

Exclusive distribution, purchasing and agency agreements all have their relevant EC 'pigeon-hole', whether it be block exemption or Notice. It is necessary to have background information concerning the parties and the transaction before an analysis under those Regulations or Notices can be made.

The RTPA analysis also involves information as to whether the goods are purchased for resale in order to ascertain whether the agreement falls within the relevant exemption in Schedule 3 to the RTPA.

QUESTION

James Smith comes to you for competition law advice concerning an agreement he entered into some years ago. The Agreement is entitled 'Agency Agreement' and under it Mr Smith is granted the 'exclusive right to sell and market Thomson's Tweeds in the UK'. Mr Smith is also given the exclusive right to sell Thomson's leather buttons, but only with the tweeds. For the buttons, he earns a 'commission' of 20 per cent. With the tweeds, it seems from the agreement that he purchases them outright from Thomson's.

The agreement states that Smith may sell only Thomson's accessories with their tweeds and must use Thomson's thread when undertaking repair work. Smith is required to resell the buttons at a fixed price stipulated by the supplier and must not sell any products within the agreement outside of the UK.

1.   What additional information would you need from James Smith in order to advise him as to whether he is an 'agent' or 'distributor' in connection with each of the two products? Discuss the impact of his being in either category.
2.   Would any of the restrictions mentioned benefit from any block exemption, if relevant?
3.   Could Smith avoid the restrictions without fear of legal action? Consider both whether the restrictions are void under Article 85(1) and also the Restrictive Trade Practices Act, or are unlawful under the Resale Prices Act.

FURTHER READING

EC law

BOOKS   *Bellamy & Child*, Sweet & Maxwell, 3rd ed., 1987, chapt.6
Christou R. – *International Agency, Distribution and Licensing Agreements*, Longman, 2nd ed., 1990 (such agreements generally)
Green N. – *Commercial Agreements and Competition Law*, Graham & Trotman, 1986, chapt.10
Hawk B.E. – *US, Common Market & International Anti-trust*, Prentice Hall Law & Business, 2nd ed. – 1990 Supplement, Volume II, Vertical Arrangements – p.403
Korah V. – *Exclusive Distribution in the EEC: Regulation 67/67 Replaced*, ESC Publishing 1984
Van Bael & Bellis – *Competition Law of the EEC*, CCH Editions, 2nd ed., 1990, chapt.3
Weijer G.M. – *Commercial Agency and Distribution Agreements: Law & Practice in the Member States of the EEC*, Graham & Trotman, 1989 (such agreements generally)
Whish R. – *Competition Law*, Butterworths, 2nd ed., chapt.17

ARTICLES   Kersten H.C. – *EEC Antitrust Policy on 'Grey Market' Exports and Imports within the Common Market* (1988) 16 IBL 134
Leigh G.I.F. – *EEC Law and Selective Distribution – Recent Developments* [1986] 4 ECLR 419
Swanson M. and Brown W. – *Agency Agreements: The Commission's New Draft Notice* [1991] 2 ECLR 82

Bayer Dental OJ 1990 L35/46   **CASES**
Belgian Travel Agents [1989] 4 CMLR 213
Brasserie de Haecht S.A. v Wilkin and Another [1968] CMLR 26
Community v Fanuc Ltd & Siemens AG [1988] 4 CMLR 945
Consten & Grundig v Commission [1966] ECR 299
Gosme/Martell – DMP OJ 1991 L185/23
Metro v Commission (No.1) [1978] 2 CMLR 1
Metro-SB-Grossmarkte GmbH & Co. KG v Commission (No.2) [1987] 1 CMLR 118
Pronuptia de Paris v Schillgalis [1986] 1 CMLR 414
Suiker Unie and others v Commission [1976] 1 CMLR 295
The Community v Konica UK Ltd & Konica Europe GmbH [1988] 4 CMLR 548
Vichy OJ 1991 L75/57

Regulation 1983/83 (exclusive distribution) OJ 1983 L173/1   **REGULATIONS**
Regulation 1984/83 (exclusive purchasing) OJ 1983 L173/5

Notice on Regulations 1983/83 & 1984/83 OJ 1984 C101/2   **NOTICES**
Agency Notice OJ 1962 2921

UK law

Green N. (see above), chapt.10   **BOOKS**
Chitty on Contracts, Sweet & Maxwell, 26th ed., 1990, Para.4405 (sched.3, para.2)
Whish R. (see above), chapt.17

9

Intellectual property and franchising

Intellectual property comes in many forms, patents for inventions, secret technical information – 'know-how', trade marks and copyright, as well as design right, registered designs and many others. Business franchising is a related field, where rights to use trade marks are granted with a business package requiring that business be carried out in a particular format or way. This chapter considers such areas in connection with competition law.

Intellectual property is a form of monopoly. It is a restriction of competition. Once a work protected by copyright, such as an oil painting or a poem, is created, the owner of that right is able to prevent others from copying the work without his consent. Patents are even more of a monopoly right. The patent holder is able to prevent any use of the invention whether the 'infringer' has copied the invention from the owner or whether he has independently discovered it himself.

Competition law of both the EC and UK has recognised, however, the necessity of some protection of intellectual property rights, provided those rights are not abused. In this chapter patents, know-how, trade marks and copyright licensing and franchising are considered. There are block or general exemptions from Article 85(1) of the Treaty of Rome in the fields of patents, know-how and franchising, which are examined here.

OWNERSHIP, EXERCISE AND LIMITED LICENCES – EC

The ownership of intellectual property rights under EC law is not of itself regarded as anti-competitive. Article 222 of the Treaty of Rome provides that the Treaty will in no way prejudice the rules in Member States governing the system of property ownership. Article 36 of the Treaty of Rome specifically provides that the provisions of Articles 30–34 (which, *inter alia*, prohibit restrictions on imports, the so-called 'free movement of goods rules') shall not preclude 'the protection of industrial or commercial property'. Industrial property' is another phrase effectively synonymous with 'intellectual property'.

Whilst the holding of rights is permissible their exercise may not in all circumstances be in accordance with the EC competition rules. There is a theory known as the 'limited licence' concept, which is supported by the UK Government in its White Paper on Restrictive Practices (discussed in Chapter 7), that the grant of any rights by the owner to a licensee is not restrictive of competition. The licensee may be given restricted rights, but were it not for the licence he would have had no rights at all. The licence restrictions can therefore hardly be described as anti-competitive, unless they go beyond the subject matter of that which was licensed, for example, by tying the licensee to the purchase of other non-related goods.

The Commission does not, however, give universal recognition to this concept and the block exemptions set out those restrictions which are permitted and those which are not. Even where a block exemption does not apply a licence may not infringe Article 85(1).[1] In *Nungesser* v *Commission,*[2] the Commission held that certain exclusive licences would not infringe Article 85(1) if they were 'open', i.e. the licensee could be granted an exclusive territory, but should not have absolute territorial protection, such that parallel imports were impeded and thus third parties affected.

In most cases the block exemptions provide the best means of ensuring that licences do not infringe Article 85(1). Even where there is no block exemption, for example for trade marks, the block exemptions for other areas at least give an indication of how the Commission would regard certain restrictions for instance in the context of patent licensing,[3] and many of those principles are likely to be relevant in the trade mark context too.

ARTICLE 86

Where a company is in a dominant position, there are certain circumstances when its licensing policy may lead to its abusing that dominant position, resulting in an infringement of Article 86. Consideration was given to this in Chapter 3, to which reference should be made. A refusal to license, agreeing to license only on discriminatory terms or the acquisition of exclusive rights where a company already holds a very high percentage of a particular market are examples of potential abuses in the intellectual property field.[4]

FREE MOVEMENT OF GOODS RULES

Reference has been made above to the rules of free movement of goods under Articles 30–34 of the Treaty of Rome and Article 36, which seeks to ensure that such rules do not prevent the protection of intellectual property. In the context of all intellectual property licensing in the EC these rules cannot be ignored. The essential effect is that once goods which have been manufactured under intellectual property rights, whether patents or copyright and possibly goods produced under secret know-how or goods which have been marked by the licensor under trade marks, have been put on the market in any Member State of the EC *by the licensor or with his consent* then the intellectual property rights in relation to such goods are exhausted. The licensor cannot invoke his intellectual property rights to prevent imports of those goods into other Member States.[5]

It is open to a patent holder to choose never to license anyone with a patent. If such a patent holder holds patents in all EC Member States then it can prevent any products made in infringement of its patents being sold in the EC. However, there may be territories of the EC where patent protection cannot be taken out for particular types of product. It used to be impossible to obtain patent protection for pharmaceutical products in Italy, for example. In such countries anyone could make products which would infringe, for example, a UK patent, without the risk of infringement proceedings, provided the products were not then imported into the UK.

1 See Chapter 2 for consideration of restrictions under Art.85(1)
2 [1983] 1 CMLR 278

3 Reg. 2349/84 OJ 1985 L113/134

4 See *Volvo* v *Veng* [1989] 4 CMLR 122, *Renault* [1990] 4 CMLR 265, *Pitney Bowes* v *Francotyp-postalia* [1990] 3 CMLR 466, *Magill TV Guide* [1989] 4 CMLR 757, (and CFI – OJ 1991 L201/13) and *Tetra Pak* [1991] 4 CMLR 334

5 Except to the extent that there may be national compulsory licences or 'licences of right' statutes or where such licensing amounts to an abuse of a dominant position

However, if such a patent holder chooses not to manufacture in that territory in which there is no patent protection it could prevent imports of the product into the rest of the EC where the product is protected by patents. It was so held in *Merck v Stephar*.[6] In that case, Merck sold a drug called Moduretic in Holland, where it was patented. Merck chose to market the product in Italy, even though there was no patent protection there. An importer from Italy to Holland could not be sued by Merck for patent infringement in Holland as Merck's rights were exhausted. This would not have been the case if it had ensured it had not sold products in Italy where there was no patent protection.

It is only the actual goods put on the market in relation to which rights are exhausted in this way, not similar or competing goods. Putting products on the market in the EC does not mean that anyone can manufacture them in infringement of patent. There is merely a right to resell them anywhere in the EC.

Rights will be exhausted not only where the patent holder has placed them on the market itself in the EC, but also where goods have been placed on the market with the consent of the patent holder. Such consent is implied where the patent holder has granted a licence of the patent, i.e. a right to a third party to manufacture the goods under the patent.

In *Centrafarm v Sterling Drug*,[7] Sterling Drug Incorporated of the USA owned the patent on a drug sold under the name 'Negram'. It licensed its patents to a UK subsidiary and a subsidiary in Holland. The UK company attempted to export the drug to Holland as the drug price was much higher in Holland. It succeeded when, on an Article 177 reference, the European Court decided that the patent owner's rights in the products were exhausted as they had been put on the market with its consent in the EC, by virtue of the licensing.[8]

The matter of what comprises 'consent' for these purposes was considered further in *Pharmon v Hoechst*.[9] Hoechst owned patents in both the UK and Holland. Under provisions of English law it was obliged to grant a compulsory licence under its patents in the UK to a company, DDSA. This company sought to export the product into Holland. The European Court determined that the rights of Hoechst were not exhausted. The compulsory licence[10] was not 'consensual', but imposed by English law and Hoechst could prevent the imports into Holland.[11]

The exhaustion of rights doctrine applies equally to trade marks and copyright. In summary:

1. An intellectual property owner cannot prevent imports of products which would be an infringement of his intellectual property rights where those rights have been exhausted.
2. Rights will be exhausted where in relation to particular physical goods, the goods have been placed on the market anywhere in the EC by the owner of the rights or with his consent, i.e. once the owner sells the goods he cannot use his intellectual property rights to prevent their resale anywhere in the EC.
3. Goods placed on the market by a licensee of the rights are placed on the market with the consent of the owner of the rights.

6 [1981] 3 CMLR 1, on copyright see *Ministère Public v Tournier* [1991] 4 CMLR 248 (ECJ)

7 [1976] 1 CMLR 1, [1974] ECR 1147

8 See also *Parke, Davis v Probel* [1968] CMLR 47, [1968] ECR 55, *Sirena v Eda* [1971] CMLR 260, [1971] ECR 69 and *Deutsche Grammaphon v Metro* [1971] CMLR 631, [1971] ECR 487
9 [1985] 3 CMLR 775

10 Probably also the granting of a 'licence of right' under the Patents Act 1977
11 For forced expropriation of trade marks leading to their being in different ownership see the 'common origin' doctrine discussed below in this chapter

4. Where intellectual property protection is unavailable in an EC Member State and the owner makes sales there or his licensees do, then rights are exhausted, so that he cannot prevent export of any goods manufactured by anyone in that territory to the territories of the EC where he has intellectual property protection.

The exhaustion of rights doctrine and the free movement of goods rules help to ensure that there is a single market in the EC and assist those seeking to make parallel imports of products from one Member State to another. In the absence of such rules, patent holders would be able to carve up the EC market territorially by the use of their national intellectual property rights.

'COMMON ORIGIN' DOCTRINE

Until 17 October 1990 there was an additional limb to the exhaustion of rights doctrine. Where trade marks had a common origin, for example where one company used to own them, and their ownership in different EC Member States became split because of forced expropriation in wartime, rights were exhausted, even where the same trade mark had been applied to them, which would otherwise be an infringement of trade mark rights.

In *Van Zuylen Frères* v *Hag*,[12] the 'Hag' trade mark for decaffeinated coffee was at issue. The two companies concerned both owned 'Hag' trade marks but for different Member States, and indeed had been companies within the same group until the shares of one had been sequestrated as enemy property. Both companies were lawfully using trade marks in different EC Member States. One sought to market goods in the territory of the other under the trade mark and the case determined that as the trade marks had had a common origin the trade mark owner could not rely on his rights to prevent imports under free movement of goods principles. The fact that the trade marks had parted from the same ownership without any consent from the owner of the mark did not prevent the rights being exhausted.

In an unusual partial reversal of earlier law, in *S.A. CNL – Sucal N.V.* v *Hag G.F. A.G.*,[13] the European Court held that where marks had come under different ownership without consent then the exhaustion of rights principle would not apply. This is logical, and consistent with the exhaustion of rights principles generally, but appears to leave common origin principles in place where the mark was voluntarily given up or assigned in one territory. For such voluntary assignments the owner of the mark would still be at risk of being unable to prevent parallel imports because the rights would have been exhausted even if the division of ownership of identical trade marks had taken place many decades before.

12 [1979] 2 CMLR 127

13 [1990] 3 CMLR 571

PATENT LICENSING – EC LAW

Granting permission to a licensee to manufacture products under specified patents of a licensor would not of itself infringe Article 85. However, most licensors will wish to ensure that the licensee has a restricted licence of some sort. Although in the field of intellectual property there is legislation for harmonisation of some national intellectual property rights, many such rights are still purely national. A licensor may choose to license a UK licensee to use his UK patent to manufacture in the UK and grant a licence under his French patent for manufacture in France.

Most licences contain restrictions of some sort and all such licences must be drafted having regard to Regulation No. 2349/84 of 23 July 1984 on the application of Article 85(3) of the Treaty to certain categories of patent licensing agreements.[14] This Patent Licence Block Exemption is complex and detailed, running to 24 pages in its published form and only a brief summary can be attempted here. Even where the block exemption does not apply because of the particular circumstances of the case, parties are well advised to follow its form as far as possible, as it gives a good indication of the Commission's views on many restrictive clauses in such agreements. Since 1 April 1989 a parallel Regulation No. 556/89[15] has applied to know-how licensing agreements. It may be more advantageous to bring an agreement within 556/89 than 2349/84 and there is some scope for choice between the two where an agreement involves both patents and know-how.

'Patents'

The Patent Licence Block Exemption, No. 2349/84, applies to patent licensing agreements and agreements combining the licensing of patents and the communication of know-how. The Regulation applies to licences issued in respect of national patents of EC Member States, Community patents or European patents granted by Member States and also licences of utility models and applications for registration of utility models, or 'certificats d'utilité' and 'certificats d'addition' and their applications issued in France.[16]

The Regulation also applies to licences in respect of inventions for which patent applications were made within one year from the date of entry into the agreement. Patents take some considerable time from application to grant, often years, and therefore this provision is useful to ensure that the protection of the block exemption is available for licences of applications as well as granted patents.

Assignments

The Regulation may also apply to assignments of patents. It is possible to exploit rights to a patent in two different ways. Rights to use the patent for the purposes of manufacture can be granted, i.e. a licence or permission to use. Secondly, the owner of a patent may choose to dispose of the right altogether by selling the patent. It would cease to be his patent and the change in ownership would be registered at the relevant patent office. This is an assignment.

In most cases assignments are not anti-competitive, and the solution to a situation where there are restrictions on the use of rights which the parties wish to impose upon themselves, but which do not fall within the block exemption, may be to sell the rights altogether to the other party so that the original owner of the rights is left with no rights whatsoever in relation to what was his own technology. Competition law rarely interferes to prevent such a disposal of rights, although clearly ancillary restraints on competition agreed between the parties in such agreements would be subject to scrutiny by the competition authorities in the usual way.

14 Published in the Official Journal at No L219/15, 16 August 1984

15 OJ 1989 L61/1

16 Rec.4 & Art.10

Where the risk associated with exploitation of rights remains with the assignor the block exemption may apply. It is rare, however, that an assignment would involve the reservation of such rights by the assignor of the rights. By Article 11, the Regulation also applies to assignments where the sum payable is dependent on the turnover of the assignee in respect of the patented products or the quantity of such products manufactured.

Sub-licences

A sub-licence is a licence further down the chain of ownership. If the owner of a right grants permission to another to use it that is a licence or head licence, a primary grant. The licensee who has been granted that right may also be given rights to license the rights himself, i.e. to sub-license the rights. Sub-licences are also covered by the block exemption.[17]

17 Art.11

Know-how

A bare patent licence is a practical rarity. In many cases what is as important to a potential manufacturer licensee is that he is able to obtain access through a licence of technical know-how, secret information, or the information necessary properly to exploit the invention. The licensor may supply secret technical information and be available over the telephone to answer queries concerning the manufacture of the product. He may have years of practical experience upon which the licensee could draw and may even send a team of experts out to assist the licensee and give training to the staff of the licensee.

The block exemption therefore recognises this practical reality and allows agreements which involve the licensing of both patents and know-how to be exempted under Regulation 2349/84. Such agreements are known as mixed agreements. Know-how is covered only in so far as the licensed patents are necessary for achieving the objects of the licensed technology and as long as at least one of the licensed patents remains in force.[18]

18 Rec.9

The know-how must be secret and must permit a better exploitation of the licensed patents. This therefore means that in any particular case it is necessary to make a judgment as to which of the patents or the know-how is the most important, in order to determine which block exemption will apply.

Trade marks

A patent licence may also include a licence of trade marks. Perhaps the licensee wishes to manufacture the goods under the patents and sell them using the trade marks of the licensor. The Regulation applies to patent licensing agreements containing ancillary provisions relating to trade marks, subject to ensuring that the trade mark licence is not used to extend the effects of the patent licence beyond the life of the patents.[19]

19 Rec.10

The word to note here is 'ancillary'. The trade mark licensing provisions must be an ancillary part of the agreement. There is no trade mark licence block exemption at all and there may be circumstances when it is desirable to license patents with trade marks in order to benefit from the patent licence block exemption. However, this can only be achieved where the patents genuinely are the principal subject matter of the licence.

Two parties

By Article 1 of the Regulation there must only be two parties to the agreement in relation to which the parties wish to obtain the benefit of the exemption. Agreements between three or more companies would not be able to benefit from the exemption.

The form of the Regulation

The Regulation sets out provisions in patent licences which are exempted in Article 1. Article 2 contains a list of provisions which are stated, almost for the avoidance of doubt, as not generally being restrictive of competition. Article 2 states restrictions which will render the exemption inapplicable – the so called 'black-list'.

Permitted restrictions – licensor restrictions

Exclusive grant

The licensor may be restricted from licensing any other company or person in a particular territory with the licensed invention; the territory may cover all or part of the common market[20] and the Regulation applies even where the relevant territory extends beyond the EC and includes other territories.

The licensor is therefore allowed to cut himself out of the territory granted to the licensee altogether. However, the restriction, in order to be exempted under the Regulation, must only last for as long as one of the licensed patents is in force. Once there is no patent protection it would be anti-competitive to prevent the licensor from undertaking an activity which because of the expiry of the patent rights it would be perfectly legitimate for any third party to undertake. It is preferable to ensure that the licence agreement states that its duration is limited in that way, or specifies a fixed period of years which does not extend beyond the expiry date of the last of the licensed patents. Patents, unlike trade marks, are not infinitely renewable and only give the patent owner a limited number of years protection, which varies throughout the EC and may be of the order of 20 years. After that period the patent will expire.

Article 1.1.2 of the Regulation permits a restriction on the licensor himself exploiting the invention in that territory, but again only as long as there are licensed patents in force. Such exclusive licences are not incompatible with Article 85(1) where:

> they are concerned with the introduction and protection of a new technology in the licensed territory, by reason of the scale of research which has been undertaken and of the risk that is involved in manufacturing and marketing a product which is unfamiliar to users in the licensed territory at the time the agreement is made.[21]

21 Rec.11

New processes for manufacturing products which have been in existence for a long time are also likely to be treated in the same way. In all other cases, the Commission could hold such exclusive licensing arrangements to be contrary to Article 85(1) and therefore the Regulation but, because of the likely improvement to the production of goods and the promotion of technical progress associated with such exclusivity, grant them exemption.

The Commission held back the issue of Regulation 2349/84 until the decision in the *Nungesser (Maize Seed)*[22] case was available. The Court in this

22 [1983] 1 CMLR 278, [1982] ECR 2015

case determined that where an exclusive licence was 'open' and there were no restrictions on third parties, i.e. parallel importers, it would not infringe Article 85(1) at all where new technology was being introduced. This principle was followed in the Regulation. Now that the block exemption is available this is the best indicator of the types of exclusivity restriction on the licensor which would be permissible.

Informing licensee of developments

Article 2, which sets out provisions which may not necessarily infringe Article 85(1), permits an obligation on the licensor to inform the licensee of any experience gained in exploiting the technology and requiring the licensor to grant to the licensee a licence of such improvements.

Most favoured licensee clauses

Also permited (by Article 2.1.11) is an obligation on the licensor to grant the licensee any more favourable terms that the licensor may grant any other company after the agreement is entered into. Such clauses are common and are often called 'a most favoured customer clause'. The licensee is assured that he is obtaining the best terms available.

Permitted restrictions – licensee restrictions

Exclusive grant

The licensee can be restricted from exploiting the licensed invention in territories within the EC which are reserved to the licensor 'in so far and as long as the patented product is protected in those territories by parallel patents' (Article 1.1.3). This is the licensee equivalent of Article 1.1 which permits a restriction on the licensor exploiting the technology in the territory reserved to the licensee. By Recital 12, parallel patents are taken to mean patents covering the same invention. This permits a restriction on both what are known as 'passive' and 'active' sales – i.e. the licensee can be prevented from making any sales into the territory of the licensor. However, the position is not as free in relation to territories reserved to other licensees, rather than the licensor himself.

Article 1.1.4 permits a restriction on the licensee manufacturing or using the licensed product or using the patented process or the know-how in territories of the EC 'which are licensed to other licensees, in so far and as long as the licensed product is protected in those territories by parallel patents'.

As well as permitting a restriction on the licensee using or manufacturing the product in territories licensed to other licensees, the licence may restrict the licensee from pursuing an active policy of putting the licensed product on such markets and in particular restrain the licensee from engaging in advertising specifically aimed at those territories or establishing any branch or maintaining any distribution depot there, provided there are parallel patents in those territories (Article 1.1.5).

An absolute ban on exports outside the licensed territory into territories of other licensees is permitted, under Article 1.1.6, for a period not exceeding five years from the date when the product is first put on the market within the common market by the licensor or one of his licensees, in so far as and for as long as the product is protected in these territories by parallel patents. This is quite a limited provision. Where old technology is involved it may not apply at all. Once the product has been sold by the licensor or one of his other licensees anywhere in the EC for more than five years an absolute ban on exports by the licensee from his exclusive territory to the territory of other licensees is not permitted. A limited restriction under Article 1.1.5 can always be added however, so that the licensee may not actively market the products outside his territory.

If a wise consumer discovers that he can purchase the licensed products more cheaply in one particular territory of the EC and asks the licensee to supply those goods to him across EC borders, then the licence agreement between the parties cannot prevent such an unsolicited sale. In *Windsurfing International* v *Commission,*[23] the Court held that a provision in a patent licence which allowed the licensor to terminate the agreement forthwith if the licensee began to manufacture the products in territories not protected by the patent was contrary to Article 85(1). The licensee must be free to manufacture in territories where there is no patent protection.

23 [1986] ECR 611

Black-listed exclusivity provisions

In this context the provisions black-listed by Article 3.11 must be considered. By those provisions a licence agreement will not gain the benefit of the block exemption where one or both parties to the agreement is obliged, without any objectively justified reason, to refuse to meet demand from users or resellers in their respective territories who would market products in other territories within the common market.[24]

24 Note that the Regulation, by Art.9.4, allows the Commission to withdraw the benefit of the Regulation if the licensee refuses to meet unsolicited demand from users or resellers in other licensees' territories

Where a company or individual in the territory of the licensee wishes to purchase the products, the licensee must be free under the agreement to supply that company even if he knows that the purchaser wishes to market the products in another EC country.

Also black-listed in the same way is any requirement in the licence that the parties must make it difficult for users or resellers to obtain the products from other resellers within the common market, and, in particular, that they must exercise industrial or commercial property rights or take measures so as to prevent users or resellers from obtaining outside, or from putting on the market in, the licensed territory products which have been lawfully put on the market within the common market by the patentee or with his consent.

Therefore, even where there are no territories licensed to other licensees and restrictions on export relate only to the territory of the licensor, or where the product was only put on the market within the last five years, the licensee must supply goods to companies within his territory even where they will export the goods, unless there is an objectively justified reason for refusing to supply. A ban on exports outside the territory would be permitted in those restricted circumstances, however.

Example

An example will illustrate the working of typical exclusivity provisions.

Company T owns a patent to manufacture a special form of lamp. The patent has ten years to run. For six years Company T has been selling the lamp in the UK. It holds patents in most EC countries and decides that it will begin exploitation abroad by appointing a French licensee.

As the technology was placed on the market in the EC Company more than five years ago T cannot in its licences provide that the French licensee shall not export the product outside the exclusive territory, which will be France, into territories licensed to any other licensees. Company T can, however, provide that the licensee in France shall not exploit the technology in such territories, as long as there are patents in the relevant territories. Here, however, there are no other licensees and Company T can provide that the licensee will not export the products to the UK whether in response to a solicited or an unsolicited order.

If an English company in France wished to purchase the products, the French licensee must be free to make the sale in France even where it knows that the goods will be exported into the UK.

Company T can agree not to license any other companies in France or exploit the invention in France for the duration of the French patent, provided that the company must meet demand within its territory even for goods which will be exported.

The exemption relating to restrictions on putting goods on the market will apply only where the licensee manufactures the product himself or has it manufactured by a connected undertaking or by a sub-contractor (Article 1.2). By Article 1.3, the exemption will also apply where the restrictions accepted are of a type which are of more limited scope than those mentioned in Article 1.

Trade mark

An obligation on the licensee to use only the licensor's trade mark to distinguish the licensed product is permitted, provided that the licensee is not prevented from identifying himself as the manufacturer of the product.[25]

25 Art.1.1.7

Article 2

Article 2 lists provisions which are not generally restrictive of competition.

Tie

The licensee can be obliged to purchase goods and services from the licensor or an undertaking designated by the licensor but only 'in so far as such products or services are necessary for a technically satisfactory exploitation of the licensed invention'. This is an important provision and in practice many companies hope to have ties of some sort in connection with their licensing agreements. The provision black-listed by Article 3.9 must be considered in this context too; it states that the block exemption will not apply where the licensee is induced at the time the agreement is entered into to accept further licences which he does not want or to agree to use patents, goods or services which he does not want, unless such patents, products or services are necessary for a technically satisfactory exploitation of the licensed invention.

The type of situation envisaged by these two provisions is where a licensor insists that the licensee purchases raw materials for incorporation into the finished product only from the licensor. The licensor may have technology held only by him in relation to which there are no other available sources on the market and which is not licensed to the licensee under the licence agreement. If this technology is not used then the finished product will be technically unsatisfactory.

In *Eurofix-Bauco* v *Hilti*,[26] it was decided that the tying of the purchase of nails to those of the nail gun, which was the subject matter of the agreement, infringed Article 85(1) and in *Windsurfing*[27] the tying together of the purchase of sail boards and rigs was also an infringement. This very much follows the law as set out in the block exemption.

26 OJ 1988 L65/9 and see also *Vaessen/Moris* [1979] 1 CMLR 511, OJ 1979 L19/32 and *Velcro-Aplix* OJ 1985 L233/22
27 [1986] ECR 611

The licensor may require that the licensee place the trade mark of the licensor on the products. If the finished products contained defective raw materials and were then sold on the open market under the licensor's trade mark his business reputation would be damaged. It is not necessary that the business reputation of the licensor be damaged, however, merely that the 'tie' is necessary for a technically satisfactory exploitation of the licensed product.

Minimum royalties

An obligation on a licensee to pay a minimum amount of money under the licence agreement is permitted.[28] Payment in connection with a licence agreement is usually a percentage of the value of sales which the licensee makes out of selling the product manufactured under the licence. This is called a 'royalty' and many licensors wish to ensure that they will have a certain fixed amount of income from the licence. Whether or not the licensee makes sufficient sales for the royalty percentage to exceed the minimum royalty, he would be obliged to make the required minimum royalty payment, bearing any loss where sales are insufficient.

28 Art.2.1.2

Many licence agreements back-up a royalty clause with a right to inspect the financial records of the licensee in order to check that the licensee is making all the payments that he should. The Commission prefer that such inspection be undertaken by an independent third party, so that the licensor does not have access to information which he could misuse (see *Spitzer*[29]).

29 Commission's 12th Competition Report, 1976

Field of use restrictions

A field of use restriction is a provision whereby the licensee is obliged to use the licensed technology only within a certain technological field of use. The block exemption in Article 2.1.3 permits a restriction that the licensed invention be exploited in only one or more technical fields of application covered by the licensed patent.

In practice, it can be difficult to determine what is meant by a technical field of application. Using the lamp example given above, if the technology which is licensed ensures a certain type of light or brilliancy and could be used in many fields other than lighting, to what extent can the licensee be restricted? Domestic lighting may itself be a technical field of use and therefore a restriction to that field would be acceptable under Article 2.1.3.

In *Windsurfing*[30] the Court condemned a field of use restriction that the windsurfer rig should only be used with particular types of sailboard. The

30 [1986] ECR 611

uses were held to be within the same technical field of application as the construction of sailboards for use on water.

Post-termination exploitation

A restriction on exploitation of the invention after the agreement between the parties has terminated is permitted provided that the patent is still in force.[31] If the patent has expired then such a provision would restrict a licensee from undertaking an activity which could be undertaken perfectly legitimately by any third party company; this would be contrary to Article 85(1), as was held in *Ottung* v *Klee & Weilbach A/S*.[32] As there was no longer a patent in force, such manufacture after expiry would clearly not be an infringement of the patent rights.

Article 3.2 black-lists a provision whereby the licence agreement is automatically prolonged beyond the expiry of the patents existing at the time the agreement was entered into by the inclusion subsequently of new patents, unless either party has the right to terminate the agreement at least annually after the expiry of the patents existing at the time of entry into the agreement. In *Ottung* v *Klee & Weilbach A/S*, the European Court held that an obligation to pay royalties after the expiry of the patent but whilst the agreement between the parties subsisted was not caught by Article 85(1) provided the licensee may freely terminate the agreement on reasonable notice.

The licensor is entitled to charge royalties for the know-how as long as the know-how is still secret, i.e. not in the public domain, even if this is after the expiry of the patents.

Sub-licences and assignments

The licensor may provide that the licensee may not sub-license his rights to use the patent to another company or assign the benefit of the agreement altogether to another company.[33]

Patentee's name

By Article 2.1.6, the licensee can be obliged to mark the licensed products with an indication of the name of the patentee, i.e. in most cases the licensor, the licensed patent or the patent licensing agreement. Many goods are marked 'manufactured under licence from X Co' or 'under licence of patent No. 12345'.

Confidentiality

Patents become published public knowledge. In some cases companies deliberately choose not to patent inventions which they could not afford to protect through legal action. Much more valuable to them is the secrecy of their know-how. The block exemption permits an obligation on the licensee not to divulge the know-how even after the agreement has expired.[34]

Infringements

By Article 2.1.8, the licensor can require the licensee to inform him of any infringement of the patent of which he becomes aware, require the licensee to

31 Art.2.1.4

32 [1990] 4 CMLR 915

33 Art.2.1.5

34 Art.2.1.7

take legal action against an infringer and require him to assist the licensor in any legal action against an infringer. These obligations must be without prejudice to the licensee's right to challenge the validity of the patent, a black-listed provision discussed below.

Quality

A requirement for the licensee to observe minimum quality specifications is acceptable in connection with the licensed product provided that the specifications are necessary to a technically satisfactory exploitation of the licensed invention, as is a requirement to allow the licensor to carry out related checks.[35]

Communication of experience

The parties may be obliged to communicate to each other improvements to the licensed technology which they devise and to grant each other licences of such improvements and new applications, provided that such communication or licence is non-exclusive.[36]

The parallel black-listed provision is Article 3.8. The licence must not contain a provision whereby the licensee is obliged to assign wholly or in part to the licensor rights in or to patents for improvements or for new applications of the licensed patents. Such a requirement is regarded by the Commission as giving the licensor an unjusified commercial advantage.[37]

Most favoured customer

A clause requiring the licensor to grant to the licensee any better terms offered subsequently to other licensees is permitted.[38]

No Article 1 restrictions

Even where a licence contains none of the restrictive provisions exempted under Article 1, the parties are entitled to use the block exemption where their agreement contains provisions which fall within Article 2.[39] Again restrictions which are of more limited scope than those set out in Article 2.1 are able to benefit from the exemption.

The black list

Article 3 sets out those provisions in a patent licence which render the block exemption inapplicable and which would be very unlikely to benefit from individual exemption following a specific notification. Some of these have been mentioned in the appropriate context above.

No challenge clauses

There must be no restriction on the licensee challenging the validity of the licensed patents. This means that the licensee must remain free to bring an action before the courts alleging that the patents are invalid. Article 3.1 also outlaws any clause restricting a challenge to the validity of any other industrial or commercial property rights. All the rights must be in the EC and belong to the licensor or undertakings connected with him.

There is an important caveat to this provision. The provision is 'without

35 Art 2.1.9

36 Art.2.1.10

37 Rec.24

38 Art.2.1.11

39 Art.2.2

prejudice to the right of the licensor to terminate the licensing agreement in the event of such a challenge'. The agreement can therefore provide in the termination provision that the licensor may terminate the agreement if the licensee challenges the patents. The no-challenge provision was confirmed as unacceptable by the Court in *Windsurfing*.[40]

In *Bayer v Süllhöfer*,[41] the Court held that a no-challenge provision in a free licence, such as one to settle litigation where the licensee does not suffer through having to pay royalties, was acceptable. Most no- challenge clauses in commercial patent licences would, however, contravene Article 85(1).

Duration beyond patents' life

Article 3.2 black-lists a provision extending the agreement beyond the life of the patents as discussed above (exploitation after termination).

It is permissible to spread the payments under the licence over a period extending beyond the life of the patents where this is to make payment easier for the licensee who could not afford to pay the larger sums sooner.

Non-competition restrictions

Where one party is restricted from competing with the other, or an undertaking connected with the other, or with other undertakings in the common market in respect of research and development, manufacture, use or sale the provision will be black-listed and void under Article 85(1).[42] This provision though is without prejudice to Article 1 (which permits limited export bans and territorial restriction – discussed above). It is also 'without prejudice to an obligation on the licensee to use his best endeavours to exploit the licensed invention'.

It will therefore not be possible to provide that the licensee must not handle goods which compete with those of the licensor, but a provision that the licensee must use his best endeavours to exploit the licensed technology is acceptable. Best endeavours has been held by the courts to be a very strong obligation, often tantamount to doing all within one's powers, whatever the cost, to achieve the particular objective.

It may be possible for a licensee to carry two competing ranges, but it would be for the courts to decide in any particular case whether sufficient effort had been put into the licensed products.

Royalties on non-patented products

Article 3.4 black-lists clauses requiring the licensee to pay royalties on products which are not entirely or partially patented or manufactured by means of the patented process, or for use of the know-how when it has fallen into the public domain otherwise than through the fault of the licensee or an undertaking connected with him.

Limitation on quantities

There can be no restriction on the quantity of licensed products which the licensee can manufacture or sell under the licence agreement. The number of operations exploiting the licensed invention which the licensee may carry out must not be subject to limitation.[43]

40 [1986] ECR 611

41 [1990] 4 CMLR 182. This was a case turning on its facts and not all settlement agreements avoid Article 85(1)

42 Art.3.3

43 Art.3.5

Pricing

As would be expected, by Article 3.6, any attempt to control the prices, components of prices or discounts for the licensed products is outlawed.

Customer restrictions

No restriction must be imposed on the licensee as to the customers which he may serve. In particular (by Article 3.7), there must be no prohibition on supplying certain classes of user, employing certain forms of distribution or, with the aim or sharing customers, using certain types of packaging for the products. This is subject to it being permissible to require the licensee to apply certain trade marks to the goods and apply the licensor's name or patent number on the goods.

In practice, it can be difficult to distinguish a restriction on the field of use to which technology can be put (which is a permitted restriction) and a restriction as to the customers which may be served. If the customers concerned all carry on business in a particular area, it may be possible to license the licensee for a field of use which excludes that area.

Assignments

Article 3.8, discussed above (communication of improvements), black-lists any obligation on the licensee to assign improvements to the licensor.

Ties

Any inducement of the licensee to accept goods which he does not want, unless the use of the goods are necessary to the technically satisfactory exploitation of the licensed patent, is outlawed by Article 3.9 (discussed above in connection with quality specifications).

Exclusivity

Export bans other than those permitted under Article 1 are expressly outlawed in Articles 3.10 and 3.11, discussed above.

Opposition procedure

Article 4 contains a procedure whereby companies can notify to the Commission patent licences which contain no black-listed provisions, but which contain restrictions which are not specifically exempted in Articles 1 and 2. If there is no opposition to the notification from the Commission within six months then the agreement will be exempted.

Where the normal notification is made,[44] the parties have no assurance from the Commission that their agreement is enforceable as to its restrictions until a decision or comfort letter is issued, which is usually several years after notification is made.

Patent pools

The block exemption does not apply to agreements between members of patent pools, i.e. agreements whereby companies pool their patents for their mutual benefit.

44 See Chapter 5

Joint ventures

By Article 5.1.2, the Regulation does not apply to patent licensing agreements between competitors who hold an 'interest in a joint venture or between one of them and the joint venture, if the licensing agreements relate to the activities of the joint venture'.

Reciprocal arrangements between competitors

Article 5.1.3 provides that the exemption does not apply to agreements under which one party grants to the other a patent licence and the other, whether or not in separate agreements or through connected undertakings, gives the first party a licence under patents, trade marks or reciprocal sales rights for unprotected products or communicates know-how to him. This applies only where the parties are competitors in relation to the products covered by those agreements.

Where there are no territorial restrictions within the EC on the parties to such arrangements which relate to the manufacture, use or putting on the market of products covered by the agreements, or on the use of the licensed processes, such reciprocal competitor licences could be exempted by the Regulation.[45]

45 Art.5.2

Plant breeder's rights

The exemption does not apply to the species of intellectual property known as 'plant breeders' rights', i.e. rights usually enshrined in legislation as to plant varieties.

Withdrawal of exemption

The Commission reserves the right to withdraw the exemption where there are effects in a particular case which are incompatible with Article 85(3) and in particular where a number of circumstances obtain (Article 9), including:

1. where there is no effective competition for the licensed process in the territory from other goods or services;
2. where the licensor has no right to terminate the agreement five years after it is entered into, and annually thereafter, where the licensee fails to exploit the patent properly or adequately without having a legitimate reason for such failure;
3. where the parties refuse to meet demand from resellers who would market the products in other EC territories or where the parties impede parallel importers.

Duration

Regulation 2349/84 applies until 31st December 1994, whereupon it is likely to be renewed in modified form.

Figure 9.1 summarises Regulation 2349/84.

**Patent Licensing Agreements under the Block Exemption Regulation
2349/84**

1. Need
    (a) 2 parties only
    (b) licence of patents, know-how/trade marks ancillary only

2. Exempted Restrictions – Article 1
    (a) on licensor
        – not to license others in territory as long as patents in force
        – not to exploit licensed invention itself in the territory
    (b) on licensee
        – not to exploit licensed invention in licensor's territory as long as
           patents in force
        – not to manufacture or use in other licensees' territories
        – not actively to sell in other licensees' territories
        – not to sell at all into other licensees' territories even in response to
           an unsolicited order where product only been on the market for no
           longer than 5 years in EC
        – obligation to use trade mark

3. Non-restrictive provisions – Article 2
    – licensee to buy goods from licensor, if necessary for technically
       satisfactory exploitation of technology
    – minimum royalties
    – restriction on exploitation to one field of use
    – restriction on exploitation after termination if patents still in force
    – restriction on sub-licensing and assignment
    – obligation to mark product with patentee's name
    – obligation to keep know-how secret even after termination of licence
    – obligation to inform licensor of infringements of patent, to take legal
       action and assist licensor
    – obligation to observe minimum quality specifications, if technically
       necessary
    – mutual exchange of information and licensing of improvements
    – most favoured licensee clauses

4. Black-listed provisions – Article 3
    – no challenge clauses
    – licence continues after patents expire
    – restrictions on competition
    – royalties on non-patented products
    – limitation on quantity of products which licensee may sell or make
    – restrictions as to price
    – restrictions as to customers
    – licensee obliged to assign improvements
    – tie to goods not technically necessary
    – export restriction to other licensees' territories after said 5 year period
    – restriction on sales in the territory where destination of goods is
       outside territory
    – making matters difficult for parallel importers

Fig. 9.1

> 5.　Opposition procedure for notification available
>
> 6.　Does not apply to:
> - patent pools
> - joint ventures with competitors
> - competitor reciprocal licences
> - licensing of plant breeders' rights

Fig. 9.1 (*cont.*)

PATENT LICENSING – UK LAW

Even where an agreement falls within the patent licence block exemption, it may still need to be registered at the Office of Fair Trading under the Restrictive Trade Practices Act 1976, which has been discussed in earlier chapters.

Schedule 3, paragraph 5 of the RTPA contains an exemption for patent licence agreements from the provisions of the RTPA. The Act will only apply in the first place if there are restrictions on two parties and there must be two parties to the agreement who are carrying on business in this country.

Unlike the position under EC law where there is a long list of acceptable and unacceptable provisions, the general provisions of the RTPA apply. In all cases, all the provisions of the agreement will need to be examined against the lists of restrictions in sections 6 and 11 of the RTPA in order to determine whether the agreement is registrable.

The Schedule 3, paragraph 5 exemption

The exemption exempts patent and patent application licences (and registered design licences) and assignments. It only applies, however, where the only restrictions are in respect of:

(a)　the invention to which the patent or application for a patent relates, or articles made by the use of that invention; or

(b)　articles in respect of which the design is or is proposed to be registered and to which it is applied;

The exemption applies to agreements which are otherwise registrable under either the goods or the services provisions of the RTPA.

This provision can be useful, but, if there is any restriction which is not in respect of the invention or goods made using it, then the exemption will not be available. Restrictions on dealing in competing goods would not be covered and, if there were a restriction of that sort on one party and other restrictions exempted under Schedule 3, the exemption would not apply.

A restriction on the quantity of products manufactured under the patents which the licensee could sell may be exempted under this provision as may a restriction on the customers who may be served. However, there is an argument, which was accepted in the *Ravenseft*[46] case (discussed elsewhere), that intellectual property licences are not restrictive at all as they involve the granting of licences and giving rights to a licensee which, but for the licence,

46 [1978] QB 52, [1977] ICR 136, [1977] 2 WLR 432 and see also *Automatic Telephone & Electric Co. Ltd* v *Registrar of Restrictive Trading Agreements* [1964] 1 WLR 795, where the predecessor of Sch.3, para.5 was considered, which case is cited in *Re Cadbury Schweppes Ltd & J. Lyons & Co. Ltd's Agreement* [1975] 1 WLR 1018

the licensee would not have had at all. Licensee 'restrictions' may therefore not be 'relevant restrictions' under the RTPA.

In its Guide 'Restrictive Trade Practices: Provisions of the Restrictive Trade Practices Act'[47] the OFT states:

7 Office of Fair Trading 990, p.16 and see also the irector's 1976 Report, p.36 nd Green (Further Reading) .8 /

Extension of the *Ravenseft* Principle

On the basis of the *Ravenseft* case, the OFT takes the view that a party to an agreement does not accept a restriction within the meaning of the Act where:

- it accepts a 'restriction' on its power to grant a licence or a franchise (although any accompanying restriction on the supply of goods or services could fall within the terms of the Act);
- it accepts a 'restriction' which simply limits rights it would not have without the agreement (this is called the *open door* principle);
- it accepts, by way of an apparent 'restriction', any obligation which is imposed on it by law.

It would follow from this that the OFT's view is that any restriction on a licensor preventing the licensor licensing his technology to other licensees within an exclusive territory or at all would not be regarded as restrictive, but any clause stating that he must not sell the products made using the technology may well be. Likewise, restrictions on a licensee, as discussed above, only in relation to the licensed technology will not be caught by the RTPA, but tie-ins and non-compete clauses would. Obligations of confidentiality, which may be present at law as well as through the terms of most licences, could be excluded from the RTPA by this statement.

However, this is merely the OFT view. In most intellectual property licences there is not much risk of a reference to the Restrictive Practices Court. The greater risk is that the licensee or licensor subsequently avoids the restrictions on the grounds that they are void. The Court may not necessarily agree with the OFT in its interpretation of the law, particularly since the legislature saw fit to include specific exemptions for certain types of patent licences but not all, which exemption seems unnecessary if the OFT is correct in its view.

The cheap and simple precaution of a fail-safe registration in cases of doubt is recommended.

Section 44 of the Patents Act 1977

Under section 44 of the Patents Act 1977, clauses are void in patent licences where the licensee is obliged to purchase from the licensor or his nominee 'anything other than the product which is the patented invention' as are clauses forbidding the licensee from taking competing technology, whether patented or not. Under the block exemption, the licensor can oblige the licensee to take other products where they are necessary to exploit the product in a technically satisfactory way. Here the legislative provisions diverge. There is an exemption under the Patents Act where the licensor is prepared to grant the licence without the clause. The agreement must allow the parties to escape the tie on three months' notice and on payment of compensation.

This provision can be easily overlooked and should always be considered in drafting a patent licence.

KNOW-HOW LICENSING – EC LAW

The principles in connection with the licensing of know-how under EC competition law are similar to those in relation to patent licensing. In the absence of a block exemption many typical licence agreements would be void as to their restrictions.

In *Rich Products/Jus-rol,*[48] Rich Products authorised Jus-rol to use its know-how for the manufacture of frozen yeast dough products. The Commission determined that the exclusive right granted to Jus-rol to manufacture this frozen yeast dough in the UK was anti-competitive, as was the obligation on Jus-rol not to manufacture the licensed product outside the UK. However, the Commission exempted those provisions under Article 85(3), on the basis that the exclusive manufacturing right contributed to economic and technical progress.

In *Boussois/Interpane,*[49] the German firm of Interpane licensed the French firm of Boussois with a body of technical information for coat glass. Boussois was granted exclusive rights to manufacture and sell products in France for five years. After two years Interpane could compete in France. Other licensees were prohibited from selling whether actively or passively into France for five years. The exclusivity was not limited to the contractual relationship between the parties and so was not merely an 'open' exclusive licence which might not have contravened Article 85(1). Boussois' exclusive rights were therefore held contrary to Article 85(1). Boussois was prohibited from manufacturing outside France and from selling outside France into another territory in the EC for which Interpane subsequently might appoint an exclusive licensee. This was also held to be anti-competitive.

As the know-how element of the licence was so important, the fact that there was also some patent licensing did not mean that the parties could use Regulation 2349/84. When the decision was reached in 1986 there was no know-how licensing block exemption. The restrictions were, however, exempted under Article 85(3).

'Know-how'

From 1 April 1989, Commission Regulation (EC) No 556/89 of 30 November 1988 on the application of Article 85(3) of the Treaty to certain categories of know-how licensing agreements[50] has applied. As with the patent exemption, the Regulation sets out in Article 1 the restrictive provisions which are exempted and in Article 2 provisions which are not generally restrictive of competition. Article 3 contains a black-list of unacceptable provisions.

The exemption only applies to know-how licences or mixed patent and know-how licences, including such agreements which include ancillary provisions relating to trade marks and other intellectual property rights. Article 1(7) contains a useful set of definitions and requires that information will only be 'know-how' where it is a 'body of technical information that is secret, substantial and identified in any appropriate form'.

The know-how is to be treated as 'secret', it must not generally be known or easily accessible. Each element does not need to be secret. To be substantial, the know-how must be of importance for a manufacturing

48 [1988] 4 CMLR 527

49 [1988] 4 CMLR 124 and *Delta Chemie/DDD* OJ 1988 L309/34

50 Published in the Official Journal at No L61/1, 11 March 1989

process or a product or service or for a development of them and trivial information is specifically excluded. The know-how must be useful and capable of improving the competitive position of the licensee.

The know-how to be 'identified' must be :

> described or recorded in such a manner as to make it possible to verify that it fulfills the criteria of secrecy and substantiality and to ensure that the licensee is not unduly restricted in his exploitation of his own technology.

The know-how must be set out in the licence agreement (something to be avoided if the agreement is also registrable under the UK RTPA and therefore will be placed on the Public Register) or recorded in any other appropriate form when the know-how is transferred or shortly thereafter. The separate document must be capable of being made available subsequently if the need arises.

'Mixed agreements'

The Regulation applies to mixed patent and know-how licences which are not exempted under the patent licence block exemption.

It applies to mixed agreements in which the licensed patents are not necessary for the achievement of the objects of the licensed technology, which contains both patented and non-patented elements.[51] This could be the case where such patents do not afford effective protection against exploitation of the technology by third parties. It will also apply to mixed agreements which, regardless of whether or not the licensed patents are necessary for the achievement of the objects of the licensed technology, contain obligations which restrict the exploitation of the relevant technology by the licensor or the licensee in Member States without patent protection. This applies only as long as such obligations are based in whole or in part on the exploitation of the licensed know-how and fulfil the other conditions set out in the Regulation.

51 Rec.2

Two parties

By Article 1, the Regulation applies only where there are just two under-takings party to the agreement.

Assignments

The Regulation applies to assignments of know-how where the risk associated with exploitation remains with the assignor, such as where payment for the assignment is based on sales, as would be the case where royalty payments are calculated on sales.

Exempted restrictions

Licensor not to license

A restriction on the licensor licensing other undertakings in the territory is permitted under Article 1(1)(1) for a period not exceeding ten years from the date of signature of the first licence agreement entered into by the licensor for that territory in respect of the same technology. If the first licensing agreement for the exclusive territory was more than ten years before, which is unlikely, then no restriction of this sort would be permitted.

Licensor not to exploit in the territory

By Article 1(1)(2), the licensor may himself be restricted from exploiting the licensed technology in the licensed territory, but again only for the limited ten year period stated above.

Export ban to licensor's territory

The licensee can be restricted from exploiting the licensed technology in territories of the EC reserved to the licensor for the ten year period described above.[52] These must be territories in which the licensor has not granted any licences and which he has expressly reserved to himself.[53]

Licensee to avoid other licensees' territory

The block exemption allows the licensee to be restricted from manufacturing and using the licensed product or process in territories within the EC which are licensed to other licensees, but only for a period not exceeding ten years from the date of signature of the first licence agreement entered into by the licensor within the EC in respect of the same technology.

It is important to appreciate the distinction between the ten year period which applies in relation to the first three categories of exemption in Articles 1(1)(1)–(3) and that in relation to sub-paragraphs (4) (and (5) discussed below). The ten year period for sub-paragraph (4) runs from licensing anywhere in the EC, i.e. it may well be a shorter period.

Licensee not actively to sell outside territory

The licensee can be restrained from pursuing an active policy of putting the licensed product on the market in territories of the EC licensed to other licensees for ten years from first licensing in the EC. It is also acceptable to prevent the licensee from engaging in advertising aimed at such territories and establishing a branch or maintaining a distribution depot there (Article 1(1)(5)).

Export ban to other licensees' territories

By Article 1(1)(5), there can be an absolute ban on the licensee exporting the products to territories licensed to other licensees for a period of no more than five years from the date of first signature of an EC licensing agreement for the technology.

Trade mark

The licensee can be required to use the licensor's trade mark on the product, provided the licensee is not prevented from identifying himself as the manufacturer of the goods.[55] This enables the licensor to retain his goodwill in the trade mark.

52 Art.1(1)(3)
53 Art.1(7)(12)

54 Art.1(1)(5)
55 Art.1(1)(7)

Quantity restriction

It is permissible to restrict the licensee to produce only such quantities of the goods as he needs in order to manufacture his own products and to sell the licensed product only as an integral part of, or a replacement part of, his own products or otherwise in connection with the sale of his own products. He must be free to determine the quantities required for such purposes.[56]

Parallel imports

The exemption in relation to exclusivity applies only as long as there are parallel patents in the relevant territories.[57]

Non-restrictive provisions

The following provisions are allowed as not being restrictive of competition:

1. The licensee to keep the know-how confidential even after the agreement has expired.
2. Restrictions on the licensee granting sub-licences or assigning the licence.
3. Restrictions on the licensee exploiting the know-how after termination of the agreement as long as the know-how is still secret.
4. Obligation on the licensee to communicate improvements to the licensor, provided there is no restriction on the licensee using know-how which is severable from that of the licensor or which would not involve disclosing licensor secret know-how and provided that there is mutual cross-licensing of improvements.
5. Obligation on the licensee to observe minimum quality specifications which are necessary for a technically satisfactory exploitation of the licensed technology or necessary for ensuring that the production of the licensee conforms to the quality standards that are respected by the licensor and other licensees and to allow the licensor to carry out related checks.
6. Obligations to assist with litigation and inform the licensor about infringement.
7. An obligation on the licensee to continue to pay royalties even after the know-how is publicly known, unless the licensor has been responsible for the release of the know-how into the public domain.
8. An obligation on the licensee to restrict his exploitation of the technology to one field of application or to one or more product markets.
9. An obligation to pay minimum royalties.
10. A most favoured licensee clause.
11. A requirement to mark the products with the name of the licensor.
12. An obligation on the licensee to use the licensor's know-how to construct facilities for third parties.

These provisions are very similar to those in the patent licence block exemption, but bear close scrutiny in drafting particular agreements. There are differences, for example in the field of improvements, and generally the wording is fuller and a greater variety of circumstances is covered.

56 Art.1(1)(8)

57 Art.1(4)

Black-listed provisions

Article 3 sets out those provisions which would render the block exemption inapplicable and would rarely be exempted if an individual notification were made.

Post-term use ban after know-how known

Once the know-how is in the public domain and the licence has ended there must be no restriction on the licensee using the know-how, unless the licensee is in breach of the agreement.[58] In *Rich Products/Jus-rol,*[59] the Commission had stated that such bans were acceptable except where the know-how became freely available otherwise than through the licensee or where the licensee obtained the know-how from a third party. The position now, however, is clearly that unless the licensee is in breach of the agreement there must be no post-term use ban once the information is in the public domain.

58 Art.3(1)
59 [1988] 4 CMLR 571

Assignment of improvements

The licensee may make improvements to the technology in the light of his experience in manufacturing the products. The block exemption will not apply where the licensee is obliged to assign its rights in such improvements to the licensor or grant the licensor an exclusive licence of the improvements which would prevent the licensee using his improvements to the extent that they are severable from the know-how. In many cases improvements will merely be just that – an 'improvement' to the licensed technology and have little or no independent utility. Where the improvements are not severable or they would involve divulging the licensor's know-how, the licensee can be restricted from licensing such improvements.

Where the agreement contains a restriction on the licensee from using the know-how after termination of the agreement, it is forbidden to provide for even a non-exclusive licence to the licensor of the licensee's improvements, even on a reciprocal basis where the improvements are not severable from the licensor's know-how, if the licensor's right to use the improvements is longer than the licensee's right to use the licensor's know-how.[60]

60 Art.3(2)

Ties

Article 3(3) black-lists an obligation on the licensee to accept quality specifications which he does not want or further licences or goods or services which he does not want, unless they are technically necessary for a satisfactory exploitation of the licensed technology or for ensuring that the production of the licensee conforms to the quality standards that are expected by the licensor and other licensees.

No-challenge

The licensee must not be prohibited from challenging the secrecy of the licensed know-how or the validity of the licensed patents within the EC belonging to the licensor or undertakings connected with the licensor. As under the patent licence block exemption the licensor can provide that the agreement will terminate if there is such a challenge (Article 3(4)).

Royalties on unconnected goods

Article 3(5) black-lists a requirement to pay royalties on products which are not in whole or in part produced using the licensed technology or a requirement where royalties are charged for the use of know-how which is in the public domain through action by the licensor or a company connected with him.

Customer restrictions

Neither party can be restricted as to the customers which he can serve, except as under the permitted exclusivity provisions discussed above (Article 3(6)).

Quantity restrictions

Any restriction on either party as to the quantity of licensed products which he can manufacture or sell is forbidden under Article 3(7).

Pricing

Article 3(8) black-lists any restriction on either licensor or licensee as to the prices which they charge for the licensed products.

Non-competition restrictions

Neither party must be restricted from competing with the other in the manufacture of competing products or in research or development or sale of competing products (Article 3(9)), although it is permissible to place an obligation on the licensee to use his best endeavours to exploit the licensed technology.

There is an additional right which is allowed to the licensor which is not found in the patent licence block exemption. The licensor can provide in the licence agreement that the exclusivity granted to the licensee may be terminated and no new improvements passed on to the licensee where the licensee engages in competing activities. The licensor can require the licensee to prove that he is not using the licensed technology for the production of goods and services other than those for which he is licensed.

Duration extended by improvements

Article 3(10) provides that the block exemption will not apply where the duration of the licence agreement is automatically prolonged by the inclusion of new improvements of the licensor. The extension of the length of the term of licences is permitted where the licensee is allowed to refuse to take such improvements or both parties have a right to terminate the agreement at the expiry of the initial term and at least every three years thereafter.

Restrictions beyond the permitted periods

The parties must not be restricted by the exclusivity provisions for periods greater than the ten or five year periods allowed (depending on the particular circumstances) in Article 1.[61]

61 Art.3(11)

Parallel importers

The parties must not be required to refuse without objectively justifiable reasons to meet demand from users or resellers in their respective territories, where those users would on-sell the products into other territories. Article 3(12) goes on to provide that the parties must not make it difficult for resellers to obtain products from other resellers within the EC.

Opposition procedure

It is possible to make a notification of a know-how licence agreement under Article 4 of the Regulation where there are no black-listed provisions; if in such a case the Commission does not object within six months of the date of receipt of the notification the agreements will not infringe Article 85(1).

Exclusions

The Regulation does not apply to members of patent or know-how pools (Article 5), nor to agreements between competing companies holding interests in joint venture companies or with the joint venture company. The Regulation also will not apply where competitors in relation to particular products enter into reciprocal agreements, unless there are no territorial restrictions (Article 5(2)).

Where the licensing agreement includes the licensing of other intellectual property rights (other than patents), and in particular involves the licensing of trade marks,[62] copyright or design rights or the licensing of software, it is necessary that the rights or the software are:

> of assistance in achieving the object of the licensed technology and there are no obligations restrictive of competition other than those also attached to the licensed know-how and exempted under the present Regulation.

Any restrictions which apply equally to the know-how and to the trade marks or other rights could be exempted, but if any restrictions, even of the sort exempted under the Regulation, do not also apply to the know-how then the exemption cannot be used. If there were territorial restrictions in relation to trade marks, but not in relation to the know-how, then it may be necessary to make a separate notification for specific exemption.

Withdrawal of exemption

The Commission has powers under Article 7 to withdraw the benefit of the exemption in particular cases for a number of reasons, including where there is no effective competition, where the licensor does not have a right to terminate the exclusivity after five years and annually thereafter if the licensee does not exploit the technology adequately or where unsolicited sales are not met from other licensees' territories or parallel patents are impeded.

The exemption may also be withdrawn in this way where the period during which the licensee continues to pay royalties after the know-how has become publicly known 'substantially exceeds the lead time acquired because of the head-start in production and marketing and this obligation is detrimental to competition in the market'. Withdrawal is also available to the Commission where the parties were competitors before the licence was granted and

62 See *Moosehead Whitbread* [1991] 4 CMLR 391

minimum quantity or best endeavours obligations on the licensee have the effect of preventing the licensee from using competing technologies.

Duration

By Article 12 the Regulation lasts until 31st December 1999. Regulation 556/89 is summarised in Fig. 9.2.

Know-how Licensing Agreements under the Block Exemption Regulation 556/89

1. Need
    (a) 2 parties only
    (b) licence of know-how, or mixed patent and know-how licence to which Regulation 2349/84 does not apply, ancillary trade mark, copyright or other rights
    (c) know-how must be secret, substantial and identified

2. Exempted Restrictions – Article 1
    For 10 years since first licensor licence of technology for that territory:
    – licensor not to license others in territory
    – licensor not to exploit territory
    – licensee not to exploit licensor territories
    For 10 years from first licensor EC licence of technology
    – licensee not to manufacture or use in other licensees' territories
    – licensee not actively to sell in other licensees' territories
    All above provisions – only as long as any patents continue
    – licensee to use licensor's trade mark
    – licensee to limit quantities of production of licensed product to what he needs to manufacture his own products

3. Non-restrictive provisions – Article 2
    – licensee to keep know-how secret even after termination
    – restriction on licensee assigning or sub-licensing
    – restriction on licensee exploiting know-how after termination where know-how is still secret
    – licensee to license licensor with licensee's improvements – no restrictions on licensee's use unless not severable from know-how or would reveal secret know-how, and must be reciprocal
    – minimum quality specifications which are technically necessary or necessary to ensure production conforms to that of other licensees and licensor
    – licensee to pay royalties after know-how publicly known unless licensor responsible
    – field of use restriction
    – minimum royalty
    – most favoured licensee clause
    – obligation to mark goods with licensor's name
    – licensee not to use know-how to construct facilities for third parties

---

Fig. 9.2

---

4. Black-listed provisions – Article 3
   - licensee restricted from using know-how after termination where know-how publicly known other than through breach by licensee of agreement
   - licensee obliged to assign improvements; grant licensor exclusive licence of improvements which stop licensee using his improvements (if they are severable from the know-how) or stop licensee licensing third parties with licensee improvements unless (jeopardises secrecy of know-how); or where post-term use ban & licence back of non-severable improvements (unless period same as licensor's)
   - quality specifications or ties, unless (i) necessary for technically satisfactory exploitation of know-how or (ii) to ensure production conforms to standards of licensor and other licensees
   - no challenge clause – validity of patents, secrecy of know-how
   - royalties on goods not made using know-how or not patented
   - restriction in one field of use as to customers who can be served
   - restriction on quantities which one party can make or sell
   - price restrictions
   - non-competition restrictions for competing goods (can terminate exclusivity if breached)
   - agreement extended automatically by including new licensor improvements unless licensor can refuse the improvements or rights to terminate at end of initial term or every 3 years thereafter
   - exclusivity beyond that permitted in Article 1
   - obligation to refuse to sell in territory to potential exporters
   - parallel importers impeded

5. Opposition procedure for notification available

6. Does not apply to:
   - patent or know-how pools
   - joint ventures with competitors
   - competitor reciprocal licences
   - agreements licensing intellectual property other than patents or know-how or licensing software, unless rights assist in achieving the object of the licensed technology and the only restrictions also attach to the know-how and are exempted

---

Fig. 9.2 (*cont.*)

KNOW-HOW LICENSING – UK LAW

Schedule 3, paragraphs 3 and 8 of the Restrictive Trade Practices Act 1976 exempt from the provisions of the RTPA certain know-how licensing agreements in relation to goods and services respectively.[63]

Know-how is not property. It is a right *in rem*. It is information, which may or may not be protected by copyright or rights of confidence. It is harder to bring know-how within the *Ravenseft* doctrine, discussed above in relation to patents,[64] than other intellectual property rights, which are quite clearly property.

Schedule 3, paragraphs 3 and 8

The RTPA does not apply to an agreement between two persons, neither of

63 For consideration of intellectual property generally under UK competition law, see the patent licensing section above and *Ravenseft* [1978] QB 53 *op cit* and the *OFT Guide to the RTPA* p.16
64 See Green (Further Reading) p.90

whom is a trade association, for the 'exchange of information' relating to the 'operation of processess of manufacture (whether patented or not)' where no other person is a party to the agreement and no restrictions are accepted 'except in respect of the descriptions of goods to be produced by those processes or to which those processes are to be applied'.

'Exchange of information'

This first requirement can cause problems in practice. There can be cases where there is no exchange of information, which suggests a swapping of technology or at the least some potential provision whereby the licensee will feed back his experience and improvements to the licensor.

'Operation of processes of manufacture'

The know-how may not always relate to processes of manufacture.

'Descriptions of goods to be produced'

This would exempt restrictions as to the field of use to which the technology may be put, but not restrictions as to the customers whom the licensee may serve, which could hardly be said to be a description of goods.

However, the provisions of section 9(3) should always be borne in mind. This provides that restrictions can be discounted in calculating whether there are restrictions on two parties (a necessary pre-condition for the application of the RTPA) where in an agreement for the application of a process of manufacture to goods there is a term relating exclusively to the goods to which the process is to be applied. This is of limited use in know-how licensing. It would however possibly catch a restriction on a licensee using raw materials which he purchases from the licensor only for the purposes of manufacture using the licensed technology.

The question of whether restrictions on the use of the know-how itself are relevant restrictions within the RTPA is a difficult one. Provisions such as 'the licensee shall not disclose the know-how' where this would prevent his performing services in a particular sector of business to particular customers in competition with the licensor may amount to restrictions as to the persons to whom designated services may be supplied, if the releasing of the know-how would be accompanied by training and other assistance to be given by the licensee.

Schedule 3, paragraph 8 may assist in such cases. This exempts agreements for exchange of information to be 'applied in the provision of designated services' provided that the restrictions 'relate exclusively to the form or manner in which services incorporating those techniques or processes are to be made available or supplied'.

As in the case of services there will usually be no goods supplied, rarely will section 9(3) apply. Section 18(2), the services equivalent, is of little use in discounting services restrictions as services, unlike goods, are not resold – not the same services.

As soon as there is any restriction on competing, for example, then there will be a restriction outside Schedule 3, paragraph 8 and the exemption will not be available.

In the *OFT Guide to the RTPA*[65] it is stated that restrictions arising through operation of law are not 'relevant restrictions' under the RTPA. As rights of confidence exist at law, this may render some forms of know-how licence as to their obligations of confidentiality outside the scope of the RTPA.

In all cases a detailed RTPA analysis needs to be carried out, and if in doubt the agreement should be registered with the OFT before the restrictions take effect in order to ensure the enforceability of the restrictions. Registration can be made on a 'fail-safe' basis if there is uncertainty as to whether or not an agreement infringes the RTPA.

TRADE MARK LICENSING – EC LAW

There is no block exemption for trade mark licensing agreements, although, as has been seen above, the patent and know-how Regulations permit restrictions in relation to trade mark licences, where their licensing is accompanied by patent or know-how licences and the restrictions apply to both. The trade mark licence must only be ancillary to the patent or know-how element. Franchising, considered later in this chapter, is often accompanied by a trade mark licence and in that context block exemption protection may be available. For 'stand-alone' trade mark licences there is no block exemption. Such licences could infringe Article 85(1) particularly where they contain res- trictions in the form of an exclusive grant of rights.

There is little case law concerning Article 85(1) and trade marks. The rules on free movement of goods in Article 30 of the Treaty should always be considered (see earlier in this chapter) and there has been much case law concerning when rights to a trade mark have been exhausted, once put on the market by the licensor or with his consent in any part of the EC, after which the licensor cannot prevent parallel imports of those goods.

The one principal decision concerning trade mark licences is *Campari.*[66] There the Commission held that Article 85(1) would apply to an exclusive trade mark licence. Campari agreed to restrict itself so that it did not license any other third parties with the trade mark in specified EC territories. Campari also agreed not to manufacture the product in the territory under the trade mark. These provisions were restrictive of competition, but individually exempted in this case.

A trade mark licence will usually consist of a grant to a licensee to use a trade mark of the licensor, perhaps for a particular territory, with some element of territorial protection for the parties. Under English law, such agreements are strictly not 'licences' but user agreements. In order to ensure that the licensor's registered trade mark rights are not diluted by a third party licensee using the mark and acquiring a reputation in the mark such agreements can be registered at the Trade Marks Registry as 'registered user agreements'.[67]

Again, to ensure the rights to the mark are protected, the licensor must ensure that he inserts provisions requiring the licensee to observe certain quality standards.[68] If a licensee were allowed to manufacture products of poor standard and sell them under the trade mark the public would think less of the goods and the licensor's reputation would be damaged. The trade mark

---

[65] OFT 1990, p.16

[66] [1978] 2 CMLR 397

[67] Trade Marks Act 1938, s.28

[68] If no quality control provisions are included in the user agreement the Registrar of Trademarks will exercise his discretion to refuse to register the agreement under s.28(4),(5)&(6)

would become less valuable too. Such quality control provisions would not normally infringe Article 85(1) (*Campari*).

69 [1991] 4 CMLR 391, OJ 1990 L100/32

In *Moosehead/Whitbread* [69] the Commission, where a mixed trade mark and know-how licence was held not to fall in Reg. 556/89, a no-challenge to *ownership* clause was cleared, though no-challenge to *validity* of the trade mark could infringe Article 85(1). Other restrictions are likely to be void where their know-how or patent equivalent is blacklisted in Regulations 2349/84 and 556/89 and in the franchising context – the Franchise Block Exemption, which can be used as a guide.

TRADE MARK LICENSING – UK LAW

As with patents and know-how there is a potential risk that a registered user agreement for trade marks, whether they be registered marks or unregistered tradenames, may infringe the RTPA. Where the trade marks are all registered and there is a formal registered user agreement in place, Schedule 3, paragraph 4(2) exempts such agreements from the RTPA where the only restrictions are in respect of:

(i) the descriptions of goods bearing the mark which are to be produced or supplied; or

(ii) the processes of manufacture to be applied to such goods or to goods to which the mark is to be applied.

The licensor could therefore stipulate exactly which goods upon which the mark appears the licensee may produce, such as that only red shoes manufactured in a certain way bear the mark, or the licensor may require that strict quality standards be applied. In practice a 'fail-safe' registration in cases of doubt should be made once a thorough RTPA analysis has been undertaken.

COPYRIGHT LICENCES – EC LAW

As with trade marks there is no block exemption for copyright licences. Copyright licences take a number of forms, from publishing agreements to computer software licences (considered in Chapter 11 below).

70 [1983] 1 CMLR 49

Reference should be made in relation to particular restrictive clauses to the block exemptions 2349/84 and 556/89. In *Coditel* v *Cine Vog Films (No 2)*, [70] almost the sole example of an EC decision on copyright, the Court held that an exclusive licence to show a film did not infringe Article 85(1). Unreasonable exploitation of such rights may in other cases, however, infringe Article 85(1). No challenge clauses, export bans and ties and any generally black-listed provision are likely to fall foul of Article 85(1).

COPYRIGHT LICENCES – UK LAW

Schedule 3, paragraph 5A of the RTPA exempts copyright and topography (semiconductor) right licences from the RTPA, as well as assignment agreements in this field. The restrictions must not be accepted 'except in respect of the work or other subject-matter in which the copyright or topography right subsists or will subsist'.

This is one of the few Schedule 3 exemptions to have been the subject of judicial consideration. In *Academy Sound & Vision Ltd* v *WEA Records Ltd,*[71] a High Court decision from 1982, WEA had assigned copyright in master recordings of films under a written agreement to Academy. WEA was allowed for three months to sell off its stocks of recordings and for three months Academy could manufacture such records but could not sell them until the period was over.

Academy maintained that, after the three month period, WEA had sold records in breach of its acquired copyright and in breach of the agreement between the parties. WEA alleged, *inter alia*, that the restrictions were void for want of registration under the RTPA. The judge attributed a wide meaning to the use in Schedule 3, paragraph 5A of 'in respect of the subject-matter in which copyright subsists'. Only restrictions of that type are exempted by the paragraph. He stated:

> In the context of paragraph 5A, which was clearly designed to exclude from the Act of 1976 agreements relating to copyright protected by the Copyright Act itself, the legislative intention must, I think, have been to except provisions fairly incidental to an assignment of any copyright within the Copyright Act, including the disposal of copies made by the owner of the copyright in a sound recording.

The judge did state that the construction of Schedule 3, paragraph 5A is not 'free from difficulty'. The case was not a full trial merely an application for summary judgement under Order 14, which was granted. The exemption was held to apply but the case illustrates the difficulties of relying on the Schedule 3 exemptions and fail-safe registration is the safer course in cases of doubt.

[71] [1983] ICR 586

OTHER RIGHTS

Other rights, such as those in relation to plant varieties,[72] will be considered under the general principles of Article 85(1) and (if not specifically exempted under Schedule 3 of the RTPA) under the general provisions of the RTPA.

[72] There have been a considerable number of major cases on plant variety rights and EC competition law, such as *Nungesser* [1983] 1 CMLR 278

FRANCHISING – EC LAW

Business format franchising consists of selling a package of marketing experience and other business assistance to franchisees, who will then set up businesses under the trade marks and other standard 'get-up' of the franchisor. Many high street chains are franchises. There are particular restrictive provisions which go with this form of business and which have merited particular consideration by the Commission, since the proliferation in recent times of this form of business start-up.

Typically the franchisee, i.e. the party buying the package, will be obliged to carry on business from a particular location in a certain way. The franchisor may agree to give some element of territorial protection to the franchisee, for example, agreeing not to sell a similar franchise to another potential franchisee to set up in business in the same street as the original franchisee.

The Commission considered a number of franchises under Article 85(1) before bringing out the franchise block exemption (see below), which came into force on 1st February 1989.

The cases

3 [1986] 1 CMLR 414

In its principal decision *Pronuptia*[73] the Commission considered the franchise system of Pronuptia, a French company specialising in bridalwear and accessories. It was held that the exclusivity given to the franchisees to operate under the franchisor's name in a given sales area contravened Article 85(1), as did an obligation on the franchisee to carry on the franchise business exclusively from premises approved for that purpose. The agreement was however exempted under Article 85(3).

4 [1988] 4 CMLR 592

In *Yves Rocher,*[74] the selection by Yves Rocher of only one franchisee for one area, which franchisee was granted an exclusive right to use the trade mark and know-how, was contrary to Article 85(1), but again an Article 85(3) exemption was granted.

5 [1987] 2 CMLR 389

In *Computerland,*[75] the products sold under franchise were microcomputer products and services. The obligation on the franchisee to operate from specified premises only, which prevented franchisees from opening further stores, and the exclusivity clause, which guaranteed franchisees a protected zone, were held to infringe Article 85(1). Also a provision requiring franchisees to sell only to end users of the products was held to be restrictive of competition. The franchise agreements were exempted under Article 85(3), although Computerland was obliged to send further information to the Commission and notify the Commission of substantial changes to the franchise system which it operated.

76 [1988] 4 CMLR 895

ServiceMaster Ltd (England)[76] was the first franchising decision to apply the rules to a franchise concerning the provision of services rather than the sale of goods through franchised outlets. The franchise concerned the provision of housekeeping and cleaning services to commercial and domestic customers. The Commission held that for service franchises the protection of know-how was even more important than for distribution franchise agreements, although generally the same rules applied. The clause prohibiting the franchisee from setting up further outlets outside his territory and a territorial protection clause preventing the franchisee from seeking customers outside his territory restricted competition contrary to Article 85(1). The agreement was specifically exempted under Article 85(3). The worst elements of the agreement had been agreed by ServiceMaster to be amended during the course of the notification process.

77 [1989] 4 CMLR 591

Finally, in *Charles Jourdan,*[77] the clauses granting exclusivity to the franchisee to operate under the franchisor's trade marks in the given sales area and requiring the franchisee to carry on his business activity exclusively from the premises approved for that purpose were contrary to Article 85(1). There was competition however in the same area from other forms of Charles Jourdan retail outlets. A specific Article 85(3) exemption was granted.

Drawing on its experience in these cases the Commission was able to produce a block exemption.

The franchising block exemption

78 Published in the *Official Journal* at No L359/46, 28 December 1988

Commission Regulation (EEC) No. 4087/88 of 30th November 1988 on the application of Article 85(3) of the Treaty to categories of franchise agreements[78] applies to agreements by which a franchisor grants to another, the franchisee, in exchange for financial consideration, the right to exploit the franchise for the purposes of marketing specified types of goods and/or services. The agreement must include obligations relating to the use of a common name or shop sign and a uniform presentation of premises and/or means of transport, the passing of know-how from franchisor to franchisee and continuing provision to the franchisee by the franchisor of commercial or technical assistance.[79]

79 Art.1.3(b)

A franchise, by Article 1.3(a), means:

> a package of industrial or intellectual property rights relating to trade marks, trade names, shop signs, utility models, designs, copyrights, know-how or patents, to be exploited for the resale of goods or the provision of services to end users.

The franchisor may insist that the franchisee pay a minimum proportion of the franchisor's advertising expenditure and that the franchisee must advertise in a manner approved by the franchisor.

By Article 3.2 the following obligations may also be imposed on the franchisee, without the conditions attached to the exemption in Article 3.1:

(a) *Keep know-how secret*. The franchisor may require that the franchisee keep know-how secret even after the agreement between them has terminated.

(b) *Grant back*. A provision that the franchisee communicate to the franchisor experience learnt whilst exploiting the franchise, and requiring the franchisee to grant a non-exclusive licence back to the franchisor of such experience, is permitted.

(c) *Infringements*. The franchisee can be obliged to inform the franchisor of infringements of the intellectual property rights of which it becomes aware and be required to take legal action against infringers or assist the franchisor in taking such legal action.

(d) *Know-how restriction*. A restriction on the franchisee from using the know-how except for the purposes of the franchise is acceptable, and the franchisee may be held to this obligation even after termination of the agreement.

(e) *Training courses*. A requirement that the franchisee and his staff attend training courses held by the franchisor is permissible.

(f) *Commercial methods*. The franchisor can insist that the franchisee use certain commercial methods devised by the franchisor and subsequent improvements and also that he must use the intellectual property rights included in the package.

(g) *Standards*. The franchisor may be obliged to comply with the franchisor's standards for the equipment and presentation of the premises and/or means of transport.

(h) *Checks*. Checking of the premises or transport is allowed to ensure that the franchisee is complying with the agreement. Such checks can include a check of the accounts and inventory of the franchisee.

(i) *Location.* The franchisee can be obliged not to move the location of the franchised premises without the consent of the franchisor, who may retain an absolute veto over whether to consent to such a change.

(j) *Assignment.* There can be a restriction on the franchisee assigning the franchise agreement without the consent of the franchisor.

Conditions

The exemption of restrictive provisions in Article 1 only applies[80] where the franchisee is free to obtain the franchise goods from other franchisees. Where the franchisor obliges the franchisee to honour guarantees for the franchisor's goods, that obligation must apply in respect of such goods supplied by any member of the franchised network or other distributors which give a similar guarantee, throughout the common market.[81]

The franchisee is obliged to indicate its status as an independent undertaking, although this must not interfere with the common identity of the franchised network resulting in particular from the common name or shop sign and uniform appearance of the contract premises and/or means of transport.

Black-listed provisions

Article 5 sets out those provisions the presence of which in a franchise agreement would render the exemption inapplicable.

Competitors

The block exemption will not apply where companies producing similar or substitutable goods enter into franchise agreements in relation to those goods.

Equivalent goods

The franchisee must not be prevented from acquiring goods from a third party source which are of a similar quality to those offered by the franchisor, although under Article 2(e) the franchisee may be restricted from dealing in competing goods and under Article 3.1(b) the franchisee may be obliged to purchase goods only from the franchisor if it is impracticable to lay down objective quality requirements.

Unjustified tie

Where the franchisee is obliged to sell only the franchisor's goods (without prejudice to Article 2(e)) and the franchisor refuses to designate other authorised manufacturers such a provision is black-listed, unless, in such a refusal the franchisor is protecting his intellectual property rights or maintaining a common identity for the franchised network.

Know-how use after termination

The franchisee must not be prevented, after termination of the agreement, from using the know-how once it is in the public domain other than by his own breach of an obligation.

Prices

The franchisee must be free to set whatever prices he chooses for the goods. This is without prejudice to the possibility of the franchisor recommending sale prices.

No-challenge

No-challenge clauses in connection with the intellectual property rights are forbidden, although the franchisor may terminate the agreement in the event of such a challenge.

End users

The franchisee must not be obliged to refuse to supply end users anywhere in the common market because of the place of residence of such end users.

Opposition procedure

Under Article 6, it is possible, as under the know-how and patent block exemptions, to notify the Commission of a franchise agreement which contains no black-listed provisions but which has restrictions other than those permitted in the rest of Regulation 4087/88, and if no response is heard from the Commission within six months the restrictions will be exempted from Article 85(1).

Withdrawal of exemption

By Article 8, the Commission may withdraw the benefit of the exemption in individual cases where there are effects which are incompatible with Article 85(3) and in particular where:

(a) access to markets or competition in such markets is restricted by the cumulative effect of parallel networks of similar agreements established by competing manufacturers;

(b) there is no competition for the goods or services in a substantial part of the common market;

(c) one of the parties prevents end users acquiring the goods because of their place of residence or where differences in specifications are used in order to isolate markets in different Member States;

(d) franchisees engage in concerted practices relating to the sale prices of goods or services the subject matter of the franchise; or

(e) the franchisor abuses his right to check the franchisee's premises or transport or refuses to allow a move of location or assignment of the agreement, for reasons other than protecting intellectual property rights, maintaining a common identity of the network or verifying that the franchisee abides by the provisions of the agreement.

Duration

By Article 9, the Regulation continues until 31st December 1999.

Figure 9.3 summarises Regulation 4087/88:

Franchising Agreements under the Block Exemption Regulation 4087/88

1. Need
   - (a) 2 parties only
   - (b) goods or services
   - (c) franchise or master franchise including:
     - – use of common name and uniform presentation
     - – franchisor communicates know-how
     - – continuing provision of assistance by franchisor

2. Acceptable restrictions – Article 2
   - – franchisor in territory not to:
   - (i) grant rights to third parties to exploit franchise
   - (ii) exploit franchise or itself market the goods
   - (iii) supply its goods to third parties
   - – master franchisee not to franchise outside territory
   - – franchisee only to exploit from the premises
   - – franchisee outside territory not to seek customers
   - – franchisee not to make or sell competing products (except spare parts)

3. Non-restrictive provisions – Article 3
   In so far as necessary to protect intellectual property rights or maintain common identity of network:
   - – minimum objective quality specifications
   - – where impracticable owing to subject matter to apply objective quality specifications, franchisee to buy goods only manufactured by franchisor or nominee
   - – not to compete with franchisor, including reasonable period after termination (no more than 12 months)
   - – not to acquire influential financial stake in capital of a competitor of franchisor
   - – only to sell to end users, other franchisees and resellers within manufacturer supplied distribution channels
   - – best endeavours to sell, minimum range, minimum turnover, plan orders, minimum support, customer and warranty services
   - – pay franchisor proportion of advertising revenue
   Whether necessary to protect rights or not:
   - – keep know-how confidential even after termination
   - – non-exclusive grant back of improvements
   - – inform and assist with intellectual property right infringement
   - – only use know-how for franchise purpose even after termination
   - – to attend training courses of franchisor
   - – to apply franchisor's commercial methods and use intellectual property rights
   - – to comply with franchisor standards of equipment, premises and equipment
   - – to permit franchisor checks
   - – not to change location without franchisor consent
   - – not to assign without franchisor consent

4. Conditions of exemption – Article 4
   - – that franchisee can buy from other franchisees
   - – to honour guarantees whether goods purchased from another

Fig. 9.3

franchisee or the same franchisee
  — franchisee must state status as independent entity

5. Black-listed provisions – Article 5
    — competitors enter into franchise agreements for competing goods
    — franchisee prevented from purchasing goods of equivalent quality from third party
    — franchisee obliged to purchase from franchisor who refuses to authorise another third party source
    — after termination and know-how known franchisee restricted other than when his breach revealed know-how
    — franchisee restricted as to price (recommended price may be acceptable)
    — no challenge clause (can terminate on challenge)
    — franchisee obliged to refuse to supply end users because of their place of residence

6. Opposition procedure for notification available

Fig. 9.3 (*cont.*)

FRANCHISING AGREEMENTS – UK LAW

The RTPA contains no exemption for franchising agreements.[82] Although most such agreements include a right to use a trade mark they are unlikely to be trade mark licences of the sort exempted under Schedule 3, paragraph 4.

If there are no restrictions on the franchisor at all then any number of restrictions on the franchisee will not render the agreement registrable as there must be restrictions on two parties for the Act to apply. Any restrictions as to the goods supplied by the franchisor can be discounted under section 9(3). This would include any restriction on the franchisee supplying goods purchased from the franchisor outside the territory or to particular classes of customer. If the franchisee is permitted to acquire goods from third parties, which may be necessary to obtain EC block exemption cover, then restrictions as to the sale of those goods would not be covered.

Any restriction on the franchisor as to the persons to whom he will sell goods within the franchisee's territory would be a relevant restriction too. The exclusive distribution exemption in Schedule 3, paragraph 2 may apply where the only restrictions are the exclusivity provisons, although trade mark restrictions may preclude the application of this exemption. Two Schedule 3 exemptions cannot be used for one agreement. Also the use of the Schedule 3, paragraph 2 exemption would be dependant on the agreement being one 'for the supply of goods'. The supply of goods is often only a very small part of a franchise agreement so the exemption may be of little use in practice.

In cases of doubt the agreement should be furnished to the OFT before the restrictions take effect and submitted on a 'fail-safe' basis.

82 See Howe M. –
Franchising and Restrictive Practices Law: the OFT View
[1988] EIPR 439

CONCLUSION

The licensing of intellectual property rights and franchising agreements is covered by a broad and detailed set of EC Regulations. There will also be the RTPA to consider in the UK law context. Competition Act 1980 investigations and Monopolies and Merger Commission investigations under the Fair Trading Act 1973 may also consider the licensing of intellectual property, although the small risk of such an investigation makes that legislation of less immediate impact than the RTPA, which renders restrictions void. Intellectual property agreements are often restrictive of competition and bear close analysis under competition law to ensure the enforceability of their provisions, and, where provisions are particularly restrictive, to avoid Commission fines.

QUESTION

Harry Dollar comes to see you for competition law advice. He is not interested in common European pricing and feels he can maximise his profits by exploiting price differentials for his product in different EC countries. The Germans will pay much more for his luxury mirrors than the British. He wants to set up a system across Europe, but has no more definite plans, except he feels it may be easier to license his secret know-how and patent for manufacture of the special mirror glass than manufacture himself and sell through a distribution network. He has not ruled out setting up a franchise system.

Ignoring the commercial differences and looking only to EC competition law, which block exemption would give Mr Dollar the greatest opportunity for tight territorial protection and why? He particularly wants to limit the scope for parallel importers. Can he enforce his patent to prevent imports of the mirrors into other territories? Consider the rules on free movement of goods and exhaustion of rights in this context.

FURTHER READING

EC law

ARTICLES
Lutz H. & Broderick – *Know-how Licensing under the EC Group Exemption Reg. No. 556/89* (1989) 17 IBL 373
Rothnie W. – *Hag II: Putting the Common Origin Doctrine to Sleep* [1991] 1 EIPR 24
Singleton E.S. – *A Mine of Uncertainty* (141) NLJ 1 March 1991 268
Subiotto R. – *Moosehead/Whitbread: Industrial Franchises and No-Challenge Clauses relating to Licensed Trade Marks under EEC Competition Law* [1990] 5 ECLR 226
Whaite R. – *Licensing in Europe* [1990] 3 EIPR 88

BOOKS
Bellamy & Child – *Common Market Law of Competition*, Sweet & Maxwell, 3rd ed., 1987, chapt.7 (and para.6–117 Franchising)
Green N. – *Commercial Agreements and Competition Law*, Graham & Trotman 1986, cpt.13
Hawk B.E. – *US, Common Market & International Anti-trust*, Prentice Hall Law & Business, 2nd ed., 1990 Supplement, Vol.II, Patents, *Knowhow, Trademarks and Copyrights* – p.575
Korah V. – *Franchising and EC Competition Rules, Regulation 4087/88*, ESC Publishing 1989
Korah V. – *Knowhow Licensing Agreements and EC Competition Rules, Regulation 556/89*, ESC Publishing 1989
Korah V. – *Patent Licensing and EC Competition Rules, Regulation 2349/84*, ESC Publishing 1985
Oliver P. – *Free Movement of Goods in the EC*, 2nd ed., European Law Centre, 1988
Van Bael & Bellis – *Competition Law of the EC*, CCH Editions, 2nd ed., 1990, chapt.4 (and franchising para.350)
Whish R. – *Competition Law*, Butterworths, 2nd ed., 1989, chapt. 19 (and franchising p.625)

Bayer AG and Maschinenfabrik Hennecke GmbH v *Süllhöfer* [1990] 4 CMLR 182   **CASES**
Boussois/Interpane [1988] 4 CMLR 124
Campari [1978] 2 CMLR 397
Centrafarm v *Sterling Drug* [1976] 1 CMLR 1, [1974] ECR 1147
Charles Jourdan [1989] 4 CMLR 591
Coditel v *Cine Vog Films (No.2)* [1983] 1 CMLR 49
Computerland [1987] 2 CMLR 389
Delta Chemie/DDD OJ 1988 L309/34
Deutsche Grammaphon v *Metro* [1971] CMLR 631, [1971] ECR 487
Eurofix-Bauco v *Hilti* OJ 1988 L65/9
Magill TV Guide [1989] 4 CMLR 757, OJ 1989 L78/43
Merck v *Stephar* [1981] 3 CMLR 1
Moosehead/Whitbread [1991] 4 CMLR 391
Nungesser v *Commission* [1983] 1 CMLR 278
Ottung v *Klee & Weilbach A/S* [1990] 4 CMLR 915
Parke, Davis v *Probel* [1968] CMLR 69
Pharmon v *Hoechst* [1985] 3 CMLR 775
Pitney Bowes v *Francotyp-postalia* [1990] 3 CMLR 466
Pronuptia [1986] 1 CMLR 414
Renault [1990] 4 CMLR 265
Rich Products/Jus-rol [1988] 4 CMLR 527
S.A. CNL – Sucal N.V. v *Hag G.F. A.G.* [1990] 3 CMLR 571
ServiceMaster Ltd (England) [1988] 4 CMLR 895
Sirena v *Eda* [1971] CMLR 260, [1971] ECR 69
Tetra Pak [1991] 4 CMLR 334
Vaessen/Moris [1979] 1 CMLR 511
Van Zuylen Frères v *Hag* [1979] 2 CMLR 127
Velcro-Aplix OJ 1985 L233/22
Volvo v *Veng* [1989] 4 CMLR 122
Windsurfing International v *Commission* [1986] ECR 611
Yves Rocher [1988] 4 CMLR 592

Patent Licence Block Exemption, Regulation 2349/84 OJ 1984 L219/15   **REGULATIONS**
Knowhow Licence Block Exemption, Regulation 556/89 OJ 1989 L61/1
Franchise Block Exemption, Regulation 4087/88 OJ 1988 L359/46

UK law

Burnett-Hall R. – *A New UK Competition Law and Its Application to Intellectual Property*   **ARTICLES**
    [1988] 11 EIPR 331
Howe M. – *Franchising and Restrictive Practices Law: the Office of Fair Trading View* [1988]
    ECLR 439
Singleton E.S. – *Intellectual Property Licences and UK Competition Law* (140) NLJ 16
    November 1990 1591

Chitty on Contracts, Sweet & Maxwell, 26th ed., 1990, Vol.II, paras. 4408, 4409 and 4410   **BOOKS**
Green N. (*op cit*), chapt. 13
Pearson H. & Miller C. – *Commercial Exploitation of Intellectual Property*, Blackstone Press
    1990 (on IP licensing generally)
Whish (*op cit*), chapt. 19 (and franchising p.624)

Academy Sound & Vision Ltd v *WEA Records Ltd* [1983] ICR 586   **CASES**
Automatic Telephone & Electric Co Ltd v *Registrar of Restrictive Trading Agreements* [1964] 1
    WLR 795
Re Cadbury Schweppes Ltd's Agreement [1975] 1 WLR 1018
Ravenseft Properties Ltd [1978] QB 52

10

Co-operation, joint ventures and research

Co-operation and joint ventures come in many forms. Two companies decide to pool their resources for research and development into new product ranges and the development of existing products. They each benefit from the complementary technology of the other party and the savings in research costs through funding only one research programme. The result – customers are offered a better, fuller range of products, which may be cheaper too, having been more efficiently produced. At the other extreme two competitors, who between them hold almost one hundred per cent of the market for a particular product in the EC, agree to 'co-operate' by staying out of each other's territory. Each is given a free rein within that territory and they are able to charge excessively high prices. Alternatively, they agree joint research through a joint venture company in which they both hold shares. Instead of them each developing competing technology, all effort is put into the joint venture and consumers are deprived of effective competition for the new range of products.

There are a number of different types of agreement to be considered, both under EC and UK competition law, in this chapter. First there is 'joint ventures', i.e. collaboration, usually through a separate 'joint venture company' by two separate entities, such collaboration falling short of their actually merging their two enterprises. Secondly, there are collaboration agreements for research and development, for which there is a block exemption under EC competition law. Thirdly, there are 'specialisation' agreements, under which companies or individuals jointly undertake the production of goods for which there is also a block exemption. Next are simple co-operation agreements, in relation to which the European Commission has issued a Notice and finally, sub-contracting agreements – a very one-sided form of 'collaboration', where one company simply contracts with another for that other to undertake manufacture for the first company, in relation to which there is also a Notice.

Separate though these categories may be to the Commission, in practice the boundaries are often unclear and overlapping. A number of the Regulations, Notices and case law may apply to one particular agreement. In this chapter EC competition law in all these areas will be discussed first and then UK law.

JOINT VENTURE AGREEMENTS – EC LAW

There is no block exemption for joint venture agreements, although the Commission has in the past produced a draft joint venture notice, which has not been revised for some time. It is anticipated that a revised form of this

Notice will be issued by the Commission in due course. The Merger Regulation discussed in Chapter 4 applies to forms of concentrative joint venture, but other joint ventures are not covered. The general principles of Article 85 as developed in the case law therefore provide the best picture of how a joint venture is treated under Article 85.

A typical joint venture agreement was considered by the Commission in *Re the Rockwell-Iveco Agreements*[1] in 1983. There was a basic agreement between Rockwell and Iveco for the formation of a joint venture company to manufacture and sell rear-drive axles for heavy commercial vehicles, with accompanying agreements. The agreements were treated as a composite whole by the Commission and contained provisions governing both the relationship between the parties and their vertical relationship with the joint venture company controlled by them.

The Commission considered that the two companies, Rockwell and Iveco, were to be considered at least potential competitors. Joint ventures are regarded as being restrictive of competition where the parties are competitors or potential competitors. Clearly if two companies, but for the joint venture, would have competed with each other and the effect of the venture is that they work together through one company then there is less competition in the market place. The joint venture company was concerned with the manufacture and sale of rear-drive axles. Before the conclusion of the agreement, both of the parties already manufactured those products which the joint venture company was to produce. Rockwell already exported to Europe and had a subsidiary in Europe. Iveco had not sold axles to third parties, but was regarded as a potential competitor. It had merely manufactured for the purposes of incorporating the products into other products which it sold. It did have the potential to increase production, which would have made it a competitor.

The Commission held that the joint venture had as its object and effect a restriction and distortion of competition within the common market:

> The supply structure on the market concerned is changed, since the parties forgo the opportunity of manufacturing individually the products in question and selling them on the market in competition with one another. Furthermore the agreements contain express obligations, which are considered by the parties to form an indispensable part of their arrangement and which restrict Rockwell, Iveco and the JVC [joint venture company] in their competitive behaviour.

The restrictions in the agreements were the following:

(a) JVC would market axles produced by subsidiary companies of the parties, which prior to the joint venture they marketed themselves. The parties did not therefore continue to sell those axles on their own account and would not pursue an independent market policy.

(b) There was an agreement for the licence of technology, under which Rockwell agreed to grant no more manufacturing licences for Italy and no further distribution agreements for another territory. Iveco granted the JVC an exclusive licence for Italy for the manufacture of certain axles. Rockwell and Iveco were therefore contractually restrained from entering into agreements with other licensees in those territories.

---

1 [1983] 3 CMLR 709, see also *Wano Schwarzpulver* [1979] 1 CMLR 403, where an Article 85(3) exemption was not granted as the parties were competitors and the joint venture would make them less likely to compete and ICI, one party to the joint venture, would obtain virtually all its requirements for the relevant product, black powder, from the joint venture company. The UK market would become insulated, the production of black powder would not be improved by the arrangement and there would be no benefits to consumers.

(c) The parties committed themselves to carry out investment in the field of activity of the joint venture in order to expand capacity in the territories through the JVC alone and not in competition with the JVC. The Commission stated:

> This results in a restriction of the independent competitive potential of the parties which increases in importance as their expectations are fulfilled and the free axle market enters an expansionary phase.

(d) Under the supply agreement between the JVC and Iveco's subsidiaries, for eight years from the beginning of production of the first Rockwell axle, such subsidiaries are obliged to satisfy all their requirements from the JVC. The Commission stated:

> Consequently they are legally prevented by the express purchasing obligation from satisfying at least part of their axle requirements from other manufacturers. Having regard in particular to the period of these agreements, this is likely to reduce the sales opportunities of other axle manufacturers.

In joint ventures many of these restrictions are present. The parties wish to ensure that each of them puts all their efforts into the venture and express restrictions on competing with the joint venture company are common. Also, where the joint venture company will be supplied by the parties with raw materials or other products, supply agreements between the parties and the joint venture company are necessary and these may contain restrictions on the parties supplying such products to other companies. Even where there are no express restrictions, the agreement may still be regarded by the Commission as infringing Article 85(1) because, in practice, the fact that the parties have set up a joint venture company and put money and effort into it makes it very likely that they will not then compete with the joint venture company and undermine its market position.

In the *Rockwell-Iveco* case Article 85(3) exemption was granted for those provisions which infringed Article 85(1). The Commission stated:

> The co-operation entails economic benefits for the production of goods concerned and for consumers, which could not be achieved in the absence of the joint venture and which outweigh its disadvantages.

All the restrictions were regarded as being indispensable to ensure the success of the venture as it was 'the only way of attaining the objective of the entry of a new and effective competitor by limiting the considerable business risk due to the market structure and investment expenditure'. A simple sub-contracting agreement or an assignment of know-how would not have achieved the same commercial effect. Moreover the joint venture did not afford the parties the opportunity to exclude competition in respect of the goods in question.

The agreements were exempted, subject to several conditions. The parties were required to provide that after the joint venture terminated they would be free to use the technical know-how which was in the possession of the joint venture company at the date of dissolution of the venture. The parties had to be free to compete after such dissolution without any temporal or geographical restrictions. Amendments to the agreements were required to be notified to the Commission.

This case illustrates the factors which the Commission will consider in assessing a joint venture agreement under Article 85(1).

Actual or potential competitors

The Commission will ask whether the parties are actual or potential competitors or whether there would have been a chance that they might have competed with each other in the future. In *Rockwell-Iveco*, Iveco had not sold any axles to third parties before. It was clearly not an actual competitor, but the Commission held that it was a potential competitor, as it made the axles itself for its own use and could have expanded production.[2]

As the Commission has tended to find potential competition readily in examining joint ventures, in considering joint venture agreements a cautious position should be taken, erring towards a finding of potential competition unless there is clearly none, and making a notification to the Commission of the agreement, where necessary. In considering 'competition' the question of whether the parties carry on business in the same market needs to be addressed.[3]

Restrictions on competition

The Commission will also look to whether there are restrictions on competition between the parties. Clearly the more express restrictions there are the less likely it is that the Commission would grant an exemption and the more likely it is that the joint venture would infringe Article 85(1). It is not the case that every joint venture will infringe Article 85(1) and require notification. There will be cases where there are no restrictions on competition in the agreements and the parties neither compete with each other at the time the agreement was entered into nor are potential competitors. Such joint ventures are unlikely to infringe Article 85(1).

The Commission does believe that joint ventures inherently contain restrictions on competition,[4] as the parent companies are unlikely in practice to seek to compete with the joint venture company, thereby undermining a venture which they hope will succeed.

Other factors

Although the principal consideration is how competition between the parties in the field of the joint venture will be affected, it is also relevant to consider what impact the joint venture will have on competition between the parties in the other spheres of activity in which they are engaged and what effects the joint venture will have on third parties.

In *Elopak/Metal Box*,[5] a Commission decision of 1990, the parties, who operated in the packaging industry, set up Odin, a jointly owned company, to carry out research and develop products for them. The parties were found to be neither actual nor potential competitors and it was highly unlikely that they would have developed the products on their own, so the agreements were not within Article 85(1) at all.

Odin was granted an exclusive licence of the know-how for the territory, but, as the know-how was essential to undertake the research, there were no restrictions on Odin's activities and the exclusivity was limited to a narrow field, the exclusive licence was not within Article 85(1) at all.

2 See *KEWA* [1976] 2 CMLR D15, *Vacuum Interrupters (No1)* [1977] 1 CMLR D67, *Re De Laval-Stork VOF* [1988] 4 CMLR 714 (JV between competitors contrary to Art 85(1), but exempted) and *Re the Application of United International Pictures BV (UIP)* [1990] 4 CMLR 749, joint subsidiary company, obligation to grant to it first refusal to distribute films in the EC caught by Art 85, but exempted.

3 See Chapter 3 and *United Brands* v *Commission* [1978] ECR 207

4 See *GEC/Weir* [1978] 1 CMLR D42

5 OJ L209/15, 18 August 1990. See also *Screensport* OJ 1991 L63/32 joint venture including Sky, W.H. Smith and European Broadcasting Union establishing a TV sports channel 'Eurosport' was not exempted under Article 85(3) and *Du Pont/Merck* joint venture approved in May 1991 (unreported to date)

On the break up of the venture the parties were free to use technology and compete. The Commission stated:

> In a case such as the one under consideration there can be no implicit anti-competitive impact on the activities of the parents outside the joint venture because not only were the parties not even potential competitors at the creation of Odin, but also neither party would have realistically developed the new product without the full and active participation of its partner.

This decision emphasises the distinction between joint ventures between competitors and others. Where there is no actual or potential competition between the parties ancillary licences may fall outside Article 85(1).

Article 85(3)

The Commission will exempt joint ventures where the usual criteria for Article 85(3) exemption are present as discussed in Chapter 2. As was seen in *Rockwell/Iveco*, where there is an improvement in production and distribution, promotion of technical and economic progress and benefits to consumers and where the restrictions are indispensable to achieve the benefits and competition still remains in the market place, exemptions will be granted. Also, in particular cases, the specialisation[6] and research and development[7] block exemptions may apply to joint ventures removing the need for individual notifications. The other circumstance in which an Article 85(3) notification will not be required is where the joint venture is a 'concentrative joint venture' and falls for consideration under the Merger Regulation (discussed in Chapter 4) and below.

It should always be remembered that a joint venture would not fall within Article 85(1) at all if it has no effect on trade between Member States and, in particular, where the Notice on Agreements of Minor Importance,[8] considered in Chapter 6, applies.

The Draft Joint Venture Notice

The Commission has not issued a Notice for joint ventures, although draft notices in various forms have been proposed by the Commission over the years.

From the draft Notice some useful information can be distilled, although the Notice is to a large extent now superseded by the Notice on concentrative and co-operative operations under the Merger Regulation discussed below. The draft Notice is not publicly available.

Market share

Where the parties' market shares do not together exceed 5 per cent then even if the turnover threshold in the Minor Agreements Notice is exceeded the Commission has suggested that a joint venture would not be attacked under the competition rules.

Competition

Where the parties are neither actual nor potential competitors the joint venture would not infringe Article 85(1), provided that the arrangements did

6 No.417/85 OJ 1985 L53/1
7 No.418/85 OJ 1985 L53/5

8 OJ 1986 C231/2

not appreciably affect the market position of third parties in downstream or upstream markets.

Paragraph 4 of the draft Notice states that the crucial factor in determining whether the parties are potential competitors is whether they could reasonably be expected to enter the market individually:

> If individual market entry is unlikely in the foreseeable future, the joint venture will not restrict competition, but will lead rather to the creation of new competition.

Where the parties cease to be actual or potential competitors by virtue of the joint venture, such agreement is likely to amount to a concentrative joint venture or even a merger and would be addressed under the Merger Regulation and not Article 85(1).

The Commission states in the draft Notice that the number of partners, their economic and financial strength, their market position, the market structure and the existence of market entry barriers must be taken into consideration. If the parties' combined market share does not exceed 15 per cent, the Commission considers (in the draft Notice) that the joint venture is unlikely to distort the competitive structure of the market.

A question the Commission will consider very carefully in each individual case, however, is whether the restrictions imposed on the partners do not exceed in their scope, geographical extent or duration the limits of what in a reasonable economic assessment must be regarded as essential for the formation and viability of the joint venture.

Bayer/Gist-Brocades

In *Bayer/Gist-Brocades,*[9] which was principally concerned with a specialisation agreement, the parties agreed to transfer manufacturing plants to jointly held subsidiaries. The Commission held that Article 85(1) applied as there was joint control over investment in and production of penicillin products. The joint venture would have led to the parties co-operating further down the chain of supply, at the stage of marketing finished products.

The part of the joint venture arrangement which was concerned with production was held to infringe Article 85(1) and it was held not to be indispensable for part of the arrangement which was approved, namely the part concerned with the specialisation of manufacturing.

Concentrative joint ventures

The Commission's 1990 Notice on concentrative joint ventures[10] provides that the Merger Regulation will apply to joint ventures where the joint venture company operates as an independent supplier and buyer on the market. The joint venture company must be set up on a lasting basis and must not have as its object or effect the coordination of the competitive behaviour of undertakings that remain independent of each other.

The Notice discusses these concepts at some length. A joint venture is an undertaking that is controlled by several other undertakings, the parent companies.[11] The venture need not be an incorporated company, but it must be an 'organized assembly of human resources, intended to pursue a defined economic purpose on a long-term basis'.[12] Most joint venture companies

9 [1976] 1 CMLR D98, see also [1990] 4 CMLR 516, Notice, proposed extension of Art 85(3) exemption

10 OJ 1990 C203/10

11 Notice, para.7

12 Notice, para.8

would fall within this definition. The joint venture must be jointly controlled by other undertakings. A subsidiary of one company could not therefore be a joint venture. However, there is a broad definition of control in paragraph 10, which includes rights to use the joint venture's assets, influence over its management and contracts concerning the running of its business.

The parent companies must agree on decisions concerning the activities of the joint venture. Where one company owns a majority of the shares or has the rights to appoint more than half the directors to the Board then control will not be joint.

Jointly controlled joint ventures will fall within the Merger Regulation where a positive and negative condition are satisfied.

The positive condition

Paragraph 16 of the Notice provides that to be a concentrative joint venture within the Merger Regulation 4064/89,[13] the joint venture (JV) must perform on a lasting basis all the functions of an autonomous economic entity. The decisive question, set out in paragraph 18, is whether the JV:

> is in a position to exercise its own commercial policy. This requires, within the limits of its company objectives, that it plans, decides and acts independently. In particular it must be free to determine its competitive behaviour autonomously and according to its own economic interests.

The parent companies may reserve to themselves the right to take certain decisions that are important to the development of the JV, such as alteration of its objects or increases in capital. Commercial policy must not remain in the hands of the parents.

The negative condition

There must be an absence of coordination of competitive behaviour. Where both parent companies withdraw from the market there is no such co-ordination. By paragraph 22, if the parents were not active in the relevant area of the JV then coordination is unlikely nor will this be likely where the parents limit their influence over the JV to strategic interests only. Common membership of the JV's and parent company's Boards of Directors is likely to be 'an obstacle to the development of the JV's autonomous commercial policy'. Many joint ventures have such common Board membership.

The direct or indirect, actual or potential, effects of the establishment and operation of the JV on market relationships have determinant importance.

The Notice considers four typical situations:

(a) JVs that take over pre-existing activities of the parent companies;
(b) JVs that undertake new activities on behalf of the parent companies;
(c) JVs that enter the parent companies' market; and
(d) JVs that operate in upstream, downstream or neighbouring markets.

In case (a), coordination is unlikely where the parent companies withdraw from the market. The parent companies need not withdraw from the market immediately the joint venture is found and may continue to be involved in the product market where there are widely separated geographic markets of the parent and joint venture respectively. In case (b), new activity by the JV is

13 OJ 1990 L257/14 and see *Conagralnc Idea Industrie*, unreported to date, concentrative joint venture cleared as only 10 per cent of French meat market held

unlikely to lead to coordination where the parent companies were unlikely to have entered the market because of technical or financial reasons. In case (c), where the parent companies remain active in the market in competition with the JV the Commission will presume that there will be coordination. Unless this is rebutted, the JV will not fall within the Merger Regulation. In case (d), coordination of purchasing or sales policy is likely where the JV acts in upstream or downstream markets.

Minority shareholding, cross-shareholdings, representation on controlling bodies of other undertakings, transfers of undertakings or parts of undertakings and joint acquisition of an undertaking with a view to its division may be concentrations and are considered in the Notice.

Conclusion

The Notice helps to clarify which mergers will fall within the Merger Regulation. If they fall within that Regulation then this is not necessarily advantageous (see Chapter 4). A complex Notification on form CO must be made to the Commission, however the Regulation is a 'fast-track' approval system with tight time limits on the Commission. Article 85(3) notifications take years.

The Merger Regulation does not apply to many mergers because for it to apply the merger must have a community dimension, i.e. the worldwide turnover of all the undertakings involved must exceed 5bn ECU (£3.5bn) and the total EC turnover of at least two of the parties must exceed 250m ECU (£175m). The limits may be reduced in 1993. Mergers which are not above these limits are unlikely, by Article 22 of the Merger Regulation, to be attacked under Article 85 (see Chapter 4). There would be no need to notify a small concentrative joint venture to the Commission under the Merger Regulation and it may be safe from Article 85(1) too. There may therefore be scope for ensuring that joint ventures are structured in such a way that the Merger Regulation applies to them, particularly if they fall outside the financial limits of the Regulation.

In the Commission's Notice regarding restrictions ancillary to concentrations[14] it is provided in paragraph V that various restrictions are acceptable. A restriction on the parent companies from competing with the joint venture company is permitted where it 'aims at expressing the reality of the lasting withdrawal of the parents from the market assigned to the joint venture'. This was discussed in Chapter 5.

14 OJ 1990 C203/5

Often the parties to a joint venture will wish to grant exclusive licences to the joint venture company. In the concentrative context the Commission regards the alternative as being a transfer to the joint venture company of all rights of the parties in the patents, know-how or other intellectual property rights as the parents are ceasing to carry on that business and will not require rights to the technology. In this context, an exclusive licence, being a substitute for a transfer, is acceptable.

Where there are purchase and supply agreements, these will be considered as they would if there were a transfer of an undertaking on normal Article 85(1) principles.

On 7 January 1991,[15] the Commission applied the Merger Regulation to a

15 FT 8 January 1991

concentrative joint venture for the first time. It cleared such a joint venture between Mitsubishi of Japan and Union Carbide of the USA in the market for carbon, graphite and related products. This was also the first time that the Commission had applied the Merger Regulation to two entities who were non-EC companies. The facts were that Mitsubishi had purchased a 50 per cent stake in Union Carbide's carbon business, the UCAR Carbon Company and its 19 international subsidiaries. The concentration affected markets for graphite and carbon related products, in particular graphite electrodes and flexible graphite. UCAR was held to be an independent company controlled neither by Union Carbide nor Mitsubishi. Neither parent remained active in the market either as a producer or as a trader. For these reasons, UCAR was a concentrative joint venture and there was no significant impact in the Community.

Conclusion

Unlike advising on an exclusive distribution agreement under Regulation 1983/83, considering a joint venture under the EC competition rules is not a matter of ensuring that particular restrictions are avoided. As with all EC competition law analysis, economic factors are important, even more so in the joint venture context where there is no block exemption.

The block exemptions and Notices considered in the rest of this chapter may be relevant in particular cases, as may the Merger Regulation. However, in most cases, the principal questions will be whether the parties are actual or potential competitors and whether competition is restricted by the joint venture.

RESEARCH AND DEVELOPMENT AGREEMENTS – EC LAW

Research and development is expensive to undertake and there is often no sure return on the investment. It is, however, essential to the development of new products and brings substantial benefits to consumers. If companies are allowed to bring together their research effort, then there are substantial cost savings to them and if they also can pool their existing ideas, the results of further research may be available to the public sooner than if they had each continued to 'go it alone'.

Any agreement to undertake research jointly is likely to contain an inherent restriction on the parties undertaking research alone, even if there is no express restriction to that effect. The parties may also wish to collaborate as to the selling and other exploitation of the results of their joint efforts and such joint exploitation is also likely to infringe Article 85(1). Where the parties are neither potential nor actual competitors, there may be no infringement of Article 85(1) provided that there are no restrictions as to the third parties with whom the parties may deal.

In *BP/Kellogg*,[16] Kellogg was a company specialising in the construction of ammonia plants. BP had developed a catalyst for ammonia production. The parties reached an agreement whereby they would co-operate in developing designs for constructing ammonia plants using BP's catalyst. Kellogg agreed not to carry out research into this catalyst itself and that it would inform BP

16 *BP/Kellogg* [1986] 2 CMLR 619, see also *The Community* v *Fanuc Ltd and Siemens AG* [1988] 4 CMLR 945

before spending money developing or commercialising other processes or bidding for a plant without offering the jointly developed process. BP agreed not to supply the catalyst to third parties without the consent of Kellogg and to employ Kellogg as the contractor to build the first plant using the technology if Kellogg built such plant. BP also agreed not to supply the catalyst to other companies without the consent of Kellogg.

The Commission held that the agreement infringed Article 85(1) and that Regulation 418/85 (research and development agreements) would not apply as the agreement contained restrictions as to products other than those which were the subject of the joint research and development. An exemption under Article 85(3) was granted, however.

Block exemption for research and development agreements

Regulation (EEC) No 418/85 of 19 December 1984 on the application of Article 85(3) of the Treaty to categories of research and development agreements[17] provides exemption for some research and development agreements.

17 Published in the *Official Journal*, 22 February 1985, at L53/5

The Regulation provides that Article 85(1) will not apply to agreements for the purpose of:

(a) joint research and development of products or processes and joint exploitation of the results of that research and development;
(b) joint exploitation of the results of research and development of products or processes jointly carried out pursuant to a prior agreement between the same undertakings; or
(c) joint research and development of products or processes excluding joint exploitation of the results, in so far as such agreements fall within the scope of Article 85(1).

It will be seen immediately that the Regulation does not apply to joint exploitation of research where the parties did not carry out such research jointly. Exploitation of the results, by Article 1, means the manufacture of the processes arising from the research or the licensing or assignment of intellectual property rights arising from such research.

In *KSB/Goulds/Lowara/ITT*,[18] Article 1.1(a) of Regulation 418/85 was considered. The case concerned KSB, the largest manufacturer of pumps in the world, which entered into a co-operation agreement setting up a joint venture, Quattro Tech SA, for the development of a type of multi-media pump with Lowara, Goulds and ITT. 'Joint research and development' was held to be 'widely defined' in the block exemption.

18 OJ 1991 L19/25

Joint research and development

Research and development will be 'joint' within the meaning of the Regulation where the work involved is carried out by a joint team, organisation or undertaking or where it is jointly entrusted to a third party or where it is allocated between the parties by way of specialisation in research, development or products.[19] Exploitation is carried out jointly where the parties collaborate in any way in the licensing or assignment of intellectual property or know-how.

19 Art.1.3

Conditions

The block exemption will only apply on condition that six requirements of Article 2 are met.

(a) The work must be carried out within a framework which defines the objectives of the work to be carried out and the field in which it is to be carried out.[20]

20 Considered in *KSB/Goulds/Lowara/ITT* OJ 1991 L19/25, *op cit*

(b) All the parties must have access to the results of the work.

(c) Where the agreement provides for joint research and development only and not joint exploitation, then both parties must be free to exploit the results of the work and any pre-existing knowledge necessary for such exploitation, independently.

(d) Any joint exploitation must be limited to intellectual property rights arising from the work or know-how which substantially contributes to economic progress. The results must be decisive for the manufacture of the contract products or the application of the contract processes.

(e) If a third party or joint company is charged with the manufacture of the contract products, it must be required to supply them only to the parties.

(f) Where undertakings are charged with manufacture by way of specialisation in production, they must be required to fulfil orders for supplies from all the parties.

Duration of exemption

The exemption will apply for the duration of the research programme and, where the results are jointly exploited, for five years from the time the contract products are 'first put on the market within the common market' (Article 3.1). This is only where the parties are not competing manufacturers.

Where the parties are competing manufacturers, or at least two of them are, the time period in Article 3.1 will apply only if, when the agreement is entered into, the parties' combined production of the products capable of being improved or replaced by the contract products does not exceed 20 per cent of 'the market for such products in the common market or a substantial part thereof' (Article 3.2).

21 OJ 1991 L19/25

In *KSB/Goulds/Lowara/ITT*[21] the usual difficulties in determining market share were evidenced in the context of Article 3.2. The Commission stated that it was 'also possible that KSB's market share will rise, at least in the long term', through sales of the multi-media pump, so doubts were cast on the applicability of Regulation 418/85 and the notified agreement was assessed under Article 85(3), which would not have been necessary if the block exemption had applied. Article 85(1) was declared 'inapplicable' in this case.

It is therefore essential always to establish whether or not the parties are competing manufacturers and, if they are, to ascertain whether their combined production of the existing products exceeds 20 per cent within the EC or a substantial part of it.

Where the time period in Article 3.1 has expired, the exemption will continue to apply where the parties' combined production of the new goods and their production of other goods which are equivalent or substitutable for such goods, does not exceed 20 per cent of the total market for such products in the EC or a substantial part of it.

Exemption

Article 1 exempts joint research and development and joint exploitation, which, but for the exemption, may be deemed inherently anti-competitive by the Commission, whether or not there are express restrictions on competition imposed upon the parties. Article 4 specifically exempts seven restrictions on competition imposed upon the parties.

(a) Obligations not to carry out independent research in the same field or a closely related field are exempted.

(b) Restrictions on entering into agreements with third parties in such fields are allowed.

(c) The parties may be obliged to obtain the contract products only from joint organisations of the parties, such as a joint venture company or from any other company entrusted with manufacture of the products.

(d) Restrictions on manufacturing the contract products in territories reserved for other parties are permitted.

(e) Unless two or more of the parties were competitors at the time the agreement was entered into, manufacture can be restricted to one or more technical fields of application.

(f) For five years from the time when the contract products are placed on the market in the EC for the first time, the parties may be restrained from carrying out an active policy of putting the goods on the market in territories reserved for other parties or from advertising or setting up distribution depots there. Users must, however, be able to obtain the contract goods from other suppliers and the parties must not make it difficult for users to obtain the products.

(g) The parties can be obliged to communicate experience to each other and grant each other non-exclusive licences for improvements.

The exemption applies where there are restrictions of more limited scope than those expressly permitted under Article 4.

Non-restrictive provisions

Article 5 lists provisions which are permitted and which are not generally restrictive of competition, following the format of other block exemptions.

The parties can be obliged to communicate patented or non-patented technical knowledge necessary for the research to be undertaken. Each party may have its own research effort to put into the 'pot', to form the basis upon which the joint research would be undertaken. A restriction on using know-how received from the other party in this way, other than for the purposes of the research and subsequent exploitation, is allowed.

The principal protection for the contract products may be intellectual property rights, the only source of protection in some instances against competitors copying the results produced at the expense of the company undertaking the research. It is therefore acceptable to require that each party maintain and enforce intellectual property rights for the contract products. Obligations to inform the other party of infringement of such rights and to assist with actions are therefore allowed.

Each party may be bringing a different contribution to the joint research venture. To allow for such discrepancies of contribution, the parties may have unequal royalty payments. The parties may share royalties received from third parties with other parties.

Obligations to supply other parties with minimum quantities of contract products and to observe minimum standards of quality are allowed.

Black-listed provisions

Where the provisions of Article 6 are present in a research and development agreement then the exemption will not apply. Such provisions would be unlikely to be exempted by the Commission on an individual notification and therefore are to be avoided. They are known as the 'black-list'.

Unconnected restrictions on research

The exemption will not apply where the parties are restricted in the carrying out of independent research in a field unconnected with the research programme (Article 6(a)).

No-challenge

The parties must not be restricted from challenging the validity of intellectual property rights which the parties hold in the EC and which are relevant to the programme. Nor must they be restricted from challenging such rights after termination or expiry of the agreement (Article 6(b)).

Quantities

There must be no restriction on the quantity of products which the parties may produce or sell or the number of operations employing the contract process which they may carry out (Article 6(c)).

Prices

Article 6(d) proscribes any restriction as to the prices which the parties may charge for sales of the contract products to third parties.

Customers

Restrictions on the customers who may be served are black-listed in Article 6(e), although under Article 4.1(e) restrictions on technical fields of application are permitted except where the parties are competitors.

Sales outside territory

Where restrictions on exports exceed the time period permitted under Article 4.1(f) discussed above, such provisions will be black-listed (Article 6(f)).

Third party manufacture

By Article 6(g), there must be no restriction on the parties allowing third parties to undertake manufacture for them, unless the parties have agreed to joint manufacture. This provision was considered in the *KSB* case,[22] where the agreements provided that Lowara would exclusively manufacture the products for the parties to the co-operative venture. As there was no separate manufacture, the fact that there would not be a right to use a third party manufacturer did not preclude the application of the block exemption. This was despite the fact that the machine tools were the property of the independent participants.

Parallel importers

Where the parties are obliged to refuse to meet demand in their territories for the contract products from persons who would market the contract products in other territories of the EC, the block exemption will not apply, nor will it apply where parallel imports are impeded (Article 6(h)).

Opposition procedure

There is provision in Article 7 for the parties to make a notification of agreements which do not fall within the block exemption, but which do not contain any black-listed provisions. If the Commission does not respond adversely within six months then the agreement will not fall foul of Article 85(1).

Withdrawal of exemption

The Commission has powers to withdraw the benefit of the block exemption under Article 10 where an agreement, although falling within the exemption, does not for other reasons fulfil the criteria necessary for exemption under Article 85(3). This applies to agreements which substantially restrict the scope of third parties carrying out research in the relevant field because of limited research capacity available elsewhere. Also, the exemption may be withdrawn where access of third parties to the market for the contract products is restricted or where, for no objectively valid reason, the parties do not exploit the results of the research and development.

Where the contract products are not subjected to effective competition, the exemption may be withdrawn by the Commission.

Duration

By Article 13 Regulation 418/85 applies until 31st December 1997. Figure 10.1 summarises the block exemption.

SPECIALISATION AGREEMENTS – EC LAW

A specialisation agreement is one under which parties agree to specialise in one particular product. Such agreements are anti-competitive when made between competing companies, although there may be advantages in such rationalisation which could be of benefit to consumers.

In *Bayer/Gist-Brocades*,[23] each of the parties financed the expansion of the other's plants for the manufacture of penicillin. Although there were no express restrictions on the parties obtaining supplies of the relevant products from third parties, in practice they sourced from each other. The agreement was held to infringe Article 85(1) as the parties were competitors, although the Commission was able to grant an exemption under Article 85(3) as the agreement led to increased production and there was some remaining competition.

23 [1976] 1 CMLR D98

Research and Development Agreements under the Block Exemption Regulation 418/85

1. Agreements exempted
    (a) joint R&D and joint exploitation of results
    (b) joint exploitation of results of joint research
    (c) joint R&D, with no joint exploitation

2. Conditions (Article 2)
    (a) defined objectives and field
    (b) all parties have access to results
    (c) where just joint R&D each free to exploit results
    (d) joint exploitation only of intellectual property rights or know-how which substantially contributes to economic progress and is decisive for manufacture
    (e) joint companies and third party manufacturer appointed by the parties supply products just to the parties
    (f) undertakings manufacturing must supply all parties

3. Duration (Article 3)
    (a) parties not competitors – 5 years from first sale
    (b) parties competitors – 5 years if combined production is no more than 20% of market for contract products in EC
    (c) after period expires exemption continues if parties' combined production in all competing goods under 20%

4. Exempted restrictions (Article 4)
    (a) no independent research in the field
    (b) no agreements with third parties for independent research in the field
    (c) contract products only to be bought from agreed manufacturer
    (d) not to manufacture in reserved territories
    (e) field of use restriction
    (f) no active policy of selling for 5 years outside territory
    (g) non-exclusive licences of improvements

5. Non-restrictive provisions (Article 5)
    (a) obligation to communicate patented and unpatented information
    (b) know-how only to be used for the R&D and exploitation of results
    (c) intellectual property rights to be maintained in force
    (d) confidentiality even after termination
    (e) informing of infringements and assisting litigation
    (f) unequal royalties to match unequal input
    (g) share royalties from third parties with other party
    (h) supply minimum quantities and observe minimum standards

6. Black-listed provisions (Article 6)
    (a) restriction on research in unconnected fields
    (b) no-challenge clauses after R&D completed
    (c) quantities of contract products produced restricted
    (d) pricing restrictions
    (e) customer restrictions
    (f) export restrictions for periods longer than allowed

Fig. 10.1

```
┌──────────────────────────────────────────────────────────┐
│     (g)  cannot have third parties manufacture            │
│     (h)  refuse demand in territory for use outside or     │
│          make parallel importing difficult                │
│                                                            │
│  7.  Opposition procedure for notification available       │
│                                                            │
└──────────────────────────────────────────────────────────┘
```

Fig. 10.1 (*cont.*)

Specialisation Regulation No. 417/85

Commission Regulation (EEC) No. 417/85 of 19 December 1984 on the application of Article 85(3) of the Treaty to categories of specialization agreements[24] is the block or general exemption for specialisation agreements. It sets out those provisions of a specialisation agreement which are acceptable. Unlike other block exemptions there is no black-list of unacceptable restrictions, however, any restrictions other than those exempted or provisions permitted would render the block exemption inapplicable.

24 OJ 1985 L53/1

Agreements covered

Article 85(1) will not apply to agreements on specialisation where, for the duration of the agreement, the parties accept reciprocal obligations (Article 1):

(a) not to manufacture certain products or to have them manufactured, but to leave it to other parties to manufacture the products or to have them manufactured; or

(b) to manufacture certain products or have them manufactured only jointly.

There must therefore be an element of reciprocity, such as 'I will not manufacture sproggets if you don't manufacture widgets'.

Exempted restrictions

Article 2.1 sets out the restrictions which may be imposed by the parties:

(a) Obligations on the parties not to enter into specialisation agreements with third parties for identical or equivalent products may be imposed. The equivalent goods must be regarded by users as equivalent in view of 'their characteristics, price and intended use'.

(b) The parties may impose a restriction whereby one party obtains the products which are the subject of the specialisation exclusively from another party, except where the goods are obtainable from another source on more favourable terms and the party is not prepared to offer the products on the same terms.

(c) Regulation 417/85 permits an obligation requiring the granting to the other party of the exclusive right to distribute products which are the subject matter of the specialisation, provided that intermediaries and users can also obtain the goods from other suppliers and the parties do not render it difficult for intermediaries or users to obtain the products from such other sources.

Less restrictive provisions would also be exempted (Article 2.2).

Non-restrictive provisions

Article 2.3 permits the following provisions which are not restrictive of competition to appear in agreements of this sort:

(a) an obligation to supply other parties with products which are the subject of the specialization and of [*sic* – with?] replacement parts for them;
(b) an obligation to maintain minimum stocks of products which are the subject of the specialization and of replacement parts for them;
(c) an obligation to provide customer and guarantee service for products which are the subject of the specialization.

Market share and turnover tests

By Article 3 the exemption is only available where the products the subject of the specialisation and the other products of the parties which are equivalent do not represent more than 20 per cent of the market for such products in the common market or a substantial part of it. Also, the total turnover of the parties must not exceed 500m ECU (£350m).

This is an important provision when considering a specialisation agreement and it will always be necessary to ask whether the parties exceed the 20 per cent threshold or the aggregate turnover figure.

Opposition procedure

Where the turnover figure is exceeded, but not the market share figure, the parties may notify a specialisation agreement to the Commission under Article 4 and if the Commission does not oppose the notification within six months of the receipt of the notification by the Commission the agreement will be exempted, as has been seen above in relation to other block exemptions. This procedure is particularly useful for large companies which would otherwise find that they would always exceed the turnover figure even where their share of the relevant market of the specialisation was tiny.

Withdrawal of exemption

The Commission may withdraw the benefit of the block exemption under Article 8 where the conditions for exemption under Article 85(3) are not present and in particular where:

(a) the agreement is not yielding significant results in terms of rationalization or consumers are not receiving a fair share of the resulting benefit; or
(b) the products which are the subject of the specialization are not subject in the common market or a substantial part thereof to effective competition from identical products or products considered by users to be equivalent in view of their characteristics, price and intended use.

Concerted practices

The Regulation applies also to decisions of associations of undertakings and concerted practices.

Duration

Regulation 417/85 applies until 31st December 1997.
Figure 10.2 summarises Regulation 417/85.

Specialisation Agreements under the Block Exemption Regulation 417/85

1. Agreements exempted
   (a) reciprocal agreements not to manufacture or have other parties manufacture
   (b) reciprocal agreements to manufacture products or have them manufactured jointly

2. Exempted restrictions
   (a) not to conclude specialisation agreements with third parties for identical or equivalent products
   (b) obligation to procure products exclusively from other party or joint undertaking, except where goods can be obtained on better terms and other party will not match those better terms
   (c) obligation to grant other parties the exclusive right to distribute the products, provided users can obtain the products from other suppliers and parties do not make this difficult

3. Non-restrictive provisions
   (a) obligation to supply other party, quality standards
   (b) obligation to maintain minimum stocks and spares
   (c) obligation to provide customer and guarantee services

4. The specialisation products and parties' equivalent products must not exceed 20% of the EC market and parties' aggregate annual turnover not to exceed 500m ECU (£350m)

5. Opposition procedure where turnover figure (not market share) exceeded

---

Fig. 10.2

CO-OPERATION AGREEMENTS – EC LAW

Co-operation takes many forms. At one extreme two companies merge. At the other they agree mutually to assist each other with research. Joint venture, research and development and specialisation agreements are all forms of co-operation discussed above.

The Commission issued its Notice on Co-operation Agreements on 29 July 1968,[25] some time before the block exemptions for research and development and specialisation agreements. The Notice is still valid, however, although as it is merely a Notice and not a Regulation it is not strictly binding upon the Commission.

25 OJ 1968 C75/3

Joint procurement of information

In the Notice (paragraph II), the Commission states that it does not regard agreements for the joint procurement of information as being restrictive of competition. This would include agreements having as their sole object:

(a) An exchange of opinion or experience,
(b) Joint market research,
(c) The joint carrying out of comparative studies of enterprises or industries,
(d) The joint preparation of statistics and calculation models.

If the scope of action of the parties is limited or their market behaviour is coordinated there may be a restraint of competition (paragraph II(1)):

> This is in particular the case where concrete recommendations are made or where conclusions are given such a form that they induce at least some of the participating enterprises to behave in an identical manner on the market.

Co-operation in accounting matters

Co-operation in accounting matters, joint provision of credit guarantees, joint debt collecting associations and joint business or tax consultant agencies are not restrictive of competition under the Notice. Joint comparison of prices or application of uniform conditions may however be contrary to Article 85(1). Standardised printed forms may be used, provided there is no tacit agreement or understanding on uniform prices, rebates or conditions of sale (paragraph II(2)).

Research and development

Agreements concerning the joint implementation of research and development projects, the joint placing of research and development contracts and the sharing out of research and development projects among participating enterprises are not restrictive of competition, under the Notice (paragraph II(3)).

Commitments which restrict the parties' freedom to carry out their own research work may be anti-competitive and the block exemption Regulation 418/85 for research and development agreements may apply. Restrictions on exploitation of the results of the joint research may restrict competition. Restrictions on granting licences of intellectual property to third parties may infringe Article 85(1).

Joint use of production facilities

By paragraph II(4), the joint use of production facilities and storage and transport equipment is not restrictive of competition, although there may be restrictions if the parties do not bear the cost of using those facilities or there are concerted practices applied regarding joint production or the establishment of a joint enterprise.

Orders

A partnership between two companies who are not competitors in the relevant products or where each of them by themselves would otherwise be able to execute the orders, would be acceptable where such partnership was for the common execution of orders (paragraph II(5)).

Joint selling

Agreements for joint selling arrangements and joint after-sales and repair services, provided the 'participating enterprises are not competitors with regard to the products or services covered by the agreement', would not restrict competition (paragraph II(6) of the Notice).

Joint advertising

By paragraph II(7), joint advertising of an industry or a brand is not restrictive of competition. Any restrictions on the parties advertising individually as well may infringe Article 85(1).

Common label

Where parties agree a common label to designate a certain quality and that label is available to all competitors on the same conditions, the agreement is unlikely to infringe Article 85(1) (paragraph II(8) of the Notice). The acceptance of quality control with the use of the label is also acceptable, but the right to use the label must not be linked with obligations regarding production, marketing, price formation or with restrictions on selling any products in respect of which the label is not used and which do not conform to the quality standards.[26]

The provisions of the Notice on Co-operation Agreements are summarised in Fig. 10.3.

26 See Vollmer A.N. – *Product and Technical Standardisation under Article 85* [1986] 4 ECLR 388

SUB-CONTRACTING AGREEMENTS – EC LAW

The final piece in the EC legislative jigsaw puzzle concerning joint venture/co-operation agreements is the Commission Notice of 18 December 1978 concerning the assessment of certain subcontracting agreements in relation to Article 85(1) of the EEC Treaty.[27]

27 OJ 1979 C1/2

Sub-contracting agreements are at the opposite extreme of a fifty/fifty joint venture to which both the parties equally contribute and from which they each benefit. Sub-contracting is merely a way of having another company undertake manufacture for another. In the Notice the Commission in paragraph 1 defines such agreements as agreements under which:

> one firm, called 'the contractor', whether or not in consequence of a prior order from a third party, entrusts to another, called 'the subcontractor', the manufacture of goods, the supply of services or the performance of work under the contractor's instructions, to be provided to the contractor or performed on his behalf.

Such agreements, the Commission states, are not themselves caught by the prohibition in Article 85(1). The Notice is not a Regulation and is not binding upon the Commission, although it is a useful indication of the Commission's views on agreements of this sort. There is very little case law concerning such agreements[28] and the Notice is the best source of definitive opinion on such agreements.

28 See *ICL/Fujitsu*, OJ 1986 C210/3 and *EMI/Jungheinrich* (7th Report on Competition Policy) 1978

In such agreements the contractor commonly has to provide the subcontractor with secret information, know-how or patented information, which must only be used for the purposes of carrying out the manufacture of products under the sub-contracting arrangement. Such agreements therefore contain potential restrictions of competition.

Notice on Co-operation Agreements of 1968

Permitted co-operation

1. (a) exchange of opinion or experience
    (b) joint market research
    (c) joint comparative studies of industries and costs
    (d) joint preparation of statistics and calculation models

2. (a) co-operation in accounting
    (b) joint provision of credit guarantees
    (c) joint debt collecting associations
    (d) joint business or tax consultant agencies

3. (a) joint implementation of R&D projects
    (b) joint placing of R&D projects
    (c) sharing out of R&D projects amongst participants

4.   joint use of production facilities and storing and transport equipment

5.   setting up partnerships for common execution of orders, where parties do not compete as to work to to be done or could not alone execute the orders

6. (a) joint selling arrangements
    (b) joint after-sales and repair service, provided not competitors for the relevant products

7.   joint advertising

8.   common quality label where available to all competitors on same conditions

---

Fig. 10.3

Acceptable provisions

Paragraph 2 of the Notice states that Article 85(1) will not apply to clauses whereby the technology or equipment supplied must not be used except for the purposes of the sub-contracting agreement, where they must not be made available to a third party and where the goods, work or services produced must only be supplied to the contractor or be performed on his behalf. However, this exemption applies only if the technology is necessary for the sub-contractor to carry out the work. This requirement is satisfied where the sub-contractor needs to use intellectual property rights, or secret know-how, or plans or dies or accessory equipment, which even though not necessarily covered by intellectual property rights or secrecy, 'permit the manufacture of goods which differ in form, function or composition from other goods manufactured or supplied on the market'. Where the sub-contractor has the necessary information to undertake the manufacture already at his disposal then the exemption will not apply.

Paragraph 3 exempts any restrictions on keeping any know-how secret which has passed between either of the parties. A restriction may be imposed on the sub-contractor using the know-how even after the agreement has terminated, as long as it is not public knowledge. Also, a requirement that the sub-contractor license back to the contractor, on a non-exclusive basis, improvements of the technology is permitted. If the improvements cannot be used independently of the technology supplied originally by the contractor, the licence-back can be exclusive. Paragraph 3 goes on to provide:

> However, any undertaking by the subcontractor regarding the right to dispose of the results of his own research and development work may restrain competition, where such results are capable of being used independently.

The sub-contractor authorised to use a trade mark on the goods, may be restrained from using such trade mark in relation to other goods which are not to be supplied to the contractor.

Figure 10.4 summarises the Notice on sub-contracting agreements.

Summary of Notice on Sub-contracting Agreements of 1978

The Notice:

1. Applies to contractor who entrusts to sub-contractor the manufacture of goods or supply of services to be provided to contractor

2. Permitted provisions
    - technology or equipment provided only to be used for purposes of agreement and not to be released to third parties
    - goods produced from such technology only to be sold to contractor

The above provisions only apply *provided* sub-contractor needs the technology in the form of:

   (i)   intellectual property rights
   (ii) secret know-how
   (iii) plans or documents of contractor
   (iv) dies, tools, equipment which is distinctly the contractor's which if no intellectual property rights or secrecy permit manufacture different from that available on the market

Sub-contractor must not have technology of his own which could do the work

   - either party to keep know-how secret even after termination unless public knowledge
   - sub-contractor not to use technology after termination unless public knowledge
   - non-exclusive licence back of improvements, can be exclusive where improvements not severable, but no restrictions on sub-contractor disposing of his results
   - restriction on sub-contractor using trade mark of contractor except on goods supplied back to contractor

---

Fig. 10.4

CONCLUSION

In the field of co-operation between enterprises, whether as to research, production or selling any restrictions of competition may fall foul of Article 85(1). In particular cases, depending on the facts, agreements may fall within the block exemptions for research and development agreements or specialisation agreements or the Notices on co-operation agreements and sub-contracting agreements. Otherwise, where there is a concentrative joint venture, it may be necessary to notify the Commission under the Merger Regulation. Where none of these provisions apply, particularly where the parties are competitors, it may be necessary to make an individual notification to the Commission under Article 85(3) and Regulation 17, unless the Notice on agreements of minor importance (discussed in Chapter 2) applies.

JOINT VENTURE AGREEMENTS – UK LAW

UK competition law is much less specific and detailed than that of the EC in this field, although of importance. Joint venture agreements, research and development and specialisation agreements and co-operation and sub-contracting agreements will be considered here.

The Restrictive Trade Practices Act 1976 (considered in more detail in Chapter 2) applies to all agreements of this sort where there are two or more parties carrying on business in the UK. Where there are restrictions on two parties to the agreement of the type set out in sections 6 or 11 of the RTPA then it may be necessary to register the agreement at the Office of Fair Trading before the restrictions take effect, unless there are restrictions which can be discounted under section 9(3) or they are exempted under Schedule 3.

Many joint venture agreements are registrable under the RTPA. As has been seen in Chapter 9 there are specific exemptions in Schedule 3 for intellectual property licences, although they are not universally applicable, as well as such an exemption for exclusive supply agreements. There are, however, no specific provisions addressing co-operation between enterprises. If an agreement falls within the RTPA, its restrictions will be void if the agreement is not registered in time and, if the parties are subject to an order of the Restrictive Practices Court and infringe the legislation again, they will be in contempt of court and face fines and the possibility of individuals going to jail.

Non-competition restrictions

Where parties to a joint venture agreement agree not to compete with the joint venture company as to the selling of goods which the joint venture company is to market, then there will clearly be restrictions on two parties and a registrable agreement. Where there is no express restriction on competition, but in practice the parties will not compete with the joint venture into which they have put much effort, the agreement will not be registrable. The legislation looks to the form of the agreement and not to its effect, unlike EC competition law.

The joint venture company may be a 'subsidiary' of one of the parties. If that is the case then restrictions on that joint venture company and its parent will be regarded as restrictions on one party as those companies will be 'interconnected bodies corporate' under section 43(2) of the RTPA and, if there are no restrictions on the other 'minority' shareholder company, the agreement would avoid being registrable.

Exclusive supply, pricing and terms

Where the parties agree to supply a joint venture company and no other companies within a particular territory, as is often the case, or stipulate the prices or terms and conditions to be used by the joint venture company, then the agreement is likely to be registrable.

A multiplicity of clauses are possible in joint ventures and each would need to be assessed to determine whether it amounted to a relevant restriction under the RTPA. For example, exclusive supply agreements may be exempted under Schedule 3, paragraph 2, but only if there are no other restrictions and only two parties to the agreement (i.e. the joint venture company would have to be an interconnected body corporate with one of its shareholders so that it would be regarded as one with it for the purposes of determining whether there were two parties to the agreement or not).

Restrictions relating to the goods supplied by one of the parties to the JV may be capable of being discounted under section 9(3), such as a clause that the joint venture company will sell goods sold to it by one of the parties only to a particular customer or in a certain area.

It may be possible to amend a draft agreement to ensure that it is not registrable. In particular, it may not be commercially essential that the parties be expressly restricted from competing with the joint venture company.[29]

Section 21(2)

Where an agreement is registered, the OFT will determine whether its restrictions are of such significance as to merit a reference to the Restrictive Practices Court and in many cases a 'section 21(2) direction' will be made, i.e. there will be no reference to the Court, but the agreement, being registrable, will be placed upon the Register. Whether such a direction can be made will depend on how restrictive the agreement is, and in the process of negotiating with the OFT the parties may be required to amend the agreement to remove the restrictive provisions or water them down to a certain extent. The restrictions should be the minimum necessary to achieve the success of the joint venture.

During the s.21(2) examination process the OFT will be looking for the first time at factors other than the form of the agreement and will commonly ask questions about the relevant market and the parties' posittition within that market, all of which wil be relevant in assessing whether the direction can be given in a particular case.

National economy

Section 29 permits an exemption where an agreement:

(a) is calculated to promote the carrying on of an industrial or commercial project or scheme of substantial importance to the national economy;
(b) has as its main object the promotion of efficiency in industry or the improvement of productive capacity in industry;

29 See *Diazo Copying Materials* [1984] ICR 427, where HTL and MSL co-operated in the manufacture and marketing of a photocopier machine

(c) has an object which cannot be achieved or achieved within a reasonable time except by the agreement;

(d) has included in it only those restrictions which are necessary to achieve the object;

(e) the agreement 'is on balance expedient in the national interest'.

Mergers

As under EC competition law, there is potential overlap between merger legislation and competition legislation concerning such agreements. Section 64 of the Fair Trading Act 1973 has been discussed in Chapter 4 and the relevant question will be whether the enterprises which are parties to the venture have ceased to be distinct under section 64.

RESEARCH AND DEVELOPMENT AGREEMENTS – UK LAW

As for joint ventures, there are no specific competition law provisions directed at research and development agreements along the lines of the EC block exemption. Non-competition restrictions and restrictions relating to the sale of products produced using the resulting technology may all render the agreement registrable and that will need to be assessed in the usual way.

Section 21(2) treatment may be available, as discussed above, and agreements may be capable of exemption under section 29 as agreements important to the national economy.

SPECIALISATION AGREEMENTS – UK LAW

Again there is no UK equivalent of the block exemption Regulation 417/85. By their nature, such agreements concern the specialisation of two parties in two areas, and often a restriction on their taking part in the other party's areas. Where they both accept a restriction the agreement would be registrable. If only one party accepts a restriction then there would not be a registrable agreement.

In many cases, where such specialisation can be justified and the parties are not dominant in their respective fields, registrable agreements of this sort will be granted a section 21(2) direction and will merely be placed upon the Register.

CO-OPERATION AGREEMENTS – UK LAW

Co-operation agreements may take a number of forms, from joint ventures to the mere exchange of information concerning accounting matters.

Information exchange agreements are registrable under section 7 of the RTPA, where they relate to the exchange of information as to prices charged or to be charged for goods or the terms and conditions on which goods have been or are to be supplied.[30] Thus an agreement between company X that it will advise company Y of its prices in return for a similar favour will comprise a registrable agreement.

Sections 9(5) and 18(5) of the RTPA exempt certain standardisation

30 Only part of s.7 has been brought into force by The Restrictive Trade Practices (Information Agreements) Order, S.I. 1969 No. 1842

schemes, where they relate to compliance with a British Standard or a scheme approved by order of the Secretary of State.

SUB-CONTRACTING AGREEMENTS – UK LAW

Where a contractor company has another company undertake manufacture to satisfy the contractor's need for manufactured product for resale, it will wish to ensure that finished products are only sold to the contractor and not to third parties and that any know-how licensed to the sub-contractor is kept confidential. Is a restriction on the sub-contractor selling the goods other than to the contractor a restriction in a contract for the supply of goods relating only to the goods to be supplied and therefore capable of being discounted under section 9(3)? It would seem not. A sub-contracting agreement may well be an agreement for the supply of goods – from sub-contractor to contractor, but the restriction is not in relation to the goods supplied by the sub-contractor to the contractor, but rather as to the goods which the sub-contractor will be manufacturing using know-how of the contractor.

Such a restriction will not however render an agreement registrable under the RTPA. There would have to be another restriction as the RTPA requires restrictions on two parties to the agreement. There would need also to be a restriction on the contractor. If the contractor agreed not to put out his contracting work to any other sub-contractor, that exclusivity would amount to a restriction as to the persons from whom the contractor could obtain goods, which would not be exempted as an exclusive dealing agreement under Schedule 3, paragraph 2 of the RTPA. It may be possible for the contractor instead to restrict himself as to the persons to whom he would license a patent, invoking the *Ravenseft*[31] case to allege that such a provision was not a restriction. A 'fail-safe' registration of such an agreement may still be advisable to ensure the enforceability of the restrictions.

31 [1978] QB 52

CONCLUSION

Assessing the vast variety of co-operation agreements and joint ventures under UK competition law involves a careful vetting of all the relevant provisions of the RTPA and, by dint of informed drafting, registration may be avoidable except where for commercial reasons express restrictions cannot be forgone.

QUESTION

Planes UK manufacture wood planes for domestic use. Woods France specialises in selling wood for the DIY market throughout Europe. They come to you asking for commercial and legal guidance as to how best to cement a vague idea of co-operation which they have. They have considered merging their two companies, setting up a joint venture company to undertake all their existing plane manufacture and wood processing, each pooling their research resources to benefit from the other's specialised knowledge so that they can develop new products for each of their businesses or they may merely regularly exchange information concerning customers, prices and recent research developments.

Planes UK is subject to an order of the Restrictive Practices Court and wishes at all costs to avoid a registrable agreement. Woods France is dominant in France, and possibly in the EC, in their type of wood and they were fined by the Commission for price fixing twelve months ago.

Assuming the parties are potential but not actual competitors which route would cause the fewest competition problems? They are keen to avoid any form of notification. What further information would you need from them of an economic nature before you could properly advise them?

FURTHER READING

Joint ventures

ARTICLES   Faull J. – *Joint Ventures under the EEC Competition Rules*, [1984] 5 ECLR 358
Satzky H. – *New Antitrust Regime for Joint Ventures*, (1990) 18 IBL 518

CASES   *Re De Laval-Stork VOF* [1988] 4 CMLR 714
Diazo Copying Materials [1984] ICR 427
Elopak/Metal Box – Odin OJ 8 August 1990, L209/15
GEC/Weir [1978] 1 CMLR D42
KEWA [1976] 2 CMLR D15
Rockwell/Iveco [1983] 3 CMLR 709
Screensports OJ 1991 L62/32
Vacuum Interrupters (No1) [1977] 1 CMLR D67
Wano Schwarzpulver [1979] 1 CMLR 403

NOTICES   *Notice on concentrative joint ventures*, OJ C203/10, 14 August 1990
Notice on restrictions ancillary to concentrations, OJ C203/5, 14 August 1990

BOOKS   Bellamy & Child – *Common Market Law of Competition*, Sweet & Maxwell, 3rd ed., 1987, Para.5-064
Fine F. – *Mergers and Joint Ventures in Europe: The Law and Policy of the EEC*, Graham & Trotman, 1989
Van Bael & Bellis, *Competition Law of the EEC*, CCH Editions, 2nd ed., 1990, para.562

Research and development

ARTICLE   Venit J. – *The Research and Development Block Exemption Regulation*, [1985] 10 European Law Review 151

BOOKS   Bellamy & Child (*op cit*), para.5-005
Green N. – *Commercial Agreements and Competition Law*, Graham & Trotman, 1986, p.619
Korah V. – *Research and Development and EEC Competition Rules, Regulation 418/85*, ESC Publishing 1986
Van Bael & Bellis (*op cit*), para.515
Whish R. – *Competition Law*, Butterworths, 2nd ed., 1989, p.442

CASES   *BP/Kellogg* [1986] 2 CMLR 619
De Laval/Stork [1977] 2 CMLR D69
KSB/Goulds/Lowara/ITT OJ 1991 L19/25

REGULATION   Research and development block exemption Regulation No 418/85 of 14 December 1984, OJ L53/5, 22 February 1985

Specialisation

BOOKS   Bellamy & Child (*op cit*), para.5-028
Green (*op cit*), p.640
Van Bael & Bellis (*op cit*), para.515

Whish (*op cit*), p.460

Bayer/Gist Brocades [1976] 1 CMLR D98 and Notice [1990] 4 CMLR 516   **CASE**

Specialisation block exemption Regulation No 417/85 of 19 December 1984, OJ L53/1, 22   **REGULATION**
    February 1985

Co-operation

Vollmer A.N. – *Product and Technical Standardisation under Article 85* [1986] 4 ECLR 388   **ARTICLE**

Van Bael (*op cit*), para.525   **BOOK**

Notice on co-operation agreements, OJ C75/3, 1968   **NOTICE**

Sub-contracting

Bellamy & Child (*op cit*), para.6-170   **BOOKS**
Van Bael & Bellis (*op cit*), para.526

EMI/Jungheinrich, 7th Report on Competition Policy, 1978   **CASES**
ICL/Fujitsu, OJ 1986, C210/3

Notice on subcontracting agreements, OJ C1/2, 3 January 1979   **NOTICE**

11

Miscellaneous sectors

In this chapter particular sectors which have been addressed specifically by the competition authorities or which merit individual consideration are discussed.

MOTOR VEHICLES – EC LAW

The European Commission has recognised that exclusive and selective distribution agreements for motor vehicles fall within Article 85(3), i.e. the benefits outweigh the anti-competitive effects. Distribution agreements and selective distribution were considered generally in Chapter 8. Here consideration will be given specifically to the motor vehicle sector.

Non-distribution areas

Motor vehicles are a major industry in the EC. Much competition law has revolved around this sector, cases concerned with whether Nissan cars contain such a percentage of Japanese, as opposed to EC, manufactured components that they are deemed not manufactured in the EC and imports of them are barred by the French and cases concerning copyright in spare parts.[1] In *Volvo AB v Erick Veng (U.K.) Ltd*[2] and *Consorzio Italiano della Componentistica di Ricambio per Autoveicoli and Maxicar v Regie Nationale des Usines Renault*[3] (known as the *Renault* case and fully discussed in Chapter 3), the product was body panels for cars. Refusal to license intellectual property rights protecting a particular design of body panel was not an abuse of a dominant position. There may be such abuse, the court suggested, where there was an arbitrary refusal to supply spare parts to independent repairers, where the manufacturer was setting prices for spare parts at an unfair level or where the manufacturer decided no longer to manufacture spare parts of a particular model where many vehicles of that model were still in circulation.

Only Regulation 123/85, being specific to motor vehicles, is considered in this chapter, in addition to relevant case law in this sector discussed below. EC rules on air and maritime transport are beyond the scope of this work.

On 12th December 1984, the Commission's Regulation (EEC) No 123/85 on the application of Article 85(3) of the Treaty to certain categories of motor vehicle distribution and servicing agreements[4] came into force. The Commission also issued a Notice concerning this Regulation – Commission notice concerning Regulation (EEC) No 123/85 of 12 December 1984 on the application of Article 85(3) of the Treaty to certain categories of motor vehicle distribution and servicing agreements.[5]

Selective distribution is the selection of dealers for selling products to end users, the selection being a matter of applying criteria to the potential dealer,

1 *British Leyland v Armstrong* [1984] 3 CMLR 102 (C.A.) and [1986] AC 577 (H.L.)
2 [1989] 4 CMLR 122
3 [1990] 4 CMLR 265

4 OJ 1985 L15/16

5 OJ 1985 C17/4

such as quality standards, before admitting him to the network. The Commission has recognised that consumers may benefit from having the servicing of their vehicles undertaken by knowledgeable experts. In Recital 4 of the Regulation it is stated:

> The exclusive and selective distribution clauses can be regarded as indispensable measures of rationalization in the motor vehicle industry because motor vehicles are consumer durables which at both regular and irregular intervals require expert maintenance and repair, not always in the same place.

The Commission goes on to state that on grounds of capacity and efficiency alone there cannot be an unlimited number of dealers. Linking servicing and distribution is therefore in the interests of consumers.

The Regulation has been widely used in practice and saves individual notifications of exclusive and selective distribution agreement networks, which networks are particularly common in the motor vehicle industry.

The Peugeot cases

Automobiles Peugeot SA ('Peugeot') manufactures and sells motor vehicles. Back in 1963 Peugeot notified the Commission of its standard form distribution agreement for distribution of Peugeot vehicles in France. In 1971 it notified the Commission by letter of its agreements for the Benelux countries. The distribution agreement contained export restrictions, and the Commission issued a statement of objections which resulted in Peugeot abandoning the restrictions. The Commission required that the standard form agreement be brought into line with the principles laid down in the *BMW* case,[6] a blueprint for the block exemption to come.

There were further notifications for Germany and the UK in 1979. At the end of December 1985 Peugeot notified the Commission of amendments to its standard agreement following the entry into force of Regulation 123/85, the block exemption.

In September 1986 the Commission reached a decision in *Peugeot*[7] concerning the distribution agreement in force between 1982 and 1985 in the Benelux countries. The main provisions of the agreement were summarised by the Commission in paragraph 12 of the decision:

> Peugeot confers on the selected dealer the right to sell the products designated in the agreement (contract products), that is to say new vehicles of the Peugeot and/or Talbot makes, as well as spare parts and accessories in a defined territory (the allotted territory). In that territory, Peugeot undertakes to supply for resale the products specified in the agreement to that dealer alone. The dealer may sell new vehicles of other makes only with Peugeot's consent. He is obliged to use only the genuine spare parts made available by Peugeot and, in France, by Peugeot or its suppliers.

The provisions of the agreement which were held to infringe Article 85(1) were:

1. Peugeot's undertaking not to conclude any distribution and servicing agreements for contract products with other firms operating within the contract territory.

6 [1975] 1CMLR D1, OJ 1975 L29/1

7 OJ 1986 L295/19

2. Dealers were only permitted to sell to end users, nor to other dealers nor parallel importers or even other Peugeot dealers.
3. New vehicles of other makes could not be marketed by dealers without the consent of Peugeot.
4. The obligation only to use Peugeot spare parts.
5. Restrictions on allowing dealers actively to market the products outside their territory.

The Commission held (in paragraph 38):

> A vehicle manufacturer who makes use of the differences in the specifications of cars with a view to controlling their outlets, and who limits the availability of RHD [right hand drive] vehicles or of LHD vehicles, as the case may be, from his dealers reduces the supply of goods and opportunities for purchasing them, to the detriment of final consumers.

The favourable effects of selective distribution arrangements are thereby nullified.[8] The Commission stated that 'the obstacles placed in the way of the supply of vehicles to purchasers resident in the UK render the restrictions of competition stemming from the Peugeot distribution system unexemptable under Article 85(3)'. The price differentials between Member States were large, 40 per cent higher in the UK than in Belgium. Strenuous efforts took place to hinder parallel imports. UK potential purchasers attempting to order RHD cars direct from the Continent were systematically referred to the UK dealer.

A fine was imposed by the Commission in respect of incorrect information which was supplied to the Commission of 4,000 ECU (£2,800). No fine was imposed in relation to the Article 85(1) infringements although the finding was adverse.

More recently, in *Ecosystem SA* v *Peugeot SA,*[9] the Commission received a complaint from Ecosystem SA alleging an infringement of Article 85(1) by Peugeot and requesting that interim measures be taking against Peugeot pending a final decision in the case. Again at the heart of the matter was price differentials, in this case a price 10 per cent higher in France than in Belgium. A circular was sent to all authorised dealers not to sell to Ecosystem as it was 'exercising an activity equivalent to resale while acting under the guise of an authorised agent'.

It was decided that there was a sufficient probability of infringement for 'interim measures' to be imposed as it was likely that the circular would infringe Article 85(1), i.e. not a formal, final decision, but relief until such a final decision, against the refusal to supply. Peugeot was required to write to all its authorised dealers within the following two weeks withdrawing the circular instruction. Peugeot applied to the Court of First Instance to have the interim measures lifted, but, in *Automobiles Peugeot SA and Peugeot SA v EC Commission,*[10] the Court held that there was no serious risk that the detrimental effects of the interim measures would cause anything beyond temporary disadvantages and the application was refused.

The cases illustrate the importance of pricing as an element of competition.

8 See paragraph 44 of the *Ford* case, [1984] 1 CMLR 549, OJ 1983 L327/31

9 [1990] 4 CMLR 449

10 [1990] 4 CMLR 674

Block exemption Regulation 123/85

Exclusivity

Regulation 123/85 applies, by Article 1, where there are two parties to an agreement and where one party agrees to supply in a defined area of the common market only to the other party, or only to the other party and to a specified number of other undertakings within the distribution system:

> for the purpose of resale certain motor vehicles intended for use on public roads and having three or more road wheels, together with spare parts therefor.

Motor cycles and tractors would not therefore be covered. The Regulation applies where the supplier agrees to grant exclusive rights to the dealer for a specific territory.

By Article 2, the supplier may also be restricted from selling the contract goods to final consumers and from providing them with servicing for the contract goods in the contract territory.

Dealer obligations

Obligations which may be imposed on the dealer or purchaser of the motor vehicles are set out in Article 3:

1. Not to modify the goods unless the modification is under a contract with the final consumer and involves a particular motor vehicle purchased by that final consumer in the contract programme.
2. Not to manufacture competing goods. The supplier can therefore be assured that the dealer will be wholly devoted to the supplier's particular range of car.
3. Not to sell new motor vehicles which compete with the contract goods nor sell at the premises where the suppler's goods are sold new motor vehicles other than those offered for supply by the manufacturer. There may be no restrictions on sale of second-hand cars, whether at the premises or not.
4. Not to sell spare parts which compete with the contract goods and 'do not match the quality of the contract goods'. A restriction also on using such competing spare parts is allowed where they are used for 'repair or maintenance of contract goods or corresponding goods'.
5. Not to conclude distribution or servicing agreements with third parties for competing goods.
6. Not to conclude distribution or servicing agreements in the territory for the goods. This effectively permits a bar on the distributor from appointing sub-distributors.
7. Where the distributor is allowed to appoint sub-distributors it is permissible to require that similar restrictions to those permitted are imposed upon the sub-distributors.
8. Not to maintain branches or depots for the distribution of the contract goods outside the contract territory nor seek customers for the contract goods or corresponding goods outside that territory.
9. Not to entrust third parties with distribution or servicing of the contract goods outside the territory.

10. An obligation to supply to resellers only where the reseller is an undertaking 'within the distribution system' or to supply spare parts within the contract programme only where they are for the purposes of repair or maintenance of a motor vehicle by the reseller.

11. To sell motor vehicles to final consumers in the contract territory using an intermediary only where the intermediary has prior written authorisation.

12. To observe the obligations in paragraph 1 and paragraphs 6 to 11 above for a maximum period of one year from the termination or expiry of the agreement.

By Article 4, minimum standards of equipment, training of staff, advertising, collection, storage and delivery and repair and maintenance are allowed, as are requirements that orders be placed in certain periods. In *D'Ieteren Motor Oils* OJ 1991 L20/42 justifiable requirements to use only approved oil fell within Article 4. Minimum quantities requirements are permitted, as well as requirements to keep stocks and demonstration models, perform guarantee work, use only spare parts within the contract programme or corresponding goods.

Article 13 contains definitions used in the Regulation. It defines 'corresponding goods' as:

> those which are similar in kind to those in the contract programme, are distributed by the manufacturer or with the manufacturer's consent, and are the subject of a distribution or servicing agreement with an undertaking within the distribution system.

A requirement to inform customers of the extent to which spare parts from other sources might be used is allowed, as is a requirement on the dealer to inform customers whenever spare parts from other sources have been used.

The exemption will only apply, however, where the dealer honours guarantees and performs free servicing for motor vehicles within the contract programme or corresponding thereto which have been supplied in the EC by another undertaking within the distribution network. Sub-distributors must honour guarantees in the same way (Article 5). The Notice in paragraph I.2. explains this provision. It would apply where dealers refuse to perform guarantee work on vehicles which they have not sold and which have been imported from other Member States.

The supplier must not withhold his consent to sub-distribution agreements without an objectively justifiable reason. The supplier must not discriminate, in the standards required of the dealer, against one dealer. In discount schemes, supplies of motor vehicles within the contract programme must be distinguished from spare parts and other goods. This counters the concentration of the dealer's demand on the supplier which might follow from cumulation of discounts and allows spare parts suppliers which do not offer as wide a range of goods as the manufacturer to compete on equal terms (Recital 15 of the Regulation). The supplier must supply to the dealer any car which corresponds to a model within the contract programme which is marketed by the manufacturer with his consent in the Member State in which the vehicle is to be registered (Article 5(2)(d)).

Where the dealer has assumed obligations to improve distribution structures, the exemption of restrictions on the dealer selling competing new cars and concluding distribution agreements with third parties for competing goods will only apply where the supplier will release the dealer from the obligations if he has an objectively justified reason for being so released. Also, in such circumstances, the supplier can reserve to himself the right to appoint further specified dealers for the territory or alter the territory only where there are such justifiable reasons.

That exemption is also restricted, by Article 5(2)(2), to cases where the agreement is for at least four years (or if for an indefinite duration provided the period of notice is at least one year) or where the dealer is a new entrant and each party undertakes to give the other six months' notice of its intention not to renew an agreement concluded for an indefinite period.

The Regulation does not apply where companies are connected manufacturers, i.e. within the same corporate group, as defined in Article 13(8). Nor will it apply where the supplier restricts the dealer from selling the contract goods below certain prices or where the agreement is exempted under Regulation 1983/83, the exclusive distribution block exemption.

Withdrawal of exemption

The Commission may withdraw the benefit of the exemption under Article 10 where the agreement has effects incompatible with Article 85(3), in particular where there is no competition for the contract goods in the EC or a substantial part of it, where manufacturers make it difficult for purchasers to obtain the contract goods or servicing, where there is differential pricing between Member States and this is due to obligations exempted by the Regulation or where prices charged to the dealer are not objectively justifiable.

Duration

By Article 14 the Regulation applies until 30th June 1995. Figure 11.1 summarises Regulation 123/85.

Motor Vehicle Distribution and Servicing Agreements under the Block Exemption Regulation 123/85

1. Applies
   (a) where one party supplies motor vehicles for resale
   (b) two parties to agreement only
   (c) vehicles intended for use on public roads
   (d) vehicles having three or more road wheels

2. Exempted restrictions
   (a) supplier not to sell to final consumers or service in territory
   (b) dealer not to modify the goods
   (c) dealer not to manufacture competing goods
   (d) dealer not to sell new competing goods
   (e) dealer not to sell competing spare parts not up to quality standard
   (f) not to enter into distribution agreements for competing goods with third parties
   (g) no sub-distributors to be appointed without consent

Fig. 11.1

    (h) not to conclude distribution or servicing agreements for 'corresponding goods', i.e. those made by supplier but sold by other dealers, without consent

    (i) to impose terms similar to those above on approved sub-distributors

    (j) outside territory to maintain no branches or seek customers

    (k) not to entrust third parties with distribution outside territory

    (l) to sell goods only to resellers within the distribution system or spare parts only for repair of a motor vehicle by the reseller

    (m) only to sell the goods through final consumers' intermediaries where intermediary has prior written authorisation

    (n) to observe (b) and (h) to (m) for a year after termination of agreement

3. Permitted restrictions
    (a) dealer to observe minimum standards
    (b) dealer to order at certain times
    (c) minimum quantity obligations
    (d) keep sufficient stocks
    (e) keep demonstration models
    (f) perform guarantee work and servicing
    (g) only use spare parts within the contract programme for servicing and guarantee work
    (h) inform customers of extent spares can be bought elsewhere
    (i) inform customers whenever spare parts from other sources have been used

4. Conditions of exemption
    (a) dealer to honour guarantees for all vehicles within distribution network and impose this on sub-distributors
    (b) supplier not arbitrarily to withhold consent to sub-distribution agreements
    (c) supplier not to discriminate against dealer for minimum requirements
    (d) where quantities aggregated supplier to separate for dealer – contract goods, spares and other goods
    (e) supplier to supply to dealer for final customer any model of car marketed for Member State for which car to be registered

5. Competing goods restrictions only apply where:
    (a) supplier agrees to release dealer where good reason
    (b) allow supplier to reserve right to appoint other dealers for the territory where good reasons
    (c) agreement is for at least 4 years or is new dealer
    (d) each party gives other 6 months' notice of non-renewal of agreement for fixed duration

6. Exemption will not apply where:
    (a) parties are connected undertakings (same group)
    (b) price restrictions
    (c) Regulation 1983/83 applies

7. Withdrawal of exemption possible where:
    (a) no competition for the products
    (b) manufacturer makes it difficult for customers to buy goods
    (c) prices differ substantially in EC due to exemption
    (d) non-justifiable prices are applied

Fig. 11.1 (*cont.*)

Where the exemption does not apply individual notification on Form A/B would need to be made for specific exemption under Article 85(3).

MOTOR VEHICLES – UK LAW

There is no specific competition legislation aimed at the motor vehicle sector in the UK, although there have been Monopolies and Mergers Commission references, particularly into bus company mergers.[11] The transport and communication sector accounted for 2.5 per cent of cases examined by the Office of Fair Trading under the Fair Trading Act in 1989. General principles of UK competition law will apply.

Exclusive distributorships for motor vehicles will be treated as other distribution agreements considered in Chapter 9 and, unless falling within the limited exemption of Schedule 3, paragraph 2 of the Restrictive Trade Practices Act 1976, will need to be registered at the OFT before the restrictions take effect, provided there are restrictions on two parties.

A simple arrangement whereby the distributor agrees not to acquire goods of the same description from persons other than the supplier and whereby the supplier undertakes only to sell goods within the territory to the distributor will be exempted, despite there being restrictions on two parties. A restriction on the distributor as to persons to whom or the terms and conditions on which he may sell the goods he has purchased from the supplier would also not cause the agreement to be registrable as such provisions would comprise restrictions on the goods supplied between the parties and can be discounted under section 9(3). However, tying the purchase of other goods, including spare parts, is likely to render an agreement registrable and clearly, given the importance to the parties in being able to enforce the restrictions, the agreement should be registered on a 'fail-safe' basis if there is any doubt.

SERVICE STATION AGREEMENTS – EC LAW

Continuing with the motor vehicle sector, service station agreements fall to be considered, there being specific EC block exemption for such agreements within the exclusive purchasing block exemption considered in Chapter 9.[12]

There is no case law concerning petrol 'solus' agreements. Such agreements typically tie the service station owner to purchase petroleum from one petrol supplier only and are addressed under Title III of Regulation 1984/83. The Regulation applies, by Article 10, to agreements:

> to which only two undertakings are party and whereby one party, the reseller, agrees with the other, the supplier, in consideration for the according of special commercial or financial advantages, to purchase only from the supplier, an undertaking connected with the supplier or another undertaking entrusted by the supplier with the distribution of his goods, certain petroleum-based motor vehicle fuels or certain petroleum-based motor vehicles and other fuels specified in the agreement for resale in a service station designated in the agreement.

The essential prerequisite is that the reseller agrees to purchase only from the supplier. For the block exemption to apply there must be such a tie.

11 See *R v MMC, ex parte South Yorkshire Transport Ltd* [1991] BCC 347, where South Yorkshire Transport successfully challenges the MMC on the grounds that the merger, affecting only a small area of the UK, should not therefore have been referred to the MMC and OFT Guide for the Bus Industry to the RTPA.

12 Commission Regulation (EEC) No 1984/83 of 22 June 1983 on the application of Article 85(3) of the Treaty to categories of exclusive purchasing agreements, OJ 1983 L173/5. See also Notice OJ 1984 C101/2

Permitted restrictions

Article 10 sets out the permitted restrictions, which include an obligation not to sell fuels supplied by other undertakings at the service station. There may also be an obligation not to use lubricants or related petroleum-based products supplied by other undertakings placed upon the reseller, but only where the supplier has made available to the reseller or financed a lubrication bay or other motor vehicle lubricant equipment.

The reseller may be restricted from advertising goods supplied by other undertakings at the premises only in proportion to the share of such competing goods which the reseller actually sells at the premises. The reseller may be obliged to have any equipment supplied by the supplier serviced with him.

Black-listed provisions

The benefit of the exemption is lost where, by Article 12, the supplier restricts the reseller from obtaining goods other than motor vehicle and other fuels or services from persons other than the supplier, unless the goods fall within the lubricant or supplier supplied equipment provisions described above. This ensures that the reseller selling fresh flowers, or milk and bread, on his forecourt could not be tied to the supplier for those goods as well.

Also black-listed is any provision extending the agreement to a period of more than ten years or an agreement is concluded for an indefinite duration. The supplier must not require that the reseller impose on his successor to the business an exclusive purchasing obligation of a longer duration than that which would have applied to the reseller.

Let service stations

By Article 12.2, where the service station involves premises which the supplier lets to the reseller, exclusive purchasing agreements and bans on dealing in competing products may be imposed for the whole of the period during which the reseller operates from the premises.

Other provisions of Regulation 1984/83 apply as they apply to other exclusive purchasing agreements (discussed in Chapter 9).

SERVICE STATION AGREEMENTS – UK LAW

There are no special UK competition laws concerning service station agreements. Any restriction on competition is potentially within the RTPA, provided that there are restrictions on two parties. Also, even one-sided restrictions may be void if in restraint of trade. In *Esso Petroleum* v *Harper's Garage (Stourport) Ltd,*[13] the House of Lords held that a tie of five years was reasonable in an agreement of this sort.

The MMC has comparatively recently investigated the petrol sector, in relation to which see its Report 'Supply of Petrol'.[14] The MMC found that a monopoly situation existed for the wholesale supply of petrol enjoyed by 69 wholesalers, but that there was no adverse impact on the public interest. No evidence of collusion between the wholesalers was found and no monopoly profits. The MMC found that petrol 'solus' ties in the industry did not operate against the public interest.

13 [1968] AC 269

14 20 February 1990, Cm 972

The Report noted the recitals of Regulation 1984/83, which allow Member States to impose a shorter maximum term for such solus agreements. The UK maximum is five years. This was recommended in the 1965 Report of the Monopolies Commission into the Supply of Petrol to Retailers in the UK, which resulted in undertakings to this effect being extracted from the petrol wholesalers (quoted in the 1990 Report).

BEER SUPPLY AGREEMENTS – EC LAW

The final block exemption, or part of a block exemption, is that part of the exclusive purchasing block exemption referred to above, which relates to beer supply agreements. This is comprised in Title II of Regulation 1984/83. This provides in Article 6 that there is a block exemption for agreements between two parties in which the reseller agrees only to purchase from the supplier:

> certain beer, or certain beers and certain other drinks, specified in the agreement for resale in premises used for the sale and consumption of drinks and designated in the agreement.

Permitted retrictions

Article 7 permits an obligation on the reseller not to sell beers and other drinks which are supplied by other undertakings and 'which are of the same type as the beers or other drinks supplied under the agreement in the premises designated in the agreement'. Where the reseller sells different types of such drinks then he can be obliged only to sell them in bottles, cans or other small packages, 'unless the sale of such beers in draught form is customary or is necessary to satisfy a sufficient demand from consumers'. Beers or other drinks are of different types where they are clearly distinguishable by their composition, appearance or taste (Article 7(2)).

An obligation may be imposed on the reseller to the effect that other undertakings' goods may only be advertised at the premises in proportion to the share of those goods in the total turnover realised at the premises.

Black-listed provisions

Article 8 lists those provisions which when present in a beer supply agreement will render the Regulation inapplicable. There must be no exclusive purchasing agreements for products other than drinks or services. Crisps, nuts and bar snacks cannot therefore be restricted. The reseller must be free to obtain from third parties goods or services of his choice for which neither an exclusive purchasing obligation nor a ban on dealing in competing goods may be imposed (Article 8.1(b)).

Where the exclusive purchasing obligation relates only to specified beers, the agreement must not be concluded for a period exceeding five years or be for indefinite duration. The supplier must not oblige the reseller to impose exclusive purchasing obligations on his successor which last for longer than those which would have applied to the original reseller.[14a]

Let premises

Article 8.2 provides that where the premises are let by the supplier to the

14a Note *Stergios Delimitis* v *Henniger Bräu AG,* OJ 1991 C86/8, an ECJ decision which considers when the exemption will be inapplicable: when entry for new competitors is hard, where other breweries have no chance to supply and where tied drinks are not listed in the agreement, just in a price list

reseller the exclusive purchasing obligations and any bans on dealing in competing goods may be imposed for as long as the reseller lets the premises. In such circumstances, however, the reseller must be entitled to purchase drinks, except beer, from other undertakings offering them on more favourable terms than the supplier's standard terms, where the supplier refuses to match such better terms. The reseller must also have a right to obtain drinks (except beer), which are of the same type as those supplied under the agreement with the supplier but which bear different trade marks, from other undertakings where the supplier does not supply them.

Other generally applicable provisions of Regulation 1984/83 also apply to such agreements.

BEER SUPPLY AGREEMENTS – UK LAW

There are no specific provisions of UK competition law in this area. The RTPA may apply and, where there is exclusive dealing, the exemption in Schedule 3, paragraph 2, may apply. The beer industry is an important business sector. There has been a Monopolies and Mergers Commission investigation, the report in relation to which is entitled 'The Supply of Beer'.[15] This was considered in Chapter 3.

By statutory instruments,[16] brewers were required to reduce the number of their licensed premises or release them from all product ties. The orders required that tied tenants be allowed to choose another cask-conditioned beer from another supplier, be released from ties for wines and soft drinks and required the amendment of loan agreements.

Arguments presented by the brewing industry that as their agreements were exempted under the block exemption they could not therefore be challenged under UK competition law were rejected by the English courts. In any event, agreements exempted from Article 85(1) may infringe Article 86 where there is an abuse of a dominant position. Clearance under Article 85(3) would not save such agreements, so neither would it under UK competition law.

The Report arose from an investigation under the Fair Trading Act 1973 into a potential monopoly situation (see Chapter 3). In February 1991 the OFT warned brewers to abide by the Orders, when a tenant was apparently told that stocking a 'guest beer' was 'bound to go against him'.[17]

COMPUTER SOFTWARE LICENCES – EC LAW

Computer hardware is the physical box of the computer, literally the hard part. The software makes it operate and is usually stored on magnetic/floppy discs or on other electronic media. Computer software is protected by copyright as a literary work by the Copyright, Designs and Patents Act 1988.[18] Software is therefore usually licensed rather than sold.

Licence agreements permitting use of software typically contain many restrictions. Examples include restrictions that the software may not be copied, except for security/back-up or archive purposes and except in so far as using the software, loading it into the computer, necessarily involves copying; that it must only be used on a particular stated machine at a specified

15 9 May 1989, Cm 651

16 Supply of Beer (Tied Estate) Order 1989, S.I. 1989 No. 2390 and the Supply of Beer (Loan Ties, Licensed Premises and Wholesale Prices) Order 1989, S.I. 1989 No. 2258. See also the MMC Report *Elders IXL and Grand Metropolitan*, Cm 1227, 19 October 1990

17 OFT Press Release 31 January 1991 and FT 1 February 1991

18 Section 3(1)(b) and see also s. 17(2). Copying includes 'storing the work in any medium by electronic means' and includes making transient copies or copies incidental to use of the work. By s.9(3), computer-generated works are owned by the person by whom the arrangements necessary for the work are undertaken

location; that it may only be used by the licensee, not other companies within its group; that it may only be used for restricted business purposes of the licensee and not in the provision of bureau services.

There have been few Commission decisions concerning software. The Commission may produce a block exemption for such agreements when it has had experience of exempting such agreements under Article 85(3), although few such notifications have been made.

In *Re the IBM Personal Computer*,[19] the Commission granted negative clearance, i.e. decided that agreements did not infringe Article 85(1) at all, to a selective distribution system operated by IBM Europe SA.[20] This was based on:

> the present situation in this market in which new highly technical products are being sold mainly to inexperienced users who have not enjoyed the education in computers that is now being offered in many schools and colleges.

IBM would accept anyone into the selective distribution system who satisfied the criteria laid down. This case was not concerned with the detailed restrictions found in typical software licences, considered above.[21]

In Chapter 9 copyright licensing under EC competition law was considered. The principal cases are *Coditel v Cine Vog Films (No 1)*[22] and *Coditel v Cine Vog Films (No 2)*,[23] although these concerned copyright in films. In *Louis Erauw Jacquery v SC La Hesbignonne*,[24] it was held by the court that where products are protected by intellectual property rights of the sort which could easily be copied then territorial protection is justified where necessary to protect the secrecy of the information and would not infringe Article 85(1). Where a software manufacturer chooses to license software through a distribution system, as is often the case, such distribution licences may benefit from the decision in this case.

In *Coditel (No 2)*, the court held that an exclusive copyright licence would not necessarily always infringe Article 85(1). It stated:

> Although, therefore, the copyright in a film and the right, arising from the copyright, to exhibit a film do not by their nature fall within the prohibitions of Article 85(1), the exercise of such rights may nevertheless, under economic or legal circumstances which have the effect of substantially restricting competition in the film market, having regard to its special characteristics, fall within those prohibitions.

It will therefore be a question of determining in each case whether any exclusivity obligations substantially restrict competition. In many cases, using the block exemptions for patent and know-how licensing, particularly where the software technology is not new, specific Article 85(3) clearance will need to be sought. Where the technology is new and there is an open exclusive licence, it may be possible to allege that the exclusivity provisions are outside of Article 85(1), as in *Nungesser*[25] (see Chapter 9).

Provisions restricting use of the software to use on a particular machine at a particular location may not be restrictive of competition as they are designed to ensure that the licensor is rewarded in proportion to the use made by the licensee. If the software is used on a more powerful machine and at a number of different locations then this amounts to greater exploitation, much

19 [1984] 2 CMLR 342

20 For selective distribution, see Chapter 9

21 Nor was *Computerland* (franchising) [1987] 2 CMLR 389
22 [1981] 2 CMLR 362
23 [1983] 1 CMLR 49

24 [1988] 4 CMLR 576

25 [1983] 1 CMLR 278

in the same way as a patent licensee manufacturing more products. Greater royalties may be charged by the patent licensor under the patent licence block exemption Regulation 2349/84, i.e. the royalties can be based on the number of products manufactured.

By analogy therefore such restrictions may be permitted. However, it is conceivable that the Commission would require that the licensee be free to use the software elsewhere, having first obtained the consent of the licensor (not to be unreasonably withheld) on agreeing to pay higher licence fees. Adding such a provision to a software licence and permitting changes of location on notification to the licensor where the licensee moves premises or undergoes a corporate reconstruction would make it more likely that it would not infringe Article 85(1), in the absence of a specific block exemption.

It also seems likely, although there is no case law to this effect, that restrictions on copying software would not infringe Article 85(1). They merely ensure protection of the licensor's copyright.

Restrictions on sub-licensing and assignment are permitted under the patent and know-how block exemptions[26] and are unlikely therefore to infringe Article 85(1) in a software licence. A requirement, which is common, that the licensee assign copyright in all improvements back to the licensor is likely to infringe Article 85(1), by analogy with the patent and knowhow block exemptions. At the most, a requirement that the licensee license back on a non-exclusive basis all improvements may be acceptable. In practice, users may be members of a user group and encouraged to inform the licensor of potential improvements, which the licensor may then incorporate into the next release of the software.

In the software context, it is possible that the Commission may take a different view than for patents and permit an assignment of licensee improvements provided the licensee obtains a free licence of the improvement when incorporated into the next version.

Maintenance ties

Many software licences require that the licensee have the software maintained by the licensor and no other person. Either outside maintenance is expressly forbidden or any warranty offered with the software is negated where outside maintenance is used.

There are valid technical reasons for this. In many cases only the licensor will hold the source code of the software. Software is usually licensed in object code form only. The source code is the secret key to the software. It can be difficult to maintain the software without the source code, which as an important business asset of the licensor, the licensor is usually reluctant to license. However, maintenance may be possible without the code and a licensee could find himself in a position where he is tied to the licensor for maintenance no matter how unreasonable the maintenance charges are.

In the absence of a block exemption, it is likely that such a tie would be void under Article 85(1) only where the tie was completely unecessary from a technical point of view. In some cases refusals to license the source code to a third party maintenance provider, such as a facilities management company, may amount to an abuse of a dominant position, although this would be difficult to prove.

26 Regulations 2349/84, Article 2.1.5 and 556/89, Article 2.1.2

In *ALSATEL,*[27] a case concerning French telecommunications not com- | 27 [1990] 4 CMLR 434
puters, the terms of a contract for rental and maintenance of telephone
installations, which required that the prices for additional equipment required
as a result of modifications to installations were fixed unilaterally by the
installer, were an abuse of a dominant position and contrary to Article 86.
The Court of Justice, on an Article 177 reference, also held that the contract,
which automatically renewed for a 15 year term where the rental arising from
those modifications was increased by more than 25 per cent, was an abuse
too. Article 86 could therefore clearly apply to abusive maintenance practices
in the software industry.

The EC Software Directive

The Commission Directive on the legal protection of computer programs[28] | 28 OJ 1991 L122/42
seeks to ensure that Member States harmonise their national legislation on the
protection of computer programs. No piece of EC legislation has ever been
subjected to as much lobbying or been the subject of as much controversy as
this. In simple terms, on one side, large computer manufacturers, mainly from
the USA, want to ensure as much protection as possible and on the other side
smaller EC based manufacturers want as much freedom to use the software of
others as possible.

The directive does not address issues of competition law at all, save to the
extent that the granting of intellectual property rights may *per se* be restrictive
of competition. The principal provision is that software throughout the
Community will be protected by copyright law and issues of who will own
the copyright, how long it will last and what are restricted acts, i.e. what
amounts to an infringement of copyright, are addressed.

Article 5.3 permits a person authorised to use a computer program,
without the authorisation of the right holder:

> to observe, study or test the functioning of the program in order to determine the
> ideas and principles which underlie any element of the program if he does so while
> performing any of the acts of loading, displaying, running, transmitting or storing
> the program which he is entitled to do.

Article 6 provides that the authorisation of the owner is not needed where
reproduction of the computer code and translation of its form are
'indispensable to obtain the information necessary to achieve the
interoperability of an independently created computer program with other
programs. This applies only if the acts are carried out by a genuine licensee,
the information necessary to achieve interoperability is not available publicly
and the acts are confined to those parts of the program necessary to achieve
interoperability with it.

This provision is designed to enable licensees to achieve interoperable | 29 See *X/Open Group* [1988]
systems.[29] Such systems permit different types of computer hardware and | 4 CMLR 542, OJ 1987 L35/36
software to be used together, an objective which is regarded as being in the
interests of consumers within the EC. Information obtained through this
provision must not be used for the creation of a similar program. Also the
provisions must not be interpreted as allowing use of a right holder's
copyright such that his legitimate interests are prejudiced or where the use
conflicts with the normal exploitation of the computer program.

Member States are required to bring their national legislation into line with the Directive by January 1993.

Competition law has been used as an argument for not permitting reverse engineering or decompilation of a program. Refusal to license copyright in software by a manufacturer in a dominant position could be an abuse of that dominant position. Licensors are already therefore obliged to grant licences for such purposes in some circumstances, such that a free right to decompile should not be given.

Refusals to license could still amount to breaches of Article 86 as discussed in Chapter 3. The provisions of the Directive are expressly 'without prejudice to the application of the competition rules under Articles 85 and 86 of the Treaty if a dominant supplier refuses to make information available which is necessary for interoperability' (pre-penultimate recital).

Conclusion

Software licensing is one of the least regulated sectors from a competition law point of view in the EC. There are virtually no cases and no block exemption. Looking at the other block exemptions it is possible to present a reasonably firm picture of when provisions will infringe Article 85(1). The least restrictive provisions capable of being commercially acceptable should be inserted, with notification for Article 85(3) exemption being made where necessary in cases of doubt.

COMPUTER SOFTWARE LICENCES – UK LAW

Again there are no specific competition law provisions of UK law regulating computer software licensing, but the formalistic nature of the RTPA permits a clearer analysis to be made. As to general law, the Copyright, Designs and Patents Act 1988 addresses copyright protection of computer software.[30]

Where there are no restrictions on a licensor at all, the RTPA will not apply whether there are restrictions on use of the software or not, as there must be restrictions on two parties for the RTPA to apply.

Schedule 3, paragraph 5A

In Chapter 11 the exemption for copyright licences in Schedule 3, paragraph 5A was considered. Under paragraph 5A(3), the only restrictions permitted are in respect of the work in which the copyright subsists. Any restrictions on the use of the software are likely to fall within this exemption.

Ravenseft case

Under *Ravenseft,*[31] restrictions in an agreement for the licensing of property on the licensee are not restrictive of competition as they do not restrict a pre-existing liberty. Before the licence, the licensee was not free to use the software at all. If he had tried he would have been at risk of being sued for copyright infringement, hence restrictions which go no further than the right would not be void.

A tie, which is mentioned in the UK Government's White Paper[32] as being an example of a clause which would not be within the *Ravenseft* principle – see Chapter 6, to maintenance by the supplier would *prima facie* be a relevant

30 See footnote 18 above

31 [1977] All ER 47 and Chapt. 9

32 See Chapt. 7

restriction falling within the RTPA. It would be a restriction as to the persons from whom services could be obtained.

Exclusivity

The only restrictions on the licensor of software are likely to relate to exclusivity. Most software licences to users are not exclusive. There are rarely restrictions on two parties. However, where the licensor agrees, perhaps as part of a distribution or OEM (original equipment manufacturer) agreement, not to license the software to others within a territory or for a particular purpose, there may be an RTP restriction, as discussed in Chapter 9, although the OFT has stated that such restrictions on licensing are not 'restrictions' within the meaning of the RTPA.

One argument in this area is that restrictions on the licensing of copyright are not restrictions either as to the persons to whom goods are to be supplied (as copyright is not goods) or as to the persons to whom services are to be supplied. However, in practice, much software is bought, perhaps under what are known as 'shrink wrapped licences' (where the opening of the package supposedly amounts to agreement to the terms of the licence) in department stores and if it is not the supply of goods it must surely be the supply of a service. It is more suppliable than say the licence of a patent. If software is not 'goods' then the services exemption may apply. Section 43(1) defines 'goods' to include ships, minerals and animals (including fish). This is not of much assistance in determining whether software would be goods. In any event it seems strange, as discussed elsewhere, that the legislature would enact specific exemption for forms of copyright licence if such licences were not *per se* within the ambit of the RTPA.

Schedule 3, paragraphs 2 and 7 comprise exemptions for agreements comprising the exclusive supply of goods and services respectively. Where there are restrictions on the licensor 'selling' the software in a specific territory then, provided there are no other restrictions except an exclusive tie on the licensee, the agreement will be exempt. Where there are exclusivity provisions and the exemptions in Schedule 3, paragraphs 2 or 7 are used, it should be noted that, if there are any other provisions which fall to be exempted under another paragraph of Schedule 3, the exemption will not apply. If the licensee is restricted in such a way that paragraph 5A exemption is used, then, because of the technical wording of the RTP which has the effect that the exemption cannot be used cumulatively, the agreement will fall to be registered. This therefore makes it particularly important where there are exclusivity provisions which could otherwise be exempted to know whether the 'restrictions' on use by the licensee are 'relevant restrictions' within the RTPA. Section 9(3) may not be used to discount restrictions relating to the goods sold between the parties if the software has not been 'sold'. It may be possible to use section 18(2) where the term relates exclusively to the service supplied under the agreement between the parties.

As the position is so doubtful a fail-safe registration is advisable where the parties are not overly concerned about their agreement going on the public register, in order to ensure the enforceability of restrictions, where there are restrictions on two parties.

BIOTECHNOLOGY LICENCES – EC LAW

Biotechnology was defined by the US Congress Office of Technology Assessment as:[33]

> any technique that uses living organisms (or parts of organisms) to make or modify products, to improve plants or animals or to develop micro-organisms for specific uses.

33 Quoted in *Transferring Biotechnology* by Waddell A. Biggart, Les Nouvelles, March 1986

Genetic engineering is a form of biotechnology. Biotechnology is a field of research growing in importance and requiring carefully drafted legal agreements. It will involve patent rights and rights of know-how. Their licensing may be exempted under Regulations 2349/84 and 556/89 (patent and know-how licensing – considered in Chapter 9). Research and development agreements in connection with the development of such technology may fall to be exempted under the research and development or specialisation block exemptions (Regulations 418/85 and 417/85 – considered in Chapter 10).

The difference between biotechnology and other licensing of patents and know-how is that there will be physical material, a cell-line, which is 'licensed' or lent in some way. There may be a licence to use the cell-line or an outright sale of it, which would effectively be the sale of goods, where the seller did not wish to retain rights to use the physical biological material.

In most cases the owner of the biological material will wish to retain ownership of it and of all patents and know-how. A licence to use the material may be akin to an agreement whereby a patent licensee is given raw materials as well as the patent and is obliged to restrict use of those raw materials to manufacture of a finished product. Parallels are difficult to draw in this very special field. Some recommend that a separate bailment agreement be entered into for the right to use the biological material. Bailment is having possession of products without acquiring ownership to them.

Whatever the form of the contractual arrangements, it is likely that the Commission would consider such agreements in the light of the existing block exemptions, although where the technology is new there may be scope for argument that Article 85(1) would not apply to exclusivity obligations.

Biotechnology Draft Directive

The Commission has issued a draft Directive for the legal protection of biotechnological inventions.[34] If enacted the Directive would require Member States to bring their legislation in line with that of the Directive. The subject matter of an invention would not be precluded from being patented merely by reason that it is composed of living matter.

34 OJ 1989 C10/3, also Explanatory Memorandum, Commission, COM(88) 496

The Directive, although of importance in this field, would not address any specific issues of competition law in connection with agreements for biotechnology. All such agreements would remain to be assessed in accordance with normal EC rules of competition.

BIOTECHNOLOGY LICENCES – UK LAW

Licences of biotechnology may be exempted under Schedule 3 of the RTPA where they comprise licences of know-how or patents as considered in

Chapter 9 or, where a research agreement falls to be considered, then they may be of importance to the national economy and exempted (under s.29 – see Chapter 10).

There are no special UK rules and restrictions on competition and exclusivity obligations would, in particular, need to be considered against UK competition legislation in each case.

COAL AND STEEL

A number of areas of activity are dealt with separately from others under EC competition law. Air, road and maritime transport and agriculture are examples and another is coal and steel. Coal and steel will be considered here. The other areas are beyond the general nature of this book.

Coal and steel are not governed by the Treaty of Rome at all. The 1951 Treaty establishing the European Coal and Steel Community, the Treaty of Paris or ECSC Treaty, sets out the provisions governing this sector. Only Articles 60 to 67 of the ECSC Treaty are relevant to competition law. The Treaty also covers general issues such as investment and financial aid, quotas, wages and commercial policy.

Article 65 of the Treaty of Paris provides that agreements between undertakings which prevent, restrict or distort normal competition in the common market are prohibited, in particular those fixing prices, restricting production, development or investment or sharing market, customers or sources of supply. These provisions are similar to Article 85 of the Treaty of Rome. Although there is case law under Article 65, case law decided under Article 85 will also be relevant to the construction of Article 65. Agreements infringing this prohibition in Article 65 will, by Article 65(4) of the ECSC Treaty, be void.

Fines may be imposed by Article 65(5) where an undertaking has entered into an agreement which is automatically void or has enforced such an agreement. This is similar to Regulation 17, which implements Articles 85 and 86 of the Treaty of Rome.

There is an equivalent to the specific exemptions which can be granted under Article 85(3) in Article 65(2) of the ECSC Treaty. Authorisations can be granted for limited periods or subject to specific conditions. They can be renewed and revoked where there is a change of circumstances. Decisions are published together with reasons under Article 65(2) and requests for information can be made.

Article 60 of the Treaty of Paris is the equivalent of Article 86 of the usual competition rules. It prohibits unfair practices and discriminatory practices.

Article 66 provides for merger control, requiring prior authorisation of concentrations. Authorisation will be given where the transaction will not enable the companies concerned to determine prices or control production or jurisdiction.

Conclusion

When examining agreements or mergers which involve coal or steel, the Treaty of Paris provisions should be studied. Although similar to the equivalent provisions in the Treaty of Rome, the ECSC is a separate regime and its particular provisions should be examined in relevant cases. Similarly, air transport and other special sectors referred to above should be considered in the light of their special treatment under the EC competition rules.

QUESTION

Better Brewers own a network of tied pubs across the UK and France. As it was thought commercially desirable, their agreements with the tenants of the tied houses contain provisions very restrictive of competition. Advise them of the maximum ambit of restrictions which would be allowed under UK and EC competition law. They would particularly like to ensure that tenants only have Better Brewers products, including crisps and fruit machines.

FURTHER READING

Motor vehicles distribution and service station agreements

ARTICLE Groves P. – *Motor vehicle distribution: the block exemption* [1987] ECLR 77

BOOKS Bellamy & Child – *Common Market Law of Competition*, Sweet & Maxwell, 3rd ed., 1987, para.6.1-101
Green N. – *Commercial Agreements and Competition Law*, Graham & Trotman, 1986, p.486
Van Bael & Bellis, *Competition Law of the EEC*, CCH Editions, 2nd ed., 1990, para.370

CASES *BMW* [1975] 1 CMLR D1 (OJ L29/1, 3 February 1975)
British Leyland v *Armstrong* [1984] 3 CMLR 102 (C.A.) and [1986] AC 577 (H.L.)
Consorzio Italiano della Componentistica di Ricambio per Autoveicoli and Maxicar v *Regie Nationale des Usines Renault* [1990] 4 CMLR 265
D'Ieteren Motor Oils OJ 1991 L20/42
Esso Petroleum v *Harper's Garage (Stourport) Ltd* [1968] AC 269
Ford [1984] 1 CMLR 649 (OJ L327/31, 24 November 1983)
Peugeot OJ L295/19, 18 October 1986, [1990] 4 CMLR 449, [1990] 4 CMLR 674
Volvo AB v *Erick Veng (U.K.) Ltd* [1989] 4 CMLR 122

GUIDE *OFT Guide*, July 1991, RTPA and the Bus Industry

MMC REPORT *Supply of Petrol* Cm 972, 20 February 1990

REGULATIONS Regulation 123/85 on motor vehicle and servicing agreements, OJ L15/16, 18 January 1985
Title III of Regulation 1984/83 of 22 June 1983, on exclusive purchasing agreements, OJ L173/5 30 June 1983

NOTICES Commission Notice on Regulation 123/85, OJ 1985 C17/4
Commission Notice on Regulation 1984/83, OJ C101/2, 13 April 1984

Beer supply agreements

ARTICLE Maitland-Walker J. – *The EEC Beer Review* [1990] 4 ECLR 131

BOOKS Bellamy (*op cit*), para.6-081
Green (*op cit*), p.478
Van Bael (*op cit*), para.369

MMC REPORTS *The Supply of Beer* Cm 651, 9 May 1989
Elders IXL and Grand Metropolitan Cm 1227, 19 October 1990

Supply of Beer (Tied Estate) Order 1989 SI No. 2390   **STATUTORY INSTRUMENTS**
Supply of Beer (Loan Ties, Licensed Premises and Wholesale Prices) Order 1989 SI No. 2258

Title II of Regulation 1984/83 of 22 June 1983, on exclusive purchasing agreements, OJ L173/5,   **REGULATION**
  30 June 1983

Commission Notice on Regulation 1984/83, OJ C101/2, 13 April 1984   **NOTICE**

Computer software licences

Green (*op cit*), p.87   **BOOK**

ALSATEL [1990] 4 CMLR 434   **CASES**
Coditel v *Cine Vog Films (No 1)* [1981] 2 CMLR 362
Coditel v *Cine Vog Films (No 2)* [1983] 1 CMLR 49
Computerland [1987] 2 CMLR 389
Re the IBM Personal Computer [1984] 2 CMLR 342
SPRL Louis Erauw Jacquery v *SC La Hesbignonne* [1988] 4 CMLR 576
X/Open Group [1988] 4 CMLR 542, OJ 1987 L35/36

Directive of 14 May 1991 on the legal protection of computer programs OJ 1991 L122/42   **DIRECTIVE**

Biotechnology

Biggart W.A. – *Transferring Biotechnology*, Les Nouvelles, March 1986   **ARTICLES**
Cole P. – *Can I Patent my new Transgenic Guinea Pig, Daddy?* Patent World, May 1989, p.39
  and p.18 – *The Proposed Council Directive on the Legal Protection of Biotechnological
  Inventions*

Draft Directive for the legal protection of biotechnological inventions, OJ 1989 C10/3   **DRAFT DIRECTIVE**

Coal and Steel

Bellamy (*op cit*), para.1-001 and para.13-050   **BOOKS**
Green (*op cit*), pp.20–21, 48–49

Selected bibliography

Bellamy C.W. and Child G.D., *Common Market Law of Competition*, 3rd ed., Sweet & Maxwell, 1987.

Brock, *The Control of Restrictive Practices from 1956*, McGraw-Hill, 1966.

Butterworths Competition Law Handbook, 2nd ed., 1990.

Chitty on Contracts, Volume II, Sweet & Maxwell, 26th ed., 1990.

Christou R., *International Agency, Distribution and Licensing Agreements*, Longman, 1986.

Cunningham, *The Fair Trading Act 1973*, Sweet & Maxwell, 1974 and Supplement, 1978.

Fine F., *Mergers and Joint Ventures in Europe: The Law and Policy of the EEC*, Graham & Trotman, 1989.

Goyder D.G., *EEC Competition Law*, OUP 1989.

Green N., *Commercial Agreements and Competition Law, Practice and Procedure in the UK and EEC*, Graham & Trotman, 1986.

Hawk B.E., *US, Common Market & International Anti-trust*, Prentice Hall Law & Business, 2nd ed. – 1990 Supplement, Volume II.

Hermannn and Jones, *Fair Trading in Europe*, Kluwer, 1977.

Jacobs F.H. and Durand A., *References to the European Court: Practice and Procedure*, Butterworths, 1975.

Kerse C.S., *EEC Antitrust Procedure*, 2nd ed., European Law Centre, 1987.

Korah V., *An Introductory Guide to EEC Competition Law and Practice*, ESC Publishing, 4th ed., 1990.

Korah V., *Exclusive Distribution in the EEC: Regulation 67/67 Replaced*, ESC Publishing, 1984.

Korah V., *Franchising and EEC Competition Rules, Regulation 4087/88*, ESC Publishing, 1989.

Korah V., *Knowhow Licensing Agreements and EEC Competition Rules, Regulation 556/89*, ESC Publishing, 1989.

Korah V., *Patent Licensing and EEC Competition Rules, Regulation 2349/84*, ESC Publishing, 1985.

Korah V., *Research and Development and the EEC Competition Rules, Regulation 418/85*, ESC Publishing, 1986.

Lever J. (ed.), *Butterworths Competition Law*, 1991 (looseleaf).

Lindrup G. (Ed.), *Butterworths Competition Law Handbook*, 2nd ed., Butterworths, 1990.

Merkin and Williams, *Antitrust Policy in the United Kingdom and the EEC*, Sweet & Maxwell, 1984.

Millett T., *The Court of First Instance of the European Communities*, Butterworths, 1990.

Neville Brown L. *The Court of Justice of the European Communities*, Sweet & Maxwell, 3rd ed., 1989

Oliver P., *Free Movement of Goods in the EEC*, 2nd ed., European Law Centre, 1988.

Schina D., *State Aids under the EEC Treaty Article 92–94*, ESC Publishing, 1987.

Schmitthoff C.M., *The Law and Practice of International Trade*, 9th ed., Stevens, 1990.

Soames T., *UK and EC Merger Control*, Butterworths, 1991.

Stevens and Yamey, *The Restrictive Practices Court: a Study of the Judicial Process and Economic Policy*, Weidenfeld and Nicholson, 1965.

Swann, *Competition and Industrial Policy in the European Community*, Methuen, 1983.

Van Bael I. and Bellis J.-F., *Anti-dumping and other Trade Protection Laws of the EEC*, CCH Editions, 2nd ed., 1990.

Van Bael I. and Bellis J.-F., *Competition law of the EEC*, CCH Editions, 2nd ed., 1990.

Whish R., *Competition Law*, 2nd ed., Butterworths, 1989.

Wood A. (Ed.), *The Times Guide to the European Parliament*, Times Books, 1989.

Waude M. van der, Jones C. and Lewis X., *EEC Competition Law Handbook*, Sweet & Maxwell, 1990.

Index